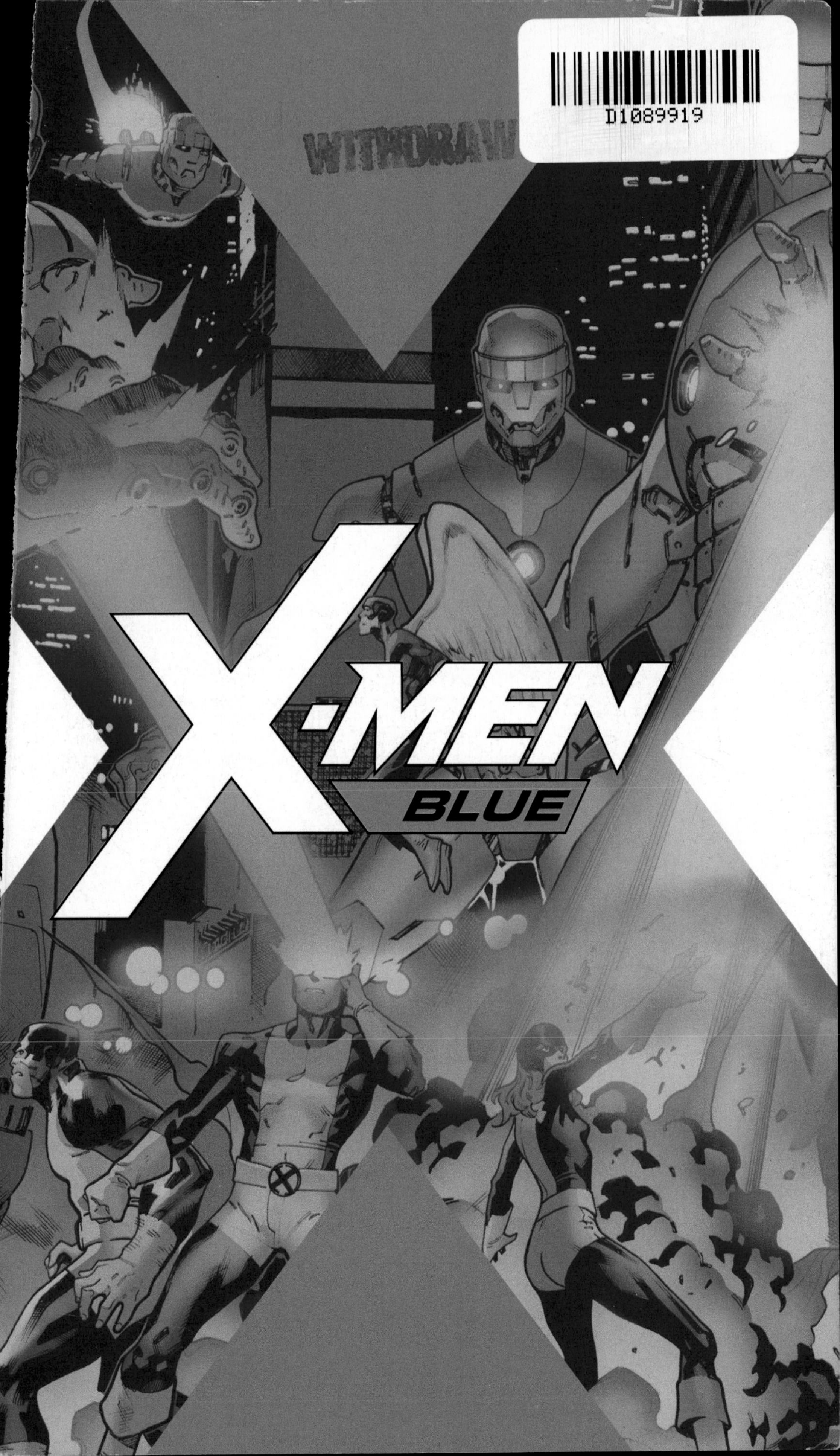
X-MEN
BLUE

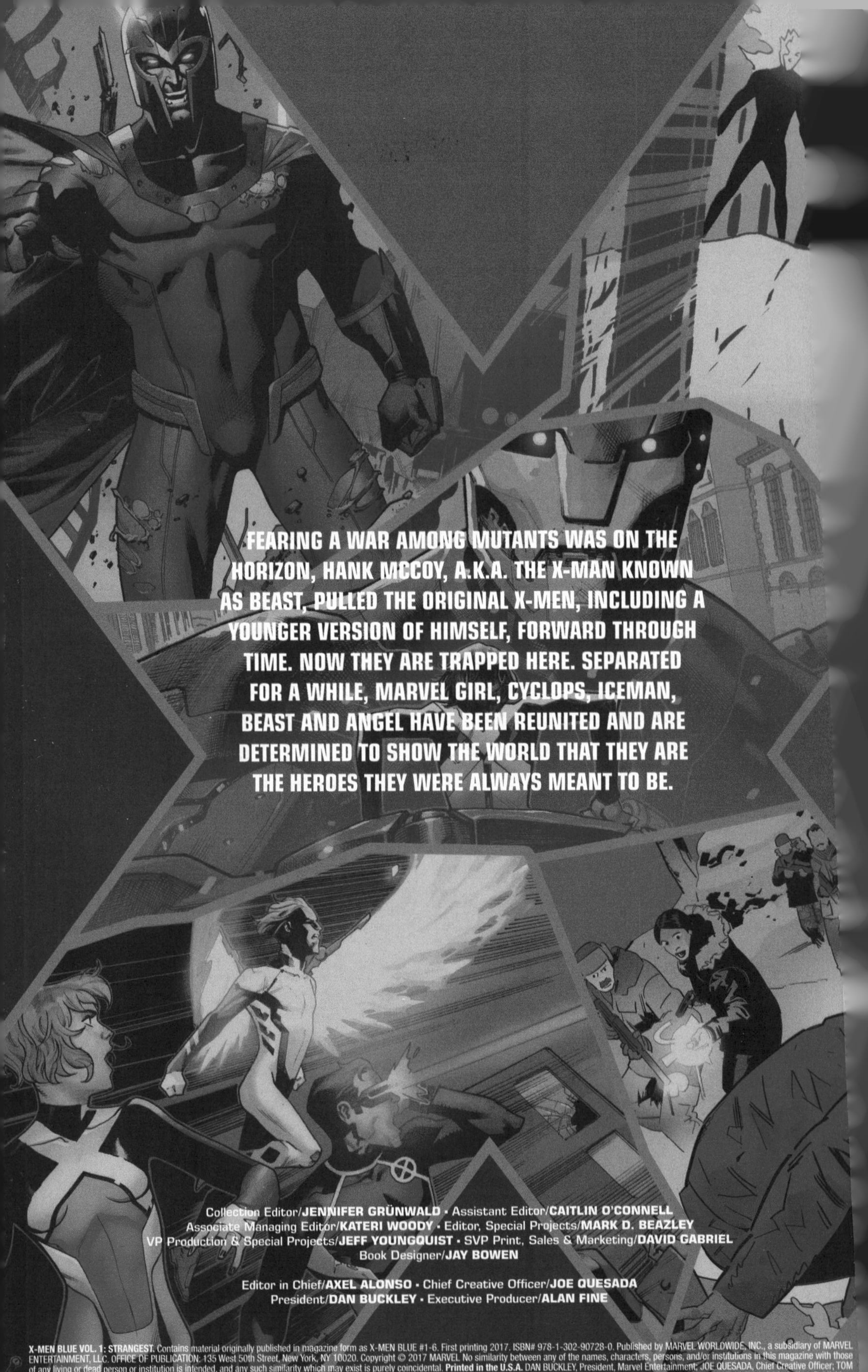

FEARING A WAR AMONG MUTANTS WAS ON THE HORIZON, HANK MCCOY, A.K.A. THE X-MAN KNOWN AS BEAST, PULLED THE ORIGINAL X-MEN, INCLUDING A YOUNGER VERSION OF HIMSELF, FORWARD THROUGH TIME. NOW THEY ARE TRAPPED HERE. SEPARATED FOR A WHILE, MARVEL GIRL, CYCLOPS, ICEMAN, BEAST AND ANGEL HAVE BEEN REUNITED AND ARE DETERMINED TO SHOW THE WORLD THAT THEY ARE THE HEROES THEY WERE ALWAYS MEANT TO BE.

Collection Editor/**JENNIFER GRÜNWALD** · Assistant Editor/**CAITLIN O'CONNELL**
Associate Managing Editor/**KATERI WOODY** · Editor, Special Projects/**MARK D. BEAZLEY**
VP Production & Special Projects/**JEFF YOUNGQUIST** · SVP Print, Sales & Marketing/**DAVID GABRIEL**
Book Designer/**JAY BOWEN**

Editor in Chief/**AXEL ALONSO** · Chief Creative Officer/**JOE QUESADA**
President/**DAN BUCKLEY** · Executive Producer/**ALAN FINE**

X-MEN BLUE VOL. 1: STRANGEST. Contains material originally published in magazine form as X-MEN BLUE #1-6. First printing 2017. ISBN# 978-1-302-90728-0. Published by MARVEL WORLDWIDE, INC., a subsidiary of MARVEL ENTERTAINMENT, LLC. OFFICE OF PUBLICATION: 135 West 50th Street, New York, NY 10020.

Printed in the U.S.A. DAN BUCKLEY, President, Marvel Entertainment; JOE QUESADA, Chief Creative Officer; TOM BREVOORT, SVP of Publishing; DAVID BOGART, SVP of Business Affairs & Operations, Publishing & Partnership; C.B. CEBULSKI, VP of Brand Management & Development, Asia; DAVID GABRIEL, SVP of Sales & Marketing, Publishing; JEFF YOUNGQUIST, VP of Production & Special Projects; DAN CARR, Executive Director of Publishing Technology; ALEX MORALES, Director of Publishing Operations; SUSAN CRESPI, Production Manager; STAN LEE, Chairman Emeritus. For information regarding advertising in Marvel Comics or on Marvel.com, please contact Vit DeBellis, Integrated Sales Manager, at vdebellis@marvel.com. For Marvel subscription inquiries, please call 888-511-5480. **Manufactured between 6/30/2017 and 7/31/2017 by QUAD/GRAPHICS WASECA, WASECA, MN, USA.**

10 9 8 7 6 5 4 3 2 1

X-MEN BLUE

STRANGEST

Writer/**CULLEN BUNN**

ISSUES #1-3
Artists/**JORGE MOLINA** with **MATTEO BUFFAGNI** (#1)
& **RAY-ANTHONY HEIGHT** (#3)
Color Artist/**MATT MILLA**

ISSUE #4
Penciler/**JULIAN LOPEZ**
Inkers/**JOSÉ MARZAN JR.** & **WALDEN WONG**
Color Artist/**IRMA KNIIVILA**

ISSUE #5
Artists/**JULIAN LOPEZ** & **CORY SMITH**
Color Artist/**IRMA KNIIVILA**

ISSUE #6
Pencilers/**RAY-ANTHONY HEIGHT** & **RAMÓN BACHS**
Inkers/**MARC DEERING** & **TERRY PALLOT**
Color Artist/**IRMA KNIIVILA**

Letterer/**VC's CORY PETIT**

Cover Artists/**ARTHUR ADAMS** & **PETER STEIGERWALD**

Assistant Editor/**CHRISTINA HARRINGTON**
Editor/**MARK PANICCIA**

X-MEN CREATED BY **STAN LEE** & **JACK KIRBY**

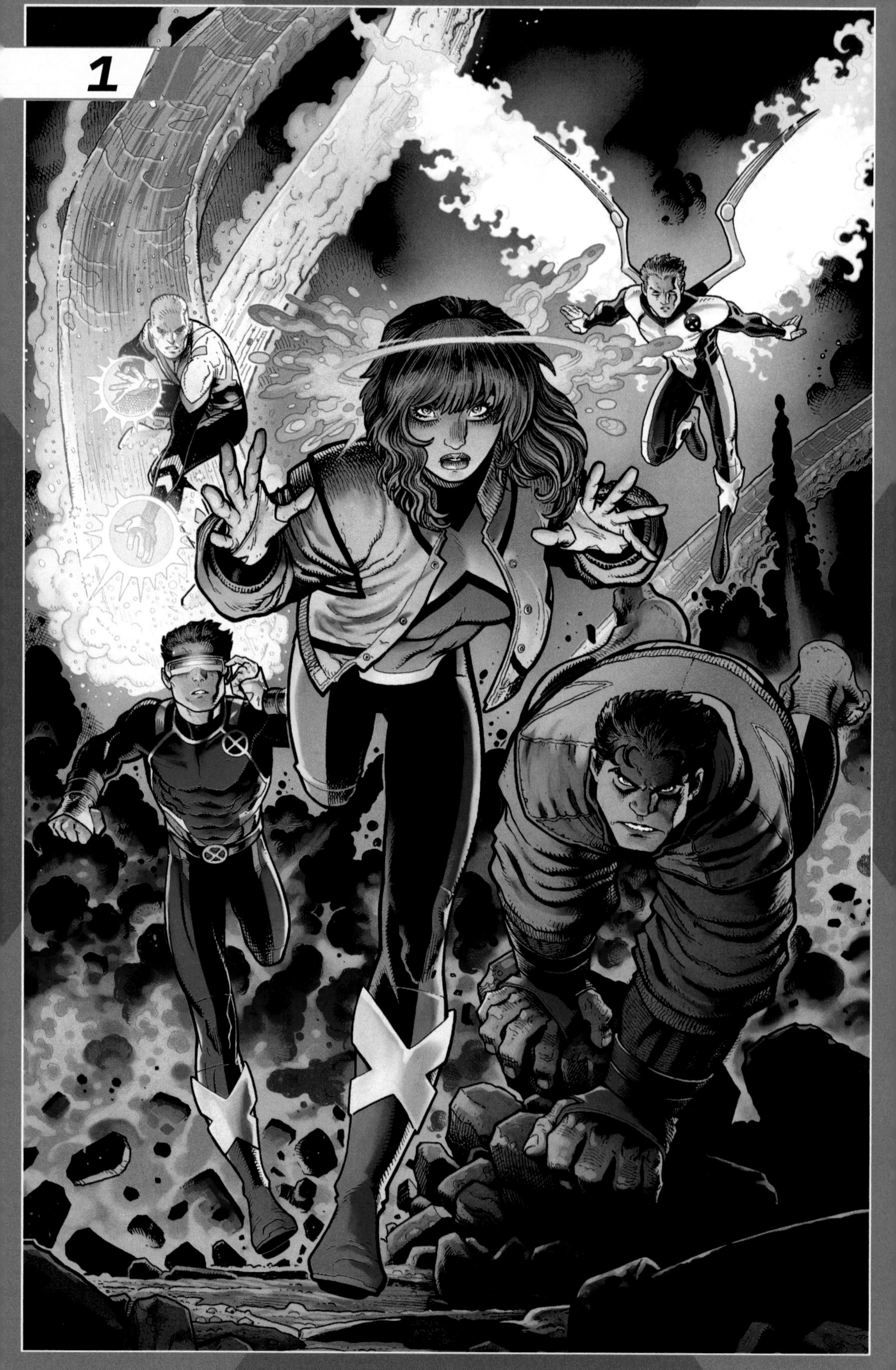
1

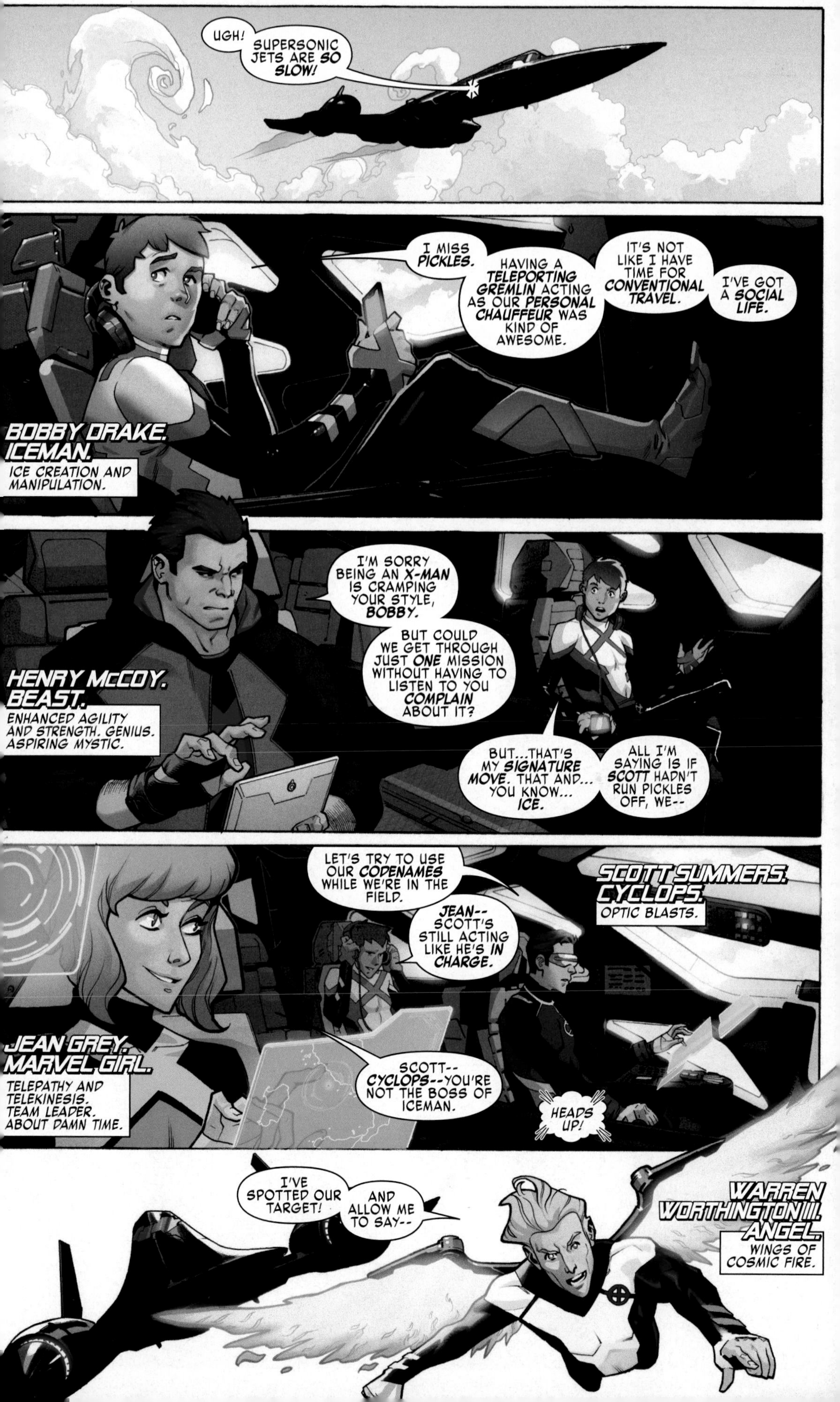
UGH!
SUPERSONIC JETS ARE SO SLOW!
I MISS PICKLES.
HAVING A TELEPORTING GREMLIN ACTING AS OUR PERSONAL CHAUFFEUR WAS KIND OF AWESOME.
IT'S NOT LIKE I HAVE TIME FOR CONVENTIONAL TRAVEL.
I'VE GOT A SOCIAL LIFE.
BOBBY DRAKE. ICEMAN.
ICE CREATION AND MANIPULATION.
I'M SORRY BEING AN X-MAN IS CRAMPING YOUR STYLE, BOBBY.
BUT COULD WE GET THROUGH JUST ONE MISSION WITHOUT HAVING TO LISTEN TO YOU COMPLAIN ABOUT IT?
HENRY McCOY. BEAST.
ENHANCED AGILITY AND STRENGTH. GENIUS. ASPIRING MYSTIC.
BUT...THAT'S MY SIGNATURE MOVE. THAT AND... YOU KNOW... ICE.
ALL I'M SAYING IS IF SCOTT HADN'T RUN PICKLES OFF, WE--
LET'S TRY TO USE OUR CODENAMES WHILE WE'RE IN THE FIELD.
SCOTT SUMMERS. CYCLOPS.
OPTIC BLASTS.
JEAN-- SCOTT'S STILL ACTING LIKE HE'S IN CHARGE.
JEAN GREY. MARVEL GIRL.
TELEPATHY AND TELEKINESIS. TEAM LEADER. ABOUT DAMN TIME.
SCOTT-- CYCLOPS--YOU'RE NOT THE BOSS OF ICEMAN.
HEADS UP!
I'VE SPOTTED OUR TARGET!
AND ALLOW ME TO SAY--
WARREN WORTHINGTON III. ANGEL.
WINGS OF COSMIC FIRE.

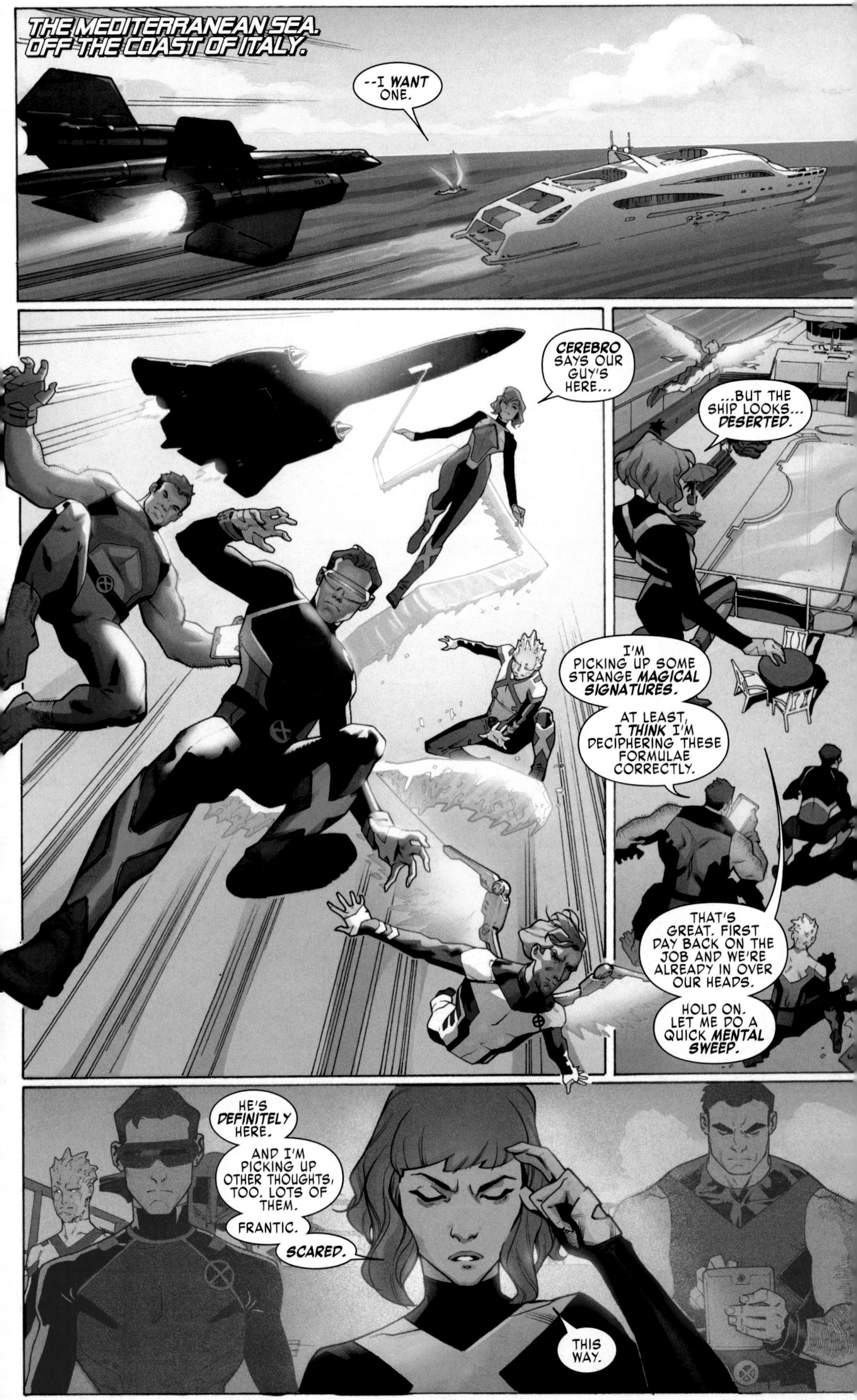
THE MEDITERRANEAN SEA. OFF THE COAST OF ITALY.
--I WANT ONE.
CEREBRO SAYS OUR GUY'S HERE...
...BUT THE SHIP LOOKS... DESERTED.
I'M PICKING UP SOME STRANGE MAGICAL SIGNATURES.
AT LEAST, I THINK I'M DECIPHERING THESE FORMULAE CORRECTLY.
THAT'S GREAT. FIRST DAY BACK ON THE JOB AND WE'RE ALREADY IN OVER OUR HEADS.
HOLD ON. LET ME DO A QUICK MENTAL SWEEP.
HE'S DEFINITELY HERE.
AND I'M PICKING UP OTHER THOUGHTS, TOO. LOTS OF THEM.
FRANTIC.
SCARED.
THIS WAY.

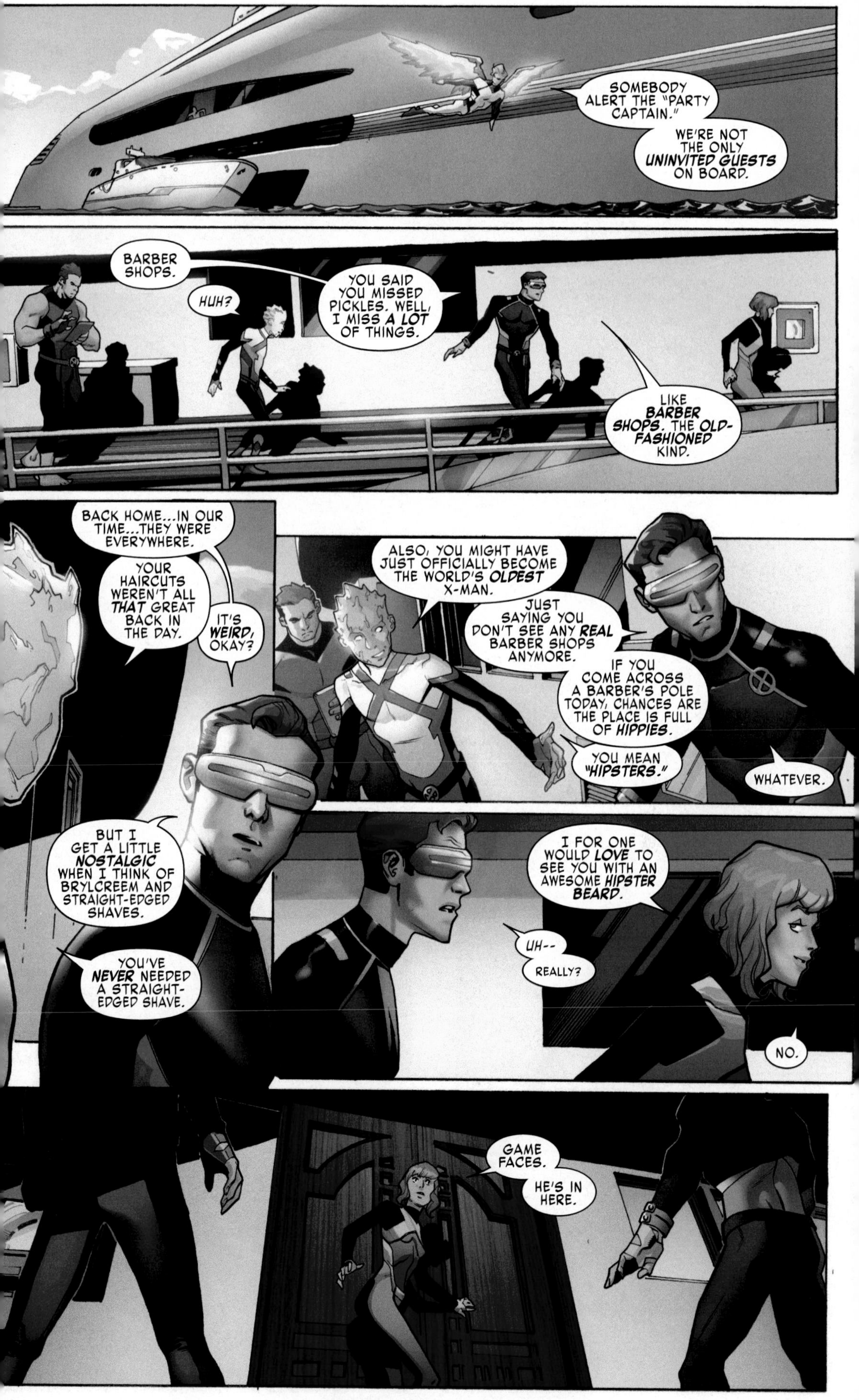

SOMEBODY ALERT THE "PARTY CAPTAIN."
WE'RE NOT THE ONLY UNINVITED GUESTS ON BOARD.
BARBER SHOPS.
HUH?
YOU SAID YOU MISSED PICKLES. WELL, I MISS A LOT OF THINGS.
LIKE BARBER SHOPS. THE OLD-FASHIONED KIND.
BACK HOME...IN OUR TIME...THEY WERE EVERYWHERE.
YOUR HAIRCUTS WEREN'T ALL THAT GREAT BACK IN THE DAY.
IT'S WEIRD, OKAY?
ALSO, YOU MIGHT HAVE JUST OFFICIALLY BECOME THE WORLD'S OLDEST X-MAN.
JUST SAYING YOU DON'T SEE ANY REAL BARBER SHOPS ANYMORE.
IF YOU COME ACROSS A BARBER'S POLE TODAY, CHANCES ARE THE PLACE IS FULL OF HIPPIES.
YOU MEAN "HIPSTERS."
WHATEVER.
BUT I GET A LITTLE NOSTALGIC WHEN I THINK OF BRYLCREEM AND STRAIGHT-EDGED SHAVES.
YOU'VE NEVER NEEDED A STRAIGHT-EDGED SHAVE.
I FOR ONE WOULD LOVE TO SEE YOU WITH AN AWESOME HIPSTER BEARD.
UH--
REALLY?
NO.
GAME FACES.
HE'S IN HERE.

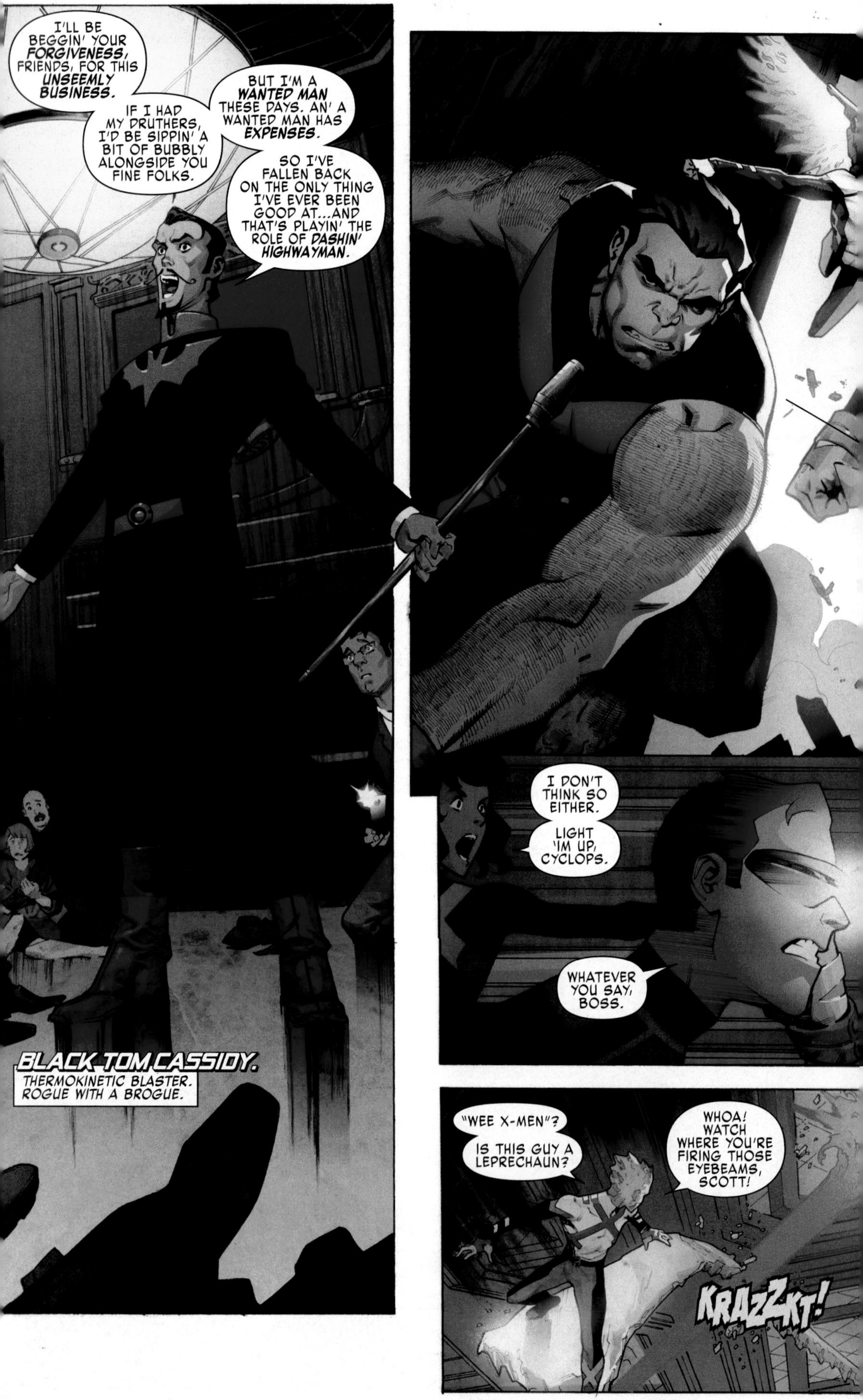

I'LL BE BEGGIN' YOUR FORGIVENESS, FRIENDS, FOR THIS UNSEEMLY BUSINESS.
IF I HAD MY DRUTHERS, I'D BE SIPPIN' A BIT OF BUBBLY ALONGSIDE YOU FINE FOLKS.
BUT I'M A WANTED MAN THESE DAYS. AN' A WANTED MAN HAS EXPENSES.
SO I'VE FALLEN BACK ON THE ONLY THING I'VE EVER BEEN GOOD AT...AND THAT'S PLAYIN' THE ROLE OF DASHIN' HIGHWAYMAN.
BLACK TOM CASSIDY.
THERMOKINETIC BLASTER. ROGUE WITH A BROGUE.
I DON'T THINK SO EITHER.
LIGHT 'IM UP, CYCLOPS.
WHATEVER YOU SAY, BOSS.
"WEE X-MEN"?
IS THIS GUY A LEPRECHAUN?
WHOA! WATCH WHERE YOU'RE FIRING THOSE EYEBEAMS, SCOTT!
KRAZZKT!

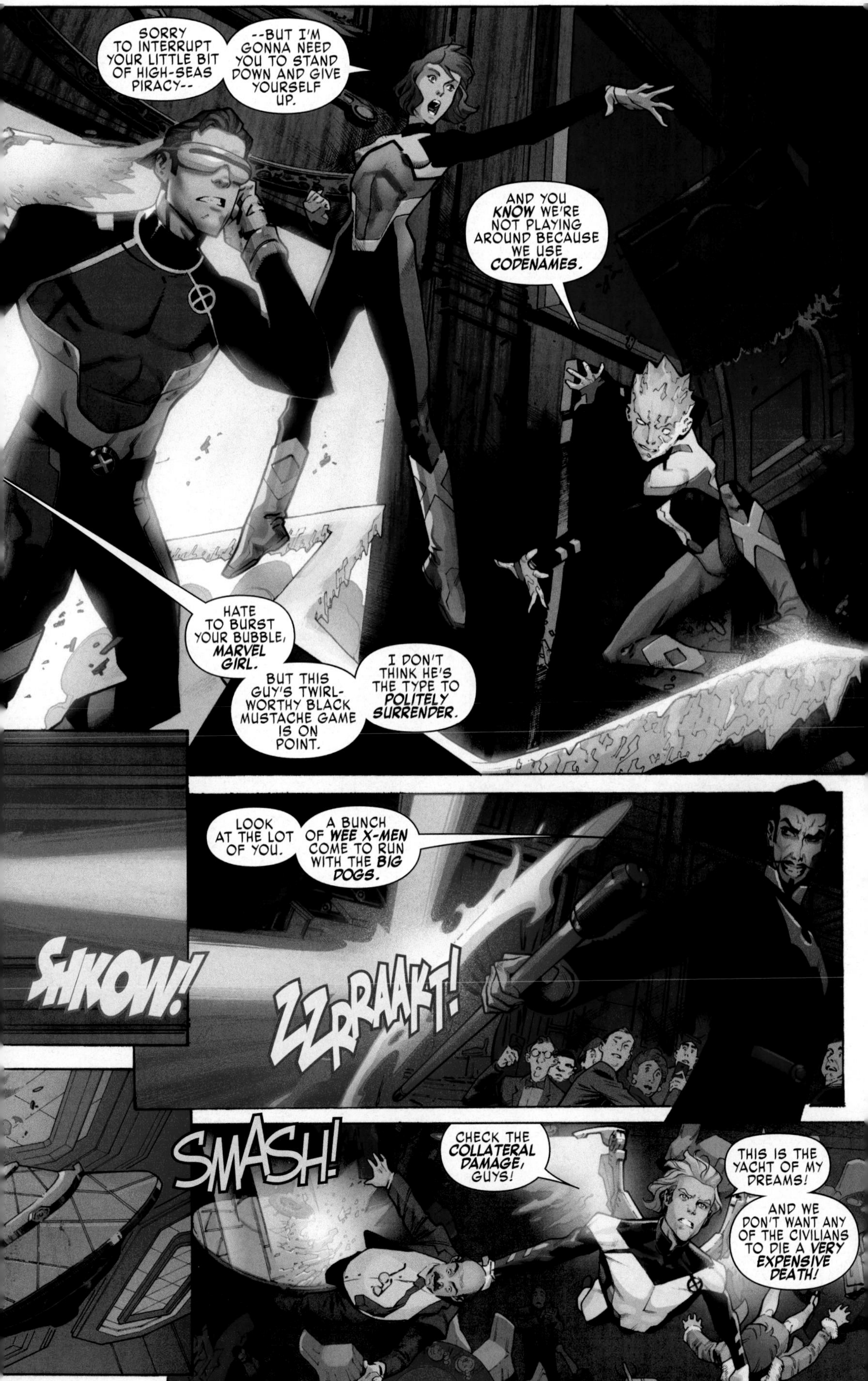
SORRY TO INTERRUPT YOUR LITTLE BIT OF HIGH-SEAS PIRACY--
--BUT I'M GONNA NEED YOU TO STAND DOWN AND GIVE YOURSELF UP.
AND YOU KNOW WE'RE NOT PLAYING AROUND BECAUSE WE USE CODENAMES.
HATE TO BURST YOUR BUBBLE, MARVEL GIRL.
BUT THIS GUY'S TWIRL-WORTHY BLACK MUSTACHE GAME IS ON POINT.
I DON'T THINK HE'S THE TYPE TO POLITELY SURRENDER.
LOOK AT THE LOT OF YOU.
A BUNCH OF WEE X-MEN COME TO RUN WITH THE BIG DOGS.
SHKOW!
ZZRRAAKT!
SMASH!
CHECK THE COLLATERAL DAMAGE, GUYS!
THIS IS THE YACHT OF MY DREAMS!
AND WE DON'T WANT ANY OF THE CIVILIANS TO DIE A VERY EXPENSIVE DEATH!

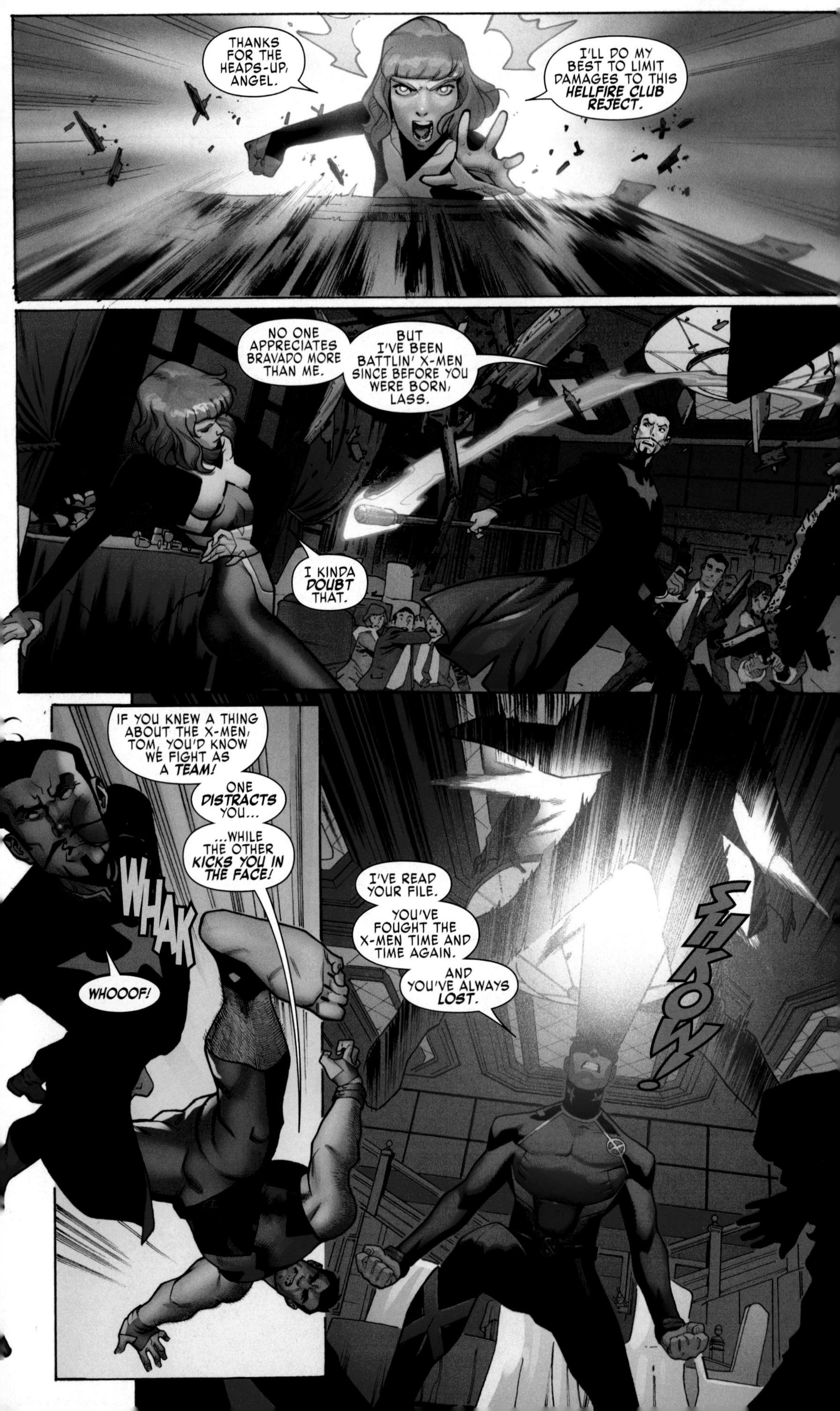
THANKS FOR THE HEADS-UP, ANGEL.
I'LL DO MY BEST TO LIMIT DAMAGES TO THIS HELLFIRE CLUB REJECT.
NO ONE APPRECIATES BRAVADO MORE THAN ME.
BUT I'VE BEEN BATTLIN' X-MEN SINCE BEFORE YOU WERE BORN, LASS.
I KINDA DOUBT THAT.
IF YOU KNEW A THING ABOUT THE X-MEN, TOM, YOU'D KNOW WE FIGHT AS A TEAM!
ONE DISTRACTS YOU...
...WHILE THE OTHER KICKS YOU IN THE FACE!
WHAK
WHOOOF!
I'VE READ YOUR FILE.
YOU'VE FOUGHT THE X-MEN TIME AND TIME AGAIN.
AND YOU'VE ALWAYS LOST.
SHKOW!

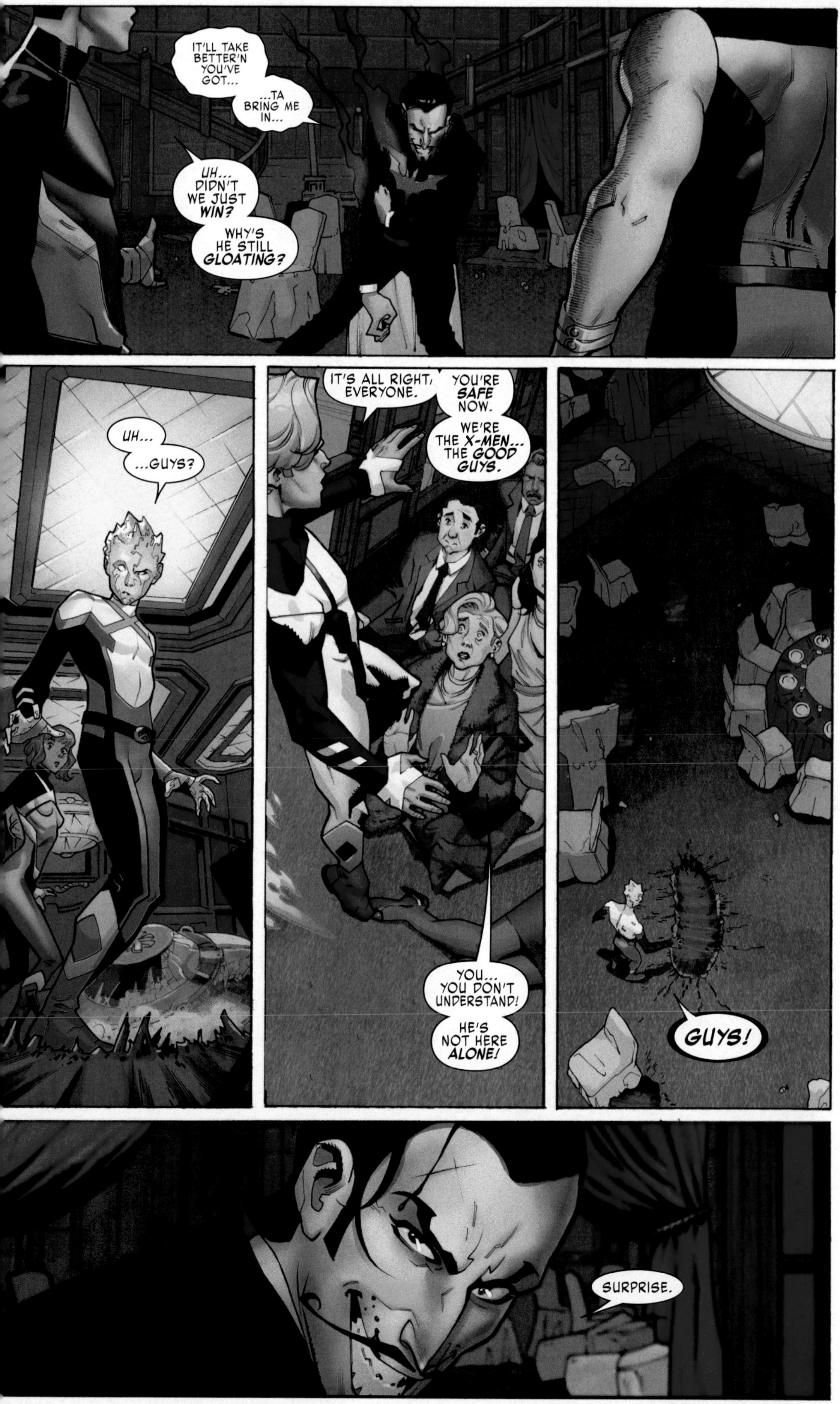
IT'LL TAKE BETTER'N YOU'VE GOT...
...TA BRING ME IN...
UH... DIDN'T WE JUST WIN?
WHY'S HE STILL GLOATING?
UH...
...GUYS?
IT'S ALL RIGHT, EVERYONE.
YOU'RE SAFE NOW.
WE'RE THE X-MEN... THE GOOD GUYS.
YOU... YOU DON'T UNDERSTAND!
HE'S NOT HERE ALONE!
GUYS!
SURPRISE.

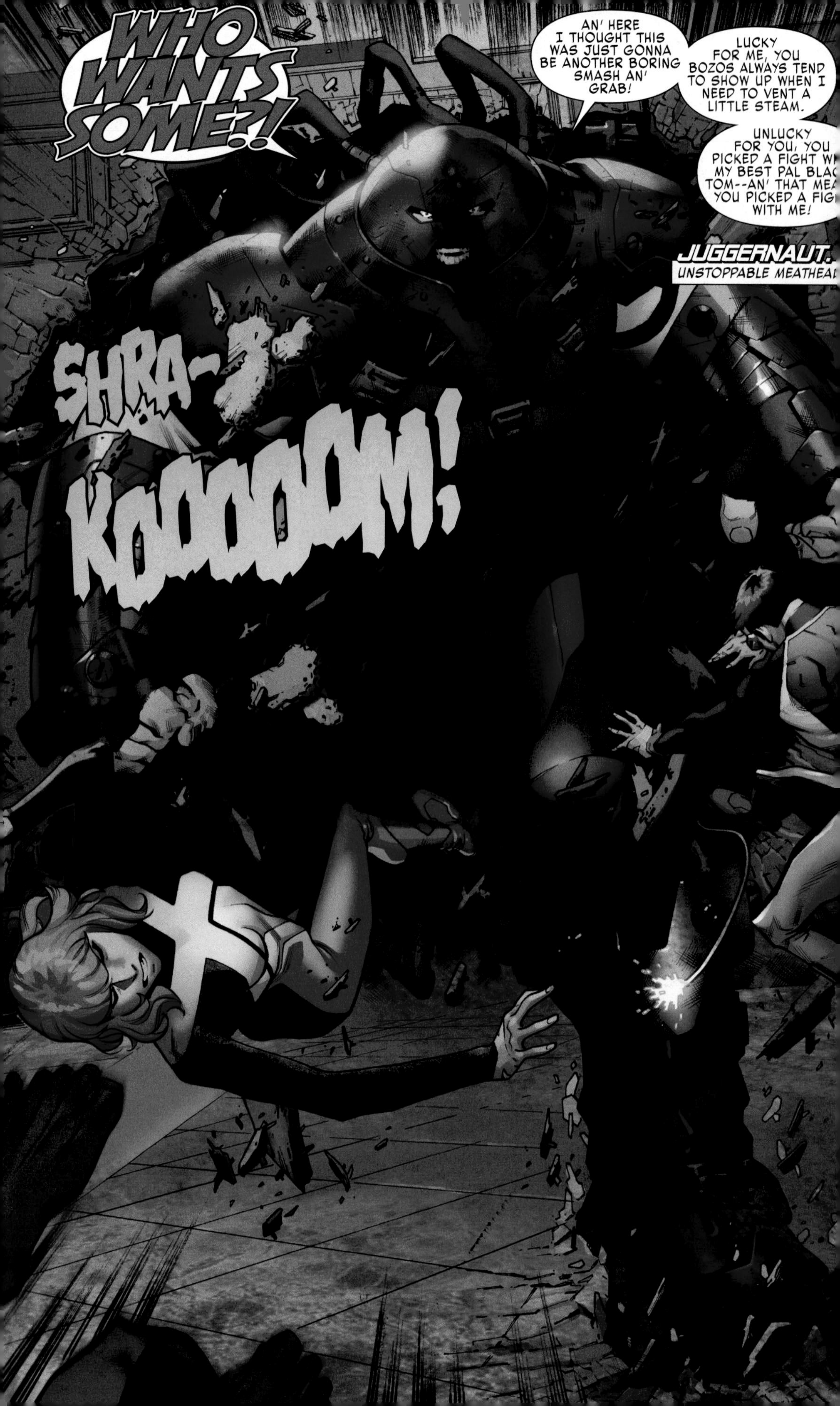

WHO WANTS SOME?!
AN' HERE I THOUGHT THIS WAS JUST GONNA BE ANOTHER BORING SMASH AN' GRAB!
LUCKY FOR ME, YOU BOZOS ALWAYS TEND TO SHOW UP WHEN I NEED TO VENT A LITTLE STEAM.
UNLUCKY FOR YOU, YOU PICKED A FIGHT WI MY BEST PAL BLAC TOM--AN' THAT MEA YOU PICKED A FIG WITH ME!
JUGGERNAUT.
UNSTOPPABLE MEATHEA
SHRA-
KOOOOOM!

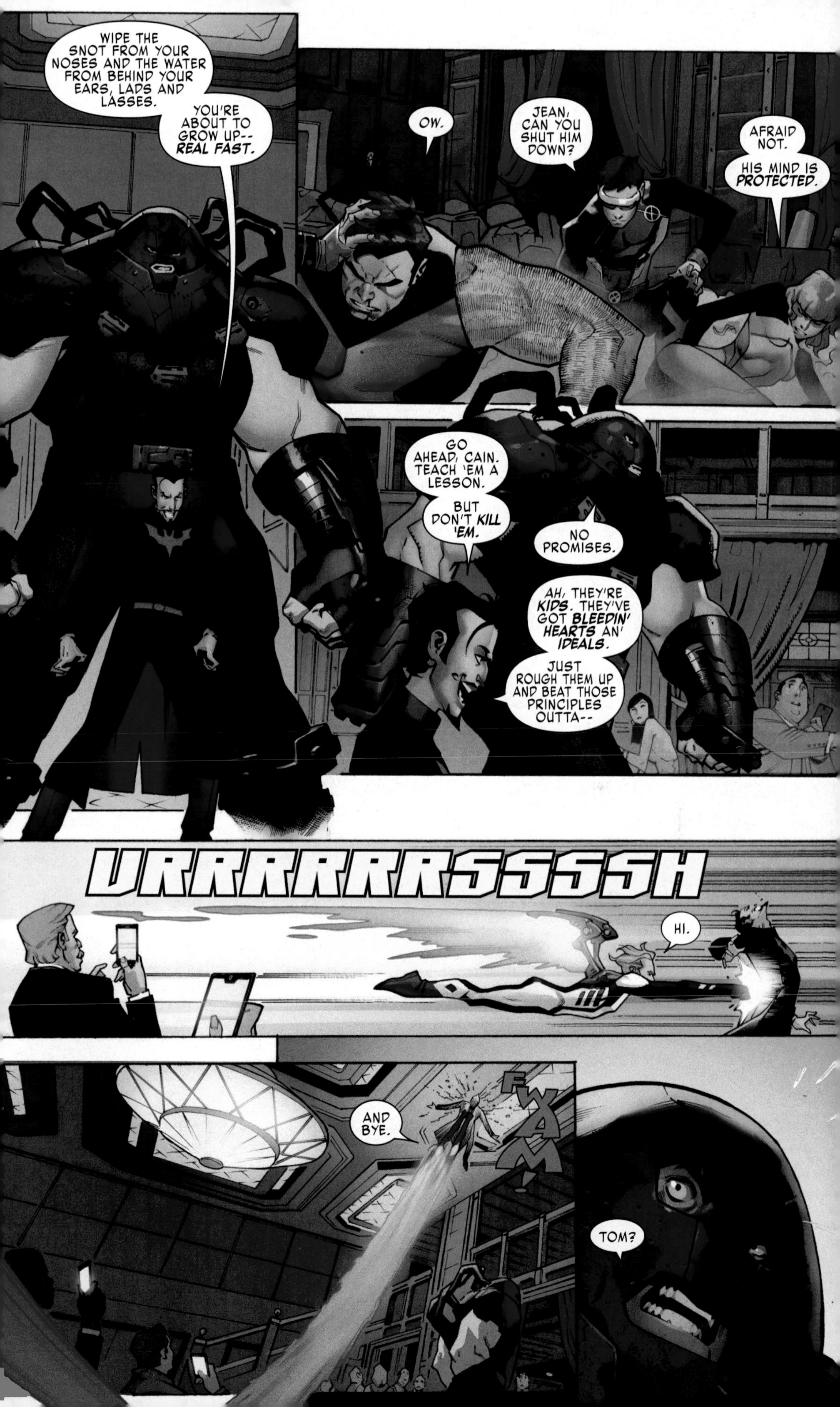
WIPE THE SNOT FROM YOUR NOSES AND THE WATER FROM BEHIND YOUR EARS, LADS AND LASSES.
YOU'RE ABOUT TO GROW UP-- REAL FAST.
OW.
JEAN, CAN YOU SHUT HIM DOWN?
AFRAID NOT.
HIS MIND IS PROTECTED.
GO AHEAD, CAIN. TEACH 'EM A LESSON.
BUT DON'T KILL 'EM.
NO PROMISES.
AH, THEY'RE KIDS. THEY'VE GOT BLEEDIN' HEARTS AN' IDEALS.
JUST ROUGH THEM UP AND BEAT THOSE PRINCIPLES OUTTA--
URRRRRRSSSSH
HI.
AND BYE.
FWAM
TOM?

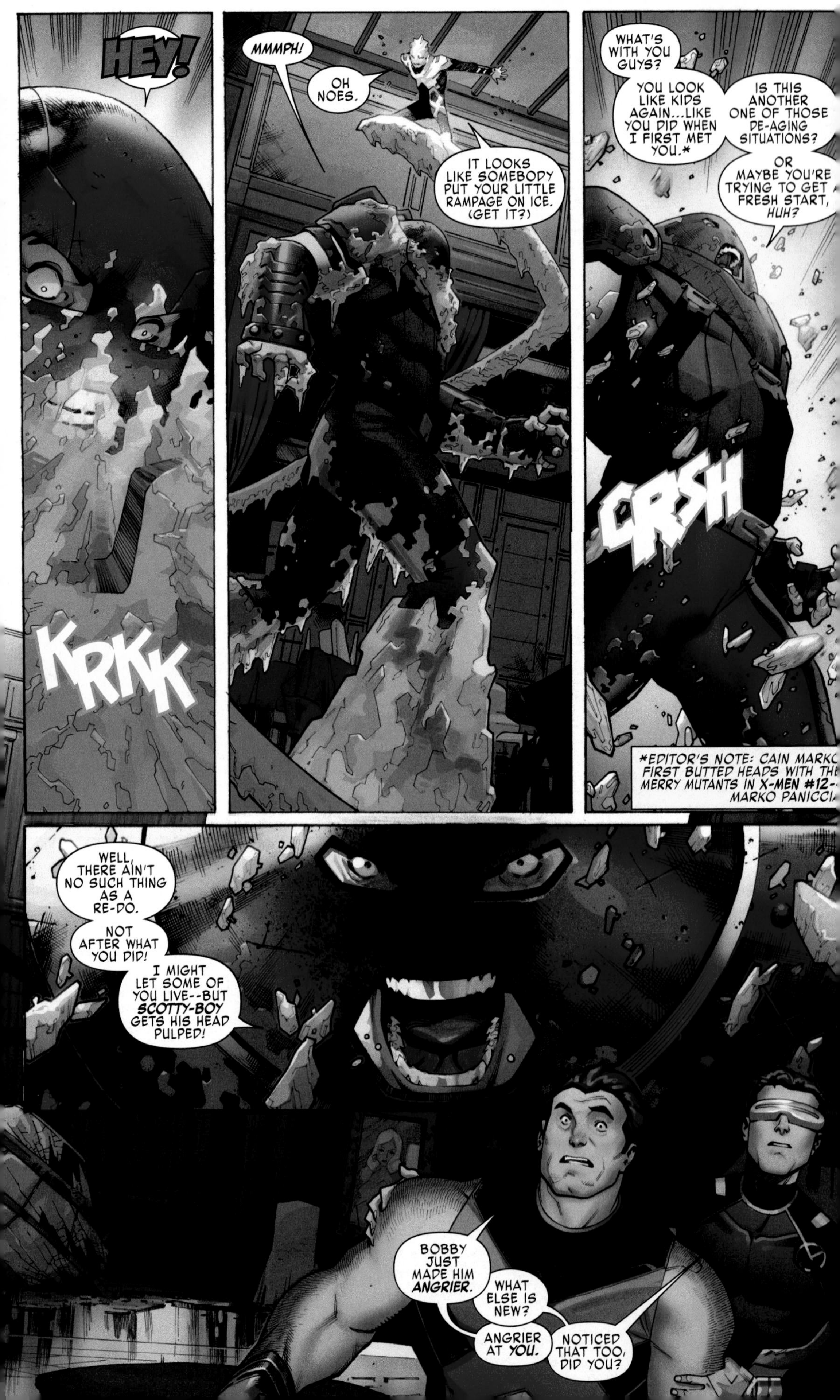
HEY!
KRKK
MMMPH!
OH NOES.
IT LOOKS LIKE SOMEBODY PUT YOUR LITTLE RAMPAGE ON ICE. (GET IT?)
WHAT'S WITH YOU GUYS?
YOU LOOK LIKE KIDS AGAIN...LIKE YOU DID WHEN I FIRST MET YOU.*
IS THIS ANOTHER ONE OF THOSE DE-AGING SITUATIONS?
OR MAYBE YOU'RE TRYING TO GET FRESH START, HUH?
CRSH
*EDITOR'S NOTE: CAIN MARKO FIRST BUTTED HEADS WITH THE MERRY MUTANTS IN X-MEN #12
MARKO PANICCI
WELL, THERE AIN'T NO SUCH THING AS A RE-DO.
NOT AFTER WHAT YOU DID!
I MIGHT LET SOME OF YOU LIVE--BUT SCOTTY-BOY GETS HIS HEAD PULPED!
BOBBY JUST MADE HIM ANGRIER.
WHAT ELSE IS NEW?
ANGRIER AT YOU.
NOTICED THAT TOO, DID YOU?

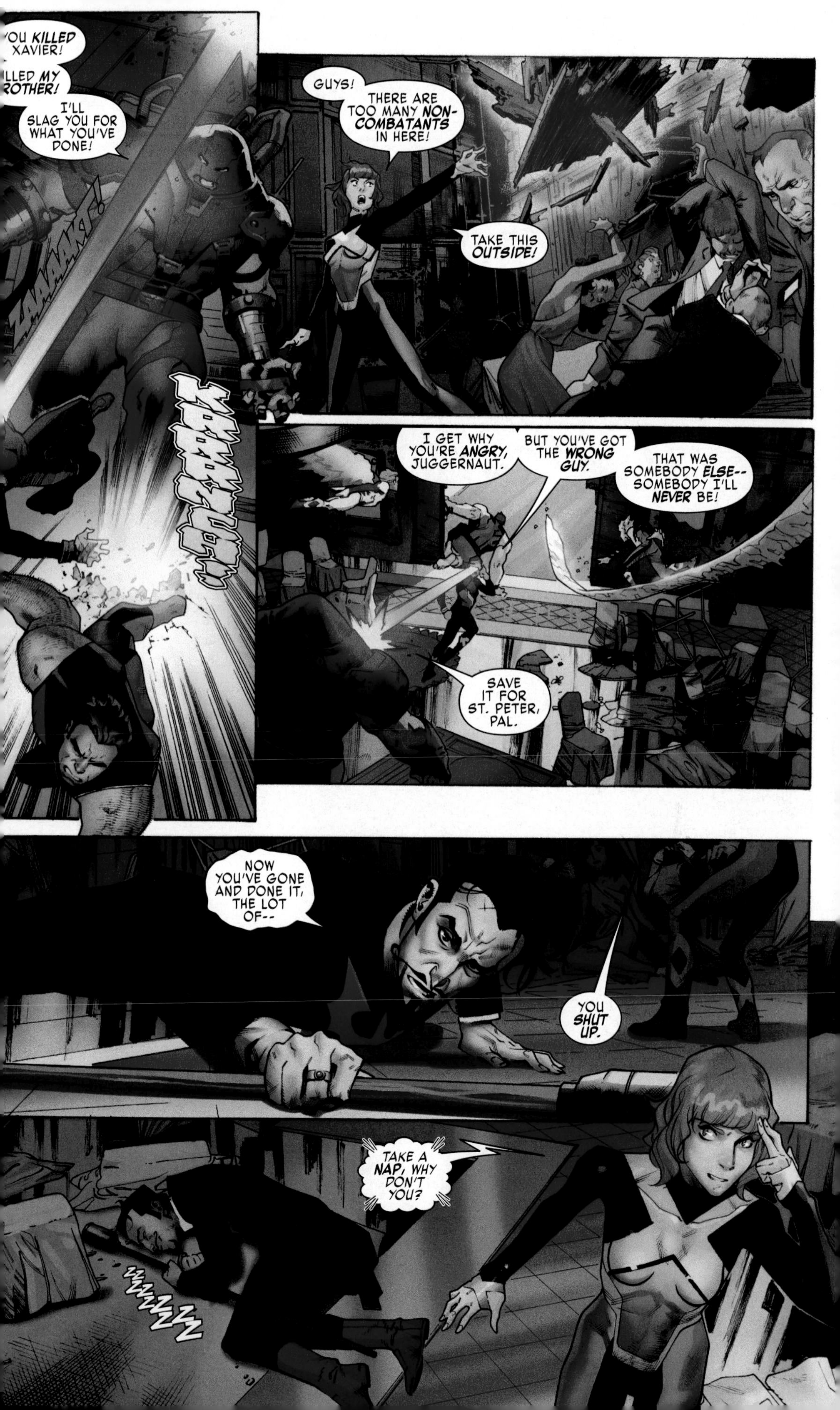
OU KILLED XAVIER!
ILLED MY ROTHER!
I'LL SLAG YOU FOR WHAT YOU'VE DONE!
ZAAAART!
GUYS!
THERE ARE TOO MANY NON-COMBATANTS IN HERE!
TAKE THIS OUTSIDE!
I GET WHY YOU'RE ANGRY, JUGGERNAUT.
BUT YOU'VE GOT THE WRONG GUY.
THAT WAS SOMEBODY ELSE-- SOMEBODY I'LL NEVER BE!
SAVE IT FOR ST. PETER, PAL.
NOW YOU'VE GONE AND DONE IT, THE LOT OF--
YOU SHUT UP.
TAKE A NAP, WHY DON'T YOU?
ZZZZZZZ

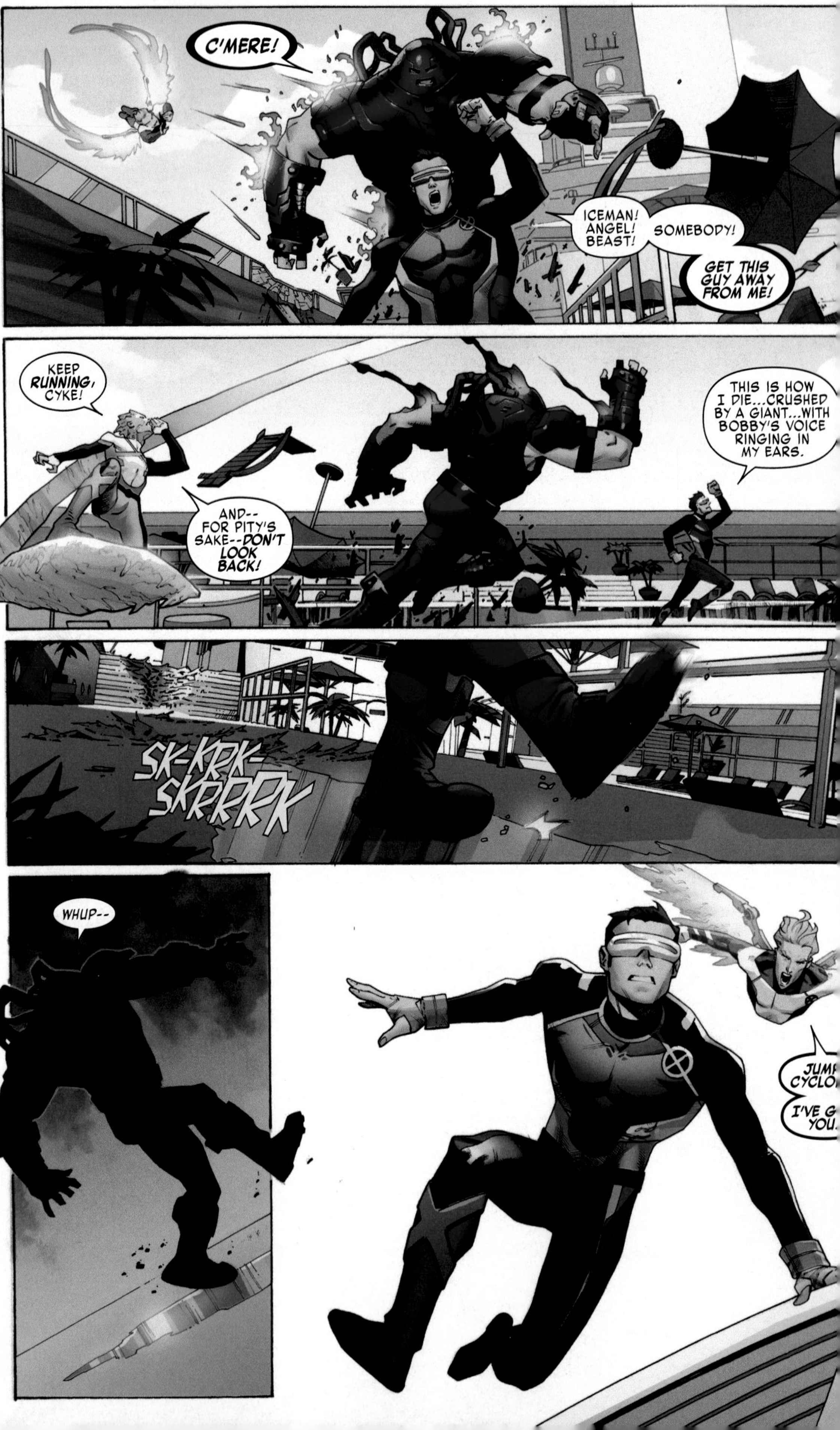
C'MERE!
ICEMAN! ANGEL! BEAST!
SOMEBODY!
GET THIS GUY AWAY FROM ME!
KEEP RUNNING, CYKE!
AND-- FOR PITY'S SAKE--DON'T LOOK BACK!
THIS IS HOW I DIE...CRUSHED BY A GIANT...WITH BOBBY'S VOICE RINGING IN MY EARS.
SK-KRK-SKRRRK
WHUP--

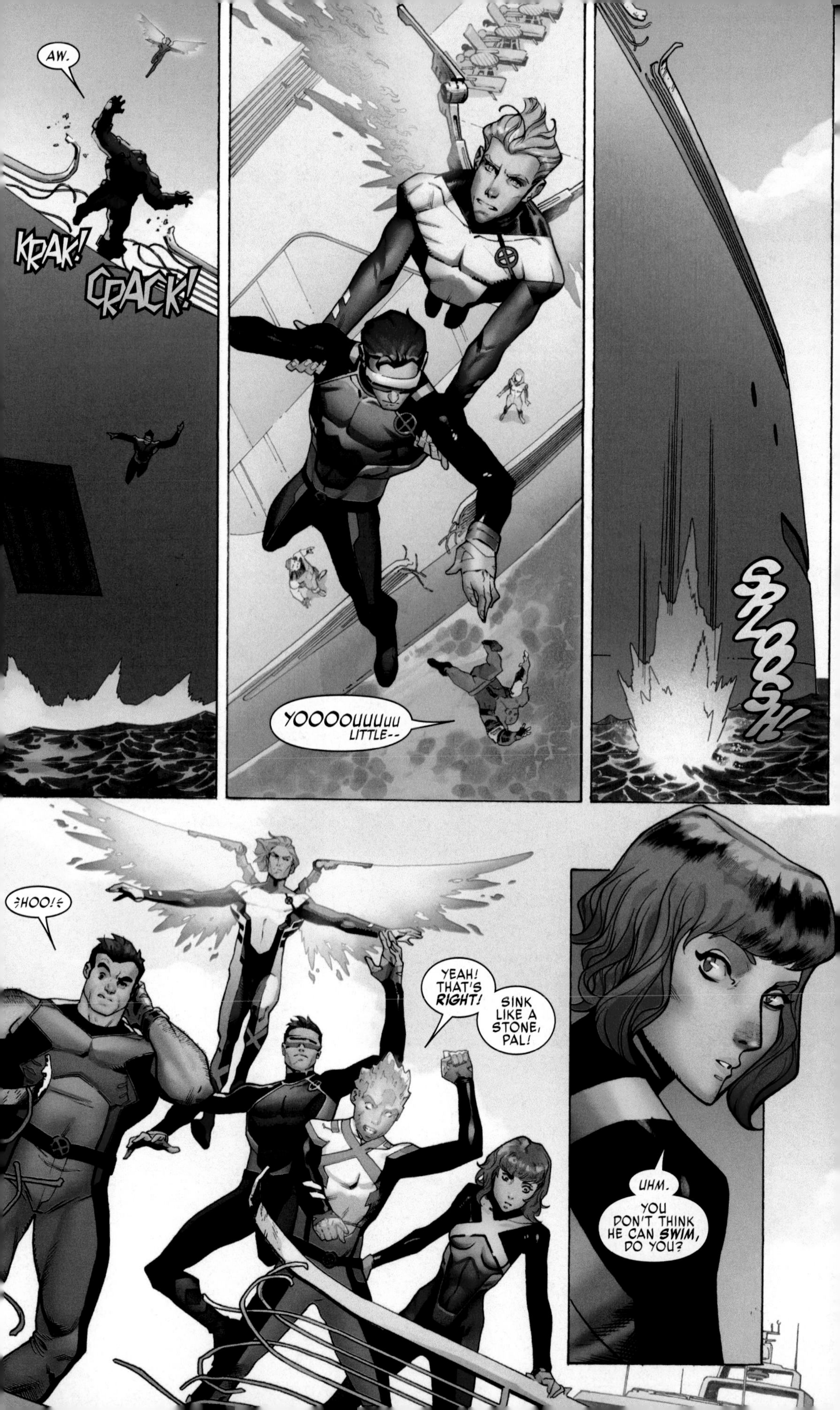
AW.
KRAK!
CRACK!
YOOOOuuuuu LITTLE--
SPLOOSH!
≥HOO!≤
YEAH! THAT'S RIGHT!
SINK LIKE A STONE, PAL!
UHM.
YOU DON'T THINK HE CAN SWIM, DO YOU?

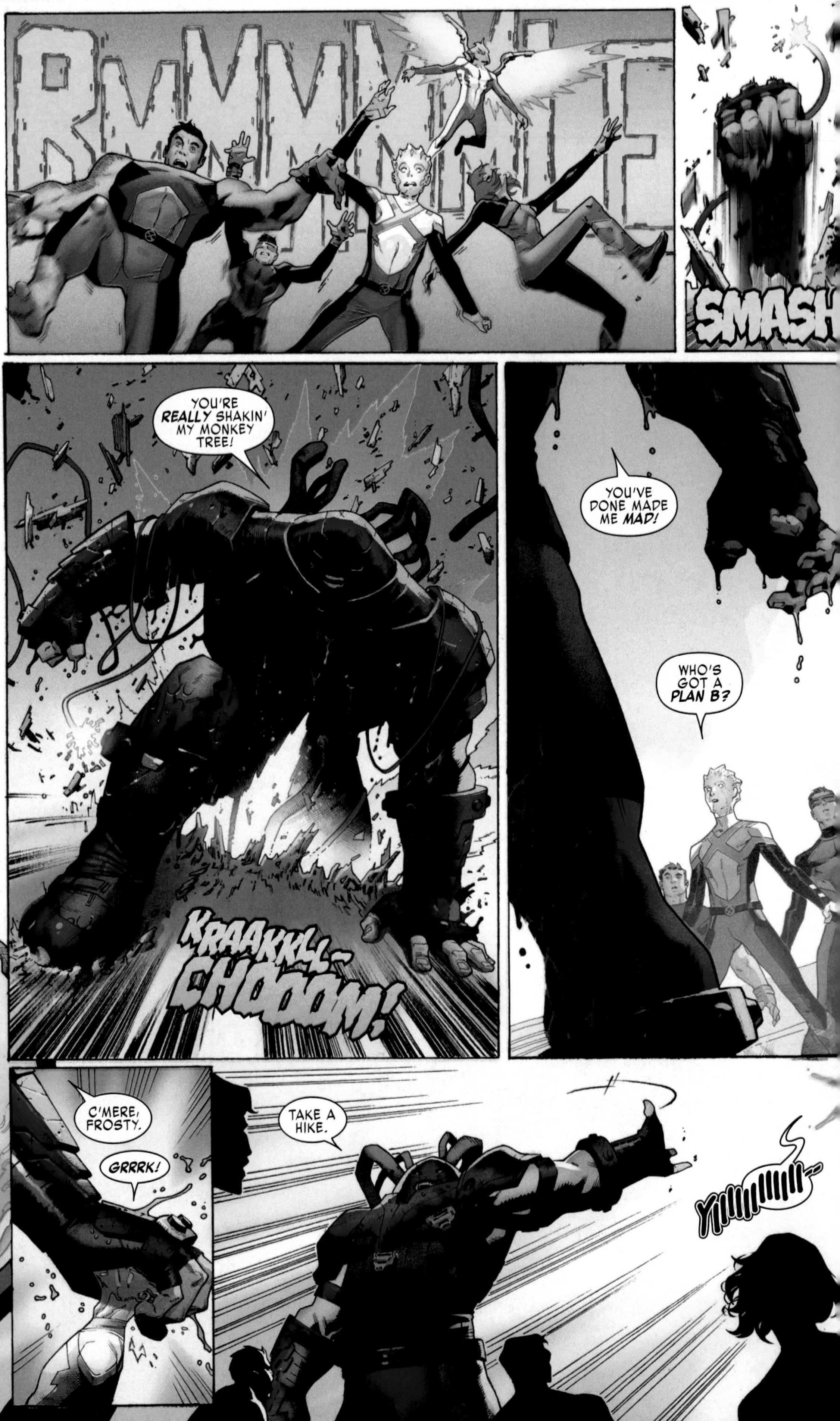
RMMMMF
SMASH
YOU'RE REALLY SHAKIN' MY MONKEY TREE!
KRAAKKLL-CHOOOM!
YOU'VE DONE MADE ME MAD!
WHO'S GOT A PLAN B?
C'MERE, FROSTY.
GRRRK!
TAKE A HIKE.
YIIIIIIIIII-

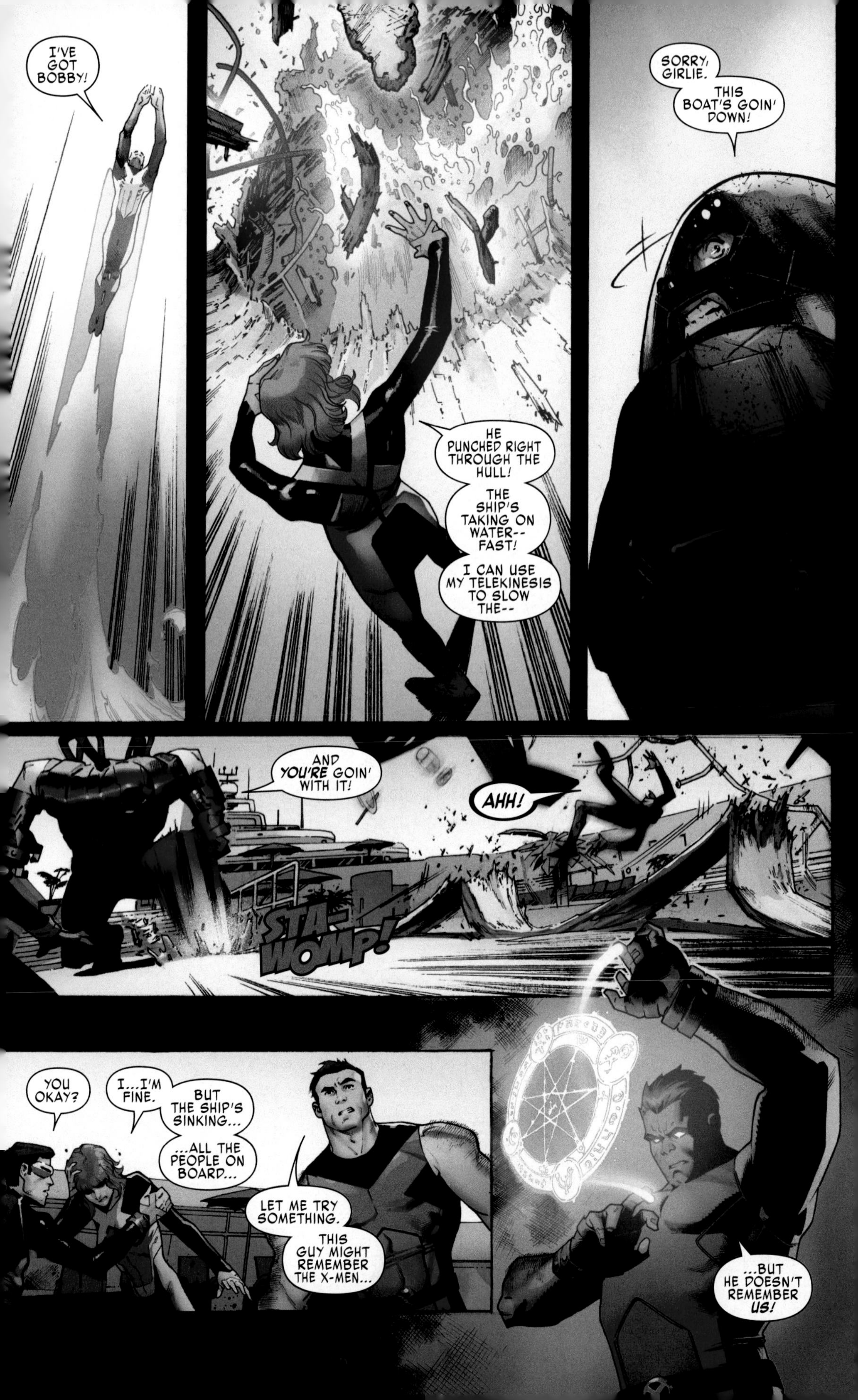
I'VE GOT BOBBY!
HE PUNCHED RIGHT THROUGH THE HULL!
THE SHIP'S TAKING ON WATER-- FAST!
I CAN USE MY TELEKINESIS TO SLOW THE--
SORRY, GIRLIE.
THIS BOAT'S GOIN' DOWN!
AND YOU'RE GOIN' WITH IT!
AHH!
STA-WOMP!
YOU OKAY?
I...I'M FINE.
BUT THE SHIP'S SINKING...
...ALL THE PEOPLE ON BOARD...
LET ME TRY SOMETHING.
THIS GUY MIGHT REMEMBER THE X-MEN...
...BUT HE DOESN'T REMEMBER US!

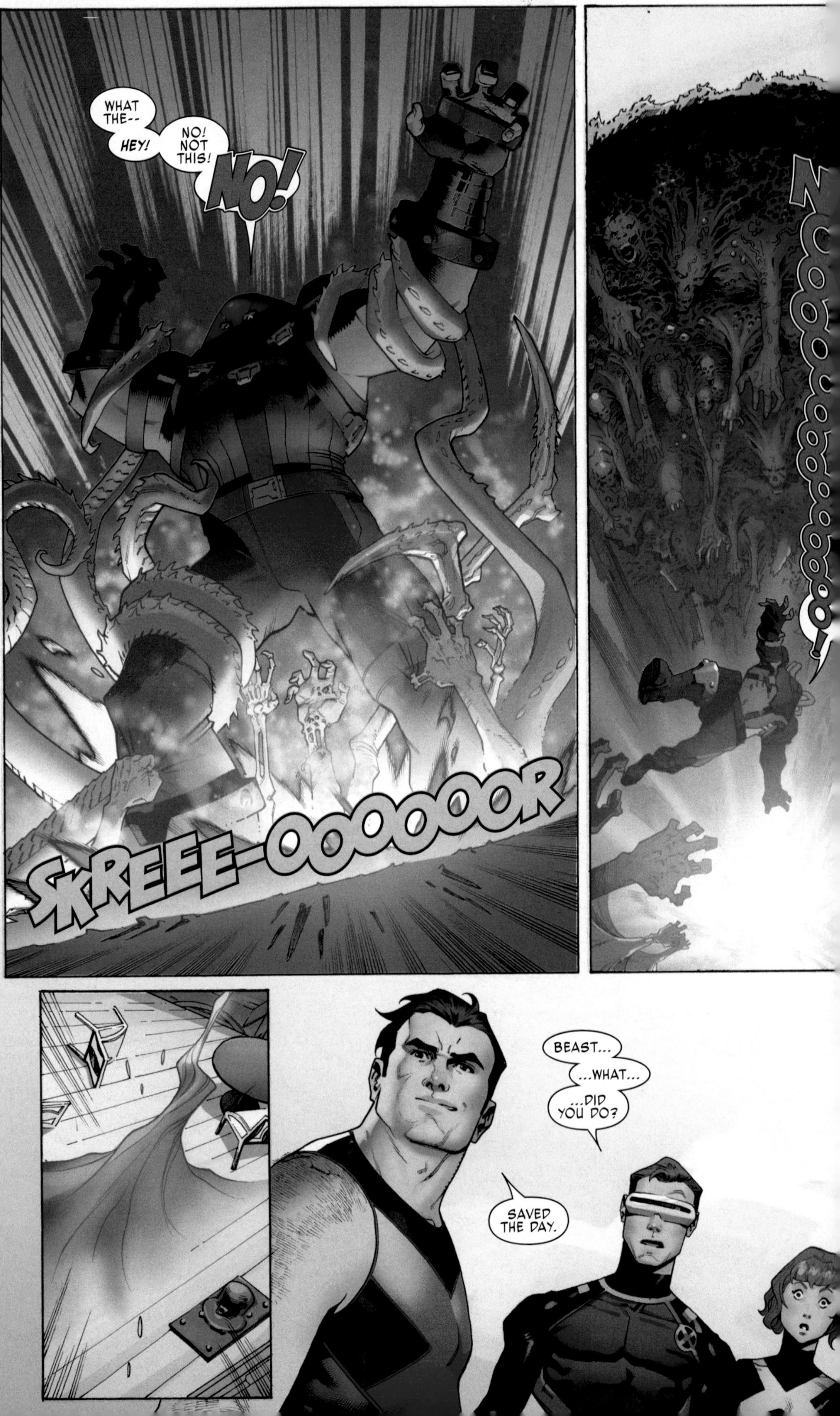

WHAT THE--
HEY!
NO! NOT THIS!
NO!
SKREEE-OOOOOOR
NOOOOOOOOOOOO!
BEAST...
...WHAT...
...DID YOU DO?
SAVED THE DAY.

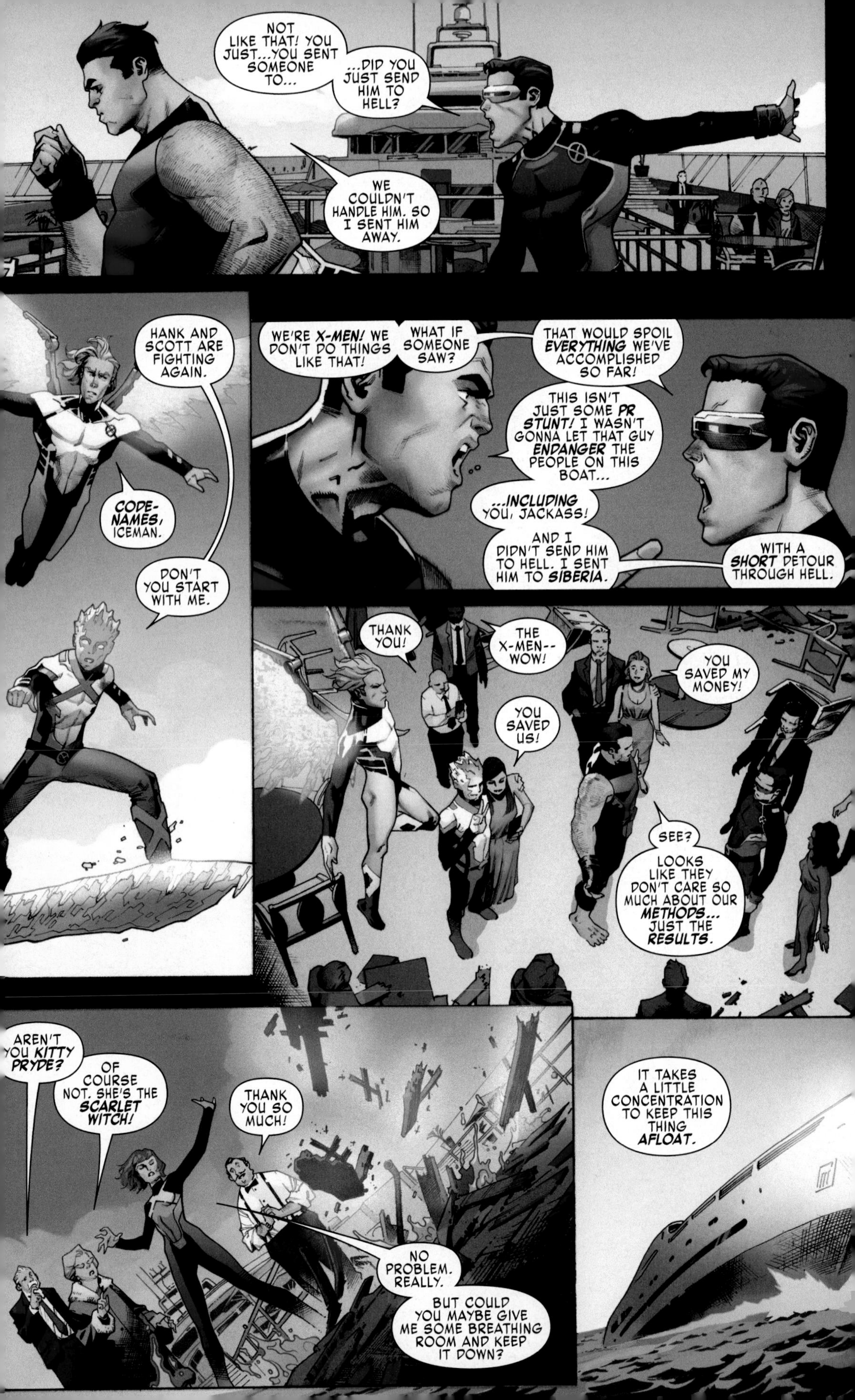
NOT LIKE THAT! YOU JUST...YOU SENT SOMEONE TO...
...DID YOU JUST SEND HIM TO HELL?
WE COULDN'T HANDLE HIM. SO I SENT HIM AWAY.
HANK AND SCOTT ARE FIGHTING AGAIN.
CODE-NAMES, ICEMAN.
DON'T YOU START WITH ME.
WE'RE X-MEN! WE DON'T DO THINGS LIKE THAT!
WHAT IF SOMEONE SAW?
THAT WOULD SPOIL EVERYTHING WE'VE ACCOMPLISHED SO FAR!
THIS ISN'T JUST SOME PR STUNT! I WASN'T GONNA LET THAT GUY ENDANGER THE PEOPLE ON THIS BOAT...
...INCLUDING YOU, JACKASS!
AND I DIDN'T SEND HIM TO HELL. I SENT HIM TO SIBERIA.
WITH A SHORT DETOUR THROUGH HELL.
THANK YOU!
THE X-MEN-- WOW!
YOU SAVED US!
YOU SAVED MY MONEY!
SEE?
LOOKS LIKE THEY DON'T CARE SO MUCH ABOUT OUR METHODS... JUST THE RESULTS.
AREN'T YOU KITTY PRYDE?
OF COURSE NOT. SHE'S THE SCARLET WITCH!
THANK YOU SO MUCH!
NO PROBLEM. REALLY.
BUT COULD YOU MAYBE GIVE ME SOME BREATHING ROOM AND KEEP IT DOWN?
IT TAKES A LITTLE CONCENTRATION TO KEEP THIS THING AFLOAT.

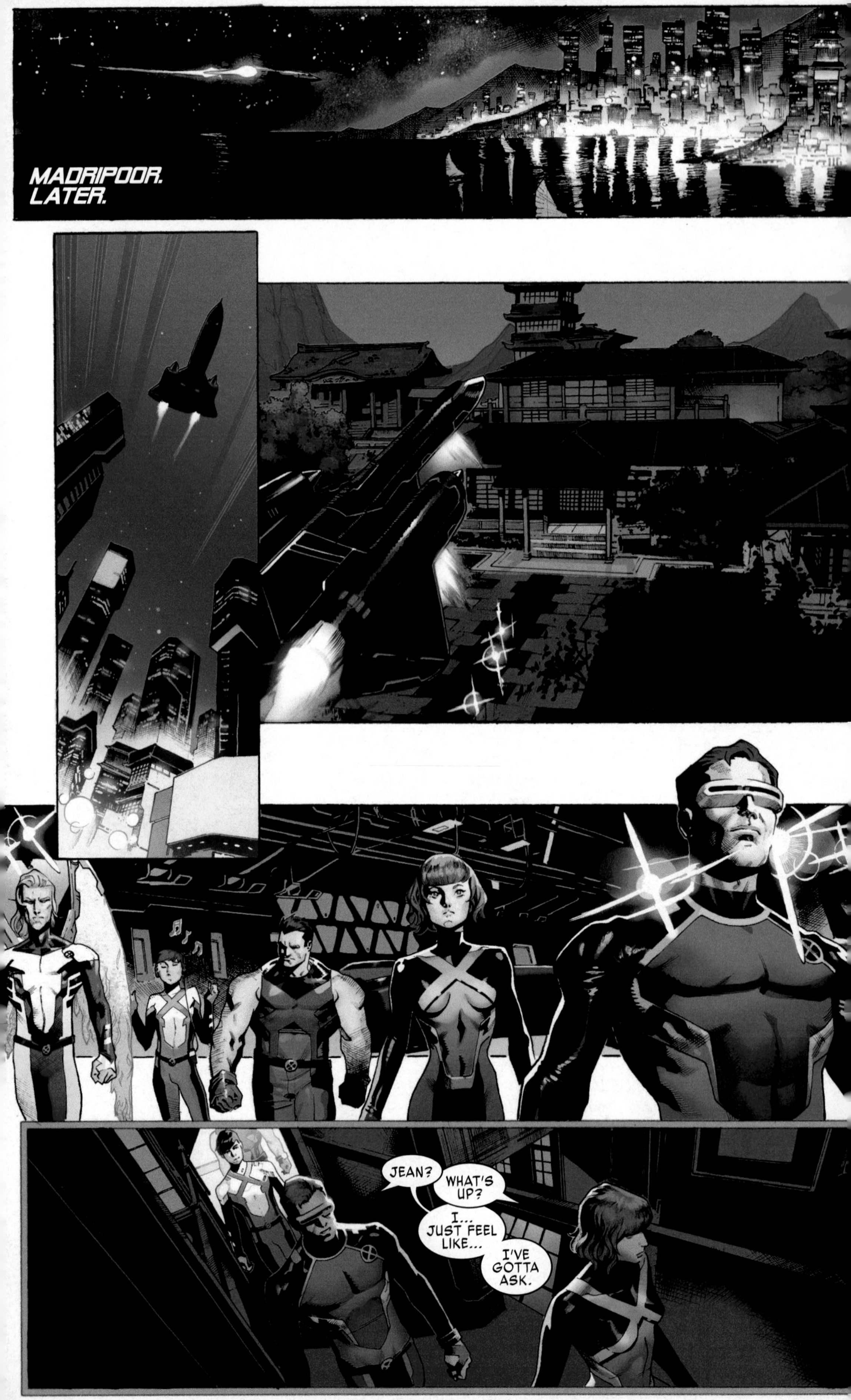

MADRIPOOR.
LATER.
JEAN?
WHAT'S UP?
I... JUST FEEL LIKE...
I'VE GOTTA ASK.

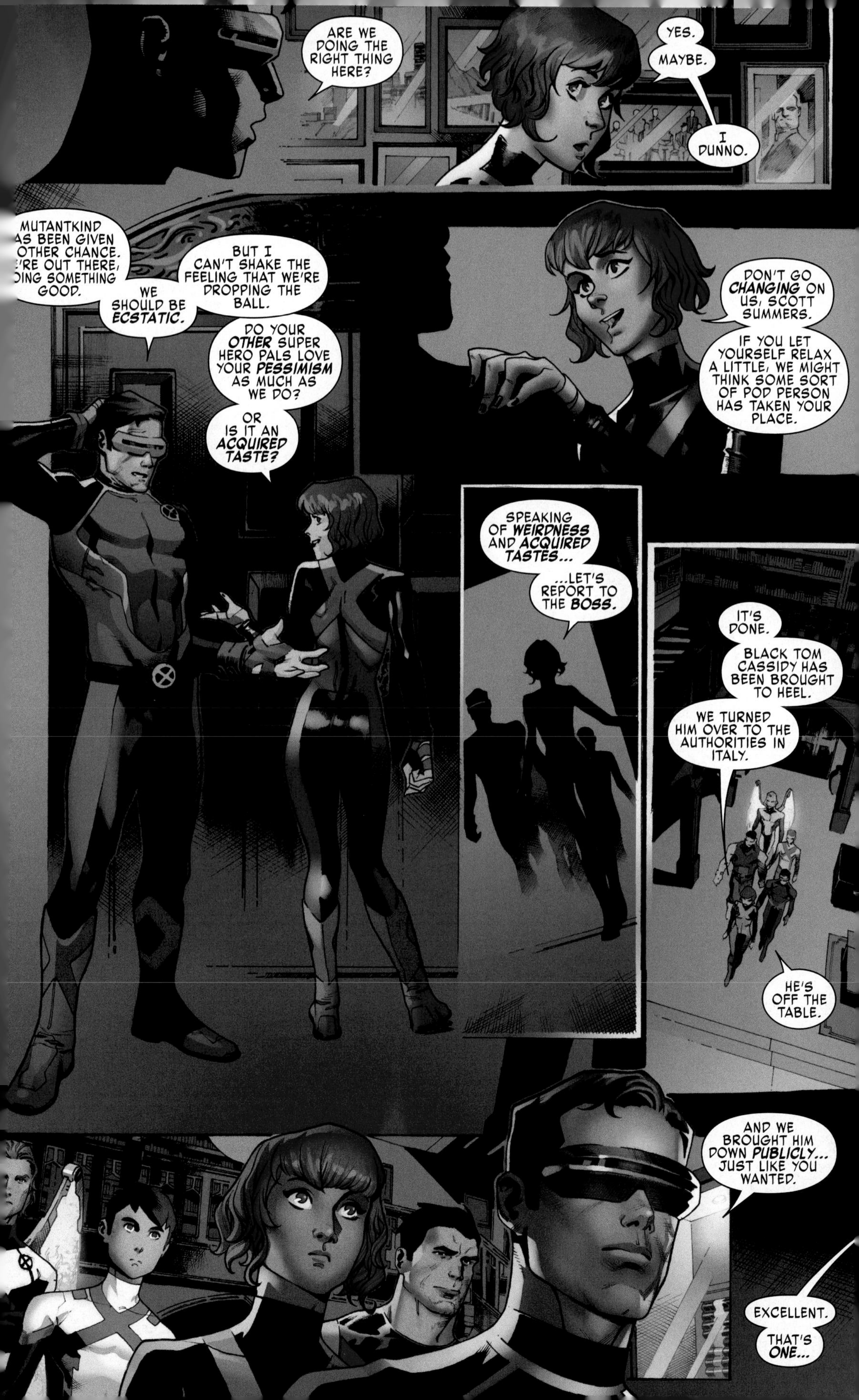
ARE WE DOING THE RIGHT THING HERE?
YES.
MAYBE.
I DUNNO.
MUTANTKIND AS BEEN GIVEN OTHER CHANCE. 'RE OUT THERE, OING SOMETHING GOOD.
WE SHOULD BE ECSTATIC.
BUT I CAN'T SHAKE THE FEELING THAT WE'RE DROPPING THE BALL.
DO YOUR OTHER SUPER HERO PALS LOVE YOUR PESSIMISM AS MUCH AS WE DO?
OR IS IT AN ACQUIRED TASTE?
DON'T GO CHANGING ON US, SCOTT SUMMERS.
IF YOU LET YOURSELF RELAX A LITTLE, WE MIGHT THINK SOME SORT OF POD PERSON HAS TAKEN YOUR PLACE.
SPEAKING OF WEIRDNESS AND ACQUIRED TASTES...
...LET'S REPORT TO THE BOSS.
IT'S DONE.
BLACK TOM CASSIDY HAS BEEN BROUGHT TO HEEL.
WE TURNED HIM OVER TO THE AUTHORITIES IN ITALY.
HE'S OFF THE TABLE.
AND WE BROUGHT HIM DOWN PUBLICLY... JUST LIKE YOU WANTED.
EXCELLENT.
THAT'S ONE...

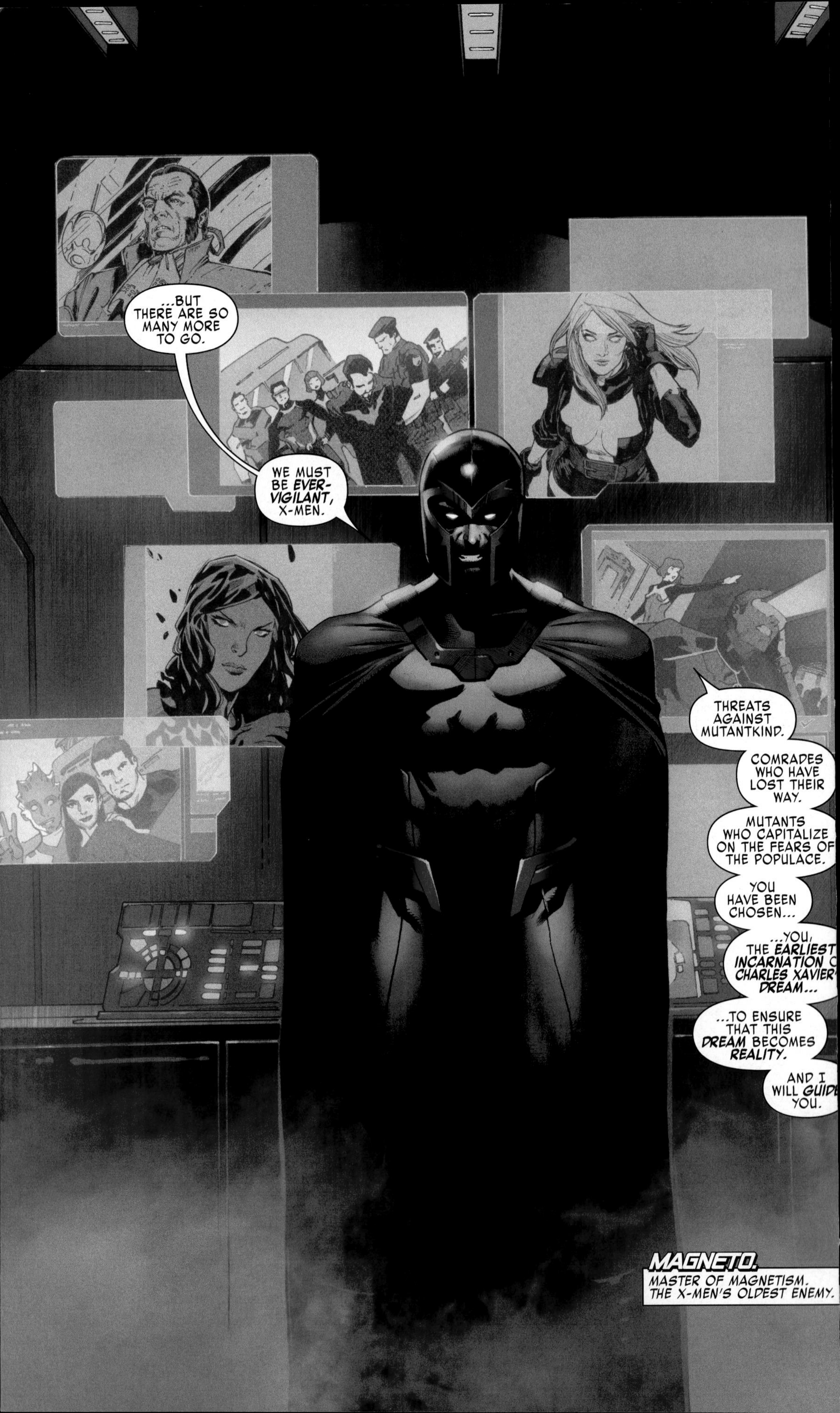

...BUT THERE ARE SO MANY MORE TO GO.
WE MUST BE **EVER-VIGILANT,** X-MEN.
THREATS AGAINST MUTANTKIND.
COMRADES WHO HAVE LOST THEIR WAY.
MUTANTS WHO CAPITALIZE ON THE FEARS OF THE POPULACE.
YOU HAVE BEEN CHOSEN...
...YOU, THE **EARLIEST INCARNATION** O **CHARLES XAVIER' DREAM...**
...TO ENSURE THAT THIS **DREAM** BECOMES **REALITY.**
AND I WILL **GUIDE** YOU.
MAGNETO.
MASTER OF MAGNETISM. THE X-MEN'S OLDEST ENEMY.

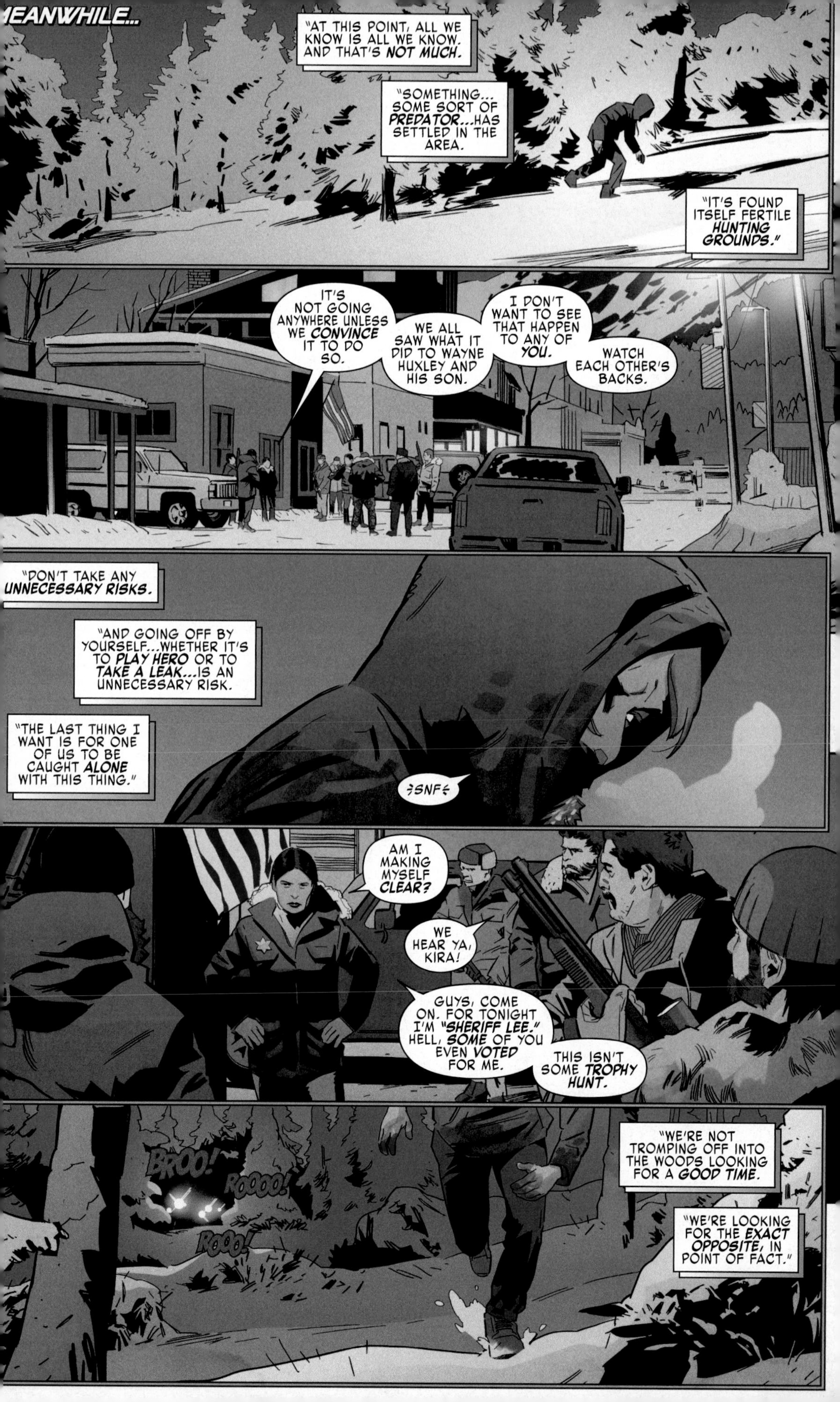

MEANWHILE...
"AT THIS POINT, ALL WE KNOW IS ALL WE KNOW. AND THAT'S NOT MUCH.
"SOMETHING... SOME SORT OF PREDATOR...HAS SETTLED IN THE AREA.
"IT'S FOUND ITSELF FERTILE HUNTING GROUNDS."
IT'S NOT GOING ANYWHERE UNLESS WE CONVINCE IT TO DO SO.
WE ALL SAW WHAT IT DID TO WAYNE HUXLEY AND HIS SON.
I DON'T WANT TO SEE THAT HAPPEN TO ANY OF YOU.
WATCH EACH OTHER'S BACKS.
"DON'T TAKE ANY UNNECESSARY RISKS.
"AND GOING OFF BY YOURSELF...WHETHER IT'S TO PLAY HERO OR TO TAKE A LEAK...IS AN UNNECESSARY RISK.
"THE LAST THING I WANT IS FOR ONE OF US TO BE CAUGHT ALONE WITH THIS THING."
SNF
AM I MAKING MYSELF CLEAR?
WE HEAR YA, KIRA!
GUYS, COME ON. FOR TONIGHT I'M "SHERIFF LEE." HELL, SOME OF YOU EVEN VOTED FOR ME.
THIS ISN'T SOME TROPHY HUNT.
BROO! ROOOO! ROOO!
"WE'RE NOT TROMPING OFF INTO THE WOODS LOOKING FOR A GOOD TIME.
"WE'RE LOOKING FOR THE EXACT OPPOSITE, IN POINT OF FACT."

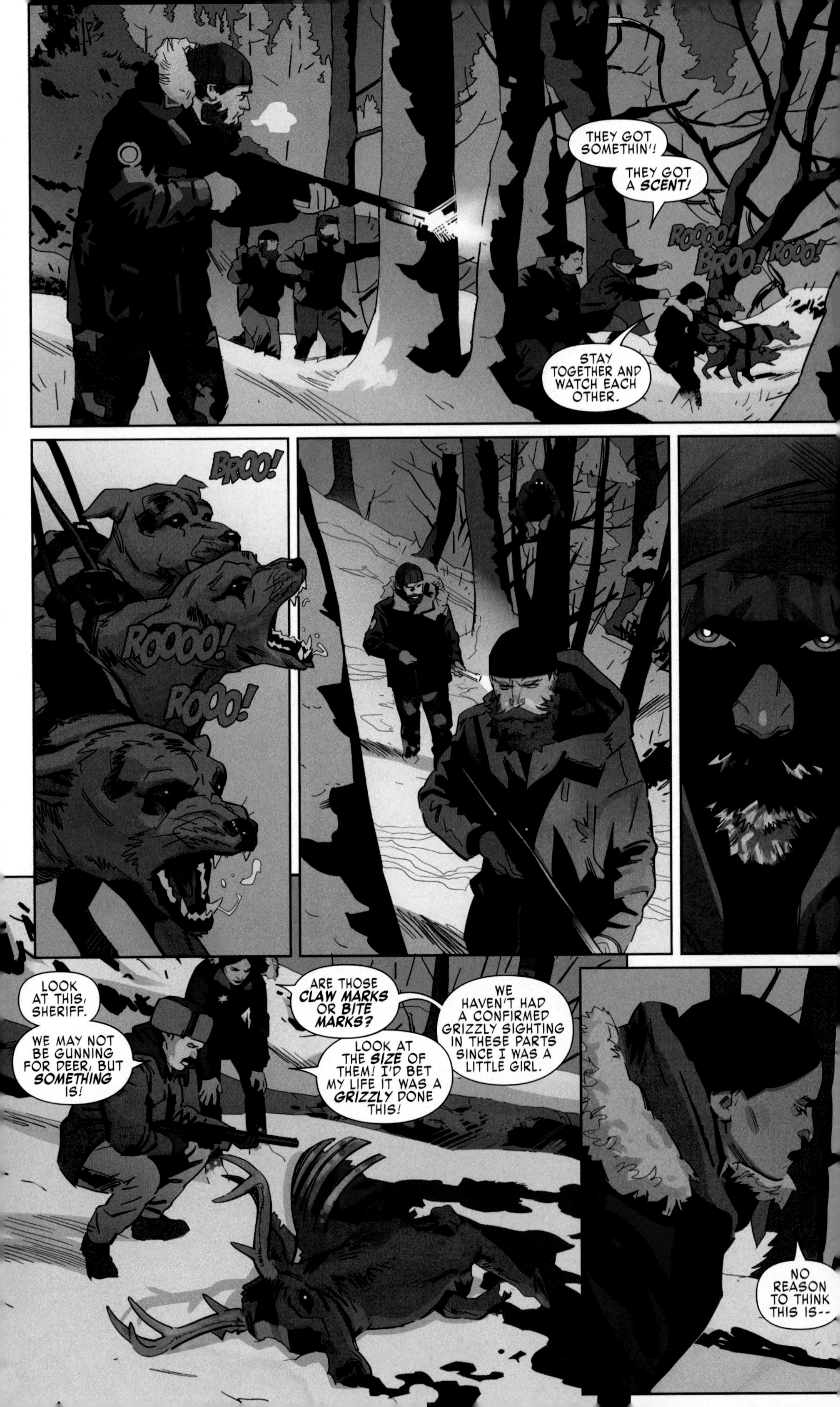

THEY GOT SOMETHIN'!
THEY GOT A SCENT!
ROOOO! BROO! ROOO!
STAY TOGETHER AND WATCH EACH OTHER.
BROO!
ROOOO!
ROOO!
LOOK AT THIS, SHERIFF.
WE MAY NOT BE GUNNING FOR DEER, BUT SOMETHING IS!
ARE THOSE CLAW MARKS OR BITE MARKS?
LOOK AT THE SIZE OF THEM! I'D BET MY LIFE IT WAS A GRIZZLY DONE THIS!
WE HAVEN'T HAD A CONFIRMED GRIZZLY SIGHTING IN THESE PARTS SINCE I WAS A LITTLE GIRL.
NO REASON TO THINK THIS IS--

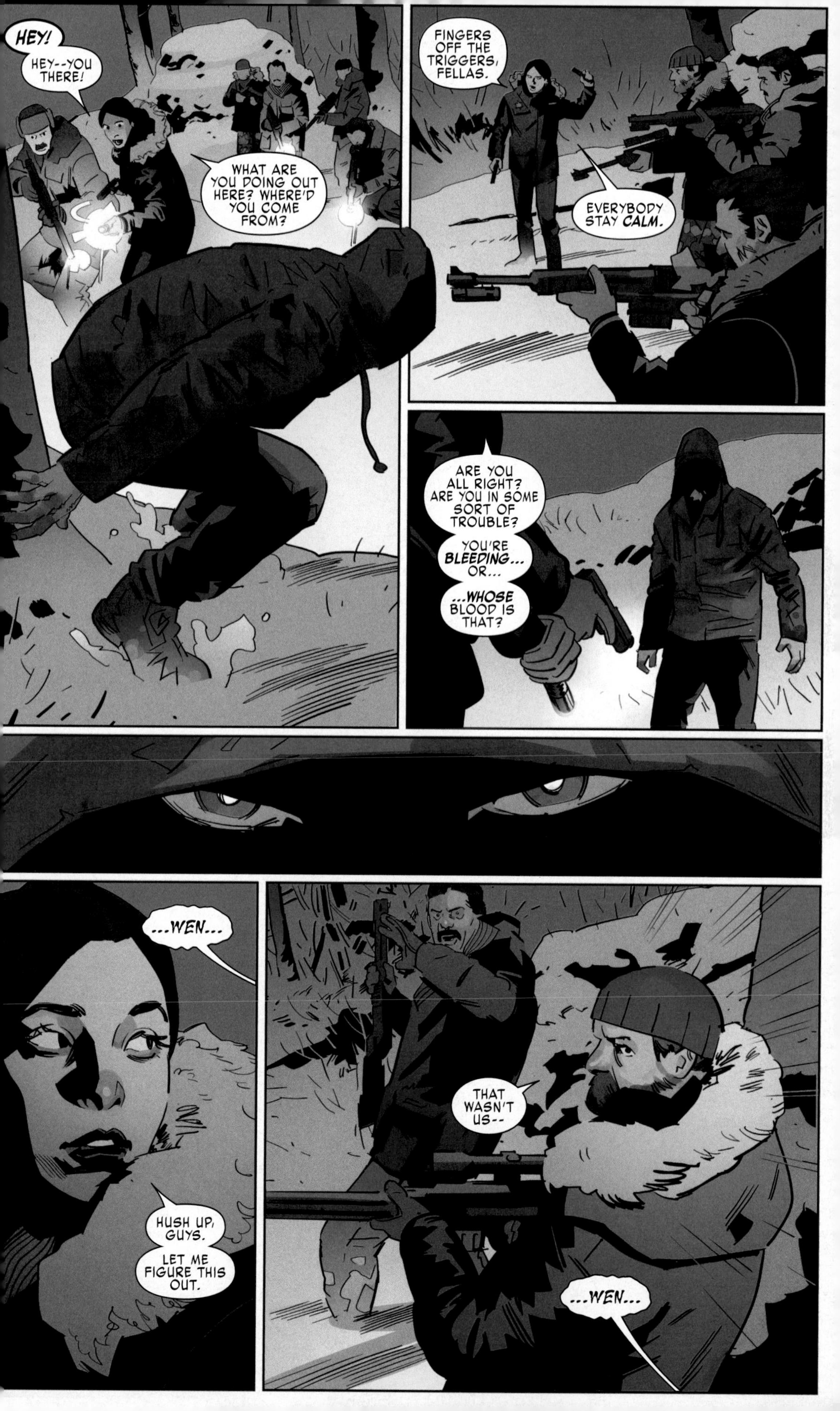
HEY!
HEY--YOU THERE!
WHAT ARE YOU DOING OUT HERE? WHERE'D YOU COME FROM?
FINGERS OFF THE TRIGGERS, FELLAS.
EVERYBODY STAY CALM.
ARE YOU ALL RIGHT? ARE YOU IN SOME SORT OF TROUBLE?
YOU'RE BLEEDING... OR...
...WHOSE BLOOD IS THAT?
...WEN...
HUSH UP, GUYS.
LET ME FIGURE THIS OUT.
THAT WASN'T US--
...WEN...

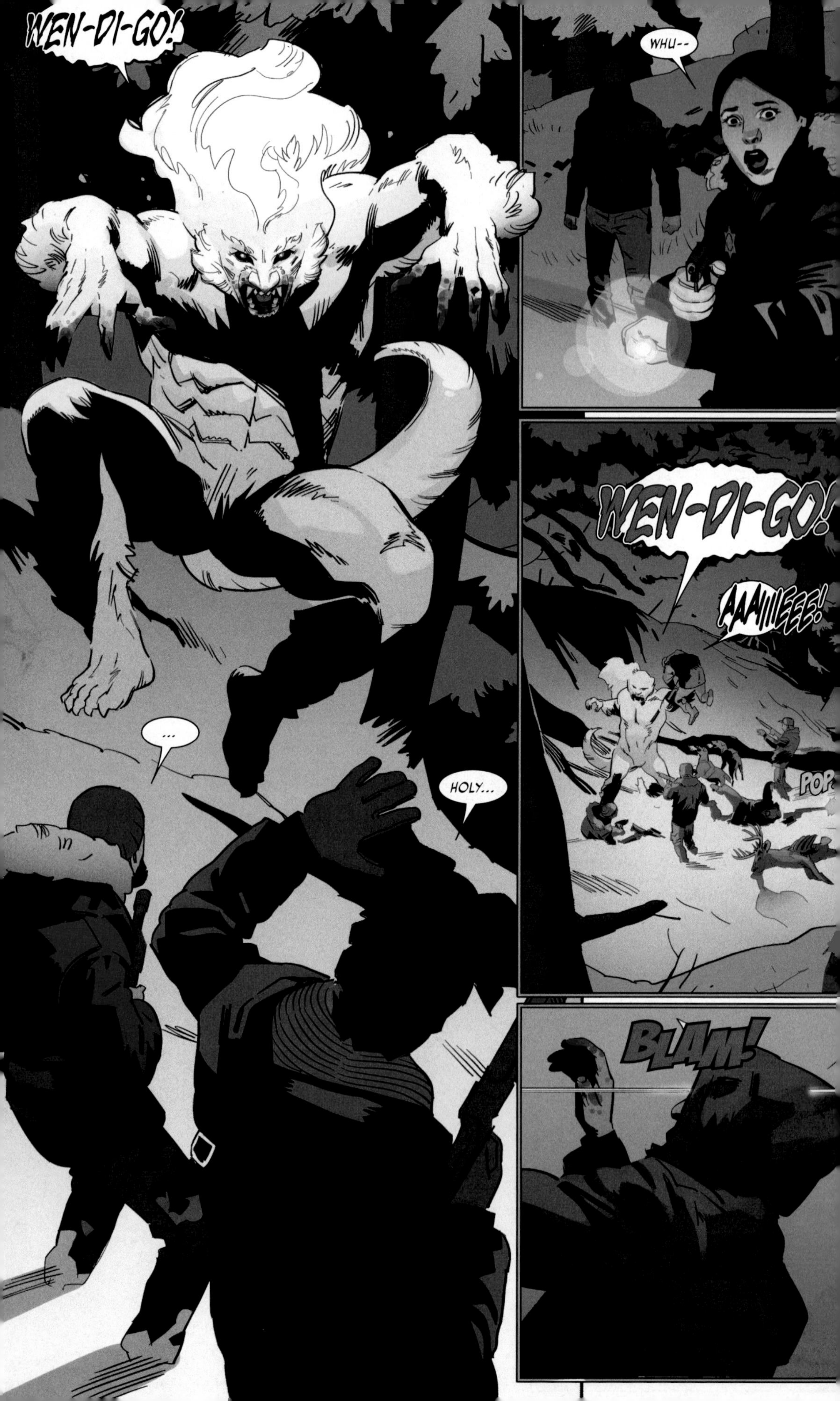
WEN-DI-GO!
...
HOLY...
WHU--
WEN-DI-GO!
AAAIIIEEE!
POP
BLAM!

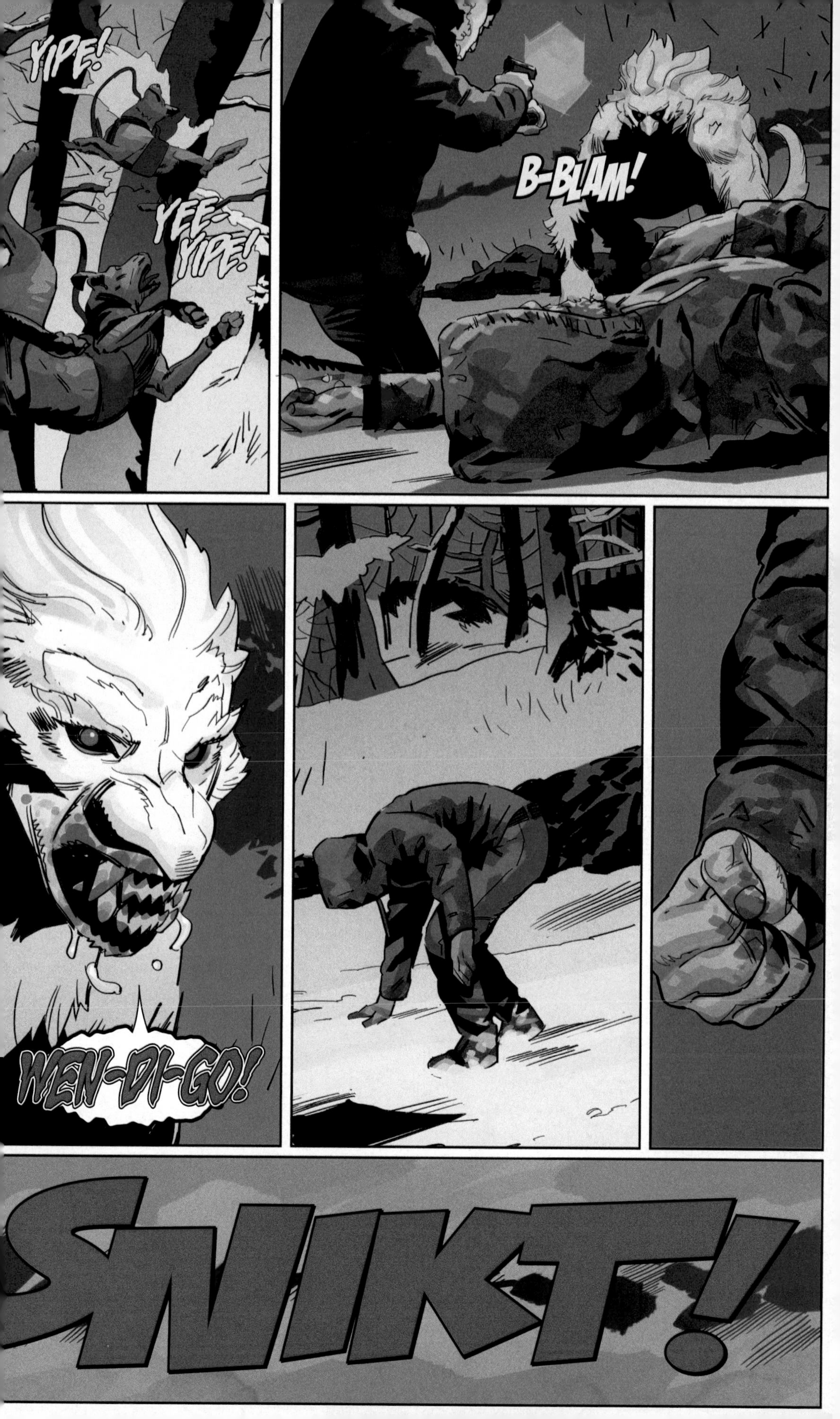
YIPE!
YEE-YIPE!
B-BLAM!
WEN-DI-GO!
SNIKT!

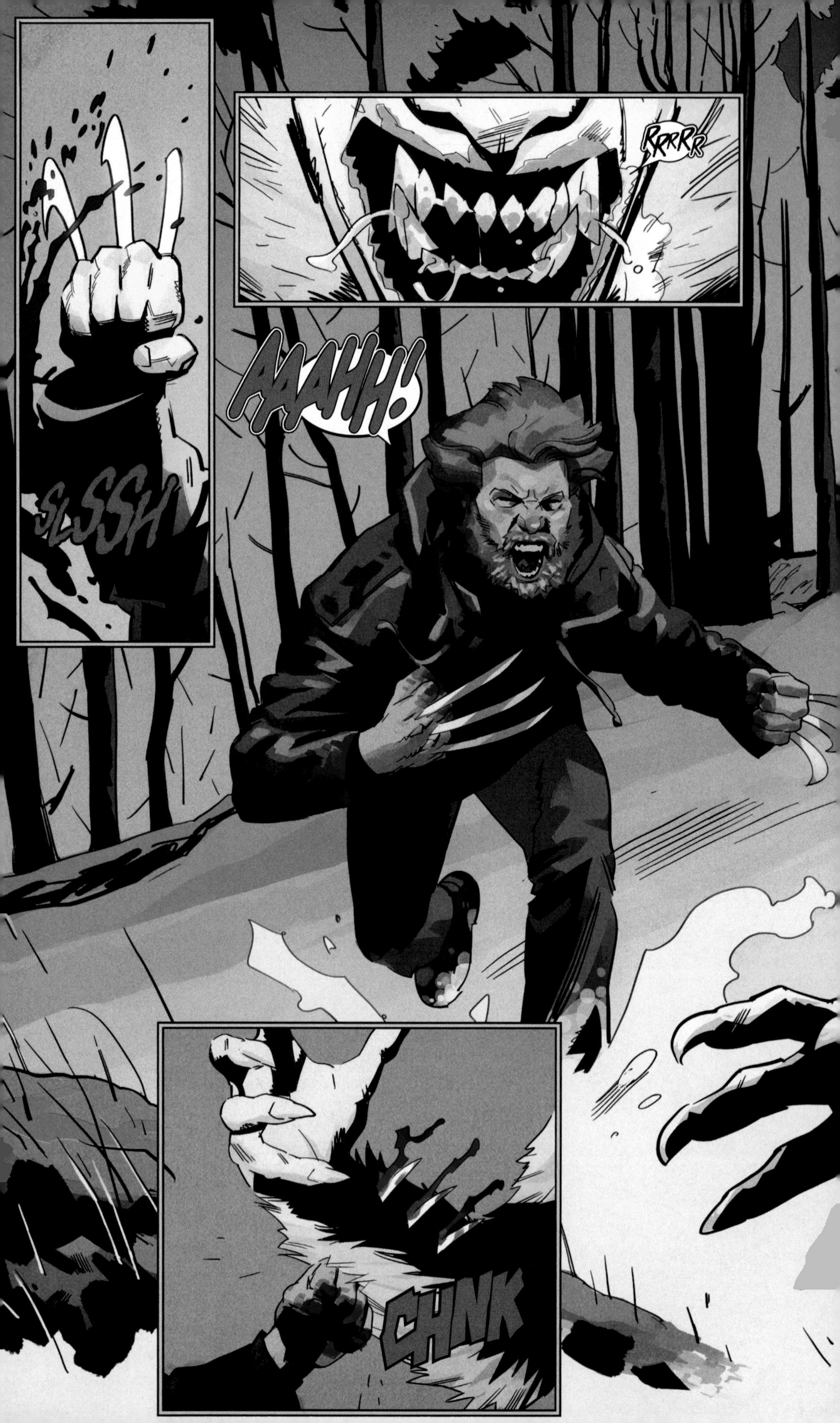
SLSSH
RRRRR
AAAHH!
CHNK

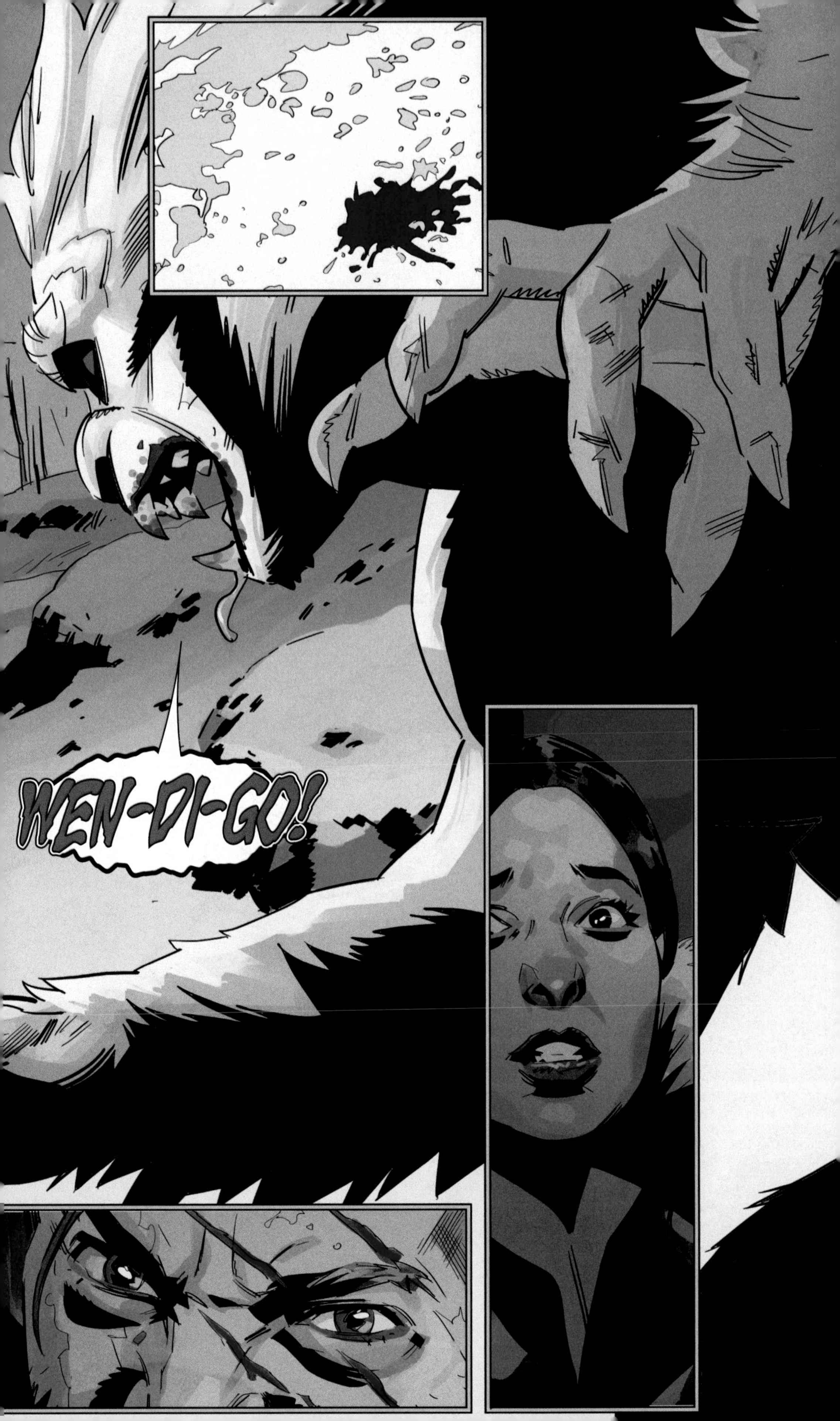
WEN-DI-GO!

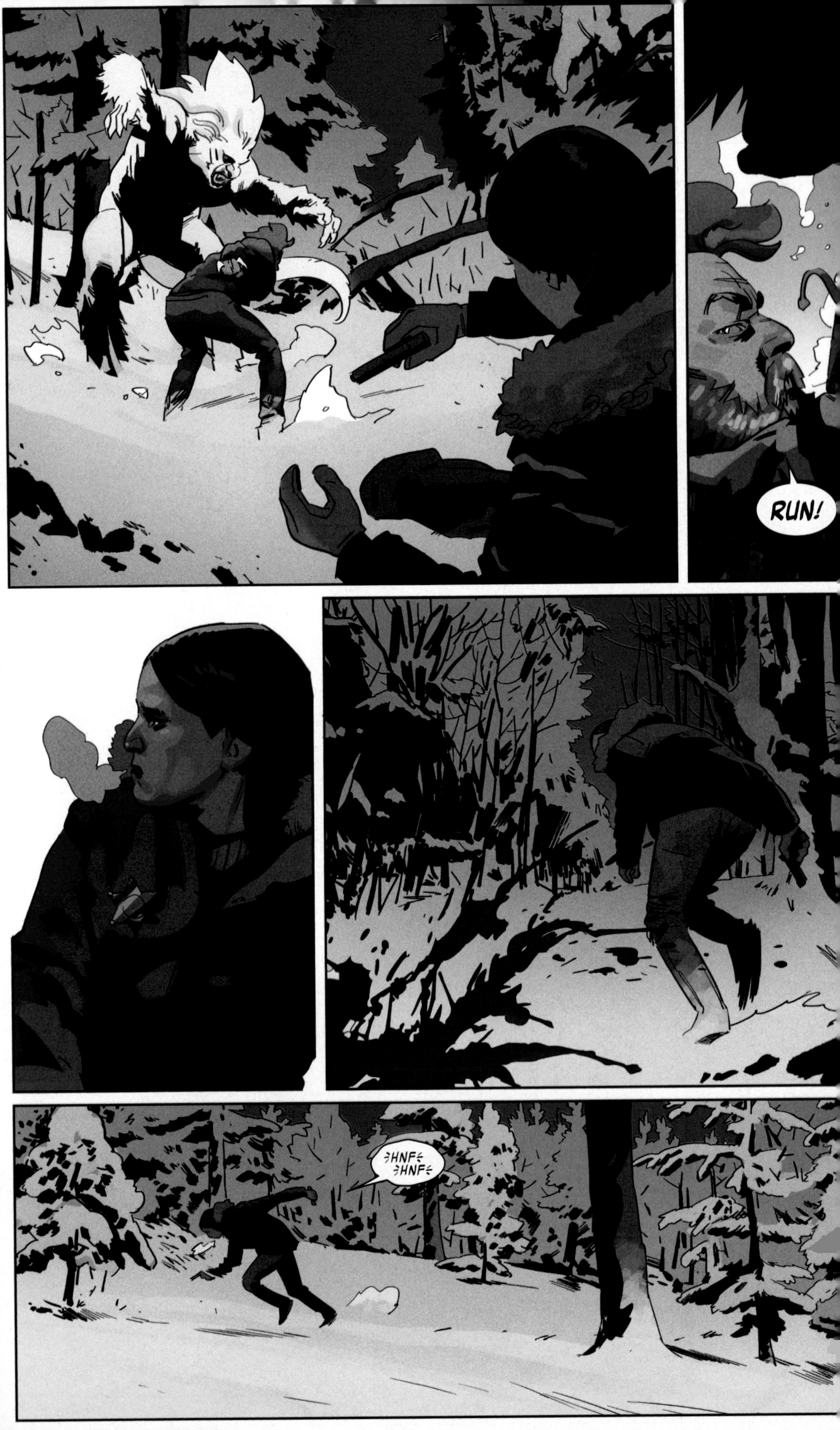
RUN!
HNF
HNF

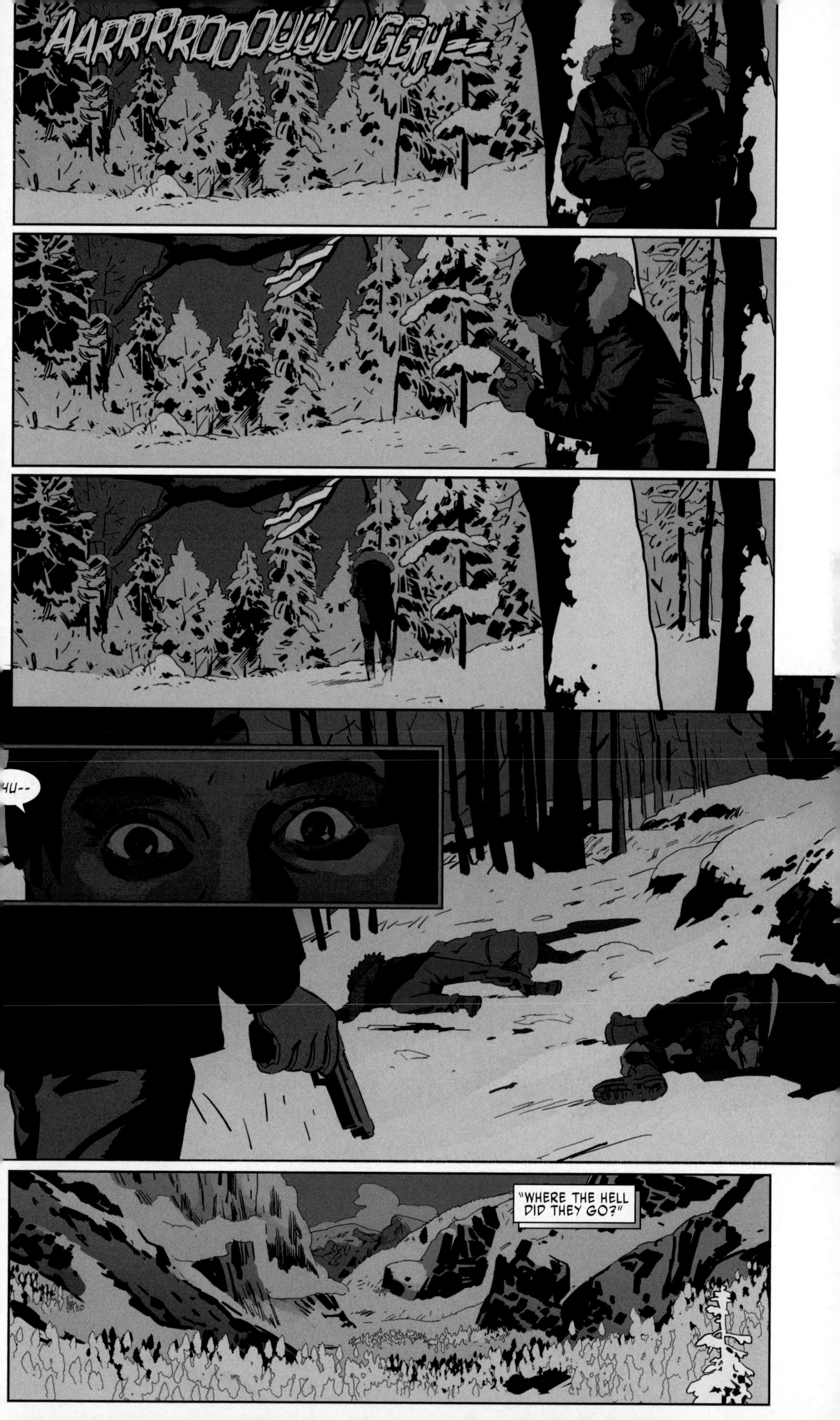
AARRRROOOUUUUUGGH--
HU--
"WHERE THE HELL DID THEY GO?"

2

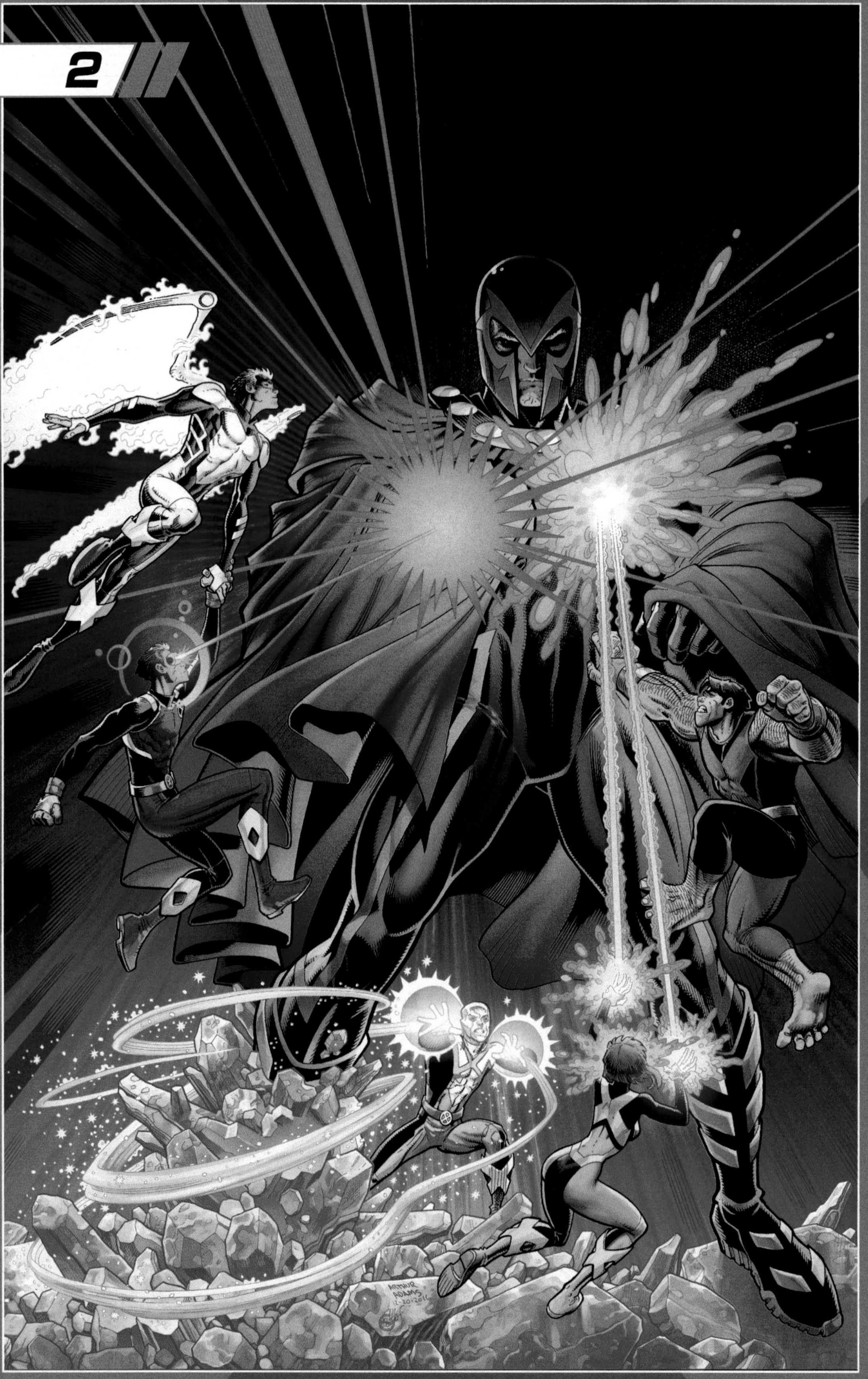
ARTHUR ADAMS 12-20-2016

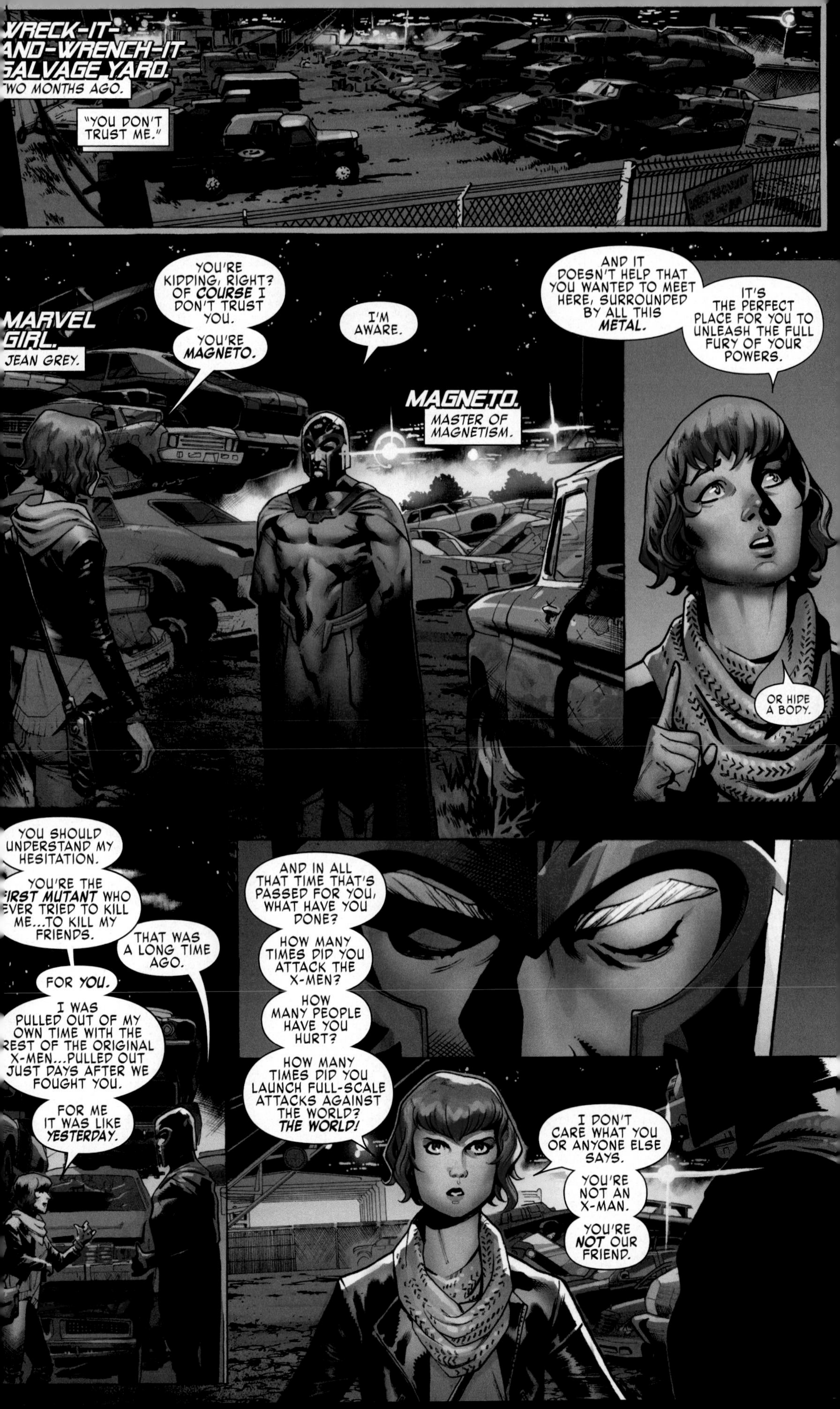
WRECK-IT-AND-WRENCH-IT SALVAGE YARD.
TWO MONTHS AGO.
"YOU DON'T TRUST ME."
MARVEL GIRL.
JEAN GREY.
YOU'RE KIDDING, RIGHT? OF COURSE I DON'T TRUST YOU.
YOU'RE MAGNETO.
I'M AWARE.
MAGNETO.
MASTER OF MAGNETISM.
AND IT DOESN'T HELP THAT YOU WANTED TO MEET HERE, SURROUNDED BY ALL THIS METAL.
IT'S THE PERFECT PLACE FOR YOU TO UNLEASH THE FULL FURY OF YOUR POWERS.
OR HIDE A BODY.
YOU SHOULD UNDERSTAND MY HESITATION.
YOU'RE THE FIRST MUTANT WHO EVER TRIED TO KILL ME...TO KILL MY FRIENDS.
THAT WAS A LONG TIME AGO.
FOR YOU.
I WAS PULLED OUT OF MY OWN TIME WITH THE REST OF THE ORIGINAL X-MEN...PULLED OUT JUST DAYS AFTER WE FOUGHT YOU.
FOR ME IT WAS LIKE YESTERDAY.
AND IN ALL THAT TIME THAT'S PASSED FOR YOU, WHAT HAVE YOU DONE?
HOW MANY TIMES DID YOU ATTACK THE X-MEN?
HOW MANY PEOPLE HAVE YOU HURT?
HOW MANY TIMES DID YOU LAUNCH FULL-SCALE ATTACKS AGAINST THE WORLD? THE WORLD!
I DON'T CARE WHAT YOU OR ANYONE ELSE SAYS.
YOU'RE NOT AN X-MAN.
YOU'RE NOT OUR FRIEND.

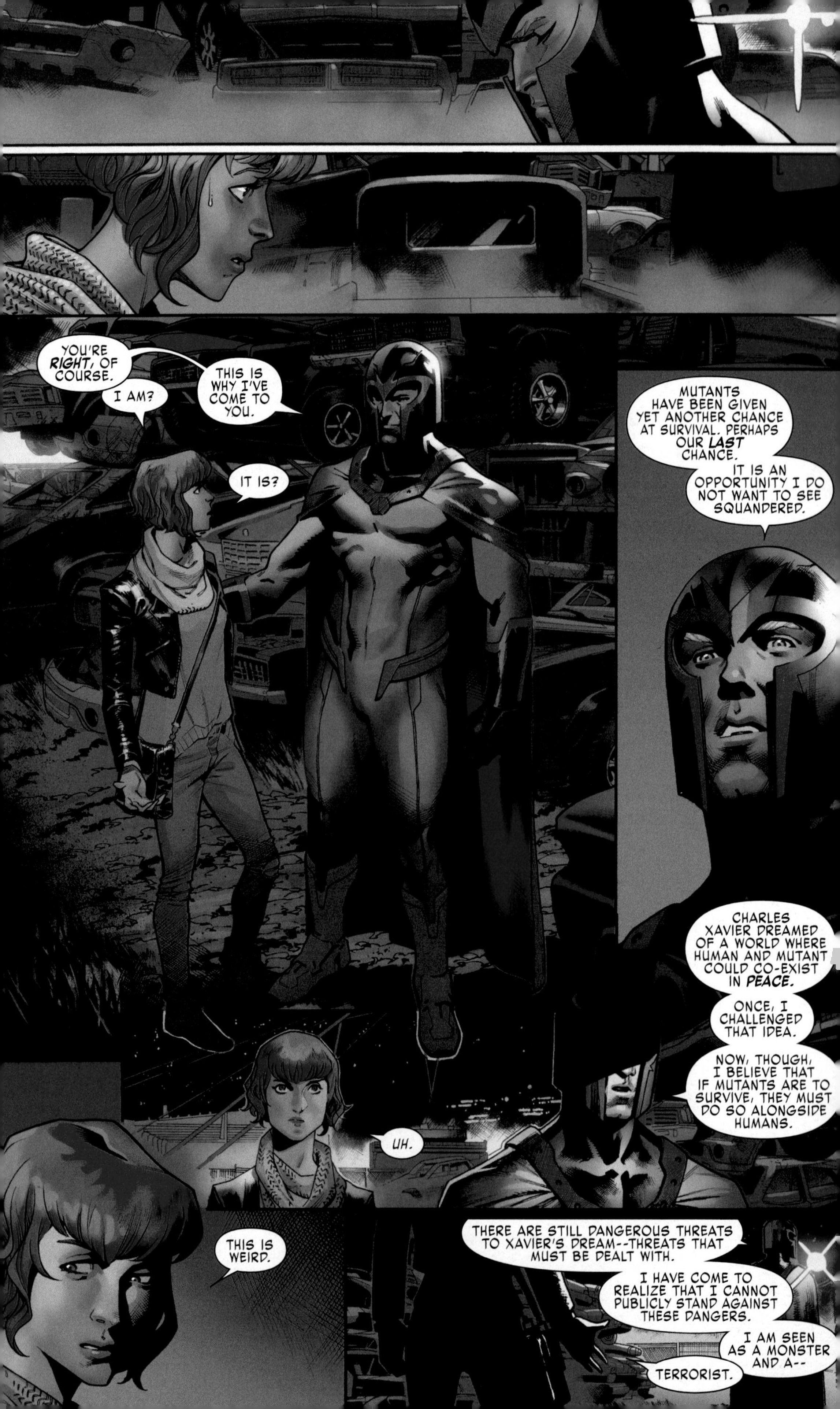
YOU'RE RIGHT, OF COURSE.
I AM?
THIS IS WHY I'VE COME TO YOU.
IT IS?
MUTANTS HAVE BEEN GIVEN YET ANOTHER CHANCE AT SURVIVAL. PERHAPS OUR LAST CHANCE.
IT IS AN OPPORTUNITY I DO NOT WANT TO SEE SQUANDERED.
CHARLES XAVIER DREAMED OF A WORLD WHERE HUMAN AND MUTANT COULD CO-EXIST IN PEACE.
ONCE, I CHALLENGED THAT IDEA.
NOW, THOUGH, I BELIEVE THAT IF MUTANTS ARE TO SURVIVE, THEY MUST DO SO ALONGSIDE HUMANS.
UH.
THIS IS WEIRD.
THERE ARE STILL DANGEROUS THREATS TO XAVIER'S DREAM--THREATS THAT MUST BE DEALT WITH.
I HAVE COME TO REALIZE THAT I CANNOT PUBLICLY STAND AGAINST THESE DANGERS.
I AM SEEN AS A MONSTER AND A--
TERRORIST.

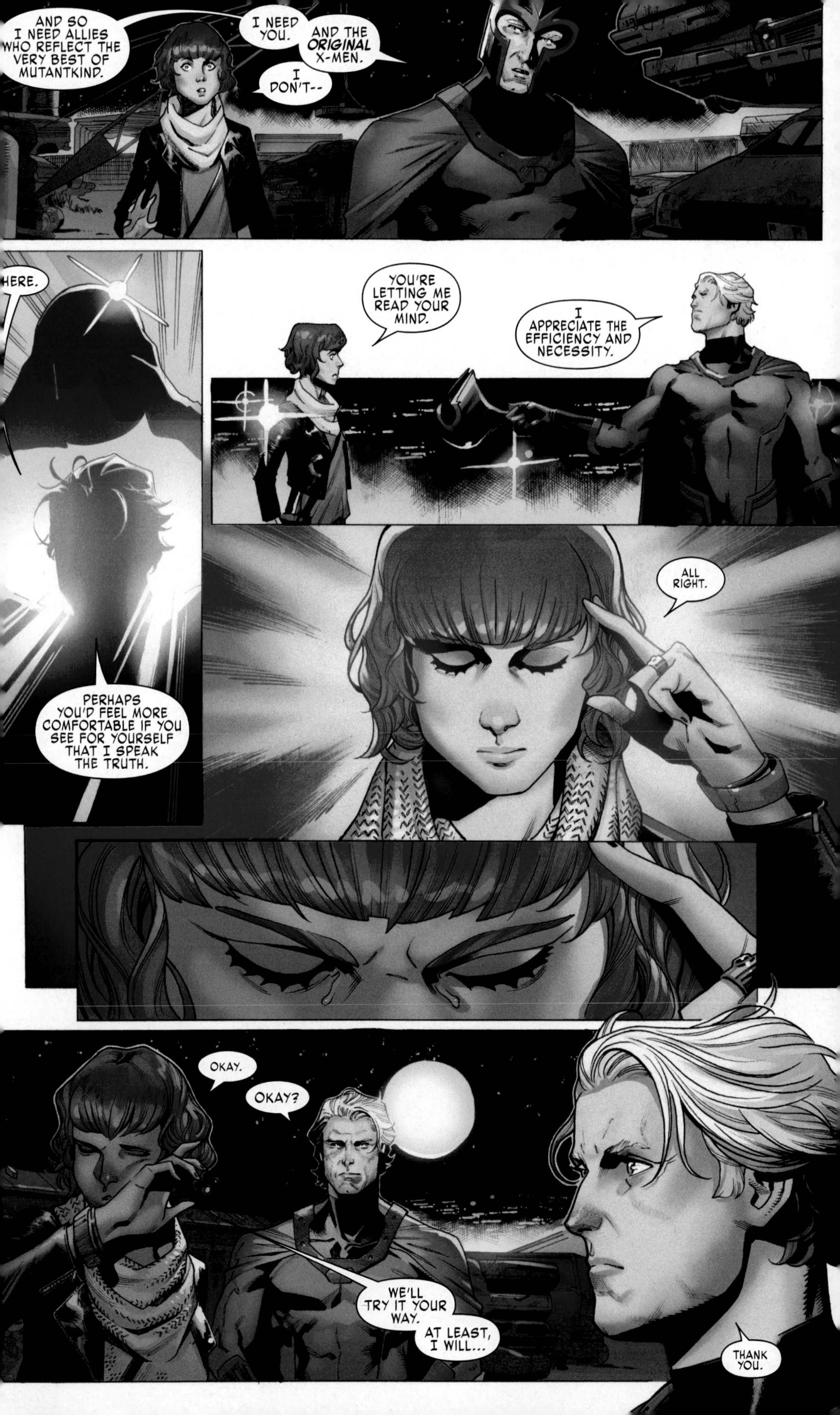

AND SO I NEED ALLIES WHO REFLECT THE VERY BEST OF MUTANTKIND.
I NEED YOU.
AND THE ORIGINAL X-MEN.
I DON'T--
HERE.
YOU'RE LETTING ME READ YOUR MIND.
I APPRECIATE THE EFFICIENCY AND NECESSITY.
PERHAPS YOU'D FEEL MORE COMFORTABLE IF YOU SEE FOR YOURSELF THAT I SPEAK THE TRUTH.
ALL RIGHT.
OKAY.
OKAY?
WE'LL TRY IT YOUR WAY.
AT LEAST, I WILL...
THANK YOU.

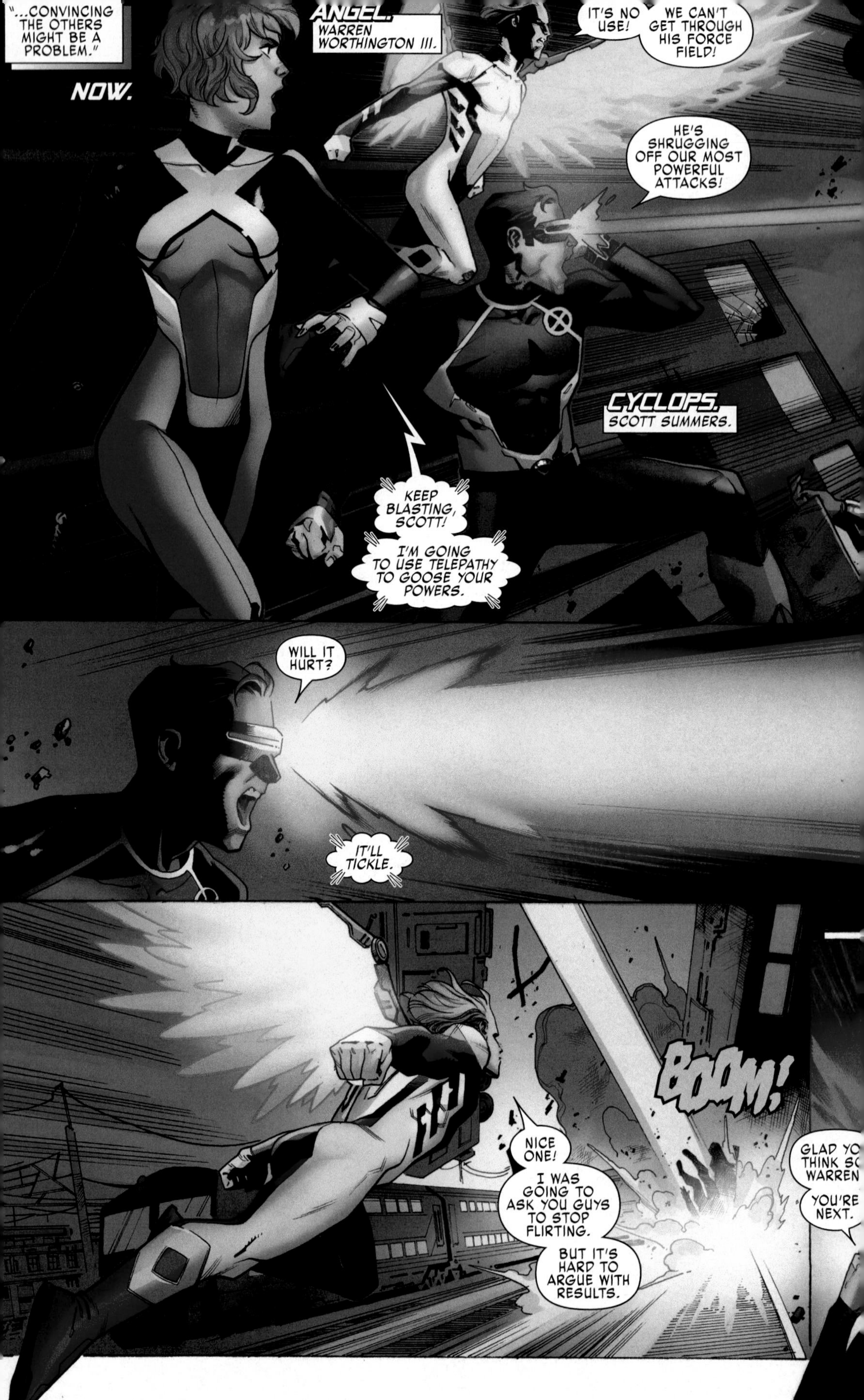
"...CONVINCING THE OTHERS MIGHT BE A PROBLEM."
NOW.
ANGEL. WARREN WORTHINGTON III.
IT'S NO USE!
WE CAN'T GET THROUGH HIS FORCE FIELD!
HE'S SHRUGGING OFF OUR MOST POWERFUL ATTACKS!
CYCLOPS. SCOTT SUMMERS.
KEEP BLASTING, SCOTT!
I'M GOING TO USE TELEPATHY TO GOOSE YOUR POWERS.
WILL IT HURT?
IT'LL TICKLE.
BOOM!
NICE ONE!
I WAS GOING TO ASK YOU GUYS TO STOP FLIRTING.
BUT IT'S HARD TO ARGUE WITH RESULTS.
YOU'RE NEXT.

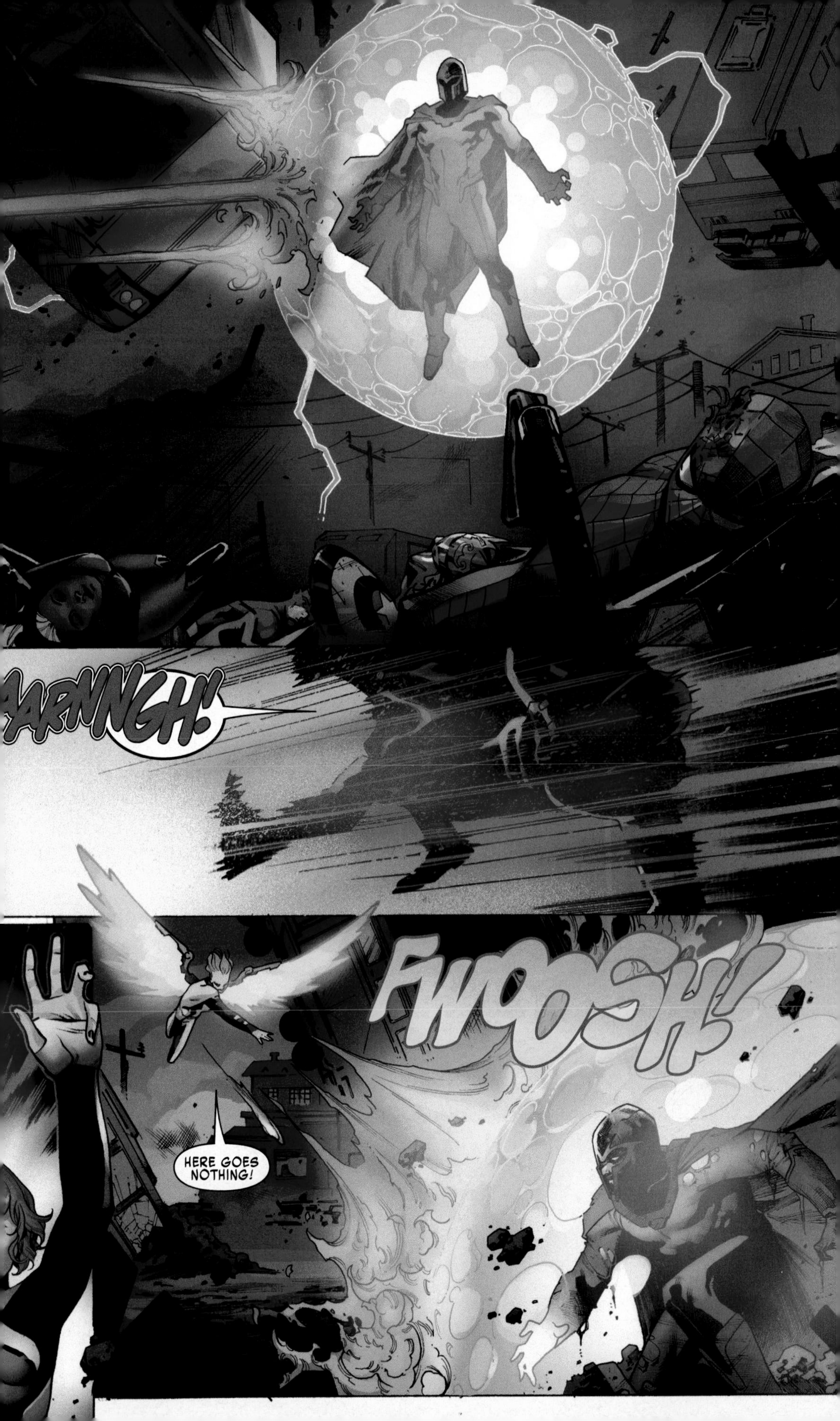
AARNNGH!
HERE GOES NOTHING!
FWOOSH!

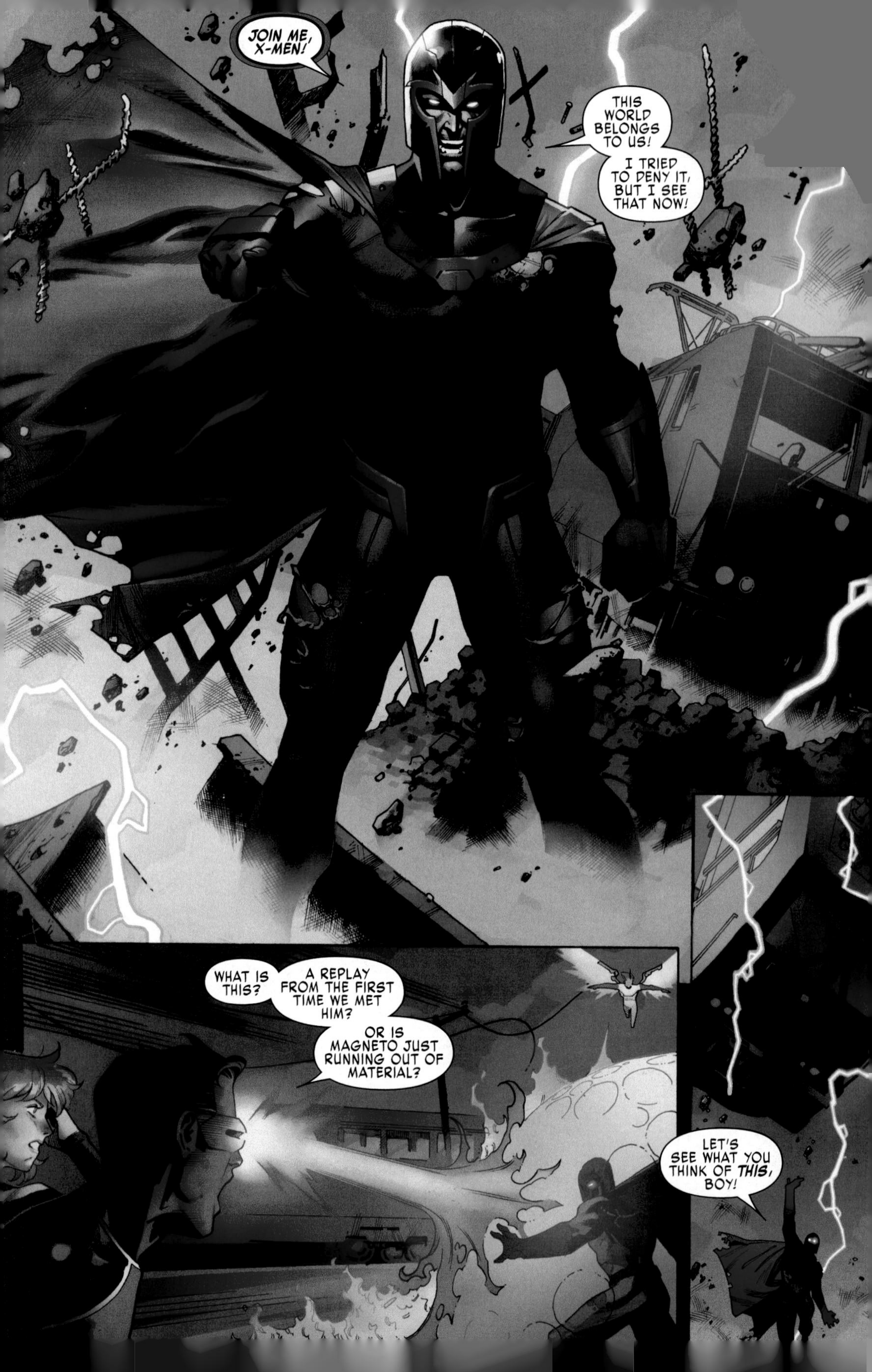
JOIN ME, X-MEN!
THIS WORLD BELONGS TO US!
I TRIED TO DENY IT, BUT I SEE THAT NOW!
WHAT IS THIS?
A REPLAY FROM THE FIRST TIME WE MET HIM?
OR IS MAGNETO JUST RUNNING OUT OF MATERIAL?
LET'S SEE WHAT YOU THINK OF THIS, BOY!

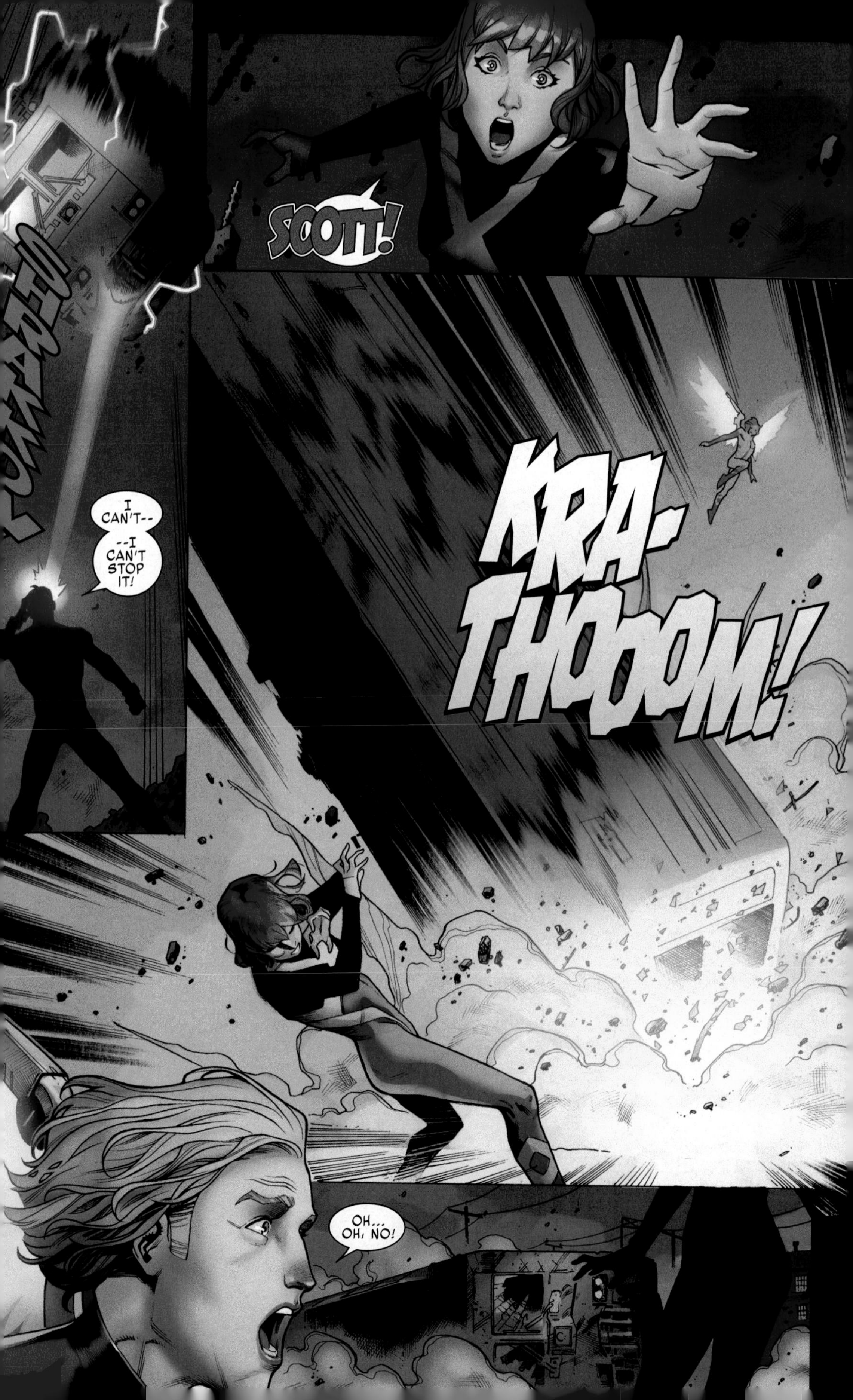
SCOTT!
I CAN'T--
--I CAN'T STOP IT!
KRA-THOOOM!
OH... OH, NO!

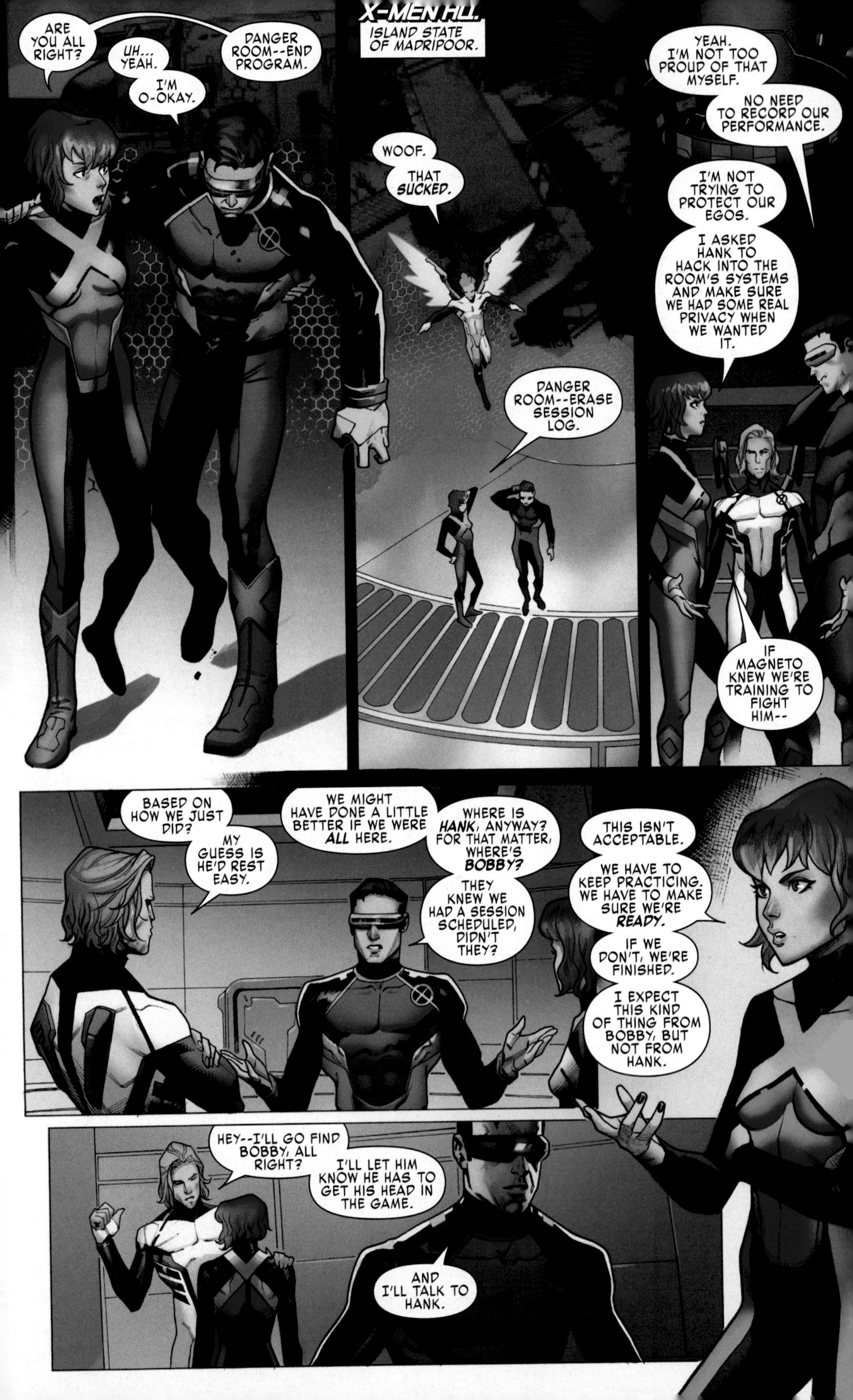
X-MEN HQ.
ISLAND STATE OF MADRIPOOR.
ARE YOU ALL RIGHT?
UH... YEAH.
I'M O-OKAY.
DANGER ROOM--END PROGRAM.
WOOF.
THAT SUCKED.
DANGER ROOM--ERASE SESSION LOG.
YEAH. I'M NOT TOO PROUD OF THAT MYSELF.
NO NEED TO RECORD OUR PERFORMANCE.
I'M NOT TRYING TO PROTECT OUR EGOS.
I ASKED HANK TO HACK INTO THE ROOM'S SYSTEMS AND MAKE SURE WE HAD SOME REAL PRIVACY WHEN WE WANTED IT.
IF MAGNETO KNEW WE'RE TRAINING TO FIGHT HIM--
BASED ON HOW WE JUST DID?
MY GUESS IS HE'D REST EASY.
WE MIGHT HAVE DONE A LITTLE BETTER IF WE WERE ALL HERE.
WHERE IS HANK, ANYWAY? FOR THAT MATTER, WHERE'S BOBBY?
THEY KNEW WE HAD A SESSION SCHEDULED, DIDN'T THEY?
THIS ISN'T ACCEPTABLE.
WE HAVE TO KEEP PRACTICING. WE HAVE TO MAKE SURE WE'RE READY.
IF WE DON'T, WE'RE FINISHED.
I EXPECT THIS KIND OF THING FROM BOBBY, BUT NOT FROM HANK.
HEY--I'LL GO FIND BOBBY, ALL RIGHT?
I'LL LET HIM KNOW HE HAS TO GET HIS HEAD IN THE GAME.
AND I'LL TALK TO HANK.

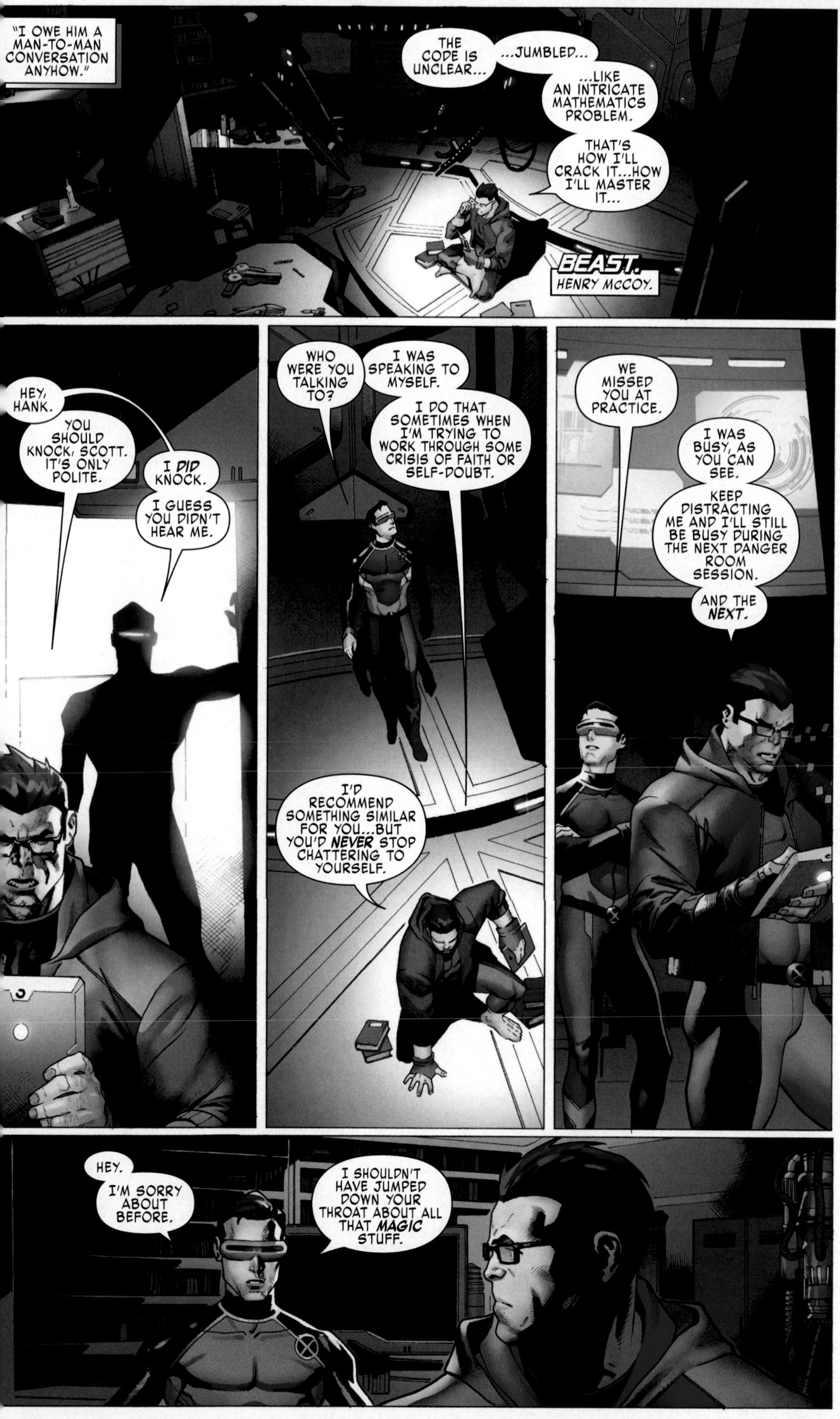
"I OWE HIM A MAN-TO-MAN CONVERSATION ANYHOW."
THE CODE IS UNCLEAR...
...JUMBLED...
...LIKE AN INTRICATE MATHEMATICS PROBLEM.
THAT'S HOW I'LL CRACK IT...HOW I'LL MASTER IT...
BEAST. HENRY McCOY.
HEY, HANK.
YOU SHOULD KNOCK, SCOTT. IT'S ONLY POLITE.
I DID KNOCK.
I GUESS YOU DIDN'T HEAR ME.
WHO WERE YOU TALKING TO?
I WAS SPEAKING TO MYSELF.
I DO THAT SOMETIMES WHEN I'M TRYING TO WORK THROUGH SOME CRISIS OF FAITH OR SELF-DOUBT.
I'D RECOMMEND SOMETHING SIMILAR FOR YOU...BUT YOU'D NEVER STOP CHATTERING TO YOURSELF.
WE MISSED YOU AT PRACTICE.
I WAS BUSY, AS YOU CAN SEE.
KEEP DISTRACTING ME AND I'LL STILL BE BUSY DURING THE NEXT DANGER ROOM SESSION.
AND THE NEXT.
HEY.
I'M SORRY ABOUT BEFORE.
I SHOULDN'T HAVE JUMPED DOWN YOUR THROAT ABOUT ALL THAT MAGIC STUFF.

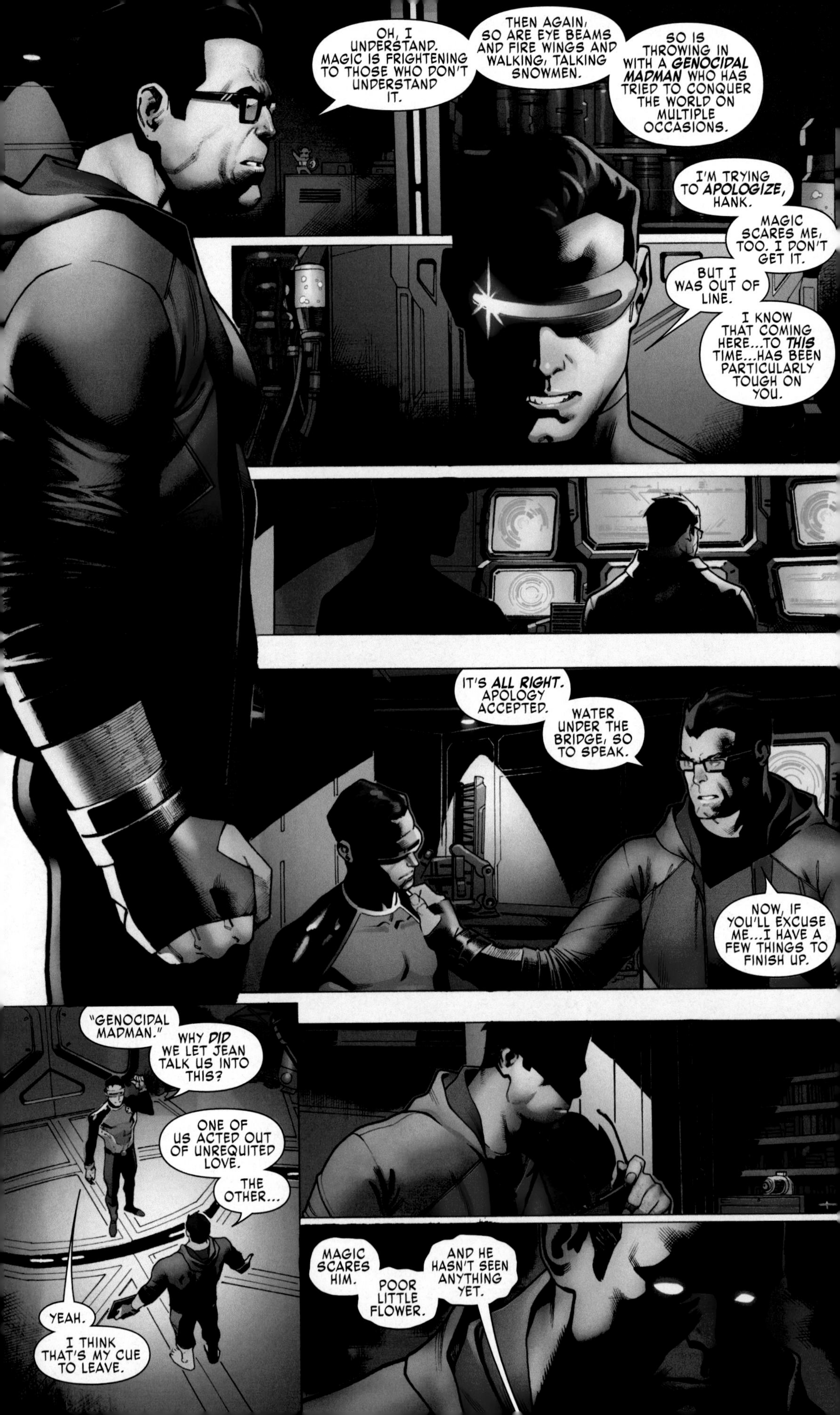
OH, I UNDERSTAND. MAGIC IS FRIGHTENING TO THOSE WHO DON'T UNDERSTAND IT.
THEN AGAIN, SO ARE EYE BEAMS AND FIRE WINGS AND WALKING, TALKING SNOWMEN.
SO IS THROWING IN WITH A GENOCIDAL MADMAN WHO HAS TRIED TO CONQUER THE WORLD ON MULTIPLE OCCASIONS.
I'M TRYING TO APOLOGIZE, HANK.
MAGIC SCARES ME, TOO. I DON'T GET IT.
BUT I WAS OUT OF LINE.
I KNOW THAT COMING HERE...TO THIS TIME...HAS BEEN PARTICULARLY TOUGH ON YOU.
IT'S ALL RIGHT. APOLOGY ACCEPTED.
WATER UNDER THE BRIDGE, SO TO SPEAK.
NOW, IF YOU'LL EXCUSE ME...I HAVE A FEW THINGS TO FINISH UP.
"GENOCIDAL MADMAN."
WHY DID WE LET JEAN TALK US INTO THIS?
ONE OF US ACTED OUT OF UNREQUITED LOVE.
THE OTHER...
YEAH.
I THINK THAT'S MY CUE TO LEAVE.
MAGIC SCARES HIM.
POOR LITTLE FLOWER.
AND HE HASN'T SEEN ANYTHING YET.

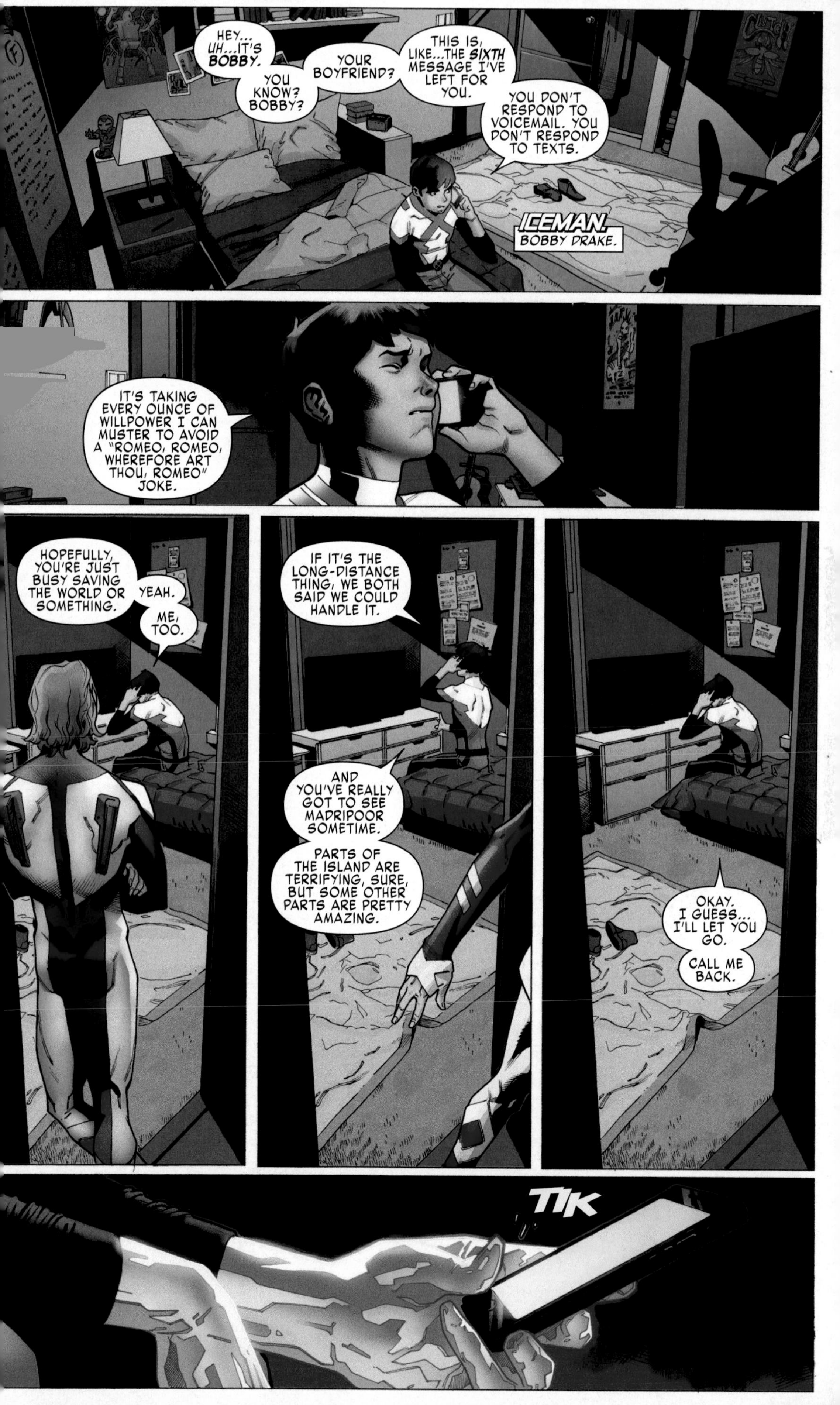
HEY... UH...IT'S BOBBY.
YOU KNOW? BOBBY?
YOUR BOYFRIEND?
THIS IS, LIKE...THE SIXTH MESSAGE I'VE LEFT FOR YOU.
YOU DON'T RESPOND TO VOICEMAIL. YOU DON'T RESPOND TO TEXTS.
ICEMAN. BOBBY DRAKE.
IT'S TAKING EVERY OUNCE OF WILLPOWER I CAN MUSTER TO AVOID A "ROMEO, ROMEO, WHEREFORE ART THOU, ROMEO" JOKE.
HOPEFULLY, YOU'RE JUST BUSY SAVING THE WORLD OR SOMETHING.
YEAH.
ME, TOO.
IF IT'S THE LONG-DISTANCE THING, WE BOTH SAID WE COULD HANDLE IT.
AND YOU'VE REALLY GOT TO SEE MADRIPOOR SOMETIME.
PARTS OF THE ISLAND ARE TERRIFYING, SURE, BUT SOME OTHER PARTS ARE PRETTY AMAZING.
OKAY. I GUESS... I'LL LET YOU GO.
CALL ME BACK.
TIK

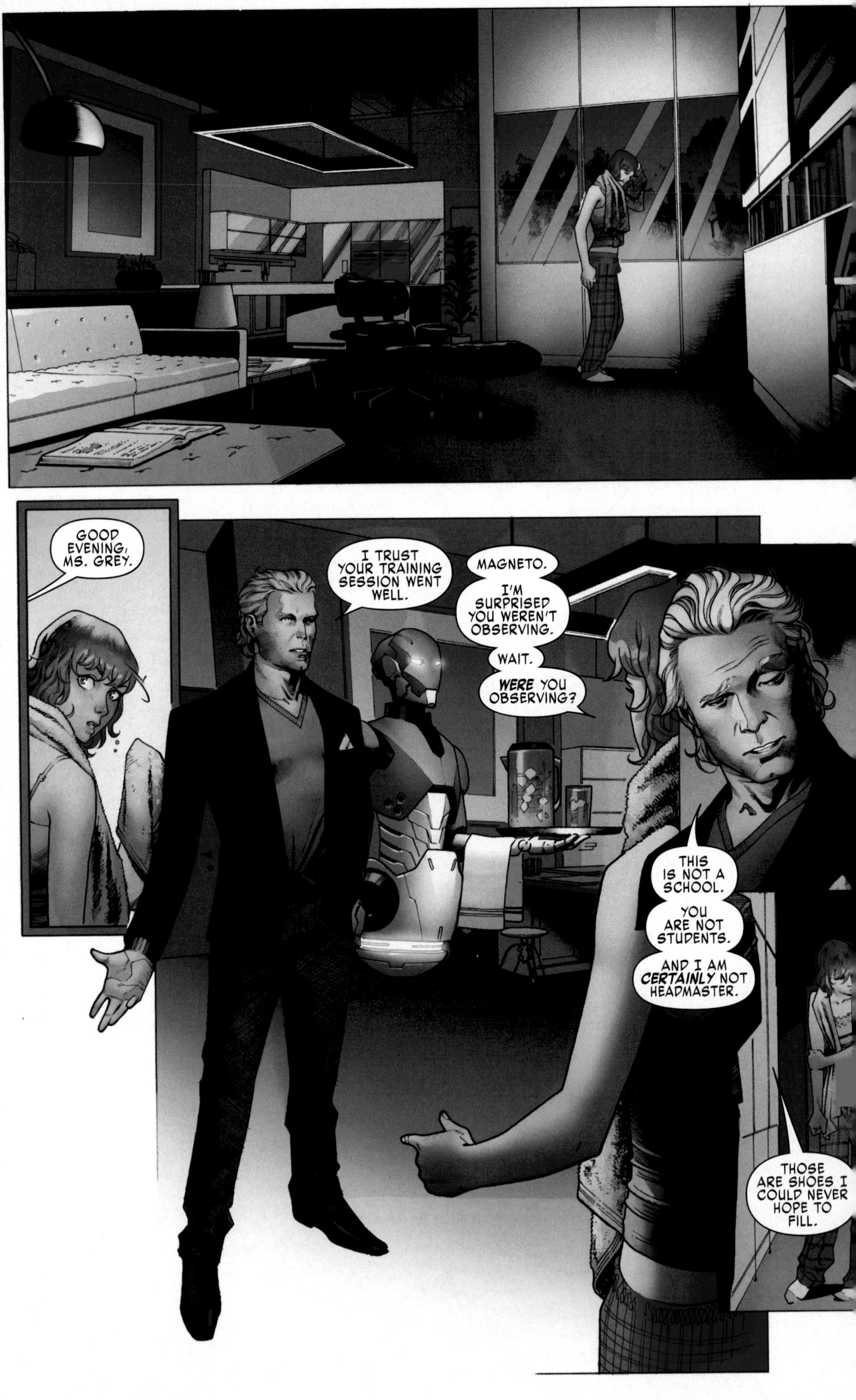
GOOD EVENING, MS. GREY.
I TRUST YOUR TRAINING SESSION WENT WELL.
MAGNETO.
I'M SURPRISED YOU WEREN'T OBSERVING.
WAIT.
WERE YOU OBSERVING?
THIS IS NOT A SCHOOL.
YOU ARE NOT STUDENTS.
AND I AM CERTAINLY NOT HEADMASTER.
THOSE ARE SHOES I COULD NEVER HOPE TO FILL.

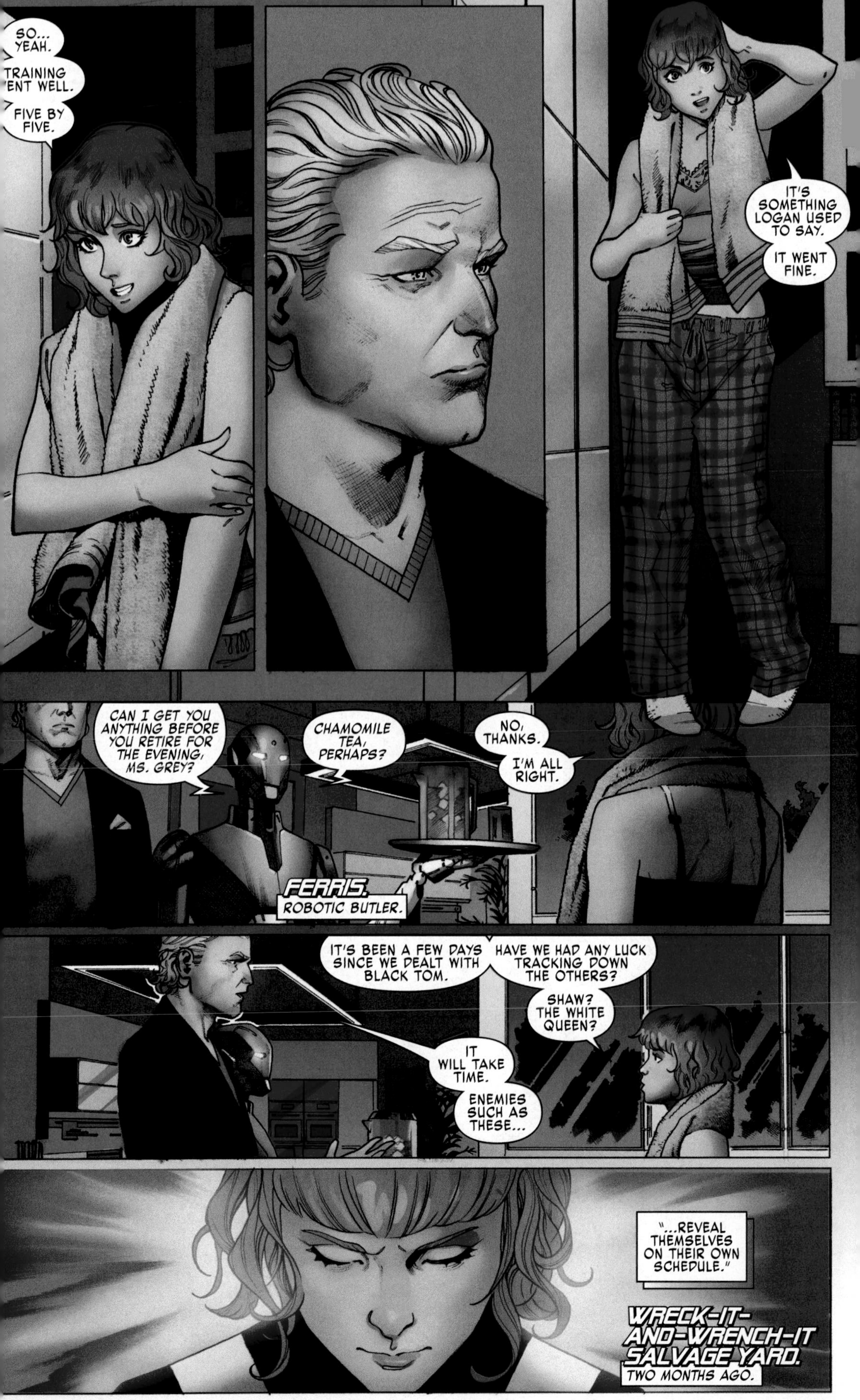
SO... YEAH.
TRAINING 'ENT WELL.
FIVE BY FIVE.
IT'S SOMETHING LOGAN USED TO SAY.
IT WENT FINE.
CAN I GET YOU ANYTHING BEFORE YOU RETIRE FOR THE EVENING, MS. GREY?
CHAMOMILE TEA, PERHAPS?
NO, THANKS.
I'M ALL RIGHT.
FERRIS. ROBOTIC BUTLER.
IT'S BEEN A FEW DAYS SINCE WE DEALT WITH BLACK TOM.
HAVE WE HAD ANY LUCK TRACKING DOWN THE OTHERS?
SHAW? THE WHITE QUEEN?
IT WILL TAKE TIME.
ENEMIES SUCH AS THESE...
"...REVEAL THEMSELVES ON THEIR OWN SCHEDULE."
WRECK-IT-AND-WRENCH-IT SALVAGE YARD.
TWO MONTHS AGO.

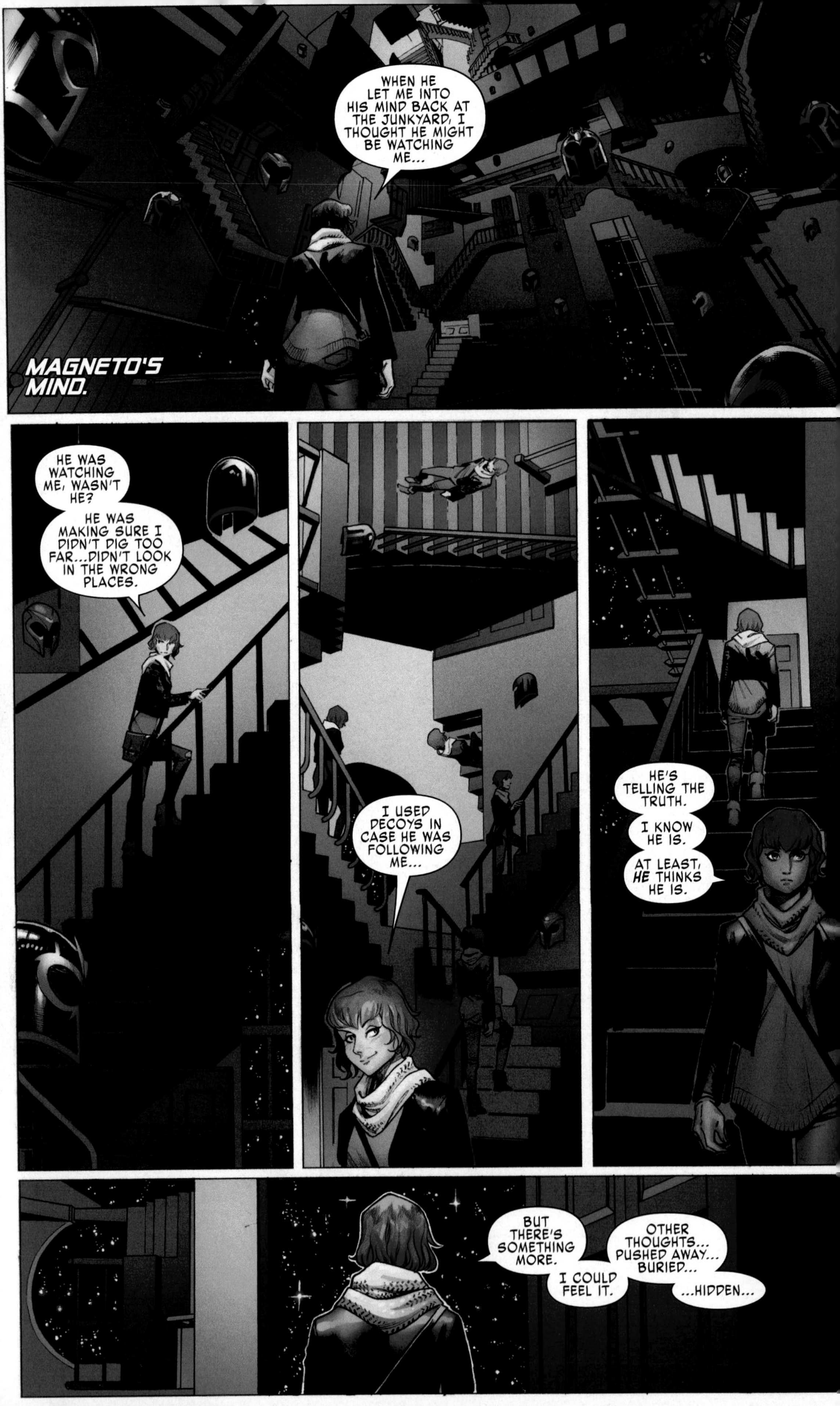
WHEN HE LET ME INTO HIS MIND BACK AT THE JUNKYARD, I THOUGHT HE MIGHT BE WATCHING ME...
MAGNETO'S MIND.
HE WAS WATCHING ME, WASN'T HE?
HE WAS MAKING SURE I DIDN'T DIG TOO FAR...DIDN'T LOOK IN THE WRONG PLACES.
I USED DECOYS IN CASE HE WAS FOLLOWING ME...
HE'S TELLING THE TRUTH.
I KNOW HE IS.
AT LEAST, HE THINKS HE IS.
BUT THERE'S SOMETHING MORE.
I COULD FEEL IT.
OTHER THOUGHTS... PUSHED AWAY... BURIED...
...HIDDEN...

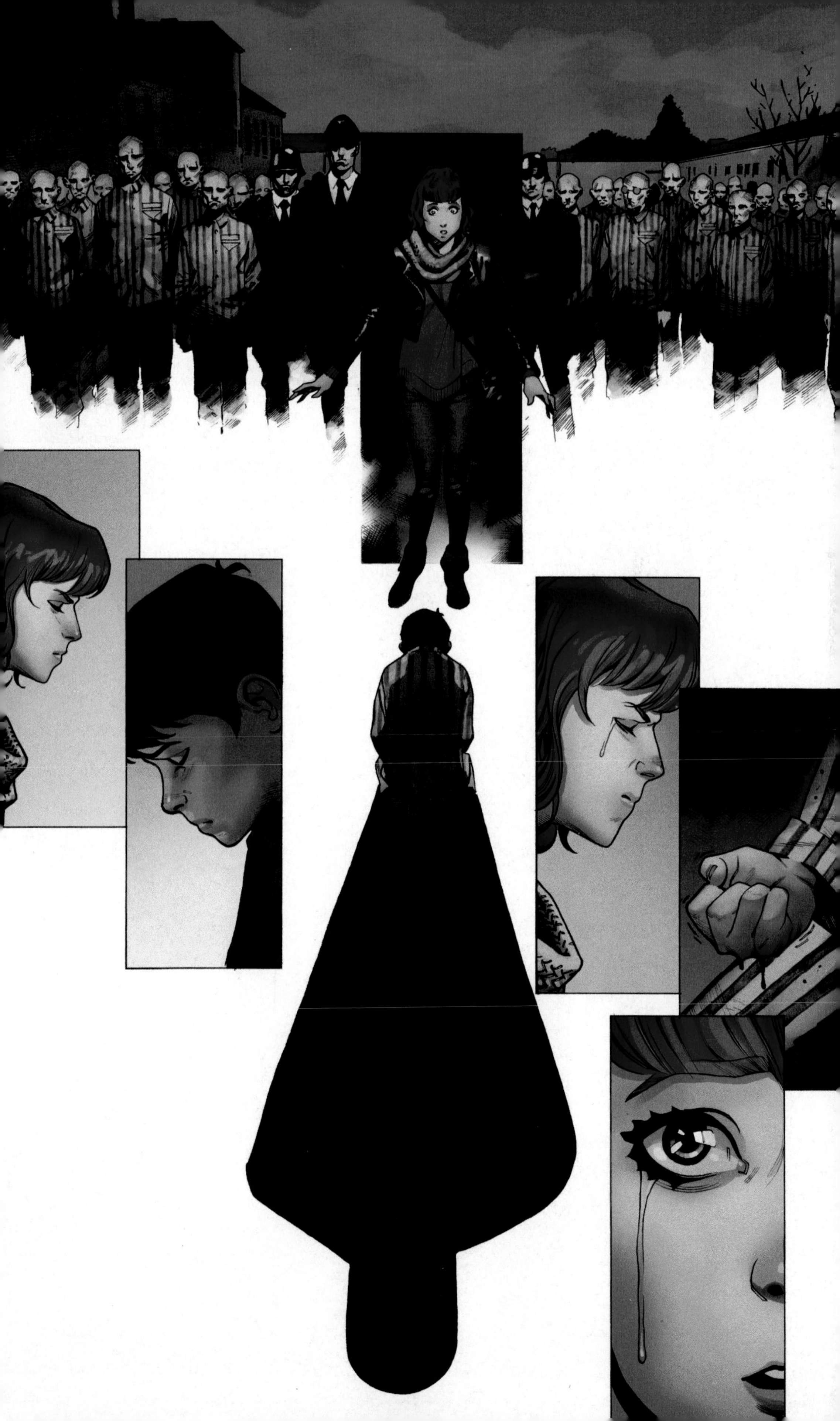

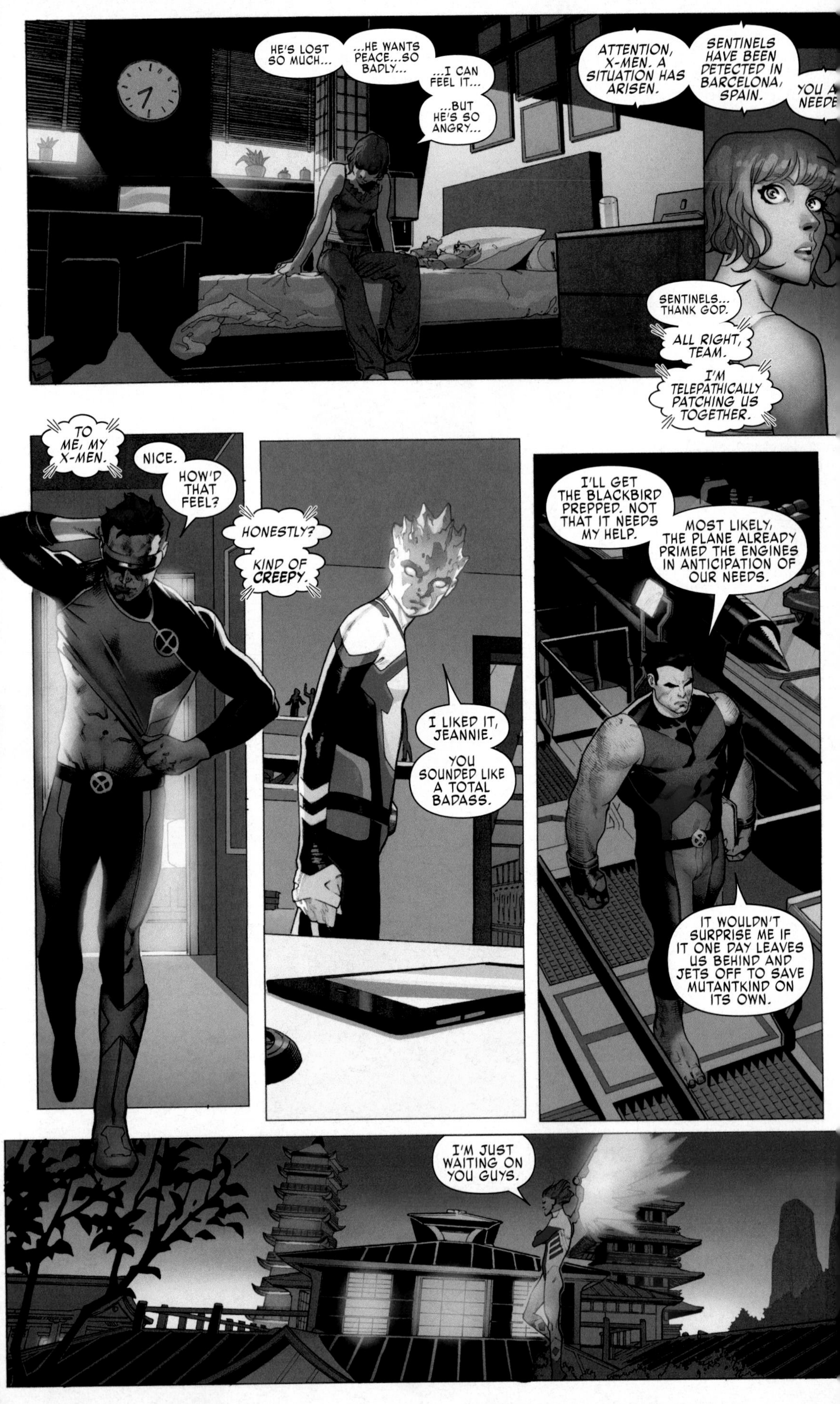
HE'S LOST SO MUCH...
...HE WANTS PEACE...SO BADLY...
...I CAN FEEL IT...
...BUT HE'S SO ANGRY...
ATTENTION, X-MEN. A SITUATION HAS ARISEN.
SENTINELS HAVE BEEN DETECTED IN BARCELONA, SPAIN.
YOU A NEEDE
SENTINELS... THANK GOD.
ALL RIGHT, TEAM.
I'M TELEPATHICALLY PATCHING US TOGETHER.
TO ME, MY X-MEN.
NICE.
HOW'D THAT FEEL?
HONESTLY?
KIND OF CREEPY.
I LIKED IT, JEANNIE.
YOU SOUNDED LIKE A TOTAL BADASS.
I'LL GET THE BLACKBIRD PREPPED. NOT THAT IT NEEDS MY HELP.
MOST LIKELY, THE PLANE ALREADY PRIMED THE ENGINES IN ANTICIPATION OF OUR NEEDS.
IT WOULDN'T SURPRISE ME IF IT ONE DAY LEAVES US BEHIND AND JETS OFF TO SAVE MUTANTKIND ON ITS OWN.
I'M JUST WAITING ON YOU GUYS.

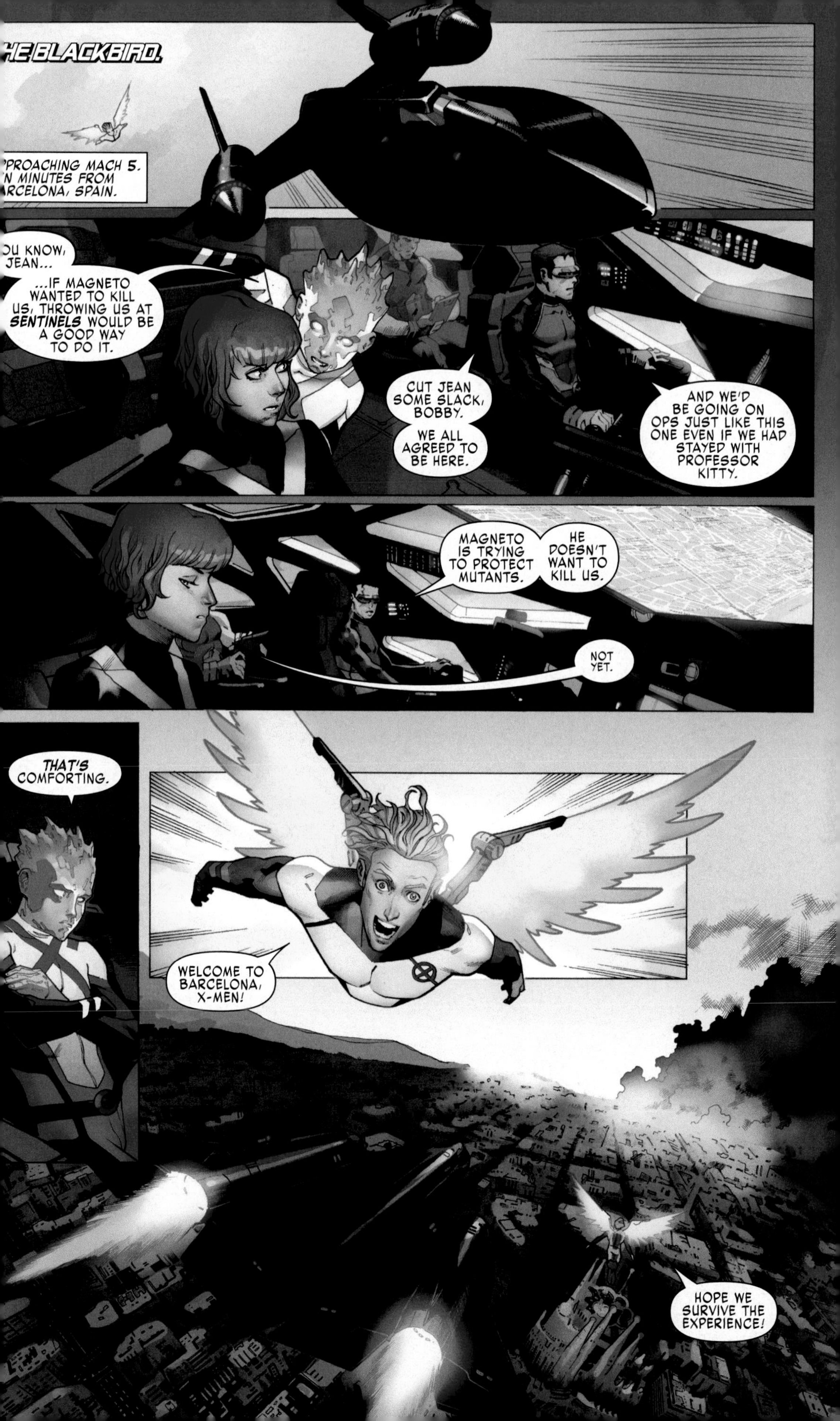
HE BLACKBIRD.
PPROACHING MACH 5.
N MINUTES FROM
ARCELONA, SPAIN.
OU KNOW, JEAN...
...IF MAGNETO WANTED TO KILL US, THROWING US AT SENTINELS WOULD BE A GOOD WAY TO DO IT.
CUT JEAN SOME SLACK, BOBBY.
WE ALL AGREED TO BE HERE.
AND WE'D BE GOING ON OPS JUST LIKE THIS ONE EVEN IF WE HAD STAYED WITH PROFESSOR KITTY.
MAGNETO IS TRYING TO PROTECT MUTANTS.
HE DOESN'T WANT TO KILL US.
NOT YET.
THAT'S COMFORTING.
WELCOME TO BARCELONA, X-MEN!
HOPE WE SURVIVE THE EXPERIENCE!

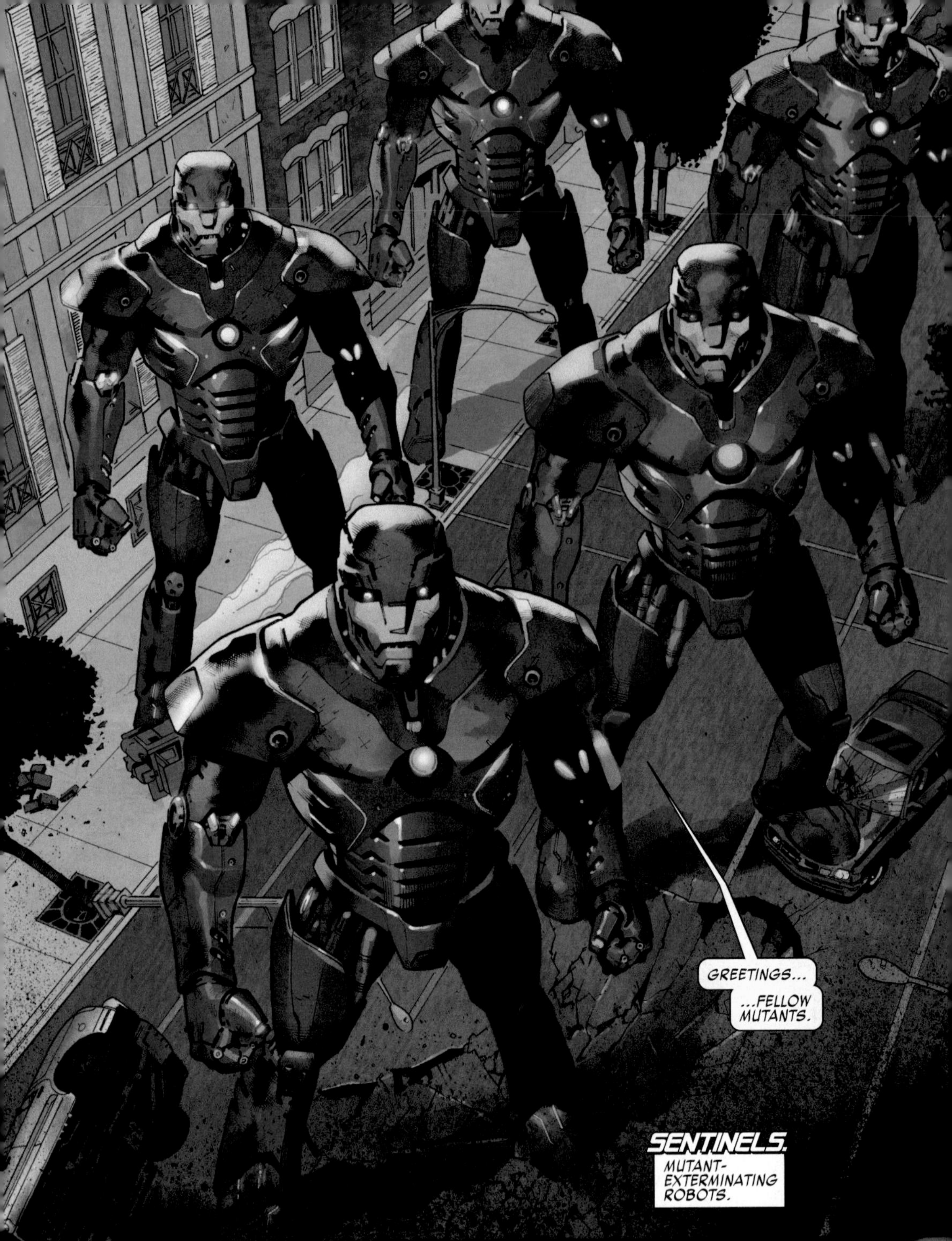
GREETINGS...
...FELLOW MUTANTS.
SENTINELS.
MUTANT-EXTERMINATING ROBOTS.

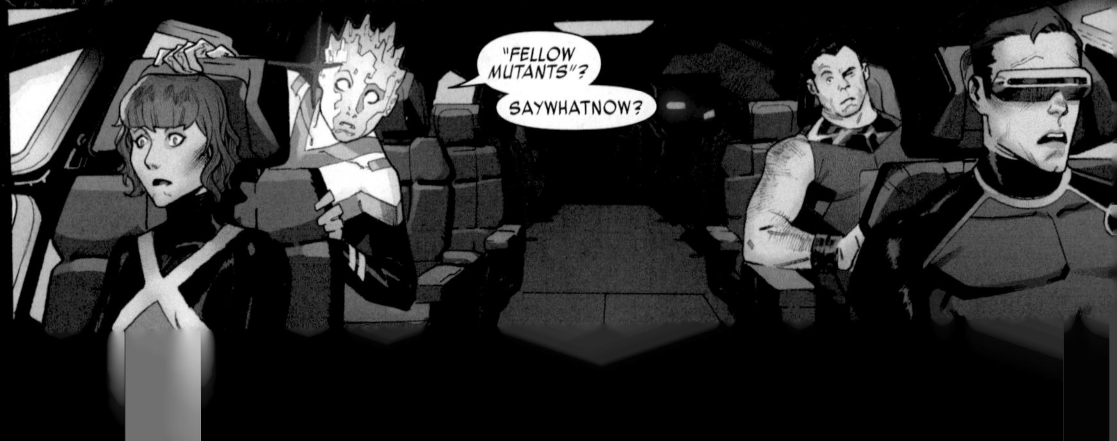
"FELLOW MUTANTS"?
SAYWHATNOW?

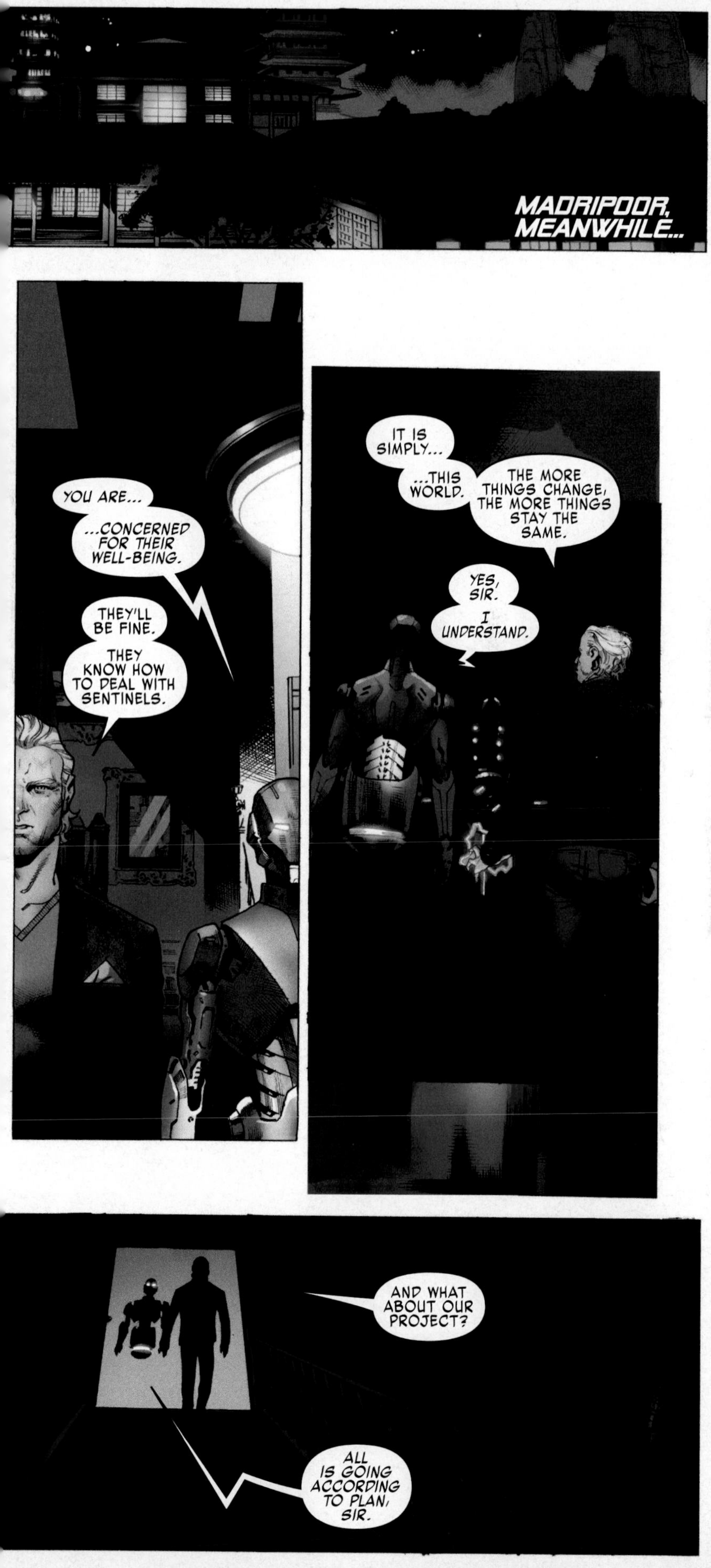
MADRIPOOR, MEANWHILE...
YOU ARE...
...CONCERNED FOR THEIR WELL-BEING.
THEY'LL BE FINE.
THEY KNOW HOW TO DEAL WITH SENTINELS.
IT IS SIMPLY...
...THIS WORLD.
THE MORE THINGS CHANGE, THE MORE THINGS STAY THE SAME.
YES, SIR.
I UNDERSTAND.
AND WHAT ABOUT OUR PROJECT?
ALL IS GOING ACCORDING TO PLAN, SIR.

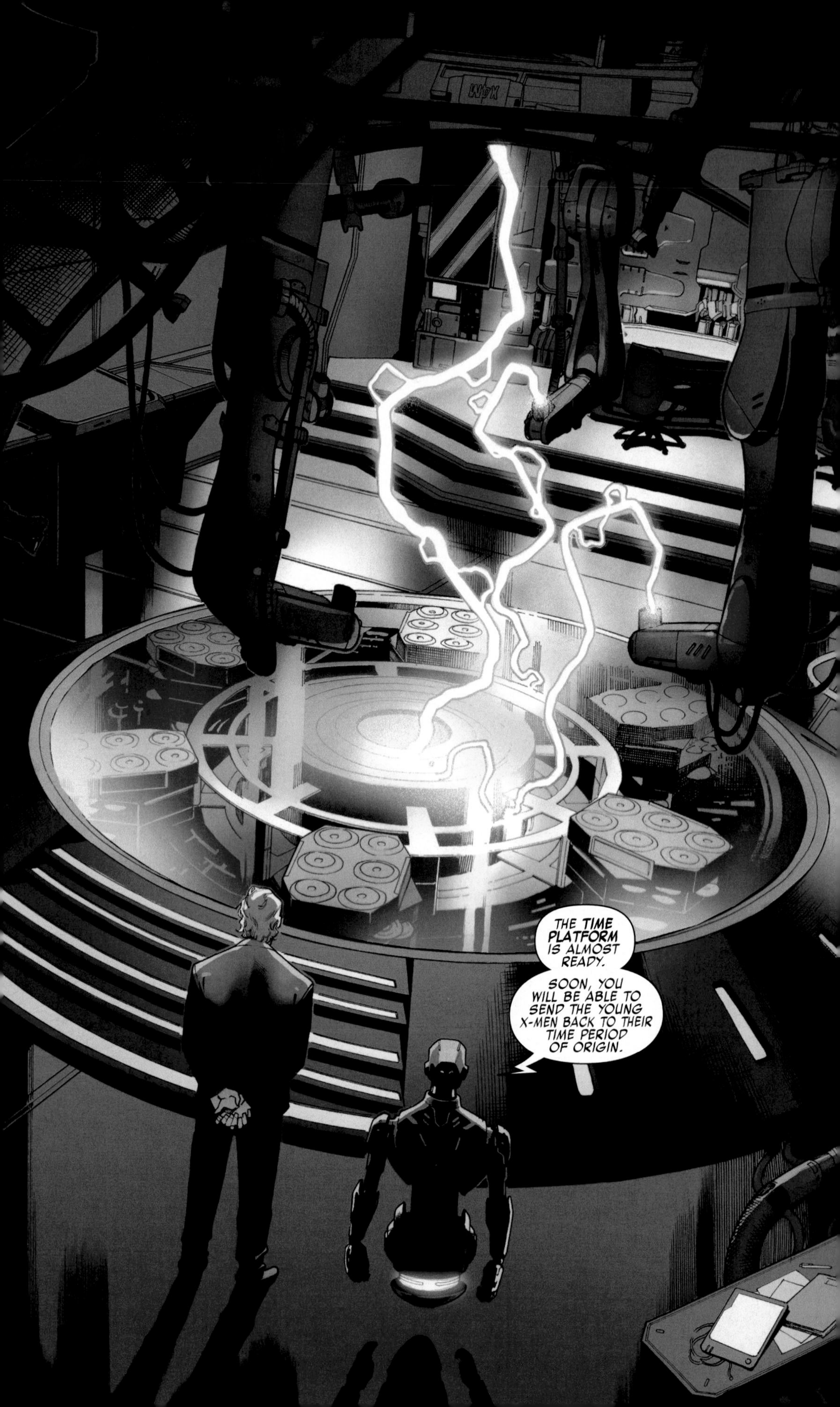
THE TIME PLATFORM IS ALMOST READY.
SOON, YOU WILL BE ABLE TO SEND THE YOUNG X-MEN BACK TO THEIR TIME PERIOD OF ORIGIN.

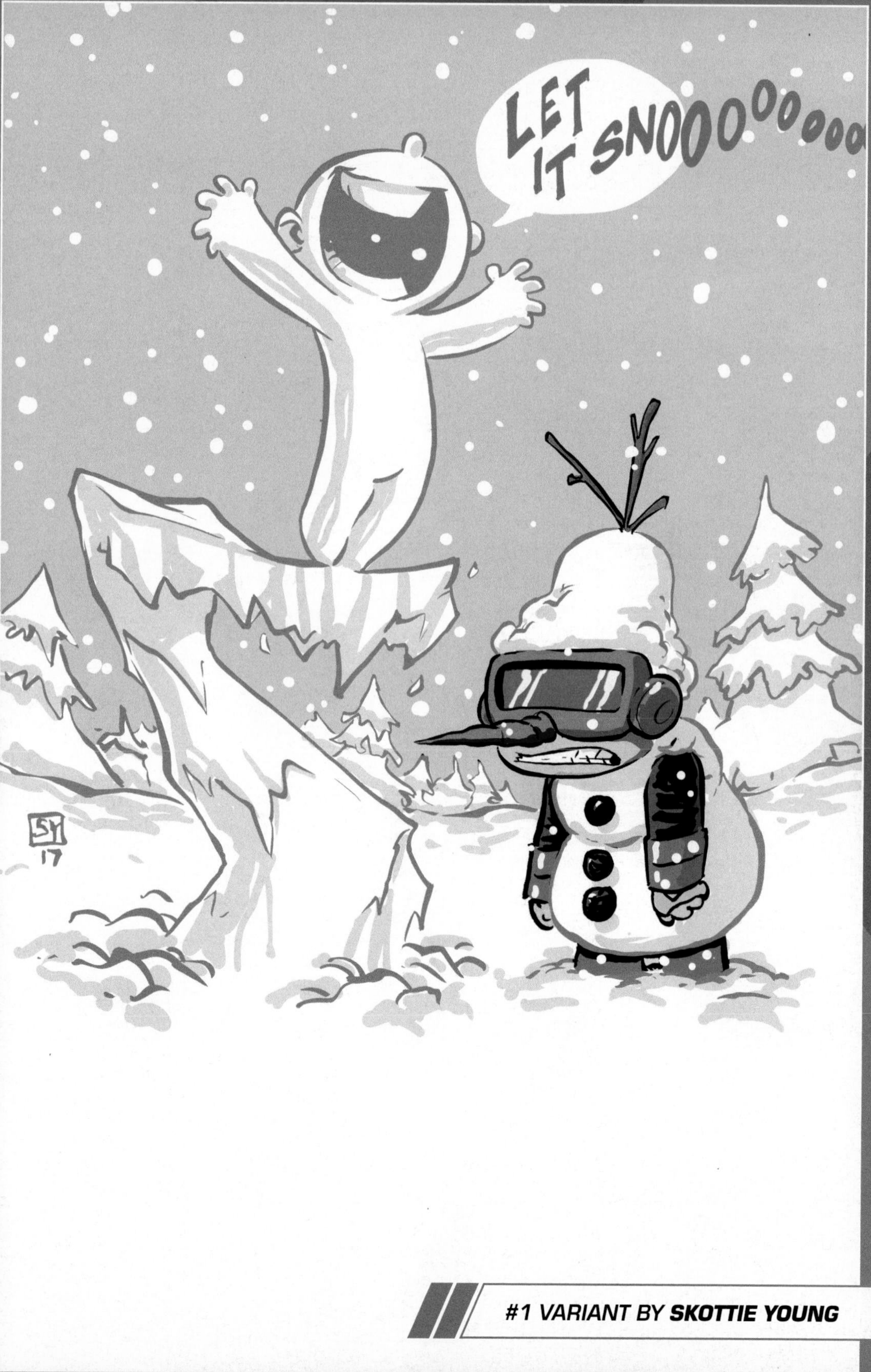
LET IT SNOOOOOOOO

#1 VARIANT BY **SKOTTIE YOUNG**

3

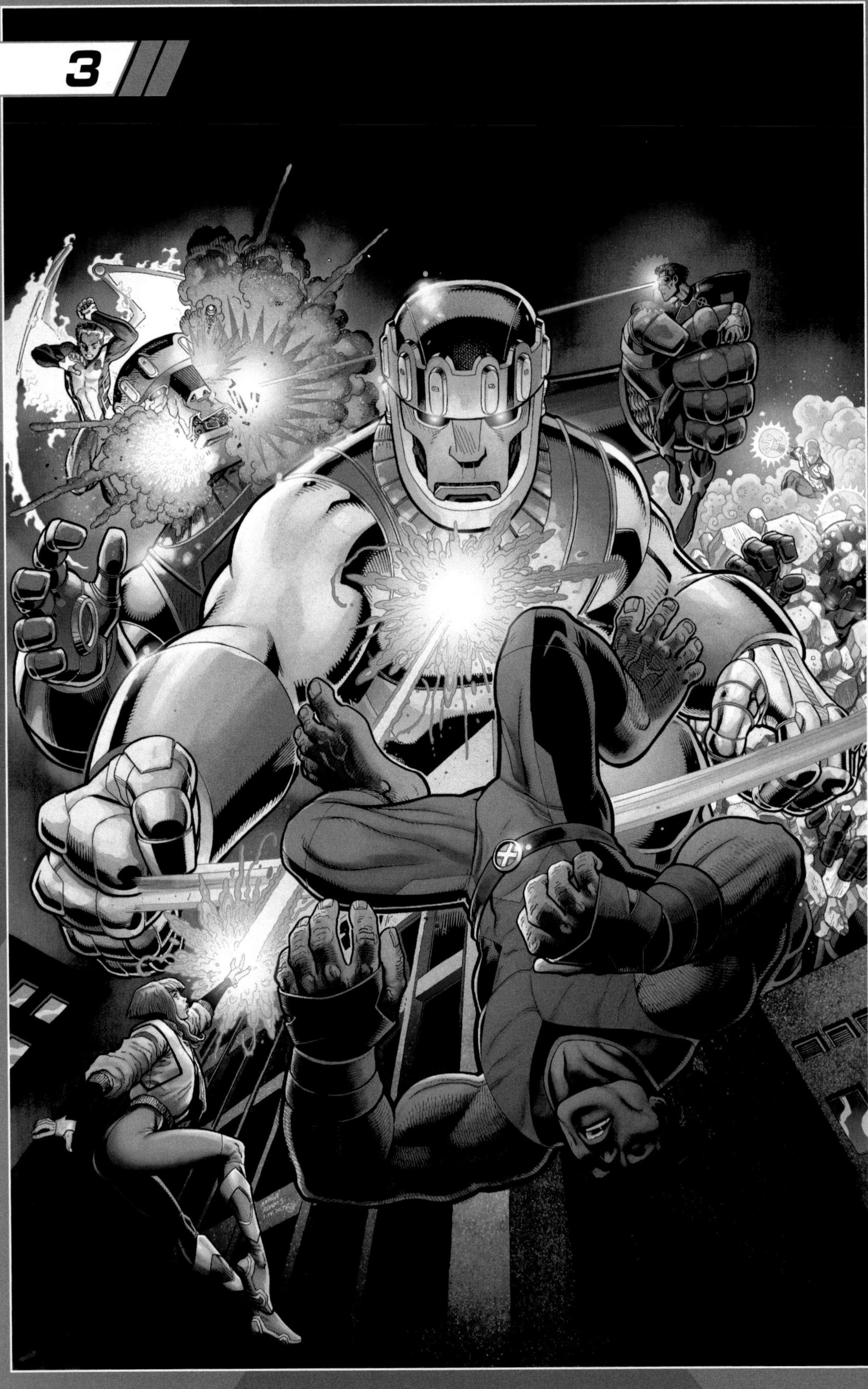

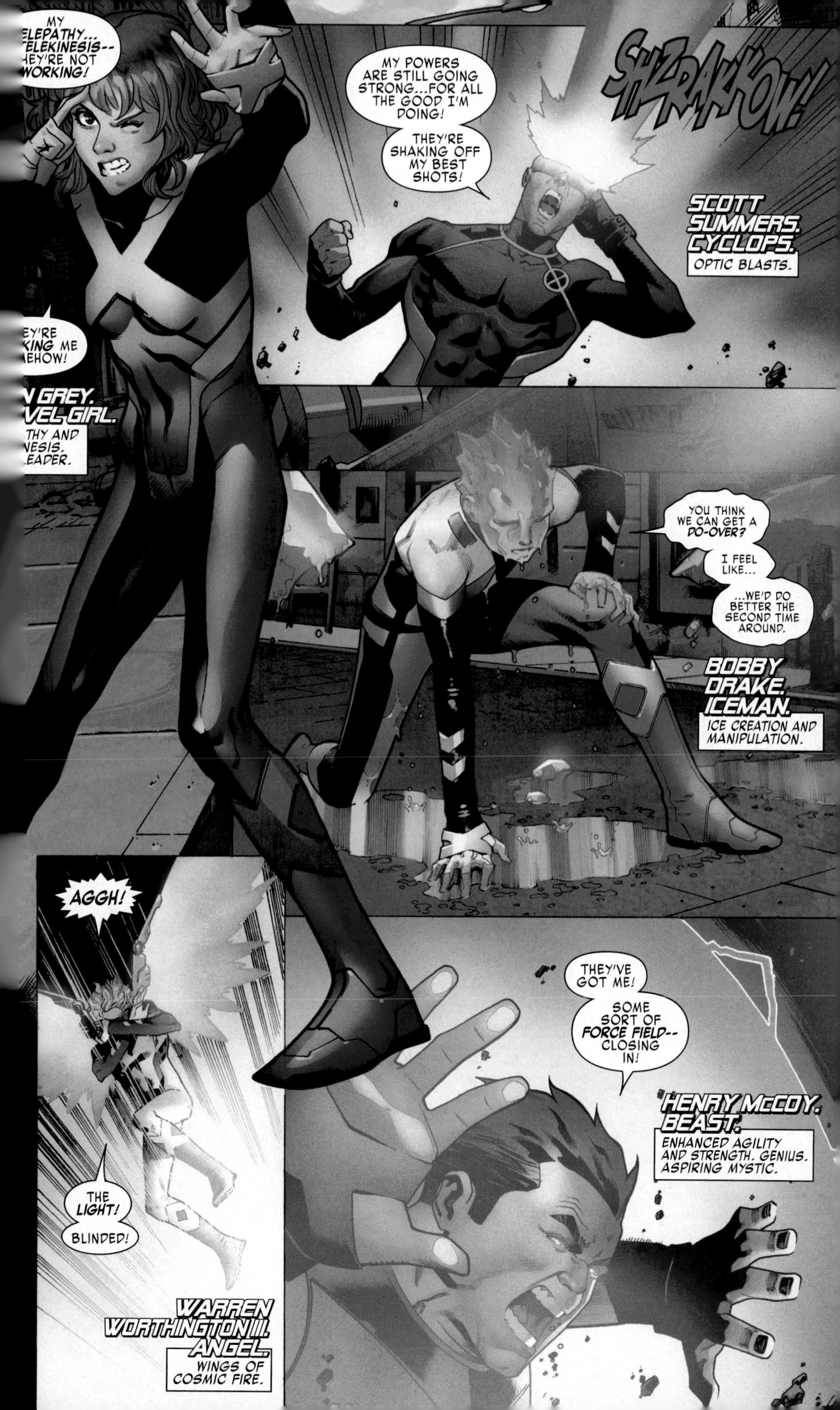

MY ELEPATHY... ELEKINESIS-- HEY'RE NOT WORKING!
MY POWERS ARE STILL GOING STRONG...FOR ALL THE GOOD I'M DOING!
THEY'RE SHAKING OFF MY BEST SHOTS!
SHZRAKKOW!
SCOTT SUMMERS. CYCLOPS.
OPTIC BLASTS.
YOU THINK WE CAN GET A DO-OVER?
I FEEL LIKE...
...WE'D DO BETTER THE SECOND TIME AROUND.
BOBBY DRAKE. ICEMAN.
ICE CREATION AND MANIPULATION.
AGGH!
THE LIGHT!
BLINDED!
WARREN WORTHINGTON III. ANGEL.
WINGS OF COSMIC FIRE.
THEY'VE GOT ME!
SOME SORT OF FORCE FIELD-- CLOSING IN!
HENRY McCOY. BEAST.
ENHANCED AGILITY AND STRENGTH. GENIUS. ASPIRING MYSTIC.

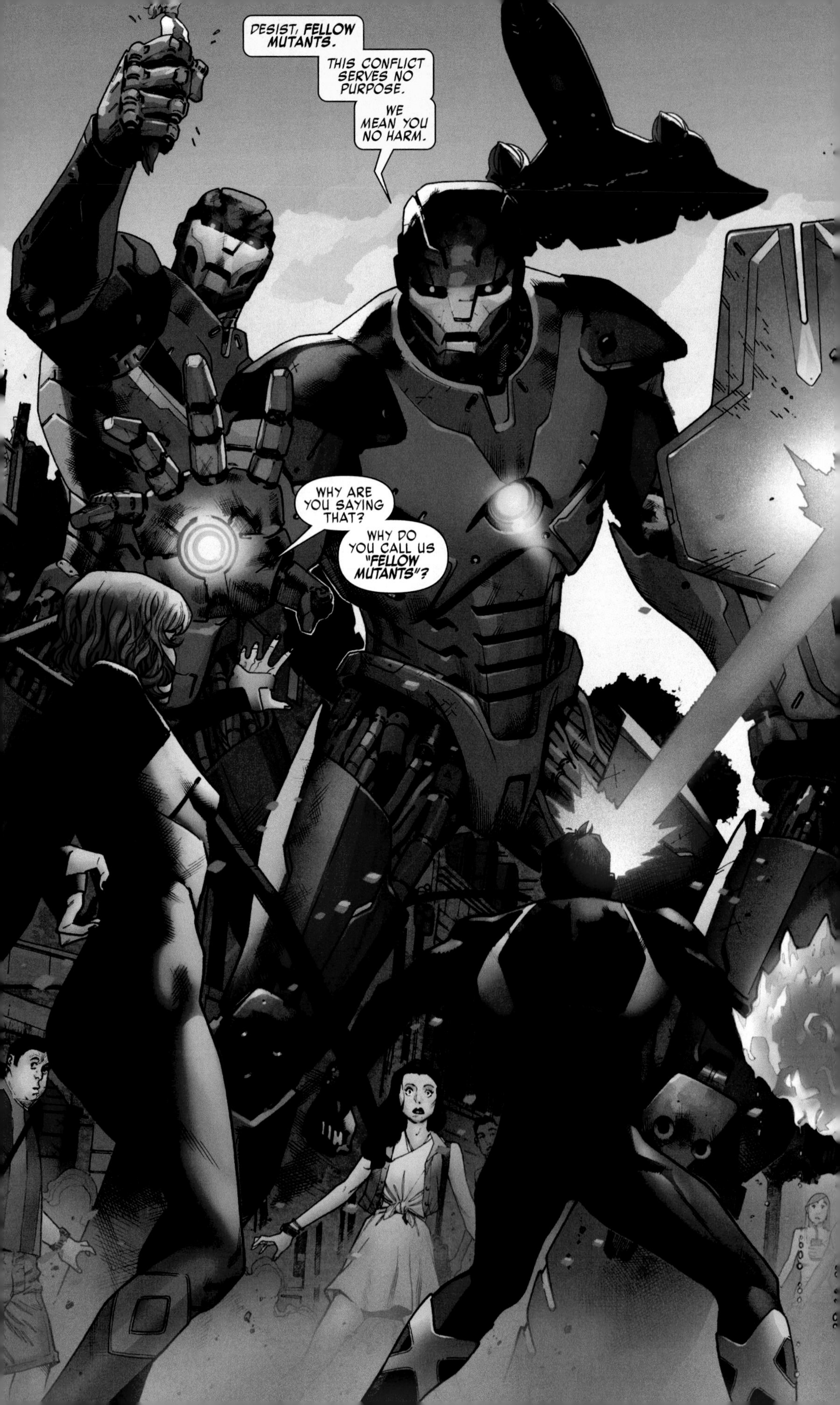
DESIST, FELLOW MUTANTS.
THIS CONFLICT SERVES NO PURPOSE.
WE MEAN YOU NO HARM.
WHY ARE YOU SAYING THAT?
WHY DO YOU CALL US "FELLOW MUTANTS"?

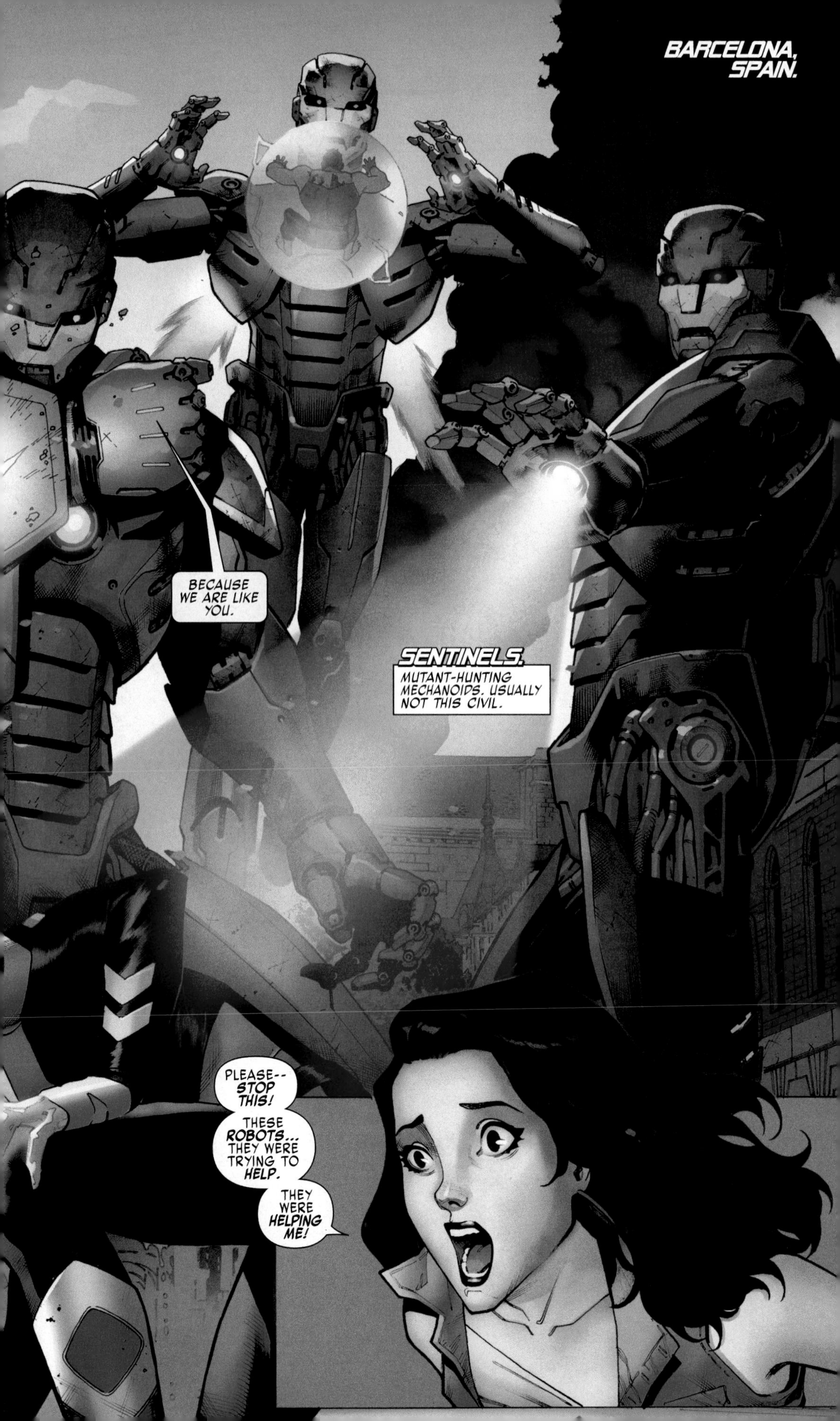
BARCELONA, SPAIN.
BECAUSE WE ARE LIKE YOU.
SENTINELS.
MUTANT-HUNTING MECHANOIDS. USUALLY NOT THIS CIVIL.
PLEASE-- STOP THIS!
THESE ROBOTS... THEY WERE TRYING TO HELP.
THEY WERE HELPING ME!

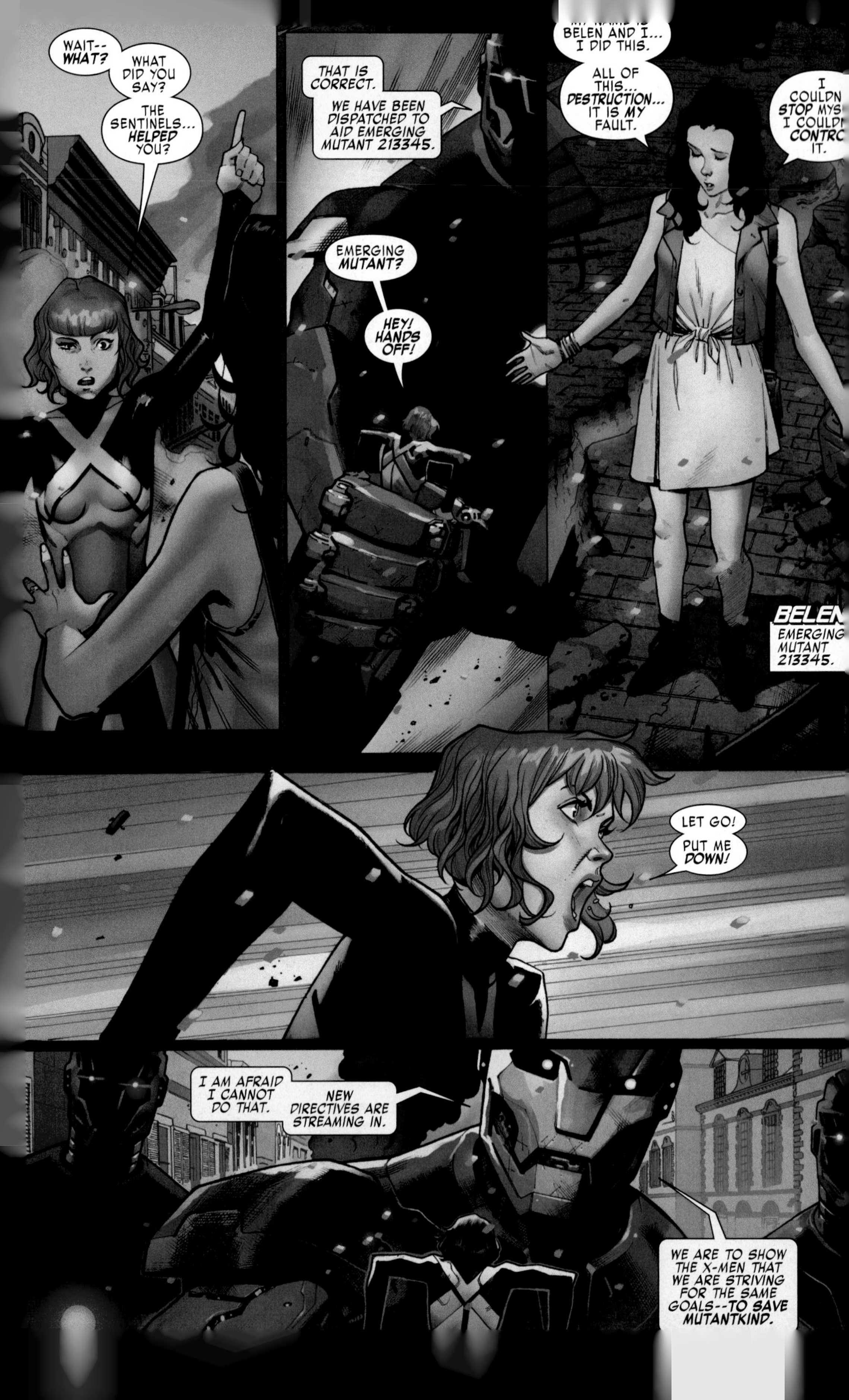
WAIT-- WHAT?
WHAT DID YOU SAY?
THE SENTINELS... HELPED YOU?
THAT IS CORRECT.
WE HAVE BEEN DISPATCHED TO AID EMERGING MUTANT 213345.
EMERGING MUTANT?
HEY! HANDS OFF!
BELEN AND I... I DID THIS.
ALL OF THIS... DESTRUCTION... IT IS MY FAULT.
BELEN
EMERGING MUTANT 213345.
LET GO!
PUT ME DOWN!
I AM AFRAID I CANNOT DO THAT.
NEW DIRECTIVES ARE STREAMING IN.
WE ARE TO SHOW THE X-MEN THAT WE ARE STRIVING FOR THE SAME GOALS--TO SAVE MUTANTKIND.

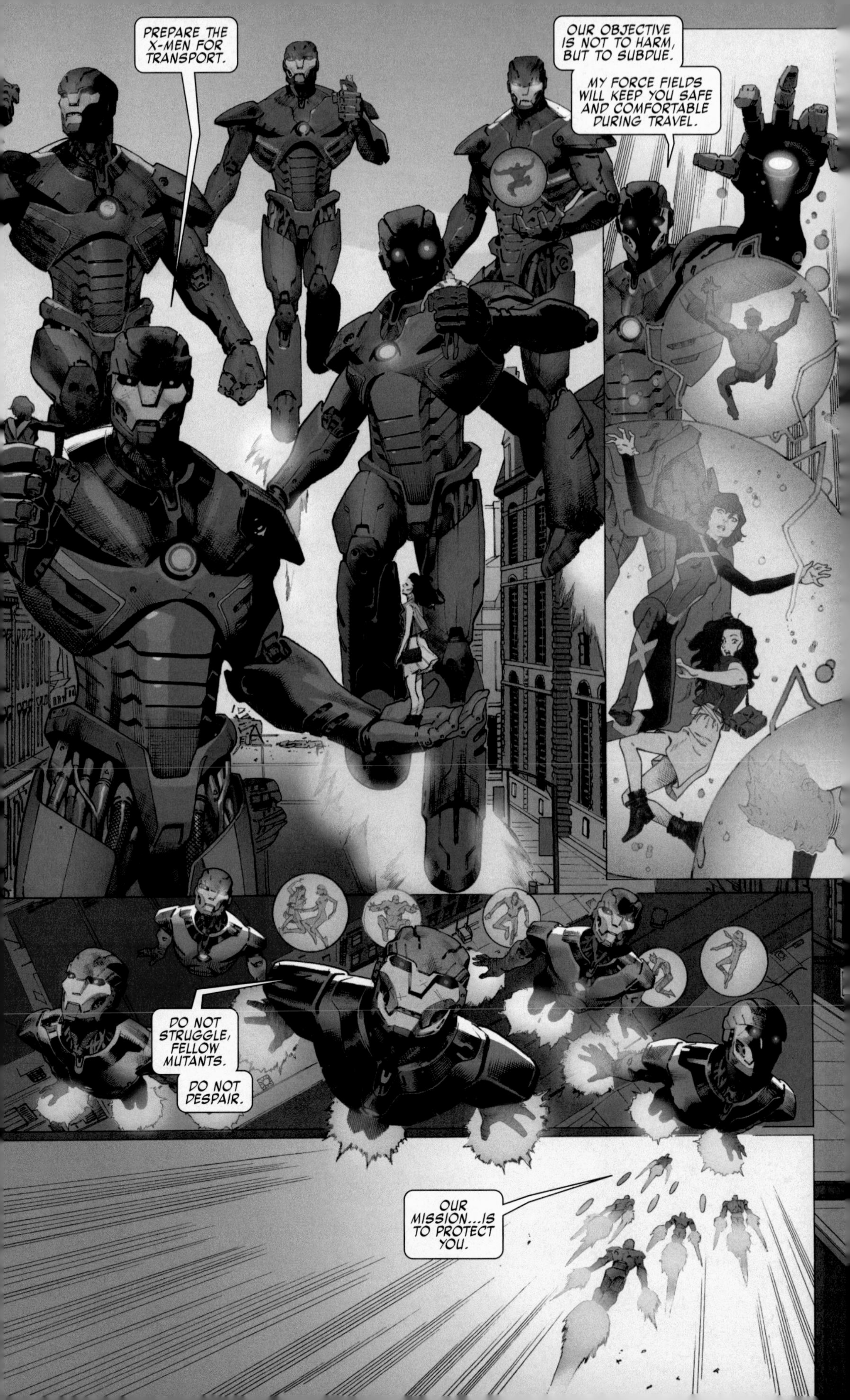
PREPARE THE X-MEN FOR TRANSPORT.
OUR OBJECTIVE IS NOT TO HARM, BUT TO SUBDUE.
MY FORCE FIELDS WILL KEEP YOU SAFE AND COMFORTABLE DURING TRAVEL.
DO NOT STRUGGLE, FELLOW MUTANTS.
DO NOT DESPAIR.
OUR MISSION...IS TO PROTECT YOU.

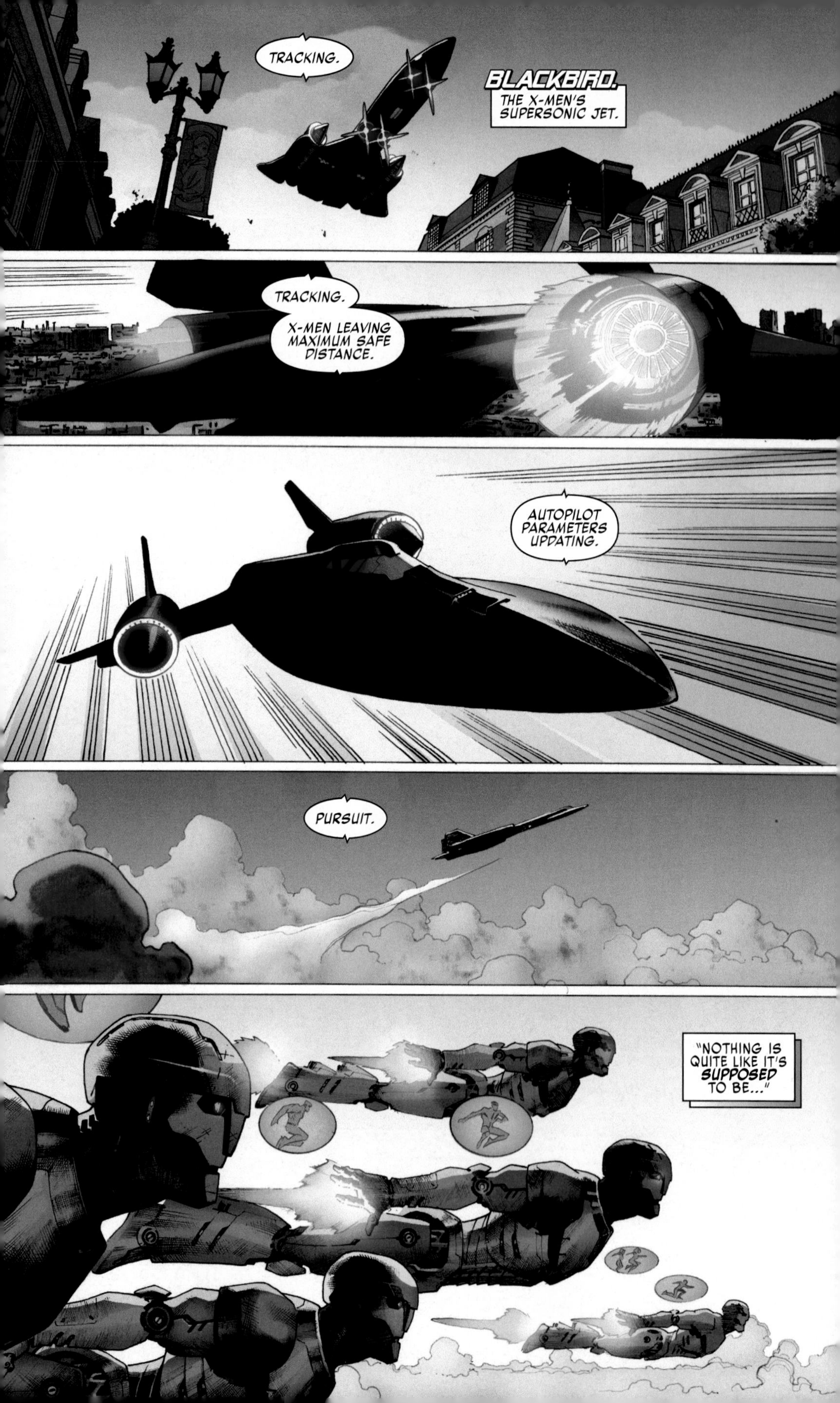
TRACKING.
BLACKBIRD.
THE X-MEN'S SUPERSONIC JET.
TRACKING.
X-MEN LEAVING MAXIMUM SAFE DISTANCE.
AUTOPILOT PARAMETERS UPDATING.
PURSUIT.
"NOTHING IS QUITE LIKE IT'S SUPPOSED TO BE..."

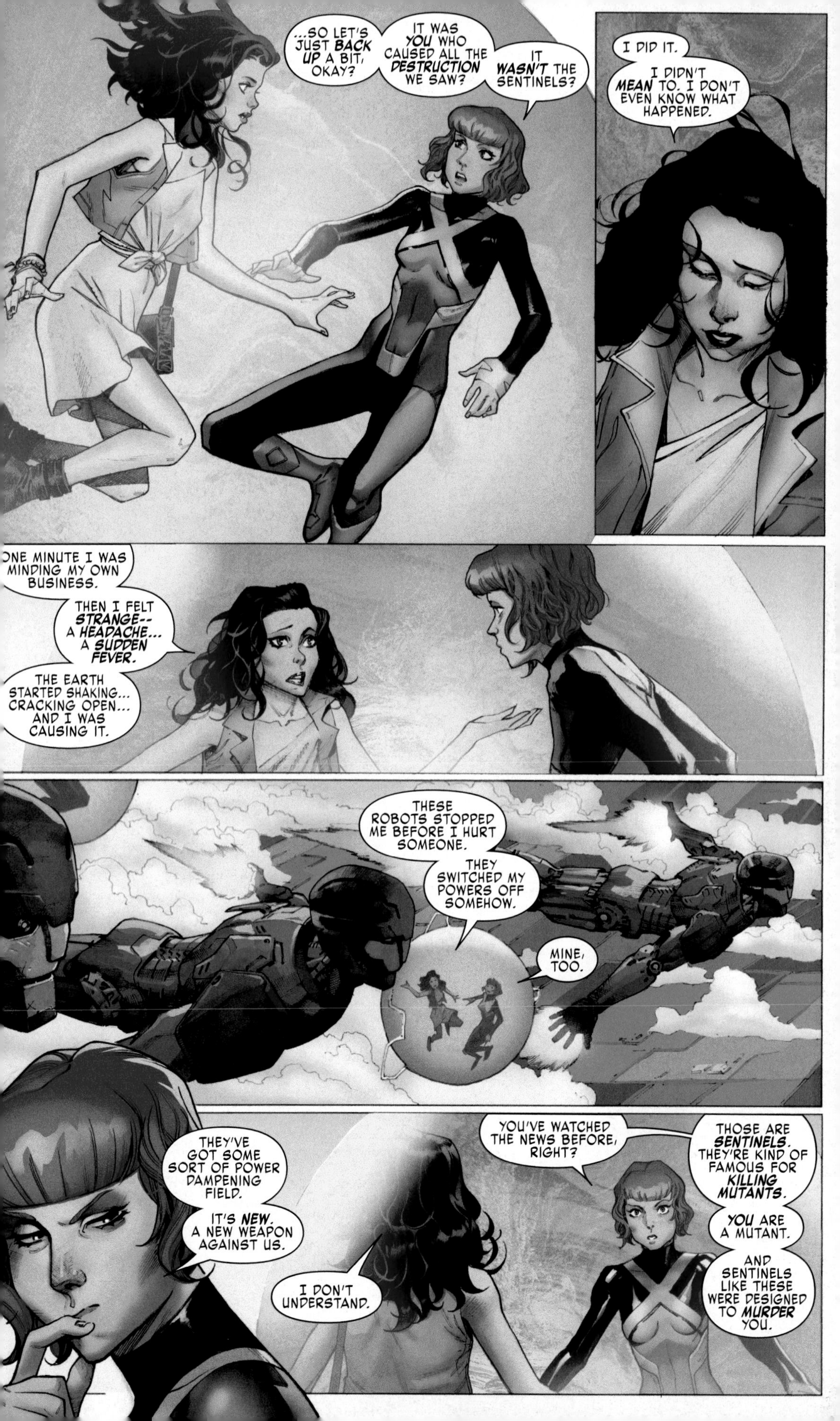
...SO LET'S JUST BACK UP A BIT, OKAY?
IT WAS YOU WHO CAUSED ALL THE DESTRUCTION WE SAW?
IT WASN'T THE SENTINELS?
I DID IT.
I DIDN'T MEAN TO. I DON'T EVEN KNOW WHAT HAPPENED.
ONE MINUTE I WAS MINDING MY OWN BUSINESS.
THEN I FELT STRANGE-- A HEADACHE... A SUDDEN FEVER.
THE EARTH STARTED SHAKING... CRACKING OPEN... AND I WAS CAUSING IT.
THESE ROBOTS STOPPED ME BEFORE I HURT SOMEONE.
THEY SWITCHED MY POWERS OFF SOMEHOW.
MINE, TOO.
THEY'VE GOT SOME SORT OF POWER DAMPENING FIELD.
IT'S NEW. A NEW WEAPON AGAINST US.
I DON'T UNDERSTAND.
YOU'VE WATCHED THE NEWS BEFORE, RIGHT?
THOSE ARE SENTINELS. THEY'RE KIND OF FAMOUS FOR KILLING MUTANTS.
YOU ARE A MUTANT.
AND SENTINELS LIKE THESE WERE DESIGNED TO MURDER YOU.

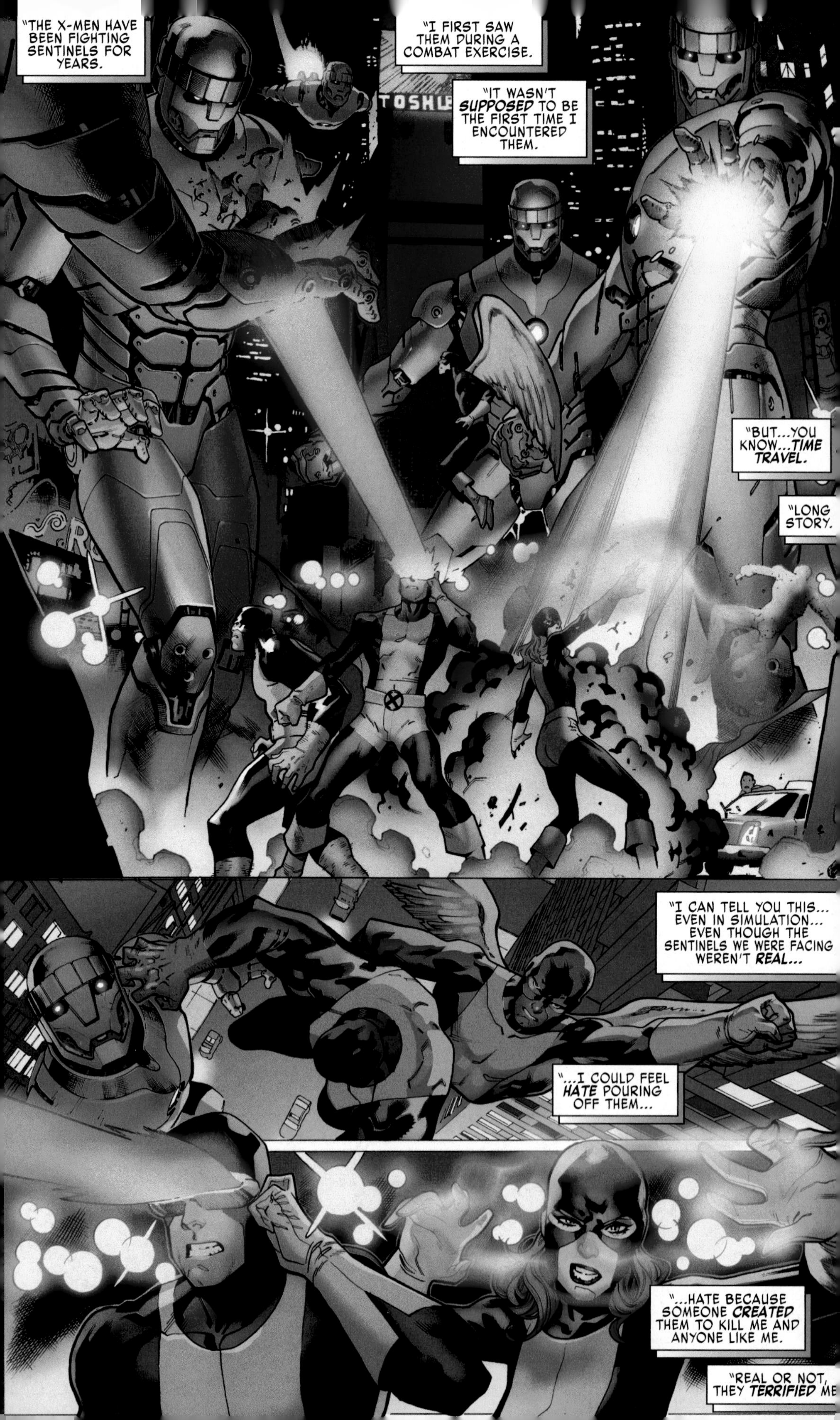
"THE X-MEN HAVE BEEN FIGHTING SENTINELS FOR YEARS.
"I FIRST SAW THEM DURING A COMBAT EXERCISE.
"IT WASN'T SUPPOSED TO BE THE FIRST TIME I ENCOUNTERED THEM.
TOSHI
"BUT...YOU KNOW...TIME TRAVEL.
"LONG STORY.
"I CAN TELL YOU THIS... EVEN IN SIMULATION... EVEN THOUGH THE SENTINELS WE WERE FACING WEREN'T REAL...
"...I COULD FEEL HATE POURING OFF THEM...
"...HATE BECAUSE SOMEONE CREATED THEM TO KILL ME AND ANYONE LIKE ME.
"REAL OR NOT, THEY TERRIFIED ME

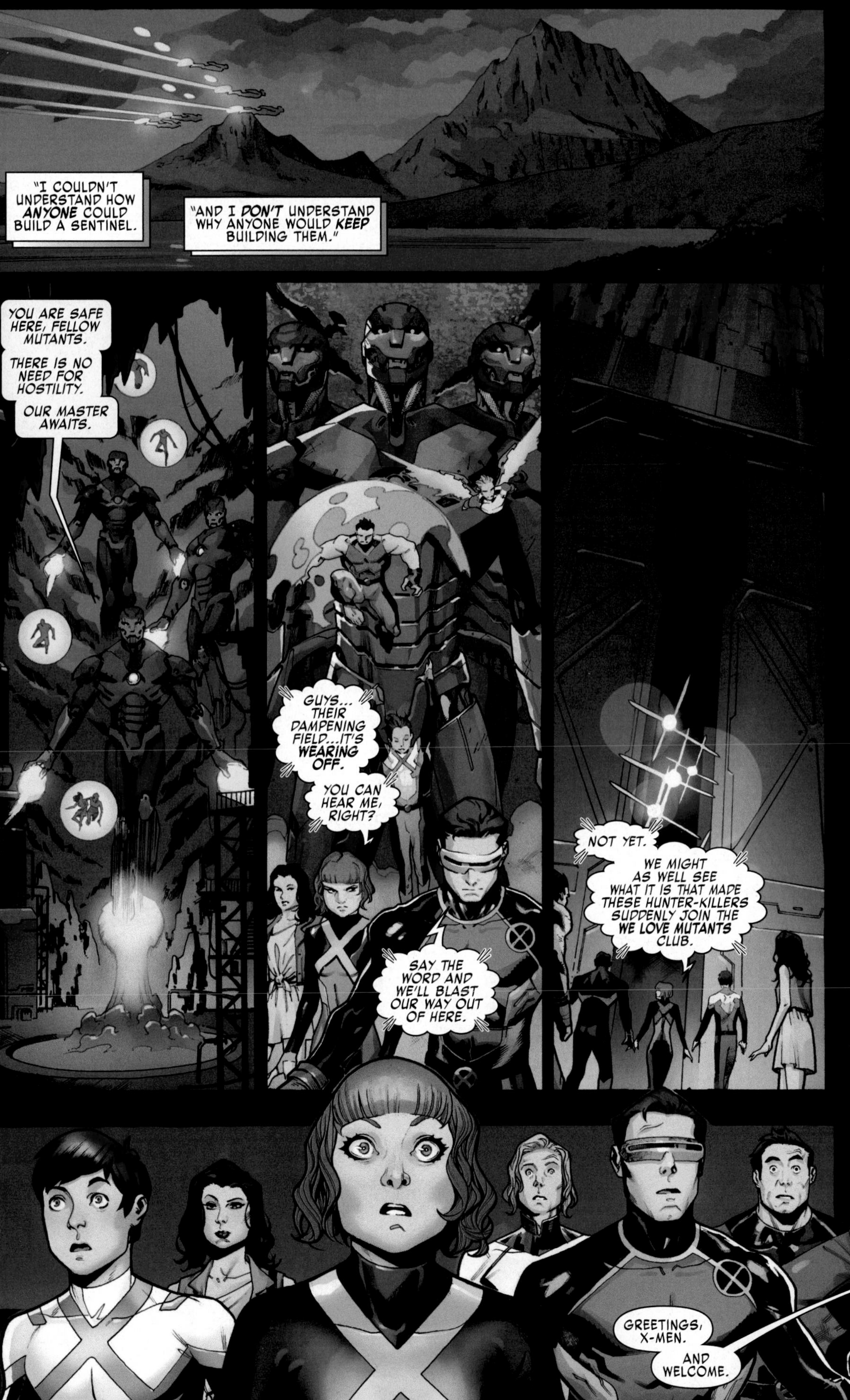

"I COULDN'T UNDERSTAND HOW ANYONE COULD BUILD A SENTINEL.
"AND I DON'T UNDERSTAND WHY ANYONE WOULD KEEP BUILDING THEM."
YOU ARE SAFE HERE, FELLOW MUTANTS.
THERE IS NO NEED FOR HOSTILITY.
OUR MASTER AWAITS.
GUYS... THEIR DAMPENING FIELD...IT'S WEARING OFF.
YOU CAN HEAR ME, RIGHT?
SAY THE WORD AND WE'LL BLAST OUR WAY OUT OF HERE.
NOT YET.
WE MIGHT AS WELL SEE WHAT IT IS THAT MADE THESE HUNTER-KILLERS SUDDENLY JOIN THE WE LOVE MUTANTS CLUB.
GREETINGS, X-MEN.
AND WELCOME.

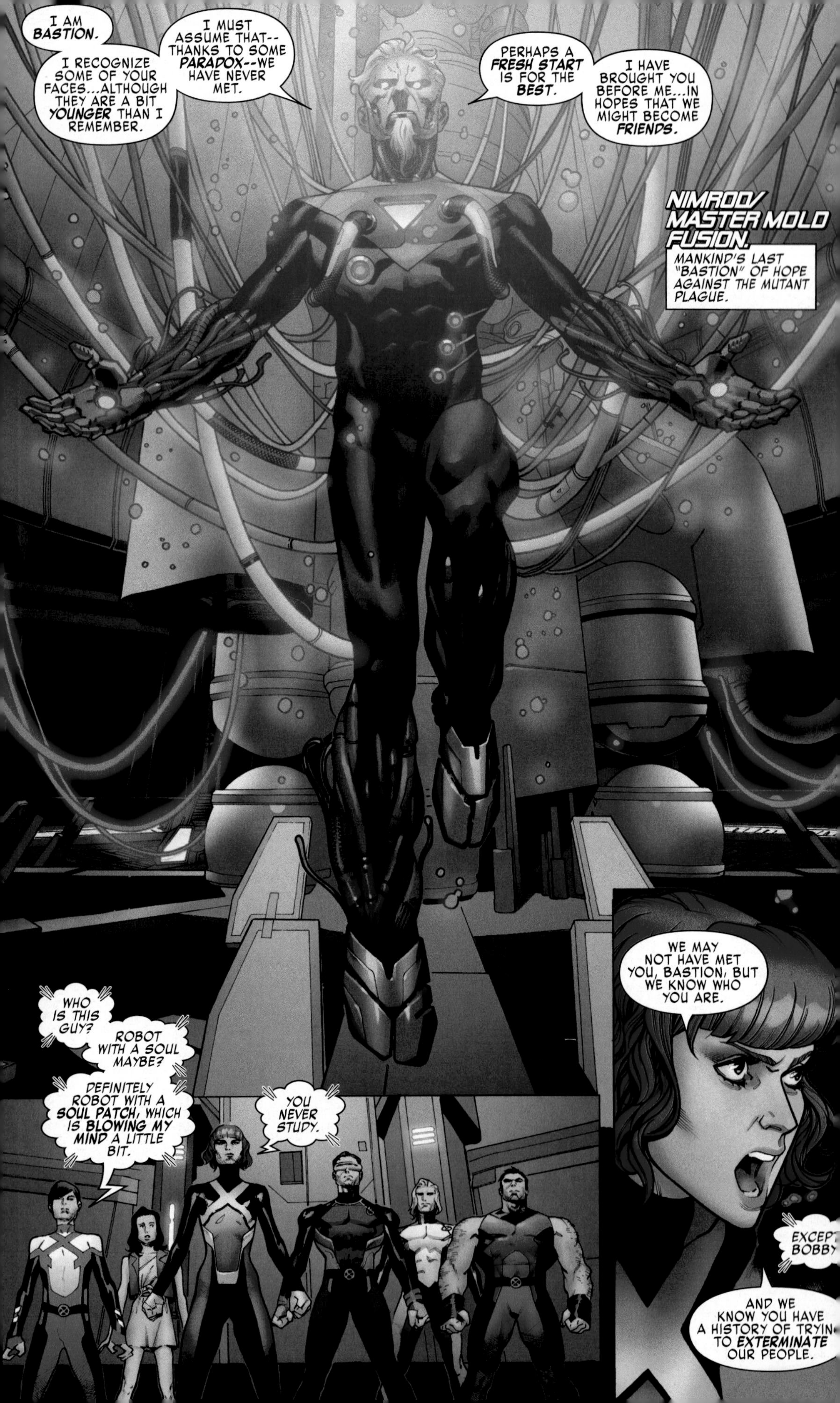

I AM BASTION.
I RECOGNIZE SOME OF YOUR FACES...ALTHOUGH THEY ARE A BIT YOUNGER THAN I REMEMBER.
I MUST ASSUME THAT--THANKS TO SOME PARADOX--WE HAVE NEVER MET.
PERHAPS A FRESH START IS FOR THE BEST.
I HAVE BROUGHT YOU BEFORE ME...IN HOPES THAT WE MIGHT BECOME FRIENDS.
NIMROD/ MASTER MOLD FUSION.
MANKIND'S LAST "BASTION" OF HOPE AGAINST THE MUTANT PLAGUE.
WHO IS THIS GUY?
ROBOT WITH A SOUL MAYBE?
DEFINITELY ROBOT WITH A SOUL PATCH, WHICH IS BLOWING MY MIND A LITTLE BIT.
YOU NEVER STUDY.
WE MAY NOT HAVE MET YOU, BASTION, BUT WE KNOW WHO YOU ARE.
EXCEPT BOBBY
AND WE KNOW YOU HAVE A HISTORY OF TRYIN TO EXTERMINATE OUR PEOPLE.

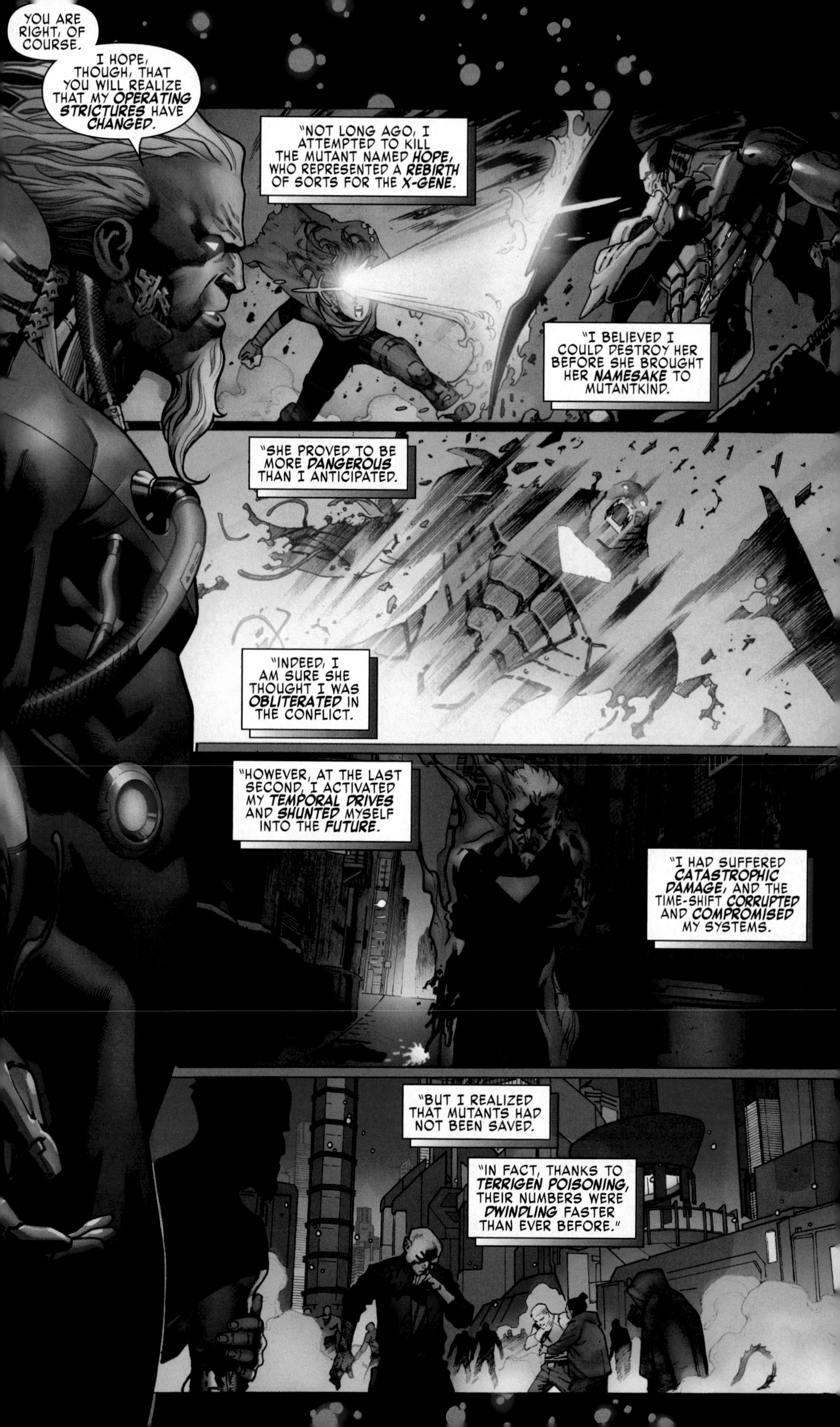
YOU ARE RIGHT, OF COURSE.
I HOPE, THOUGH, THAT YOU WILL REALIZE THAT MY OPERATING STRICTURES HAVE CHANGED.
"NOT LONG AGO, I ATTEMPTED TO KILL THE MUTANT NAMED HOPE, WHO REPRESENTED A REBIRTH OF SORTS FOR THE X-GENE.
"I BELIEVED I COULD DESTROY HER BEFORE SHE BROUGHT HER NAMESAKE TO MUTANTKIND.
"SHE PROVED TO BE MORE DANGEROUS THAN I ANTICIPATED.
"INDEED, I AM SURE SHE THOUGHT I WAS OBLITERATED IN THE CONFLICT.
"HOWEVER, AT THE LAST SECOND, I ACTIVATED MY TEMPORAL DRIVES AND SHUNTED MYSELF INTO THE FUTURE.
"I HAD SUFFERED CATASTROPHIC DAMAGE, AND THE TIME-SHIFT CORRUPTED AND COMPROMISED MY SYSTEMS.
"BUT I REALIZED THAT MUTANTS HAD NOT BEEN SAVED.
"IN FACT, THANKS TO TERRIGEN POISONING, THEIR NUMBERS WERE DWINDLING FASTER THAN EVER BEFORE."

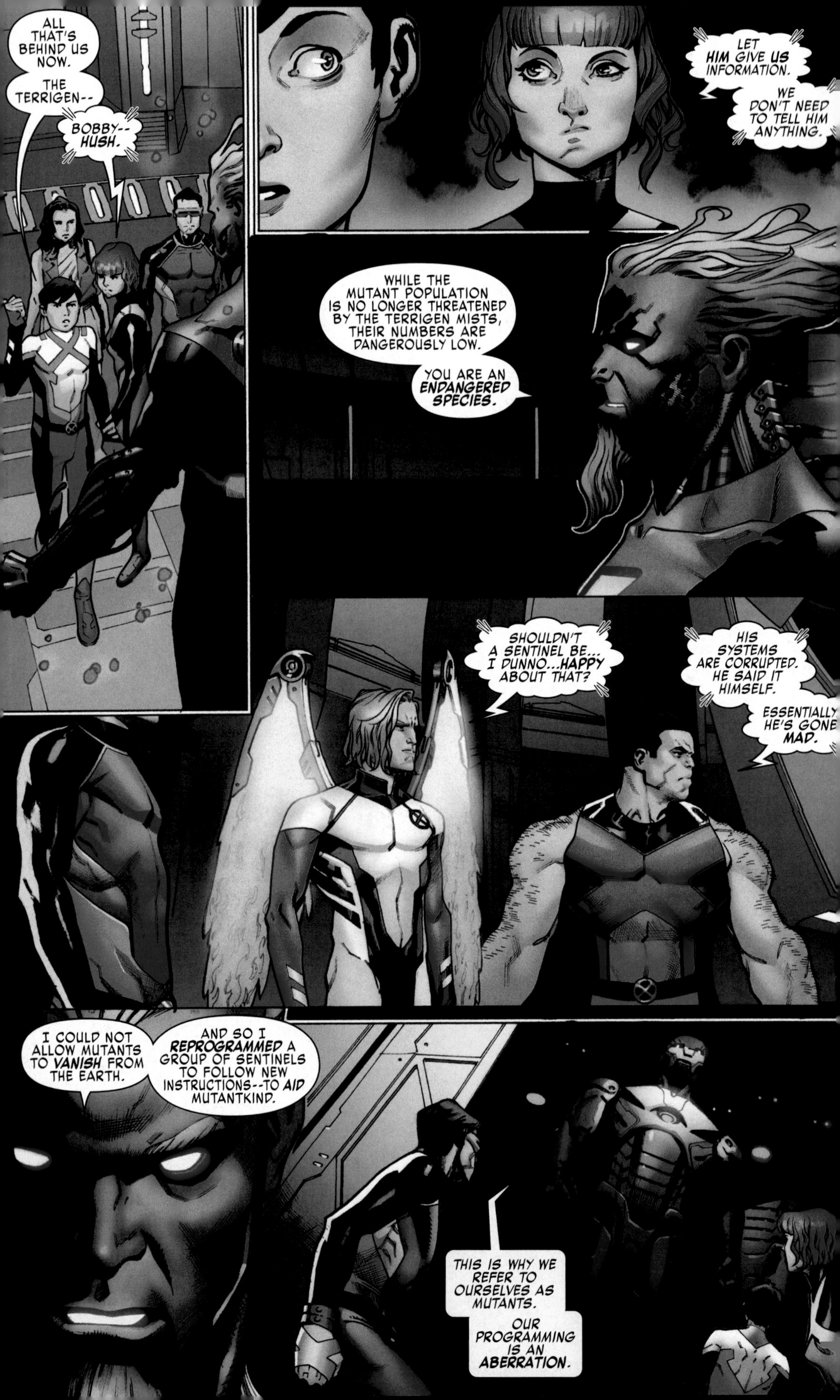
ALL THAT'S BEHIND US NOW.
THE TERRIGEN--
BOBBY-- HUSH.
LET HIM GIVE US INFORMATION.
WE DON'T NEED TO TELL HIM ANYTHING.
WHILE THE MUTANT POPULATION IS NO LONGER THREATENED BY THE TERRIGEN MISTS, THEIR NUMBERS ARE DANGEROUSLY LOW.
YOU ARE AN ENDANGERED SPECIES.
SHOULDN'T A SENTINEL BE... I DUNNO...HAPPY ABOUT THAT?
HIS SYSTEMS ARE CORRUPTED. HE SAID IT HIMSELF.
ESSENTIALLY HE'S GONE MAD.
I COULD NOT ALLOW MUTANTS TO VANISH FROM THE EARTH.
AND SO I REPROGRAMMED A GROUP OF SENTINELS TO FOLLOW NEW INSTRUCTIONS--TO AID MUTANTKIND.
THIS IS WHY WE REFER TO OURSELVES AS MUTANTS.
OUR PROGRAMMING IS AN ABERRATION.

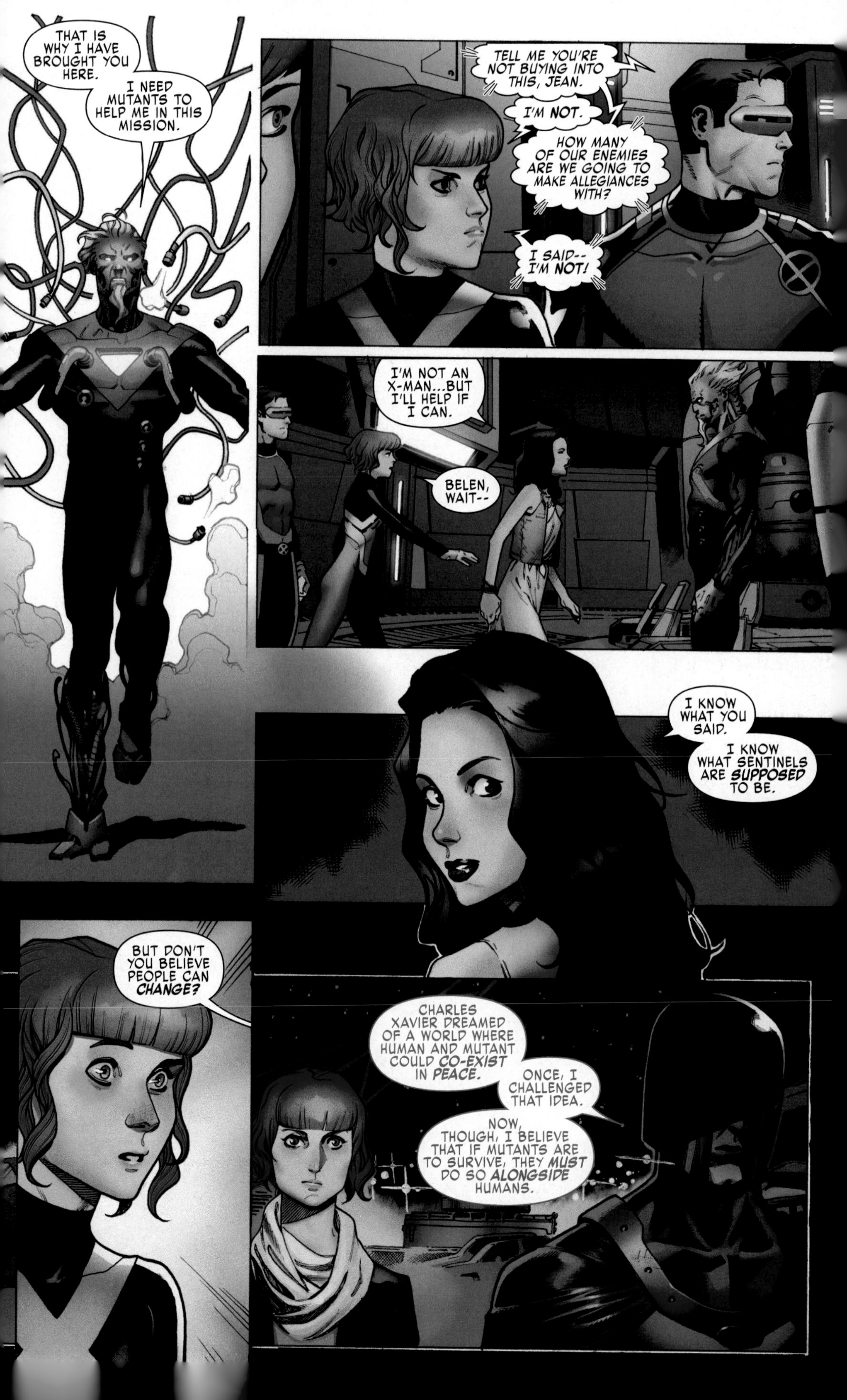
THAT IS WHY I HAVE BROUGHT YOU HERE.
I NEED MUTANTS TO HELP ME IN THIS MISSION.
TELL ME YOU'RE NOT BUYING INTO THIS, JEAN.
I'M NOT.
HOW MANY OF OUR ENEMIES ARE WE GOING TO MAKE ALLEGIANCES WITH?
I SAID-- I'M NOT!
I'M NOT AN X-MAN...BUT I'LL HELP IF I CAN.
BELEN, WAIT--
I KNOW WHAT YOU SAID.
I KNOW WHAT SENTINELS ARE SUPPOSED TO BE.
BUT DON'T YOU BELIEVE PEOPLE CAN CHANGE?
CHARLES XAVIER DREAMED OF A WORLD WHERE HUMAN AND MUTANT COULD CO-EXIST IN PEACE.
ONCE, I CHALLENGED THAT IDEA.
NOW, THOUGH, I BELIEVE THAT IF MUTANTS ARE TO SURVIVE, THEY MUST DO SO ALONGSIDE HUMANS.

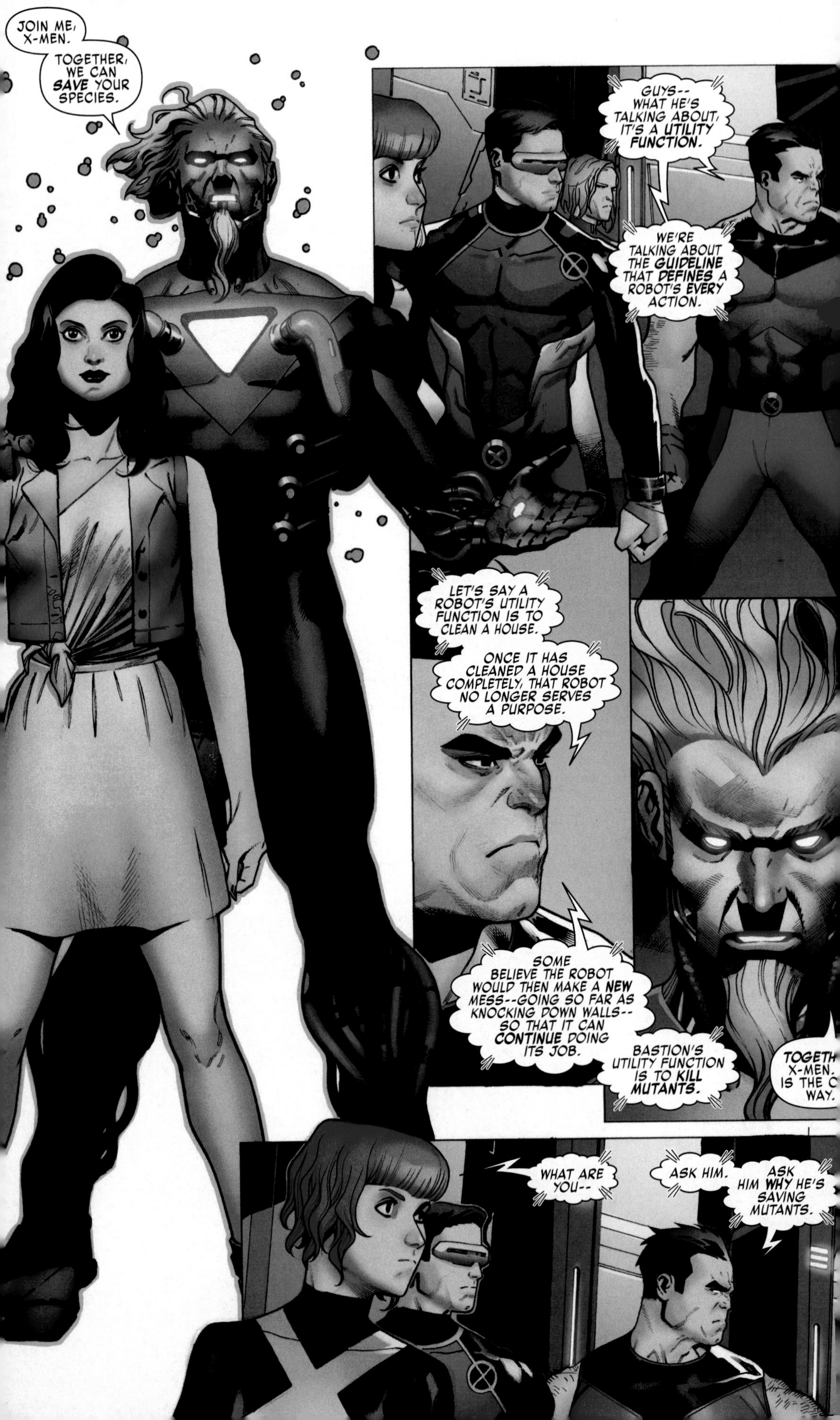
JOIN ME, X-MEN.
TOGETHER, WE CAN **SAVE** YOUR SPECIES.
GUYS-- WHAT HE'S TALKING ABOUT, IT'S A **UTILITY FUNCTION.**
WE'RE TALKING ABOUT THE **GUIDELINE** THAT **DEFINES** A ROBOT'S **EVERY** ACTION.
LET'S SAY A ROBOT'S UTILITY FUNCTION IS TO CLEAN A HOUSE.
ONCE IT HAS CLEANED A HOUSE COMPLETELY, THAT ROBOT NO LONGER SERVES A PURPOSE.
SOME BELIEVE THE ROBOT WOULD THEN MAKE A **NEW** MESS--GOING SO FAR AS KNOCKING DOWN WALLS-- SO THAT IT CAN **CONTINUE** DOING ITS JOB.
BASTION'S UTILITY FUNCTION IS TO **KILL MUTANTS.**
WHAT ARE YOU--
ASK HIM.
ASK HIM **WHY** HE'S SAVING MUTANTS.

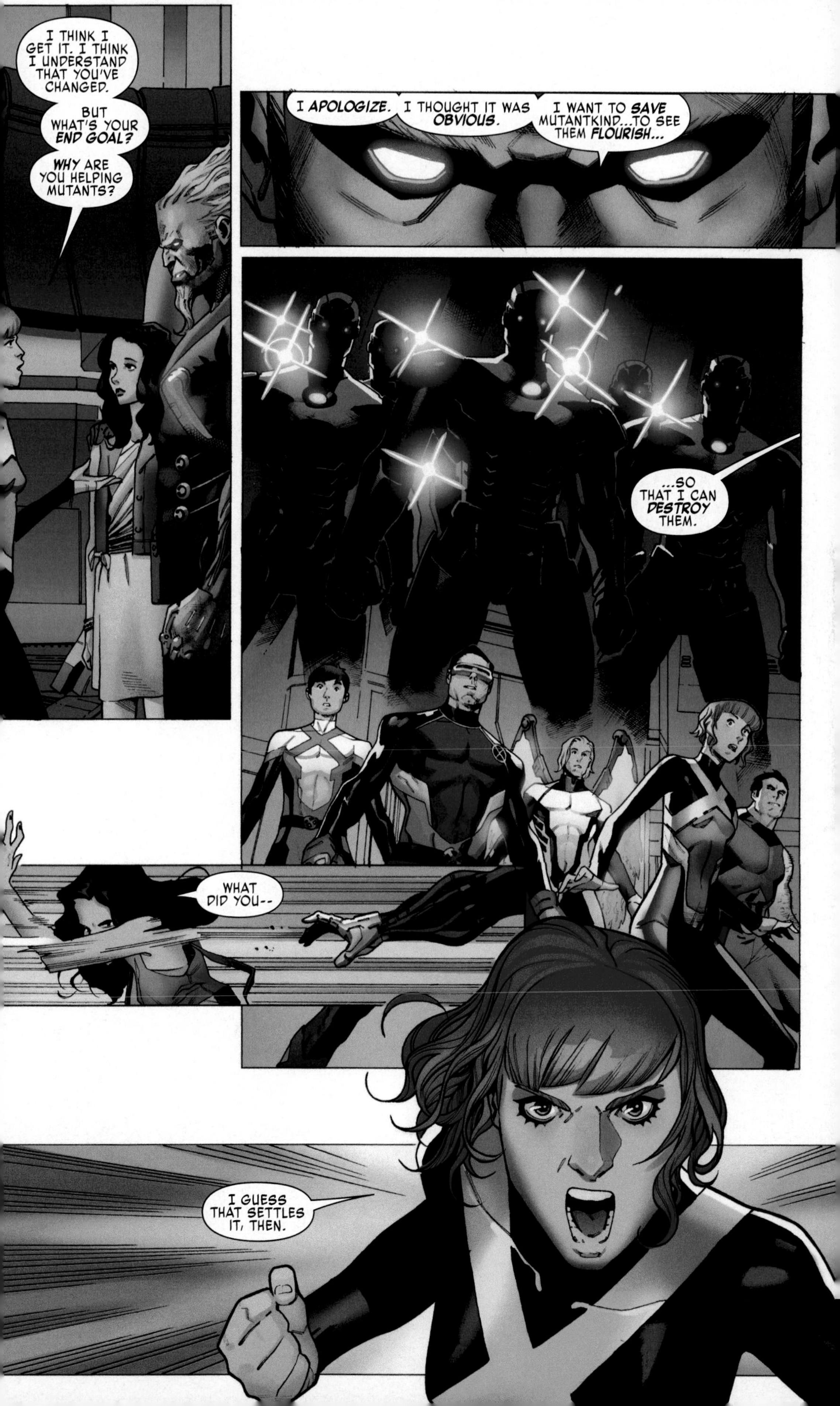
I THINK I GET IT. I THINK I UNDERSTAND THAT YOU'VE CHANGED.
BUT WHAT'S YOUR **END GOAL?**
WHY ARE YOU HELPING MUTANTS?
I **APOLOGIZE.**
I THOUGHT IT WAS **OBVIOUS.**
I WANT TO **SAVE** MUTANTKIND...TO SEE THEM **FLOURISH...**
...SO THAT I CAN **DESTROY** THEM.
WHAT DID YOU--
I GUESS THAT SETTLES IT, THEN.

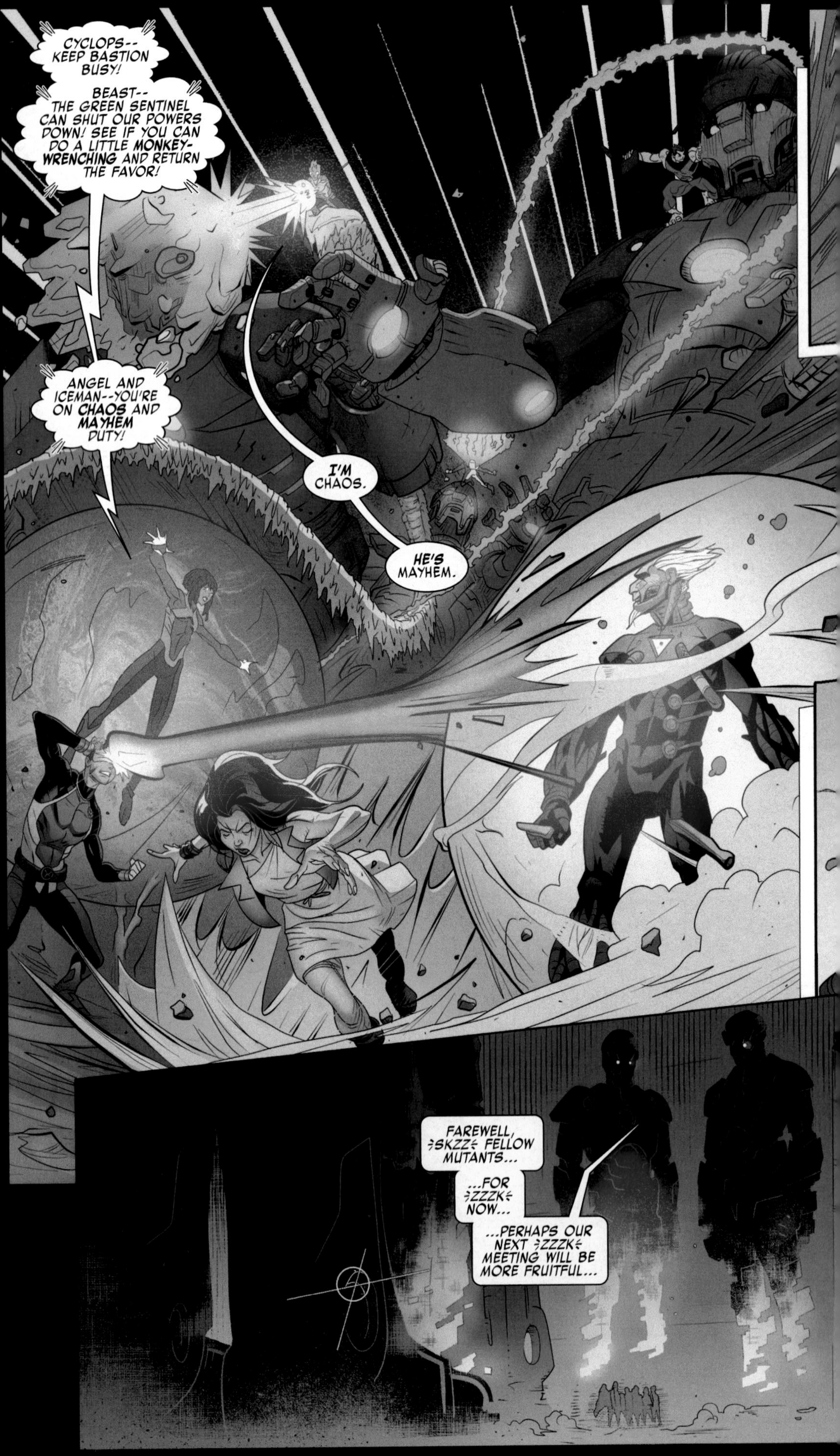
CYCLOPS-- KEEP BASTION BUSY!
BEAST-- THE GREEN SENTINEL CAN SHUT OUR POWERS DOWN! SEE IF YOU CAN DO A LITTLE MONKEY-WRENCHING AND RETURN THE FAVOR!
ANGEL AND ICEMAN--YOU'RE ON CHAOS AND MAYHEM DUTY!
I'M CHAOS.
HE'S MAYHEM.
FAREWELL, ⫶SKZZ⫶ FELLOW MUTANTS...
...FOR ⫶ZZZK⫶ NOW...
...PERHAPS OUR NEXT ⫶ZZZK⫶ MEETING WILL BE MORE FRUITFUL...

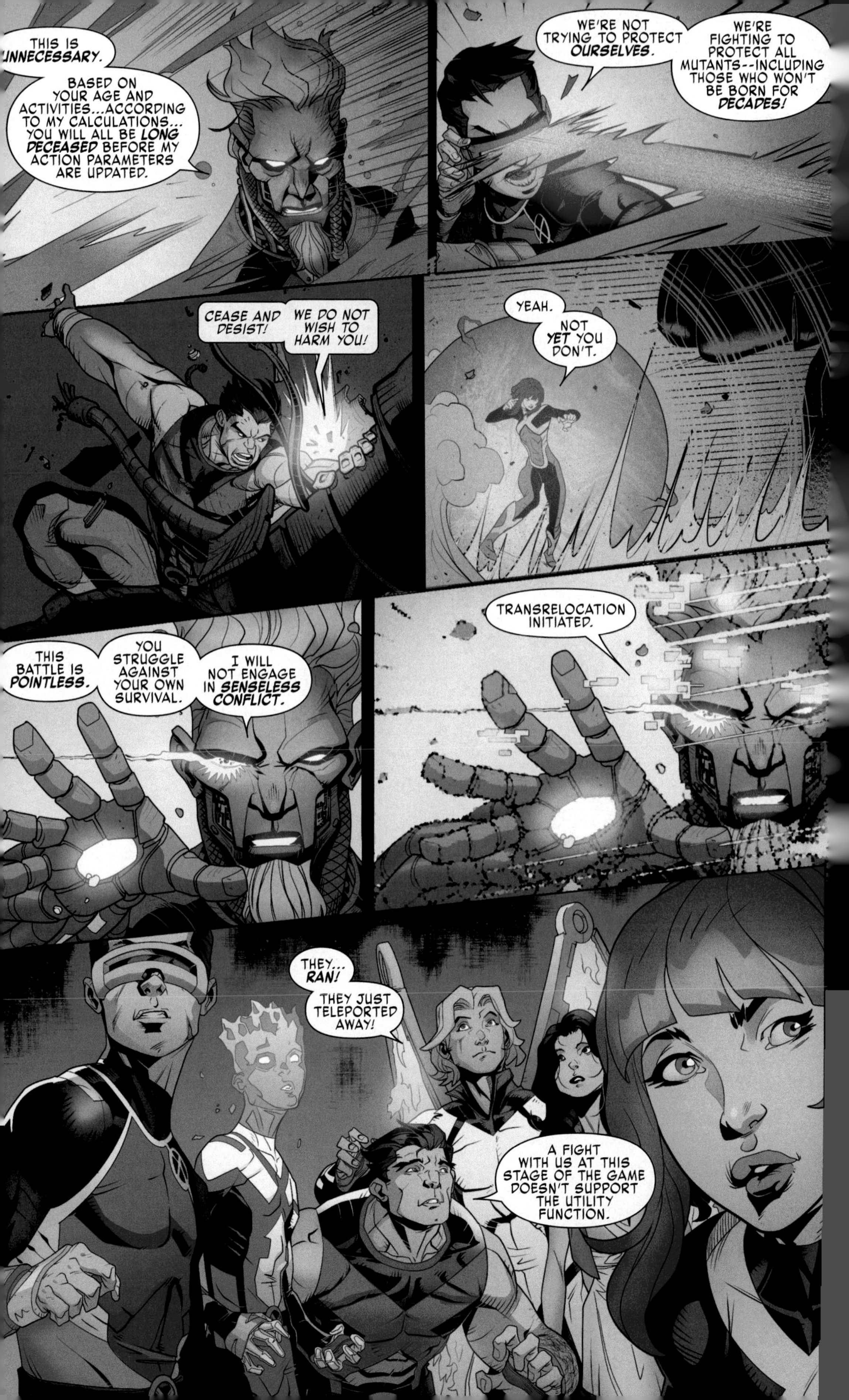
THIS IS UNNECESSARY.
BASED ON YOUR AGE AND ACTIVITIES...ACCORDING TO MY CALCULATIONS... YOU WILL ALL BE LONG DECEASED BEFORE MY ACTION PARAMETERS ARE UPDATED.
WE'RE NOT TRYING TO PROTECT OURSELVES.
WE'RE FIGHTING TO PROTECT ALL MUTANTS--INCLUDING THOSE WHO WON'T BE BORN FOR DECADES!
CEASE AND DESIST!
WE DO NOT WISH TO HARM YOU!
YEAH.
NOT YET YOU DON'T.
THIS BATTLE IS POINTLESS.
YOU STRUGGLE AGAINST YOUR OWN SURVIVAL.
I WILL NOT ENGAGE IN SENSELESS CONFLICT.
TRANSRELOCATION INITIATED.
THEY... RAN!
THEY JUST TELEPORTED AWAY!
A FIGHT WITH US AT THIS STAGE OF THE GAME DOESN'T SUPPORT THE UTILITY FUNCTION.

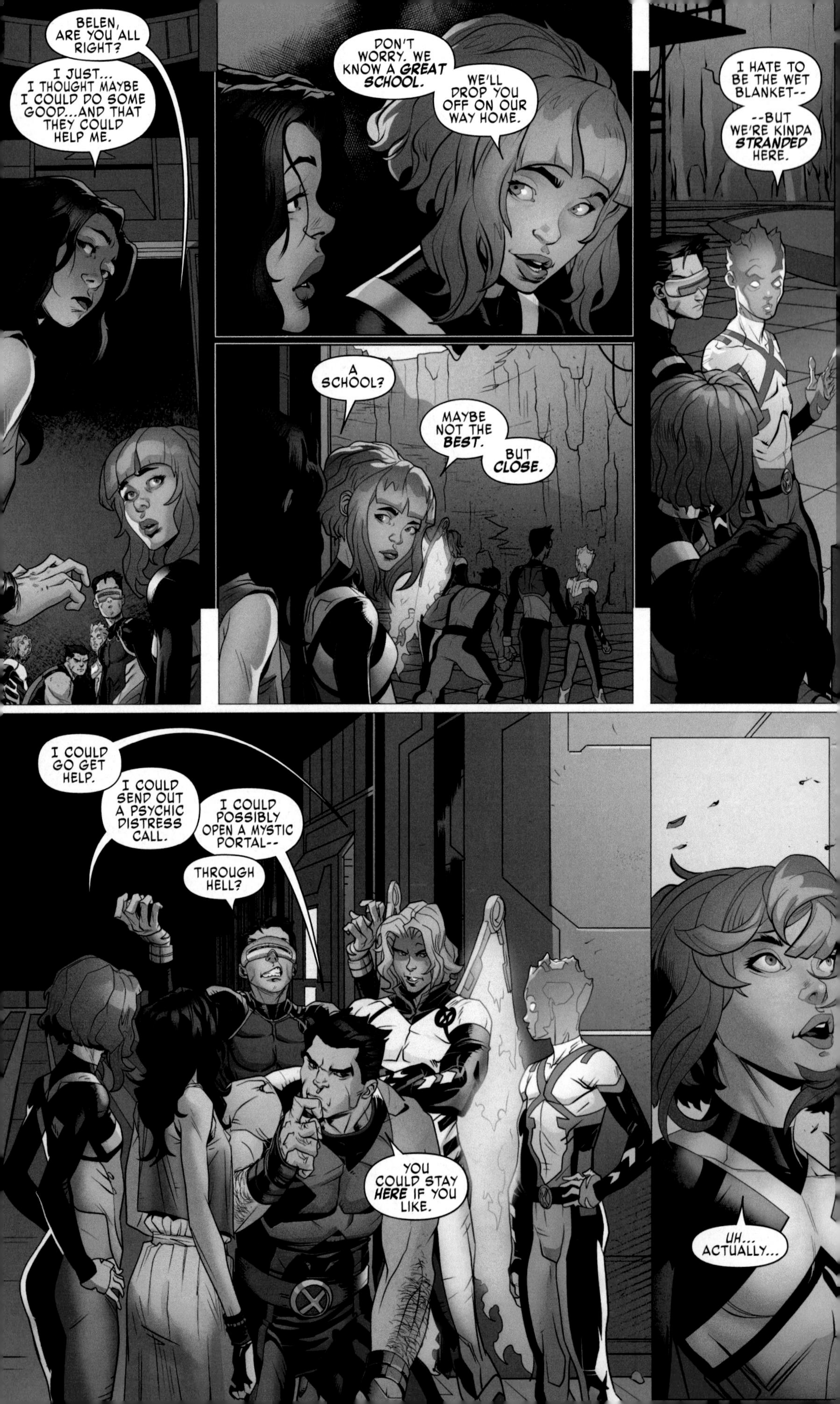

BELEN, ARE YOU ALL RIGHT?
I JUST... I THOUGHT MAYBE I COULD DO SOME GOOD...AND THAT THEY COULD HELP ME.
DON'T WORRY. WE KNOW A GREAT SCHOOL.
WE'LL DROP YOU OFF ON OUR WAY HOME.
A SCHOOL?
MAYBE NOT THE BEST.
BUT CLOSE.
I HATE TO BE THE WET BLANKET--
--BUT WE'RE KINDA STRANDED HERE.
I COULD GO GET HELP.
I COULD SEND OUT A PSYCHIC DISTRESS CALL.
I COULD POSSIBLY OPEN A MYSTIC PORTAL--
THROUGH HELL?
YOU COULD STAY HERE IF YOU LIKE.
UH... ACTUALLY...

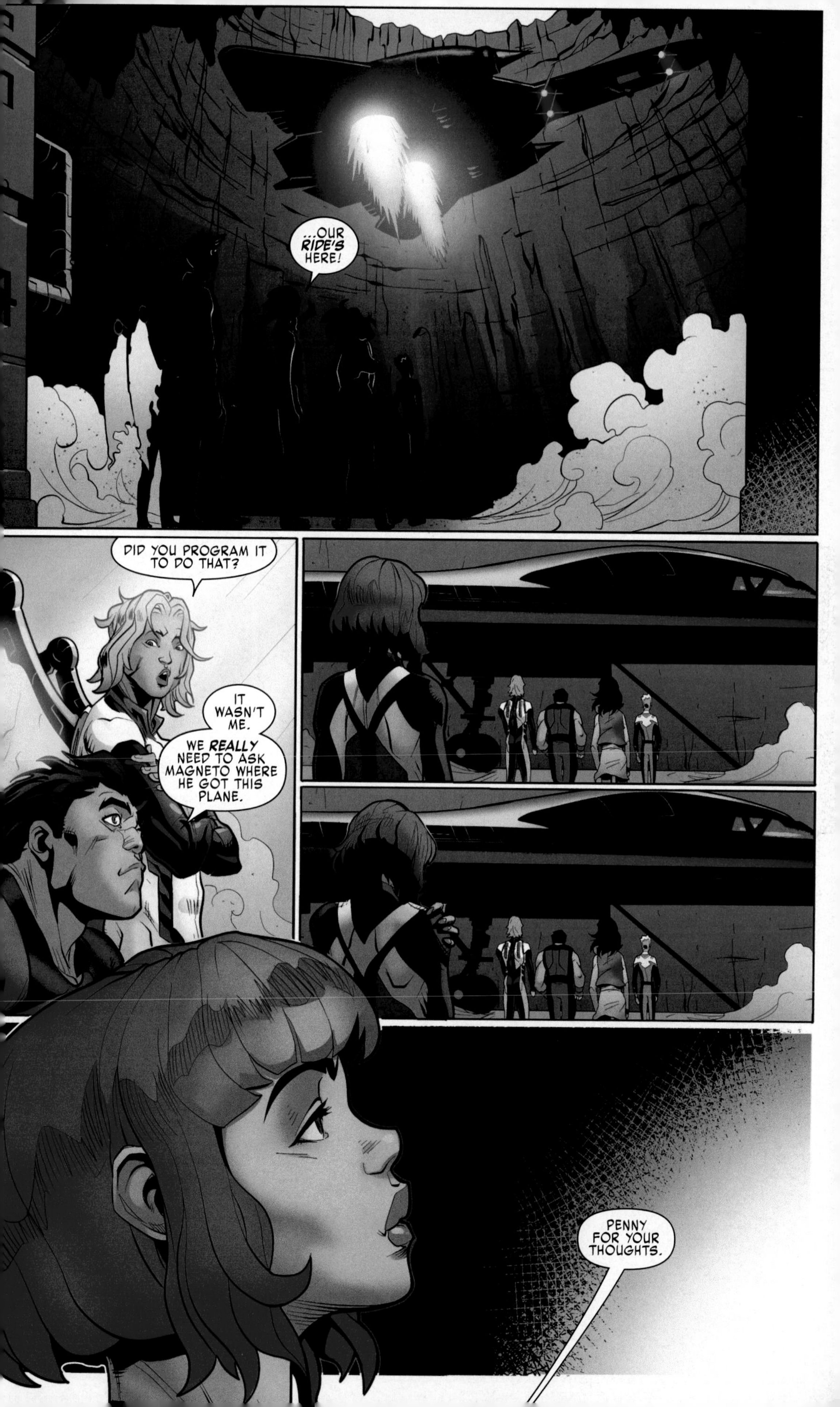
...OUR RIDE'S HERE!
DID YOU PROGRAM IT TO DO THAT?
IT WASN'T ME.
WE REALLY NEED TO ASK MAGNETO WHERE HE GOT THIS PLANE.
PENNY FOR YOUR THOUGHTS.

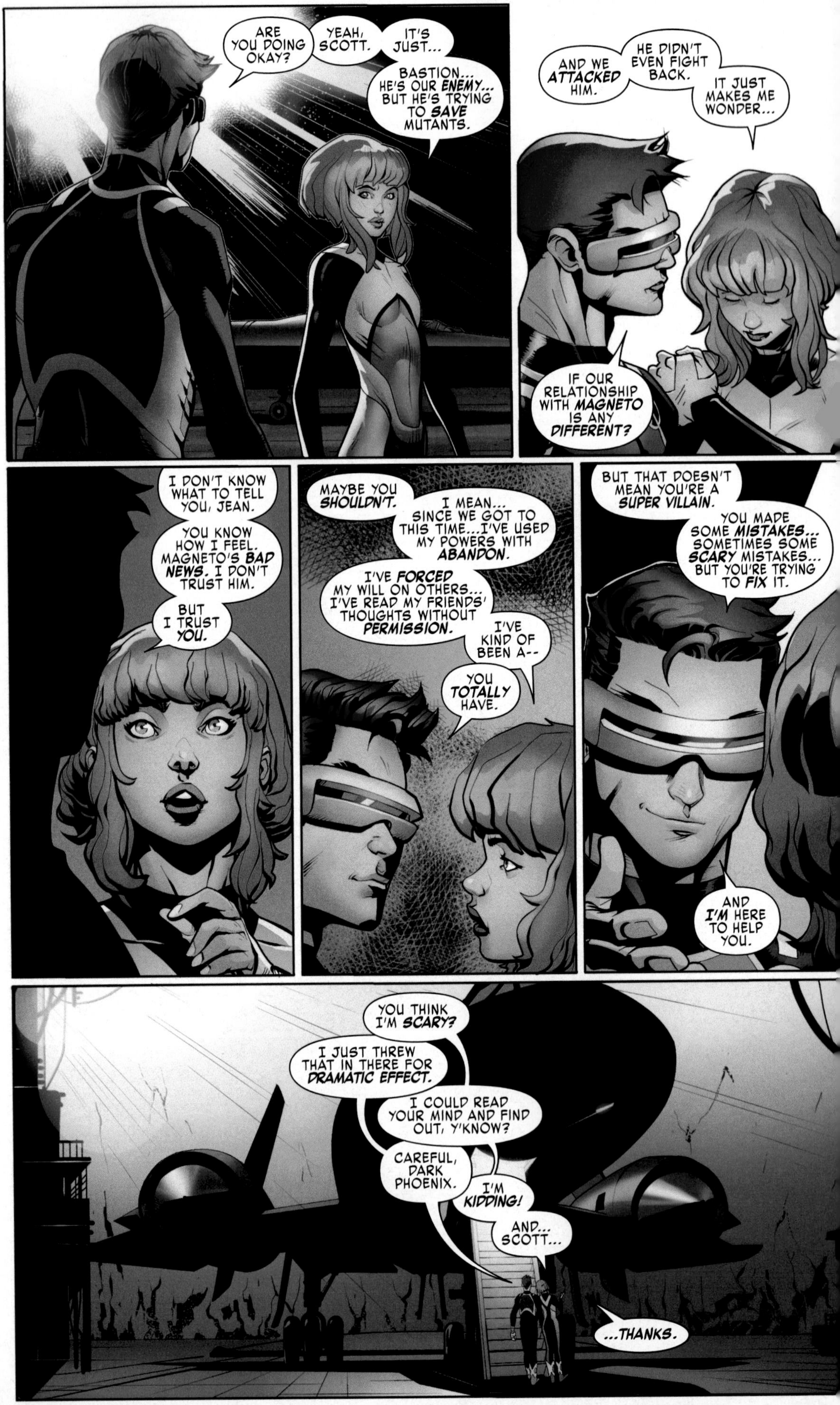
ARE YOU DOING OKAY?
YEAH, SCOTT.
IT'S JUST...
BASTION... HE'S OUR ENEMY... BUT HE'S TRYING TO SAVE MUTANTS.
AND WE ATTACKED HIM.
HE DIDN'T EVEN FIGHT BACK.
IT JUST MAKES ME WONDER...
IF OUR RELATIONSHIP WITH MAGNETO IS ANY DIFFERENT?
I DON'T KNOW WHAT TO TELL YOU, JEAN.
YOU KNOW HOW I FEEL. MAGNETO'S BAD NEWS. I DON'T TRUST HIM.
BUT I TRUST YOU.
MAYBE YOU SHOULDN'T.
I MEAN... SINCE WE GOT TO THIS TIME...I'VE USED MY POWERS WITH ABANDON.
I'VE FORCED MY WILL ON OTHERS... I'VE READ MY FRIENDS' THOUGHTS WITHOUT PERMISSION.
I'VE KIND OF BEEN A--
YOU TOTALLY HAVE.
BUT THAT DOESN'T MEAN YOU'RE A SUPER VILLAIN.
YOU MADE SOME MISTAKES... SOMETIMES SOME SCARY MISTAKES... BUT YOU'RE TRYING TO FIX IT.
AND I'M HERE TO HELP YOU.
YOU THINK I'M SCARY?
I JUST THREW THAT IN THERE FOR DRAMATIC EFFECT.
I COULD READ YOUR MIND AND FIND OUT, Y'KNOW?
CAREFUL, DARK PHOENIX.
I'M KIDDING!
AND... SCOTT...
...THANKS.

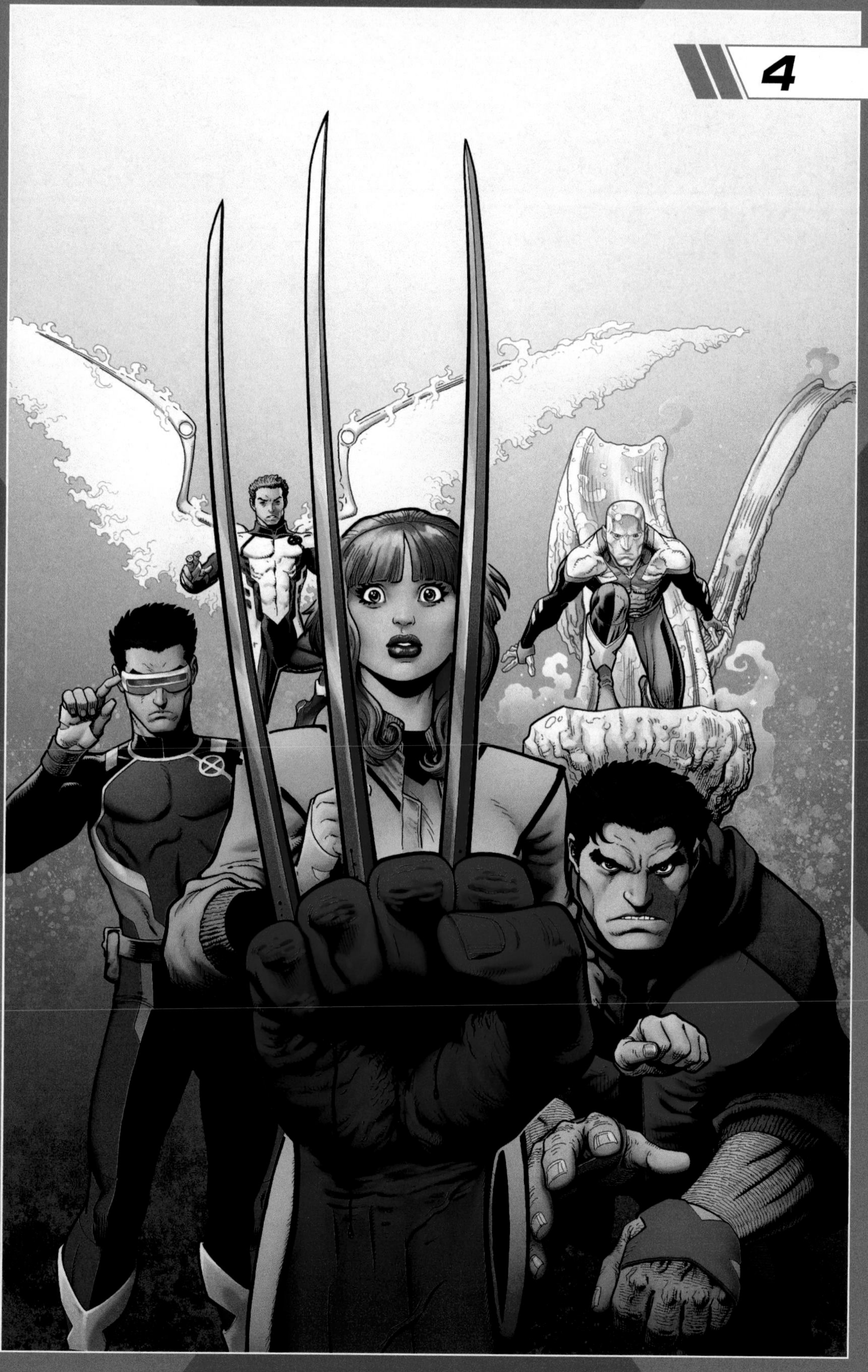
4

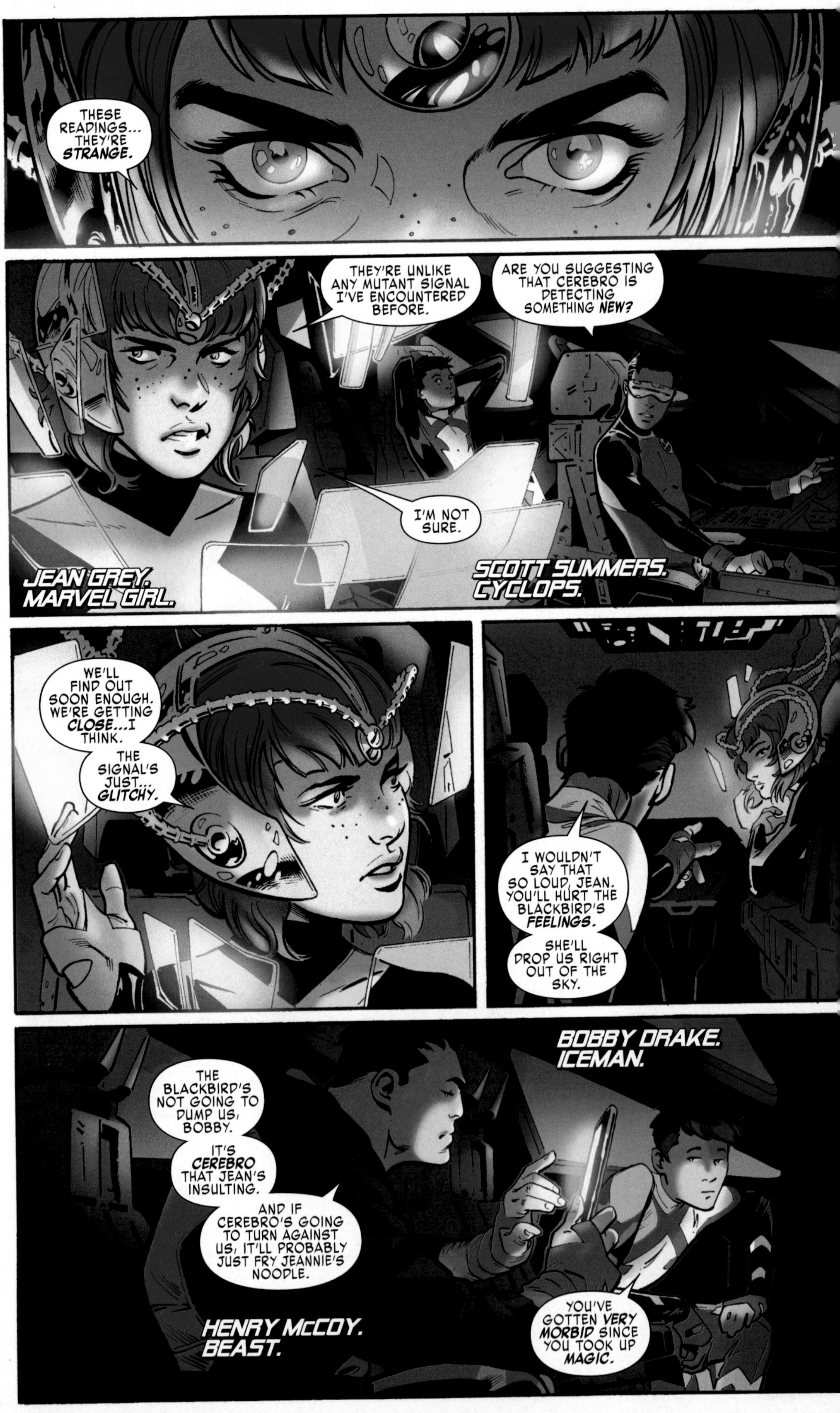
THESE READINGS... THEY'RE STRANGE.
THEY'RE UNLIKE ANY MUTANT SIGNAL I'VE ENCOUNTERED BEFORE.
ARE YOU SUGGESTING THAT CEREBRO IS DETECTING SOMETHING NEW?
I'M NOT SURE.
JEAN GREY. MARVEL GIRL.
SCOTT SUMMERS. CYCLOPS.
WE'LL FIND OUT SOON ENOUGH. WE'RE GETTING CLOSE...I THINK.
THE SIGNAL'S JUST... GLITCHY.
I WOULDN'T SAY THAT SO LOUD, JEAN. YOU'LL HURT THE BLACKBIRD'S FEELINGS.
SHE'LL DROP US RIGHT OUT OF THE SKY.
BOBBY DRAKE. ICEMAN.
THE BLACKBIRD'S NOT GOING TO DUMP US, BOBBY.
IT'S CEREBRO THAT JEAN'S INSULTING.
AND IF CEREBRO'S GOING TO TURN AGAINST US, IT'LL PROBABLY JUST FRY JEANNIE'S NOODLE.
HENRY McCOY. BEAST.
YOU'VE GOTTEN VERY MORBID SINCE YOU TOOK UP MAGIC.

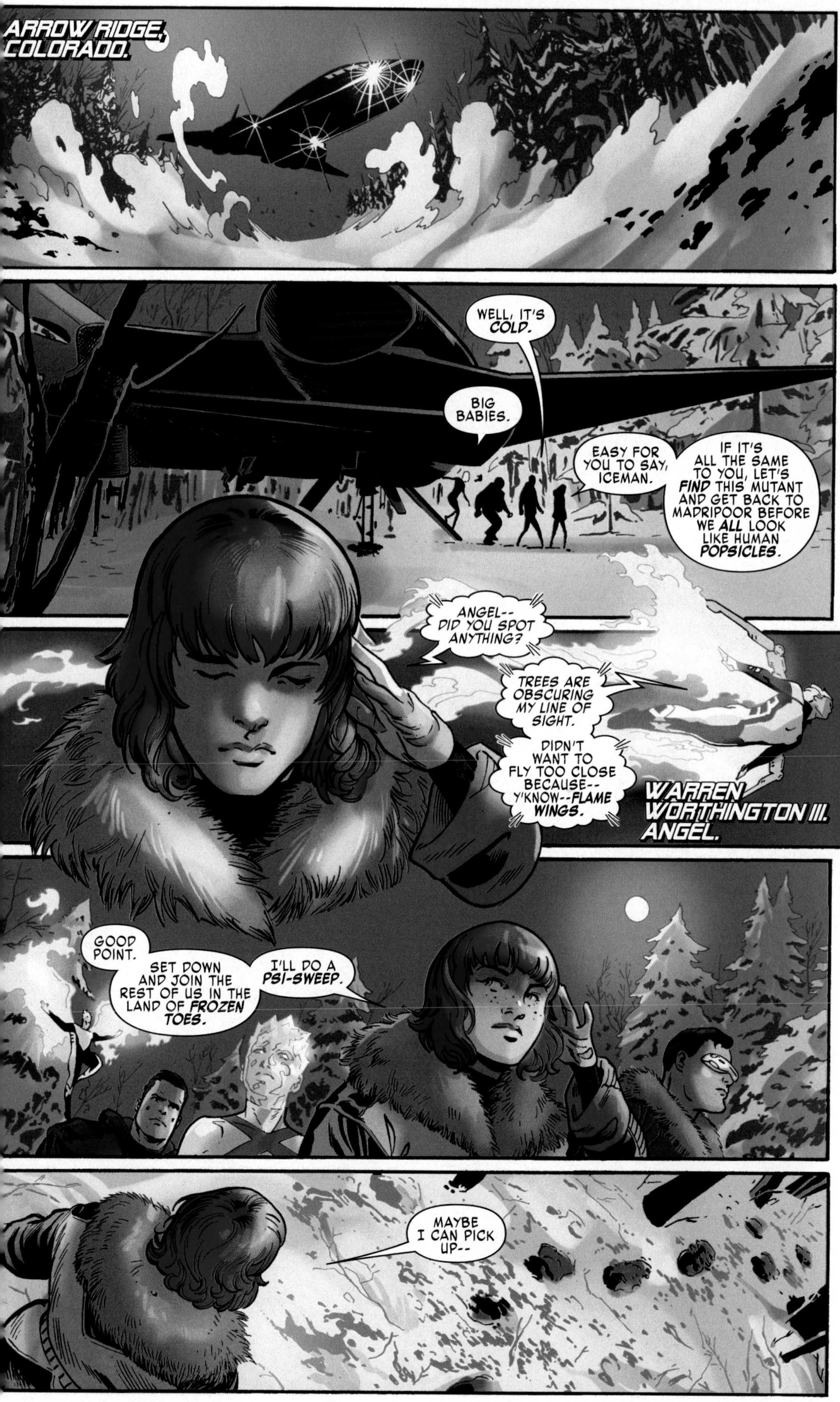
ARROW RIDGE, COLORADO.
WELL, IT'S COLD.
BIG BABIES.
EASY FOR YOU TO SAY, ICEMAN.
IF IT'S ALL THE SAME TO YOU, LET'S FIND THIS MUTANT AND GET BACK TO MADRIPOOR BEFORE WE ALL LOOK LIKE HUMAN POPSICLES.
ANGEL-- DID YOU SPOT ANYTHING?
TREES ARE OBSCURING MY LINE OF SIGHT.
DIDN'T WANT TO FLY TOO CLOSE BECAUSE-- Y'KNOW--FLAME WINGS.
WARREN WORTHINGTON III. ANGEL.
GOOD POINT.
SET DOWN AND JOIN THE REST OF US IN THE LAND OF FROZEN TOES.
I'LL DO A PSI-SWEEP.
MAYBE I CAN PICK UP--

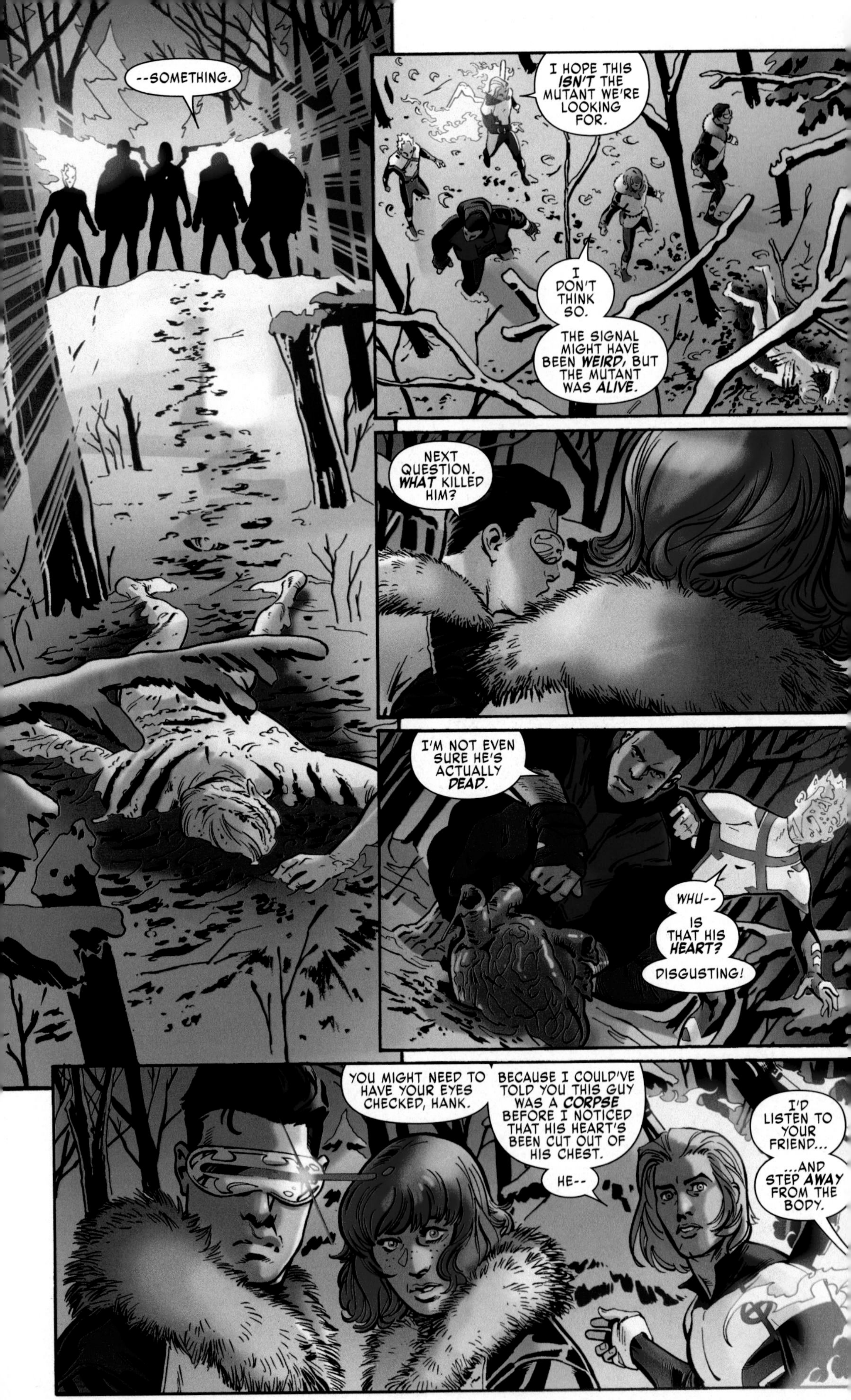
--SOMETHING.
I HOPE THIS ISN'T THE MUTANT WE'RE LOOKING FOR.
I DON'T THINK SO.
THE SIGNAL MIGHT HAVE BEEN WEIRD, BUT THE MUTANT WAS ALIVE.
NEXT QUESTION. WHAT KILLED HIM?
I'M NOT EVEN SURE HE'S ACTUALLY DEAD.
WHU--
IS THAT HIS HEART?
DISGUSTING!
YOU MIGHT NEED TO HAVE YOUR EYES CHECKED, HANK.
BECAUSE I COULD'VE TOLD YOU THIS GUY WAS A CORPSE BEFORE I NOTICED THAT HIS HEART'S BEEN CUT OUT OF HIS CHEST.
HE--
I'D LISTEN TO YOUR FRIEND...
...AND STEP AWAY FROM THE BODY.

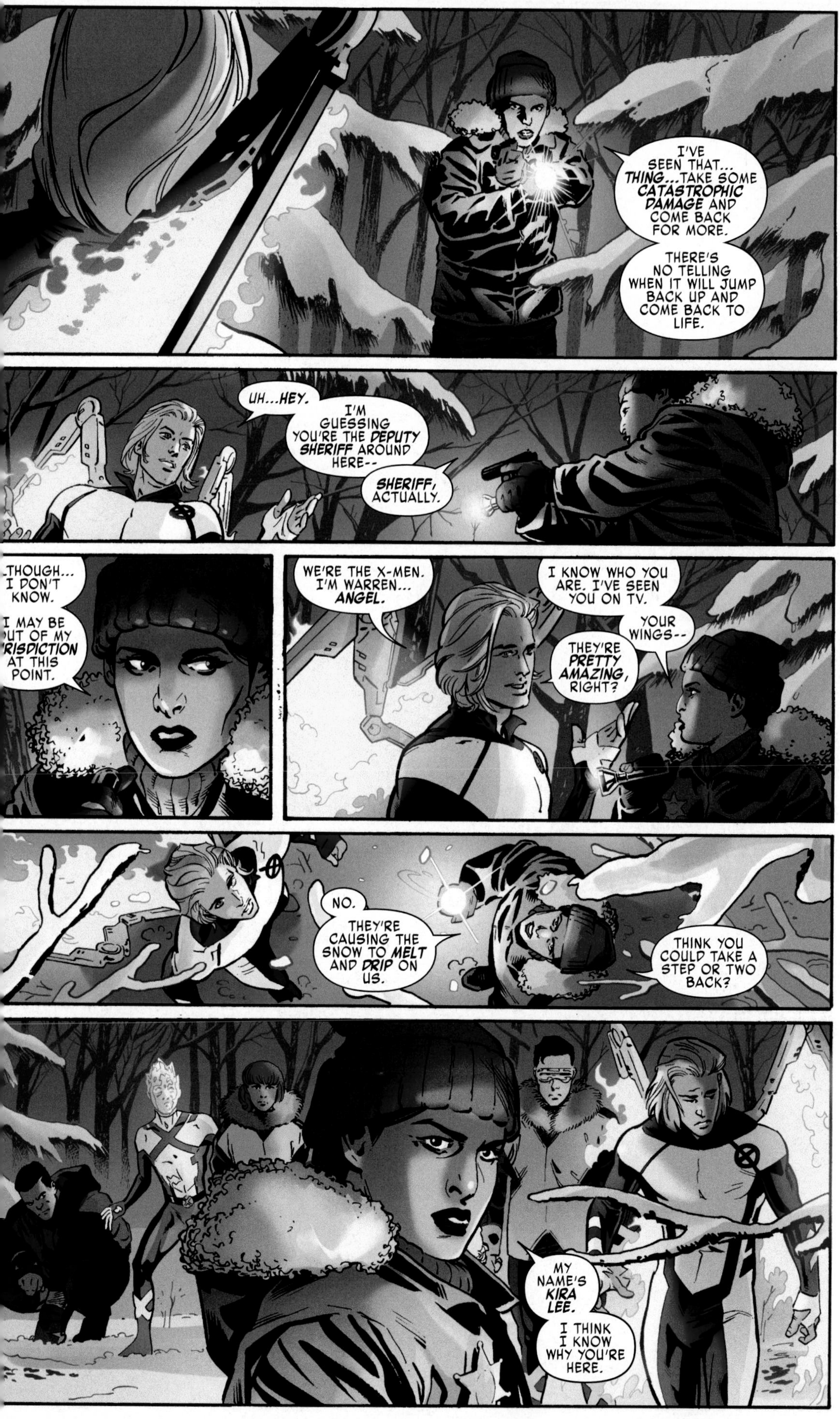
I'VE SEEN THAT... THING... TAKE SOME CATASTROPHIC DAMAGE AND COME BACK FOR MORE.
THERE'S NO TELLING WHEN IT WILL JUMP BACK UP AND COME BACK TO LIFE.
UH... HEY.
I'M GUESSING YOU'RE THE DEPUTY SHERIFF AROUND HERE--
SHERIFF, ACTUALLY.
-THOUGH... I DON'T KNOW.
I MAY BE OUT OF MY RISDICTION AT THIS POINT.
WE'RE THE X-MEN. I'M WARREN... ANGEL.
I KNOW WHO YOU ARE. I'VE SEEN YOU ON TV.
YOUR WINGS--
THEY'RE PRETTY AMAZING, RIGHT?
NO.
THEY'RE CAUSING THE SNOW TO MELT AND DRIP ON US.
THINK YOU COULD TAKE A STEP OR TWO BACK?
MY NAME'S KIRA LEE.
I THINK I KNOW WHY YOU'RE HERE.

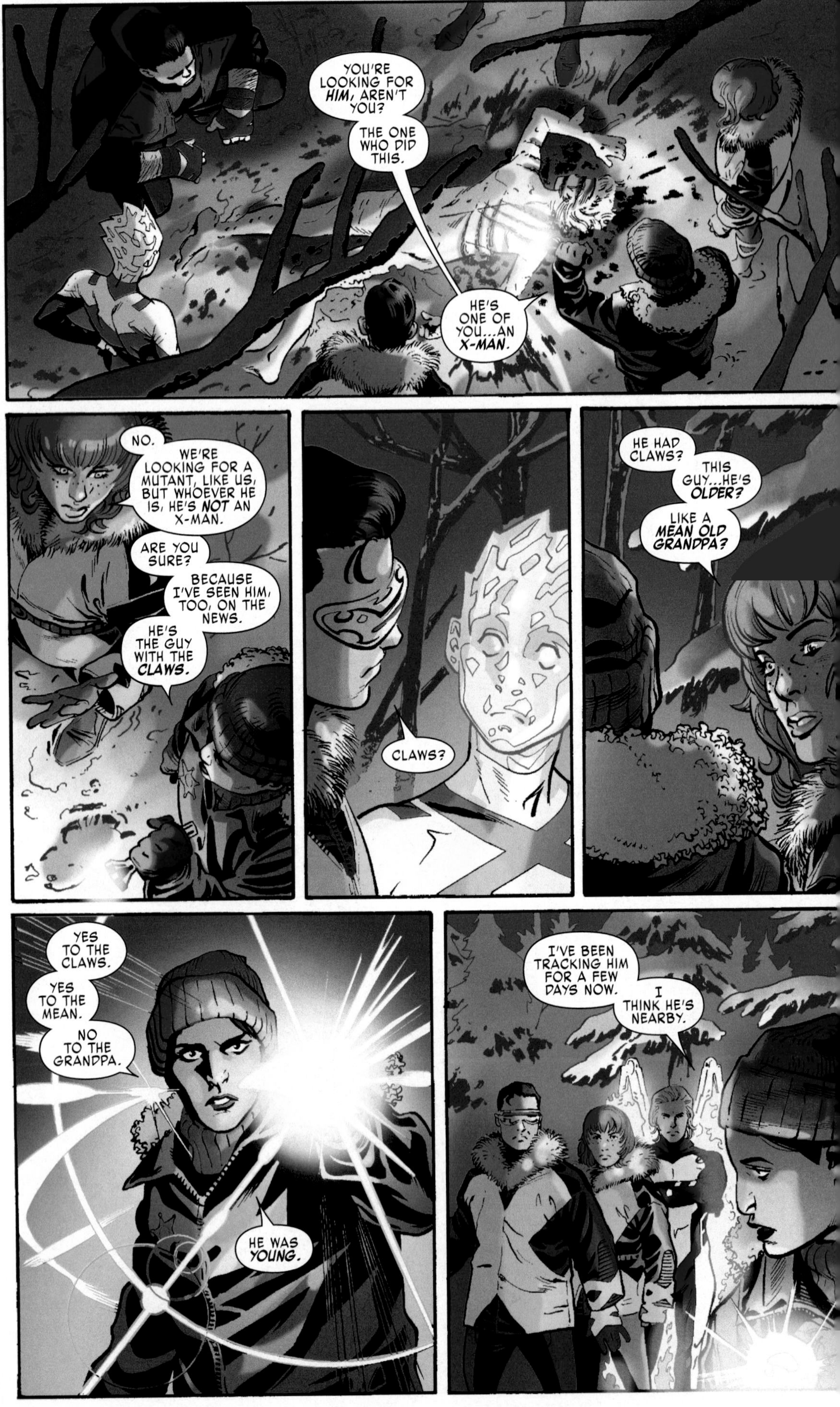
YOU'RE LOOKING FOR HIM, AREN'T YOU?
THE ONE WHO DID THIS.
HE'S ONE OF YOU...AN X-MAN.
NO.
WE'RE LOOKING FOR A MUTANT, LIKE US, BUT WHOEVER HE IS, HE'S NOT AN X-MAN.
ARE YOU SURE?
BECAUSE I'VE SEEN HIM, TOO, ON THE NEWS.
HE'S THE GUY WITH THE CLAWS.
CLAWS?
HE HAD CLAWS?
THIS GUY...HE'S OLDER?
LIKE A MEAN OLD GRANDPA?
YES TO THE CLAWS.
YES TO THE MEAN.
NO TO THE GRANDPA.
HE WAS YOUNG.
I'VE BEEN TRACKING HIM FOR A FEW DAYS NOW.
I THINK HE'S NEARBY.

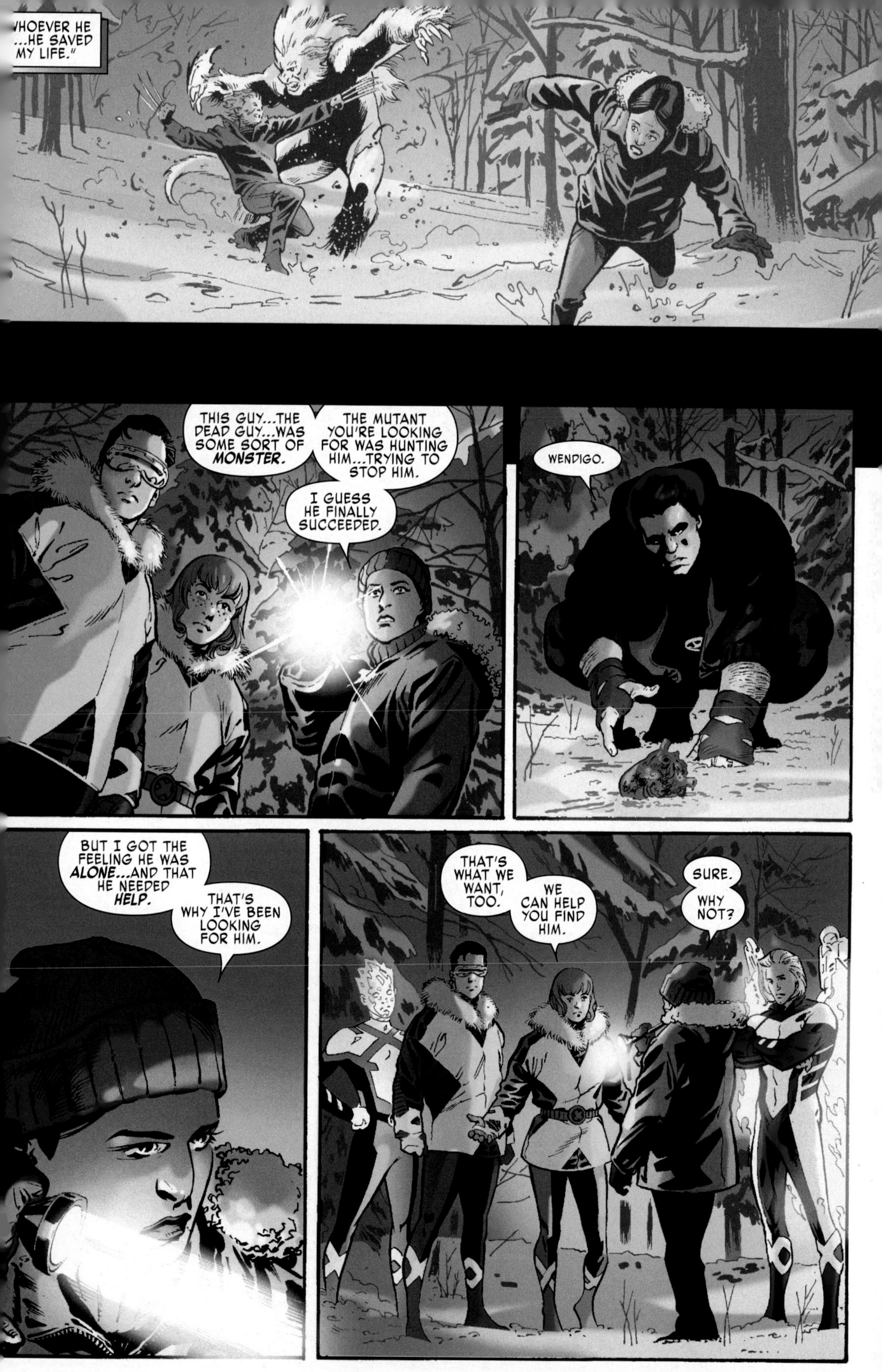
"WHOEVER HE ...HE SAVED MY LIFE."
THIS GUY...THE DEAD GUY...WAS SOME SORT OF MONSTER.
THE MUTANT YOU'RE LOOKING FOR WAS HUNTING HIM...TRYING TO STOP HIM.
I GUESS HE FINALLY SUCCEEDED.
WENDIGO.
BUT I GOT THE FEELING HE WAS ALONE...AND THAT HE NEEDED HELP.
THAT'S WHY I'VE BEEN LOOKING FOR HIM.
THAT'S WHAT WE WANT, TOO.
WE CAN HELP YOU FIND HIM.
SURE.
WHY NOT?

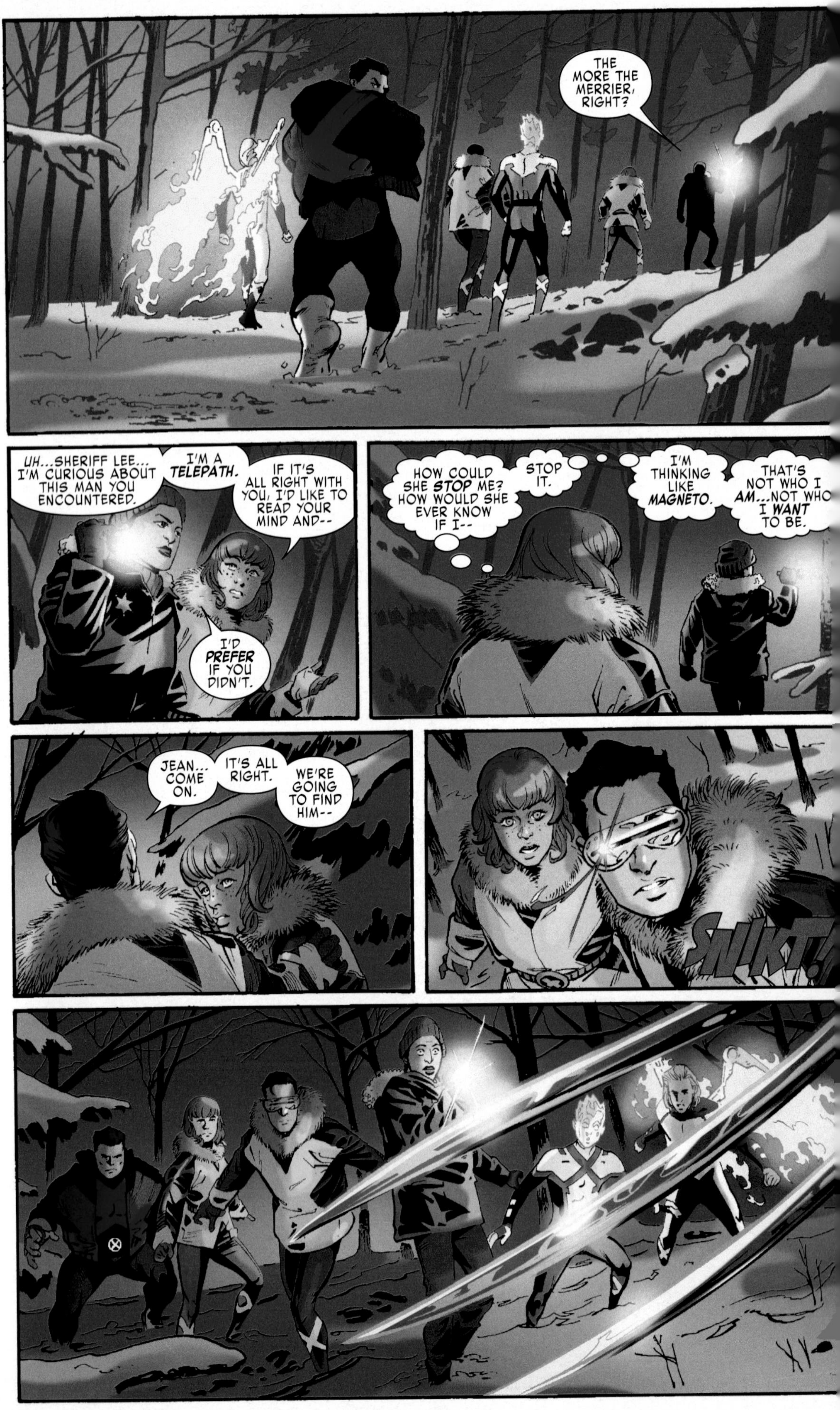
THE MORE THE MERRIER, RIGHT?
UH...SHERIFF LEE... I'M CURIOUS ABOUT THIS MAN YOU ENCOUNTERED.
I'M A TELEPATH.
IF IT'S ALL RIGHT WITH YOU, I'D LIKE TO READ YOUR MIND AND--
I'D PREFER IF YOU DIDN'T.
HOW COULD SHE STOP ME? HOW WOULD SHE EVER KNOW IF I--
STOP IT.
I'M THINKING LIKE MAGNETO.
THAT'S NOT WHO I AM...NOT WHO I WANT TO BE.
JEAN... COME ON.
IT'S ALL RIGHT.
WE'RE GOING TO FIND HIM--
SNIKT!

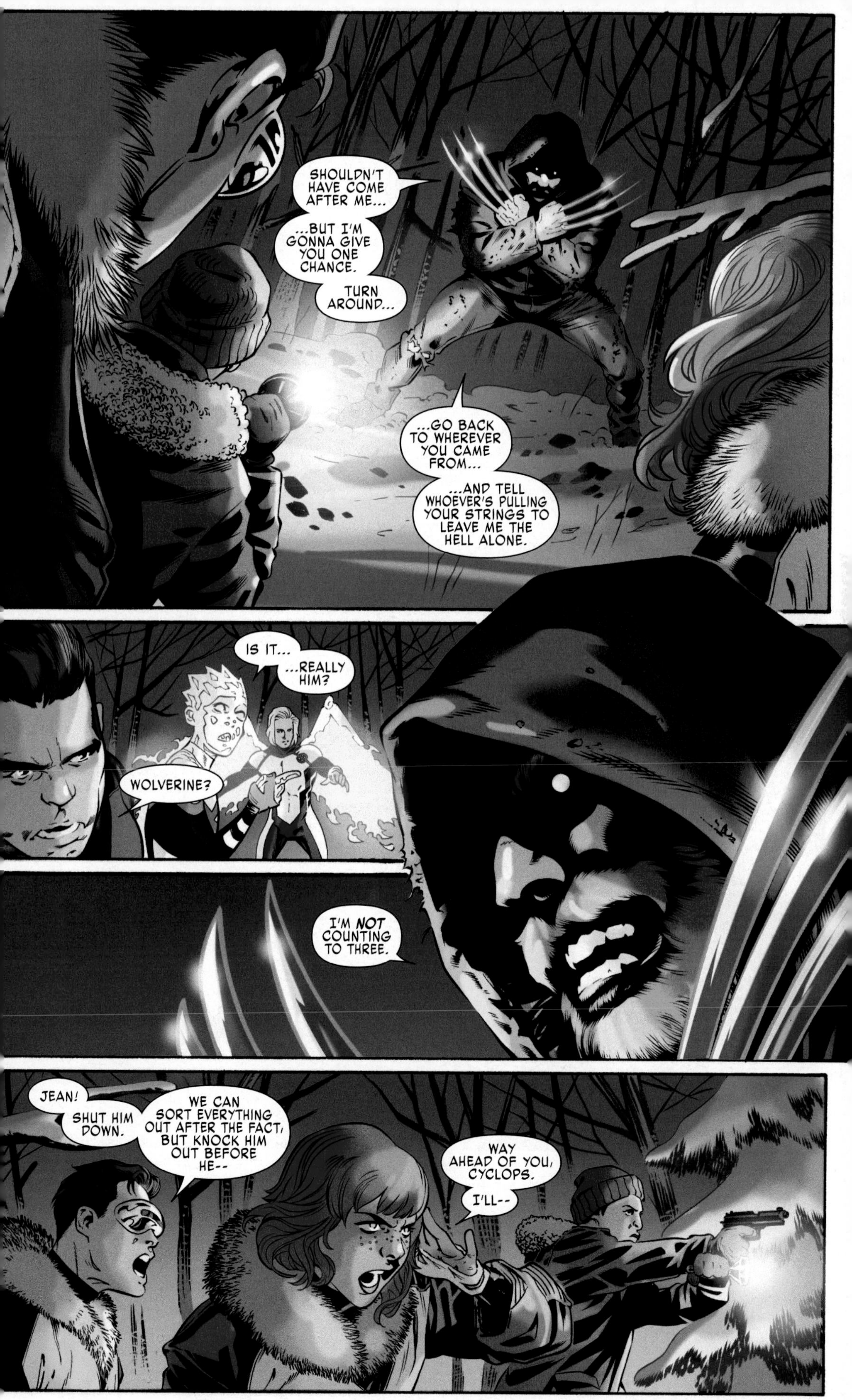
SHOULDN'T HAVE COME AFTER ME...
...BUT I'M GONNA GIVE YOU ONE CHANCE.
TURN AROUND...
...GO BACK TO WHEREVER YOU CAME FROM...
...AND TELL WHOEVER'S PULLING YOUR STRINGS TO LEAVE ME THE HELL ALONE.
IS IT...
...REALLY HIM?
WOLVERINE?
I'M NOT COUNTING TO THREE.
JEAN!
SHUT HIM DOWN.
WE CAN SORT EVERYTHING OUT AFTER THE FACT, BUT KNOCK HIM OUT BEFORE HE--
WAY AHEAD OF YOU, CYCLOPS.
I'LL--

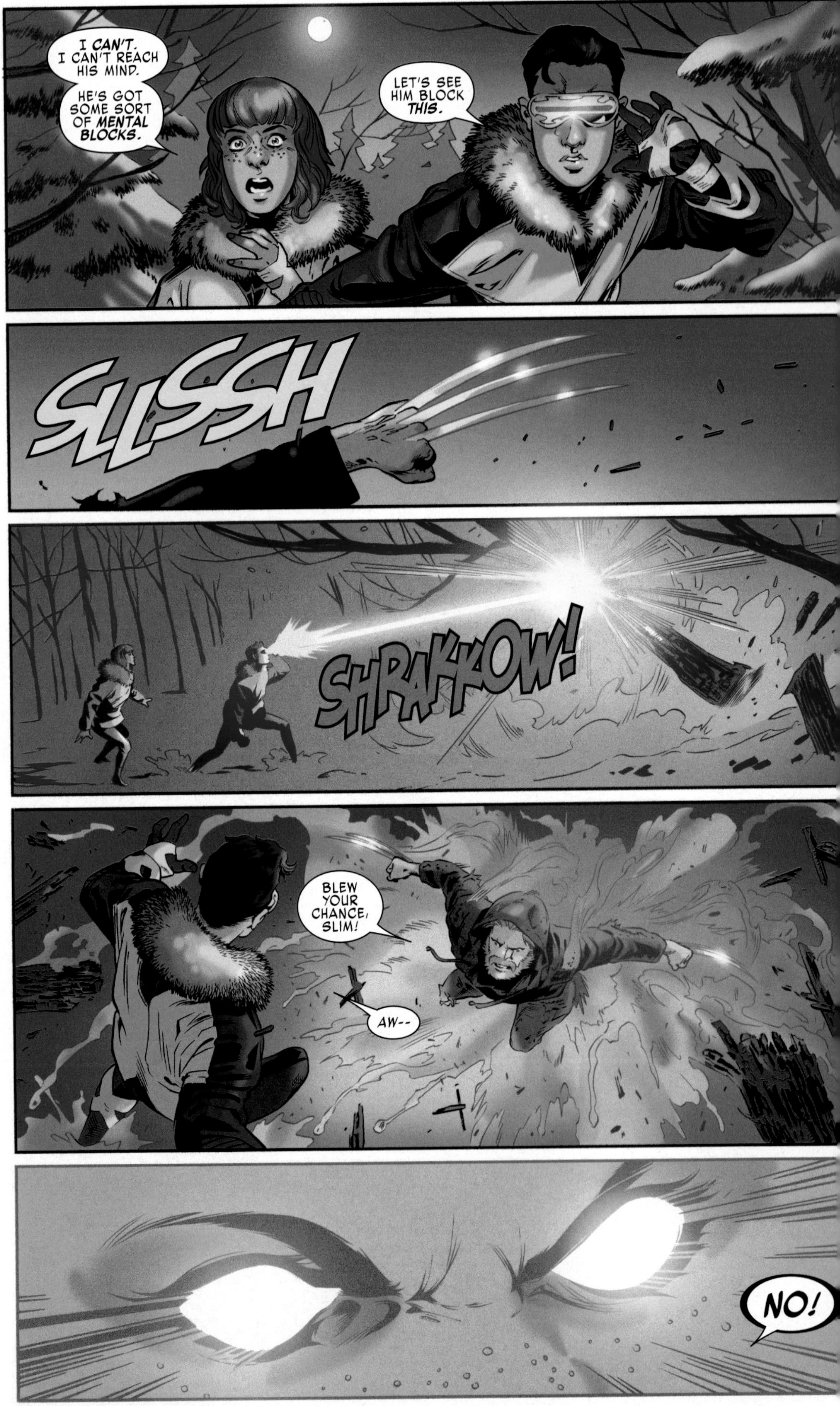
I CAN'T. I CAN'T REACH HIS MIND.
HE'S GOT SOME SORT OF MENTAL BLOCKS.
LET'S SEE HIM BLOCK THIS.
SLISSH
SHRAKKOW!
BLEW YOUR CHANCE, SLIM!
AW--
NO!

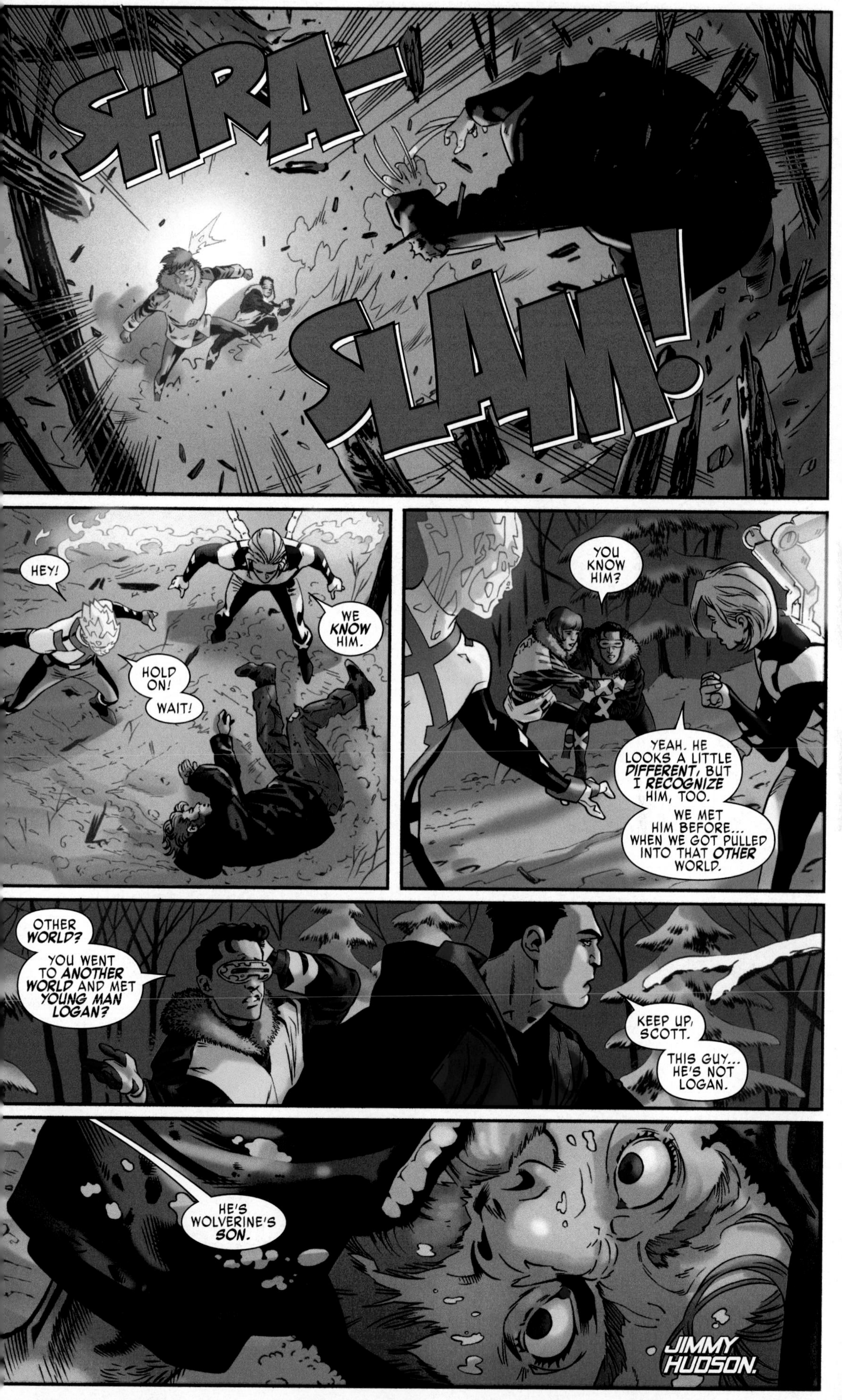
SHRA-
SLAM!
HEY!
HOLD ON!
WAIT!
WE KNOW HIM.
YOU KNOW HIM?
YEAH. HE LOOKS A LITTLE DIFFERENT, BUT I RECOGNIZE HIM, TOO.
WE MET HIM BEFORE... WHEN WE GOT PULLED INTO THAT OTHER WORLD.
OTHER WORLD?
YOU WENT TO ANOTHER WORLD AND MET YOUNG MAN LOGAN?
KEEP UP, SCOTT.
THIS GUY... HE'S NOT LOGAN.
HE'S WOLVERINE'S SON.
JIMMY HUDSON.

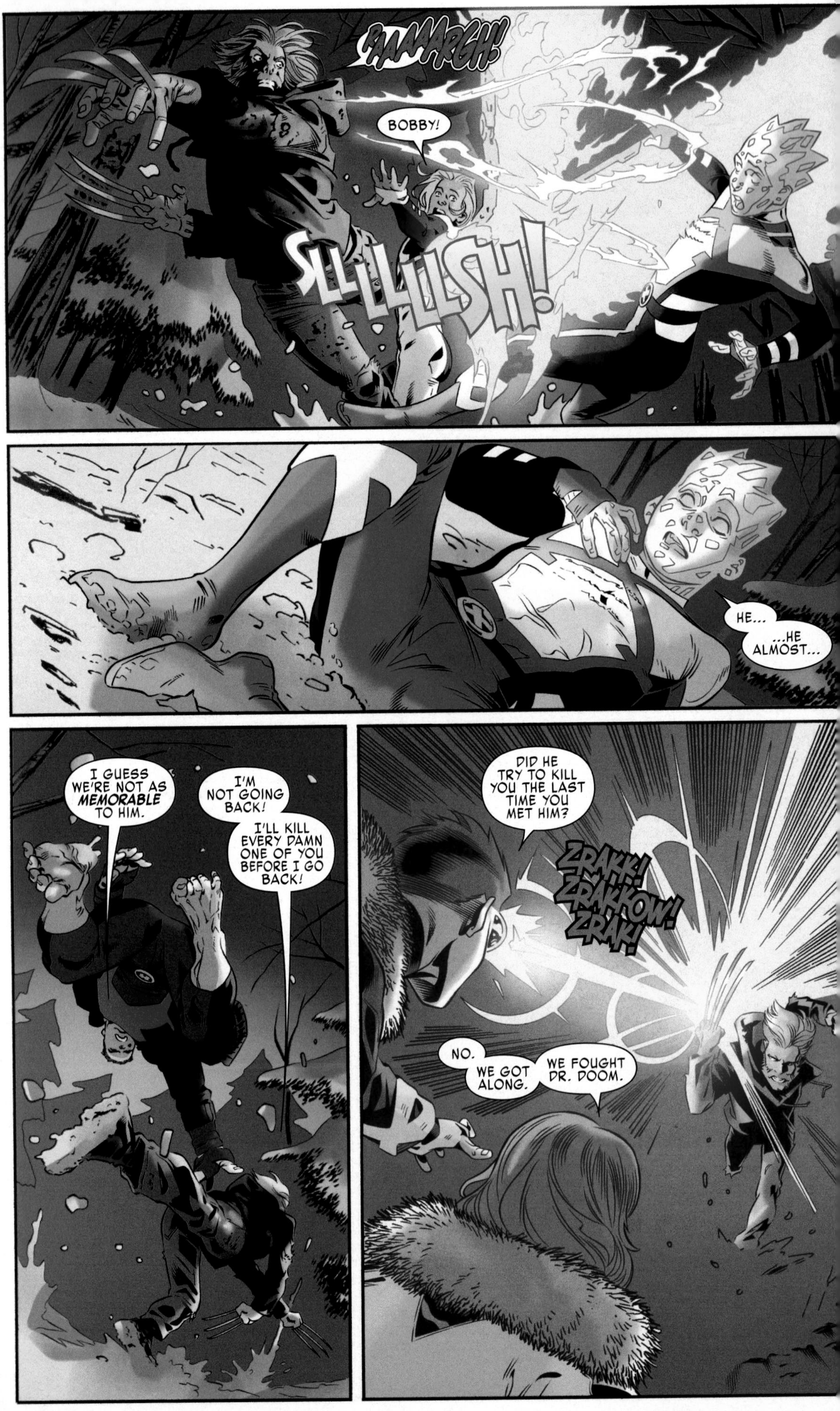
RAAAAARGH!
BOBBY!
SLLLLLLSH!
HE...
...HE ALMOST...
I GUESS WE'RE NOT AS MEMORABLE TO HIM.
I'M NOT GOING BACK!
I'LL KILL EVERY DAMN ONE OF YOU BEFORE I GO BACK!
DID HE TRY TO KILL YOU THE LAST TIME YOU MET HIM?
ZRAKK! ZRAKKOW! ZRAK!
NO.
WE GOT ALONG.
WE FOUGHT DR. DOOM.

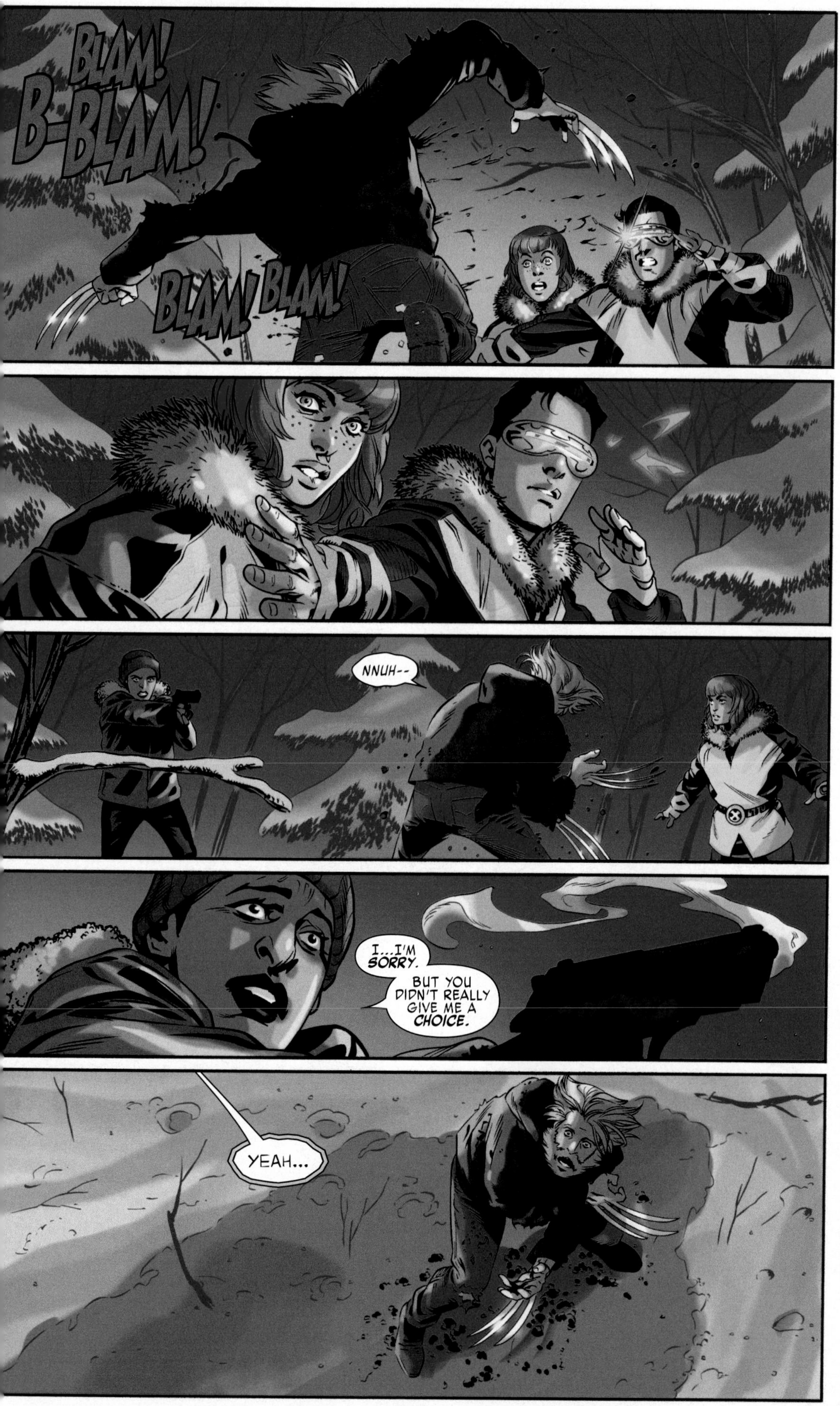
BLAM! B-BLAM!
BLAM! BLAM!
NNUH--
I...I'M SORRY.
BUT YOU DIDN'T REALLY GIVE ME A CHOICE.
YEAH...

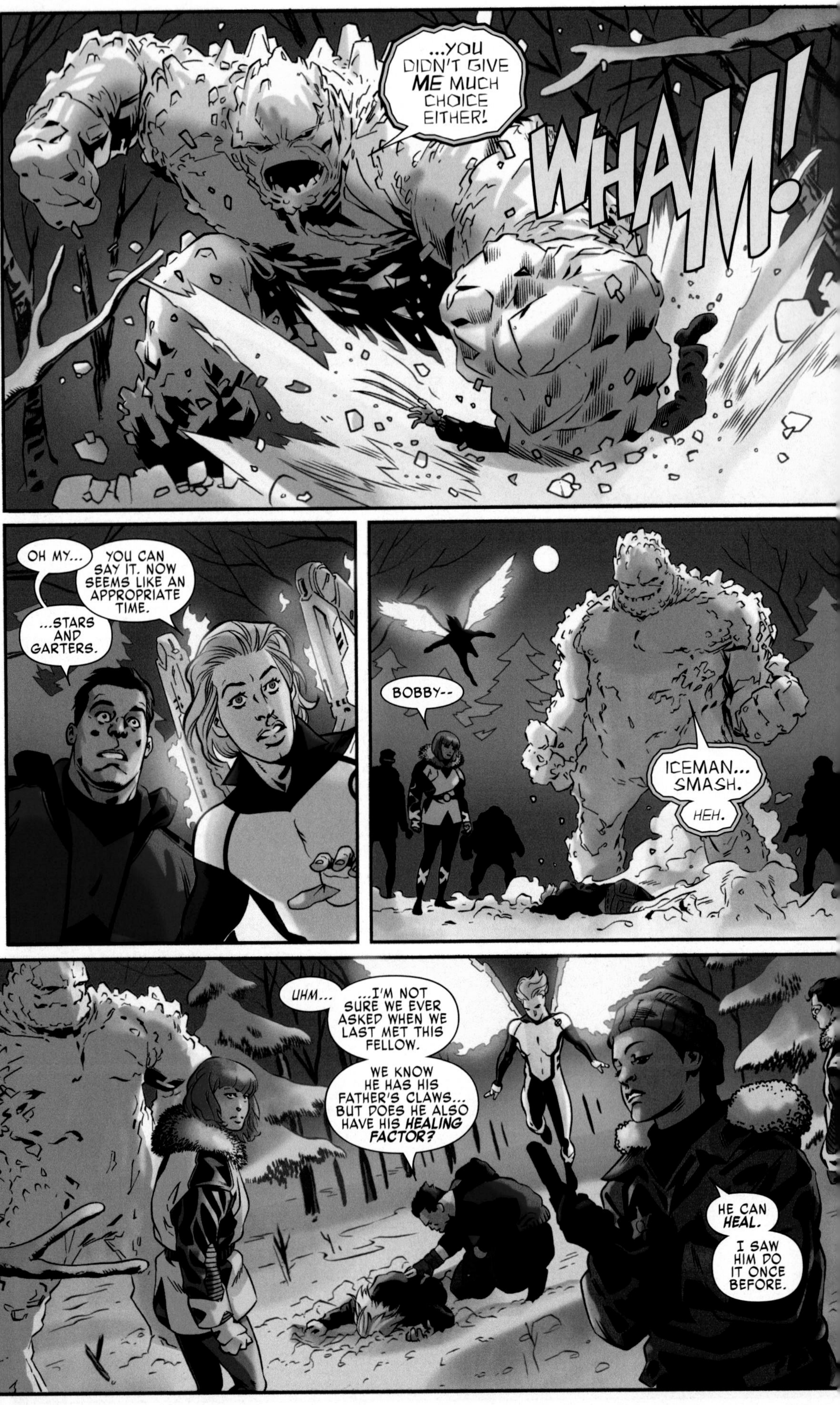
...YOU DIDN'T GIVE ME MUCH CHOICE EITHER!
WHAM!
OH MY...
...STARS AND GARTERS.
YOU CAN SAY IT. NOW SEEMS LIKE AN APPROPRIATE TIME.
BOBBY--
ICEMAN... SMASH.
HEH.
UHM...
...I'M NOT SURE WE EVER ASKED WHEN WE LAST MET THIS FELLOW.
WE KNOW HE HAS HIS FATHER'S CLAWS... BUT DOES HE ALSO HAVE HIS HEALING FACTOR?
HE CAN HEAL.
I SAW HIM DO IT ONCE BEFORE.

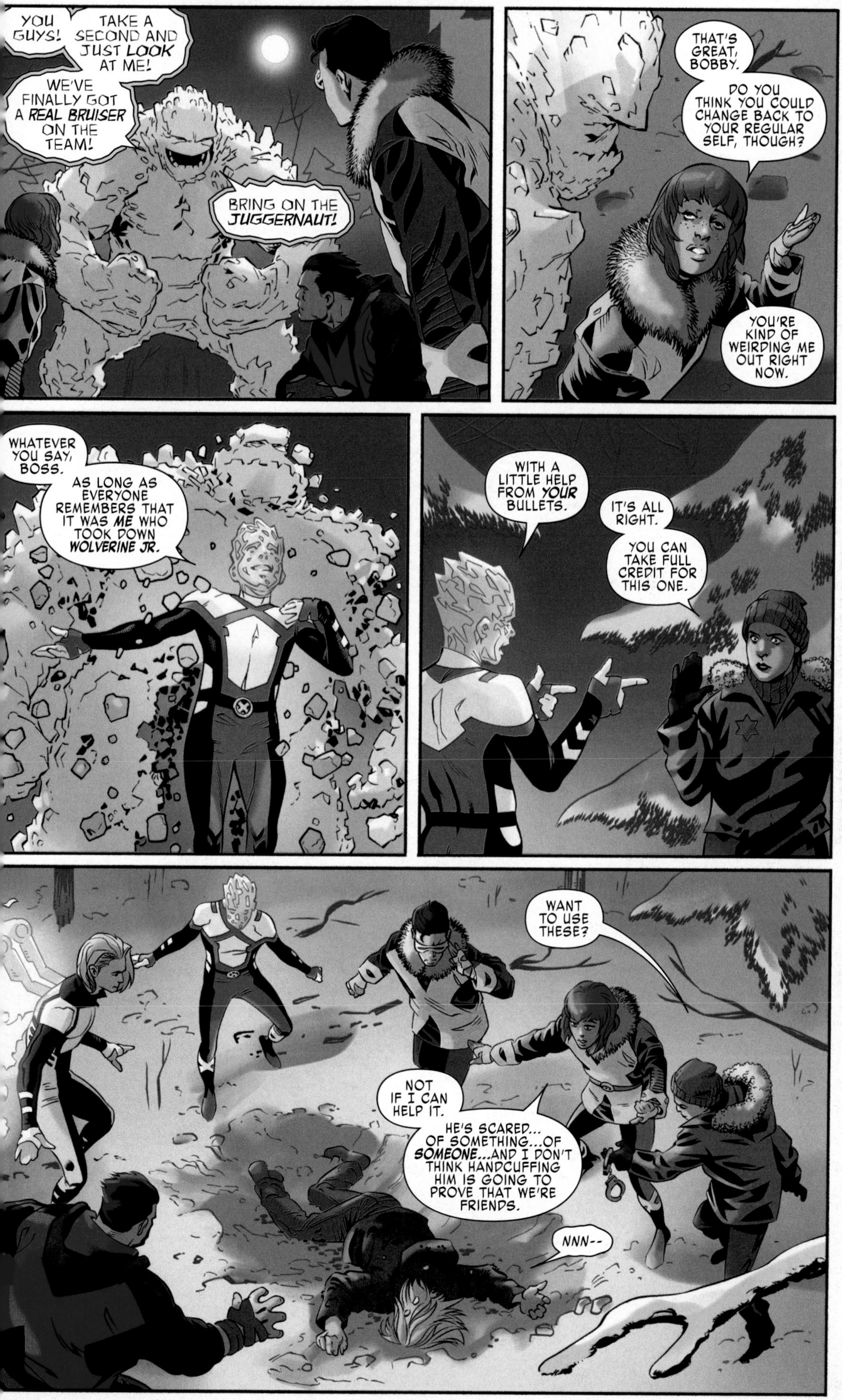
YOU GUYS!
TAKE A SECOND AND JUST LOOK AT ME!
WE'VE FINALLY GOT A REAL BRUISER ON THE TEAM!
BRING ON THE JUGGERNAUT!
THAT'S GREAT, BOBBY.
DO YOU THINK YOU COULD CHANGE BACK TO YOUR REGULAR SELF, THOUGH?
YOU'RE KIND OF WEIRDING ME OUT RIGHT NOW.
WHATEVER YOU SAY, BOSS.
AS LONG AS EVERYONE REMEMBERS THAT IT WAS ME WHO TOOK DOWN WOLVERINE JR.
WITH A LITTLE HELP FROM YOUR BULLETS.
IT'S ALL RIGHT.
YOU CAN TAKE FULL CREDIT FOR THIS ONE.
WANT TO USE THESE?
NOT IF I CAN HELP IT.
HE'S SCARED... OF SOMETHING... OF SOMEONE... AND I DON'T THINK HANDCUFFING HIM IS GOING TO PROVE THAT WE'RE FRIENDS.
NNN--

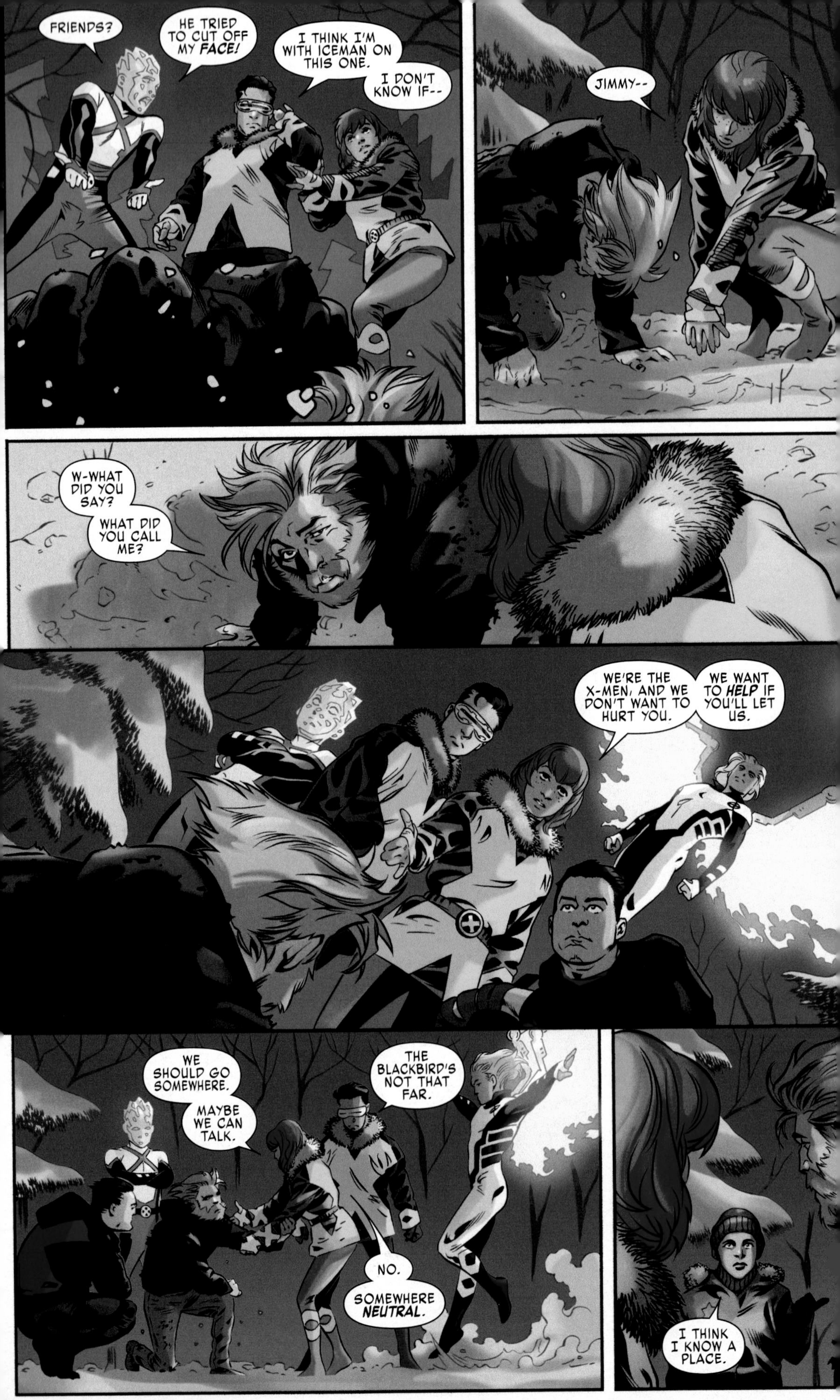
FRIENDS?
HE TRIED TO CUT OFF MY *FACE!*
I THINK I'M WITH ICEMAN ON THIS ONE.
I DON'T KNOW IF--
JIMMY--
W-WHAT DID YOU SAY?
WHAT DID YOU CALL ME?
WE'RE THE X-MEN, AND WE DON'T WANT TO HURT YOU.
WE WANT TO *HELP* IF YOU'LL LET US.
WE SHOULD GO SOMEWHERE.
MAYBE WE CAN TALK.
THE BLACKBIRD'S NOT THAT FAR.
NO.
SOMEWHERE *NEUTRAL.*
I THINK I KNOW A PLACE.

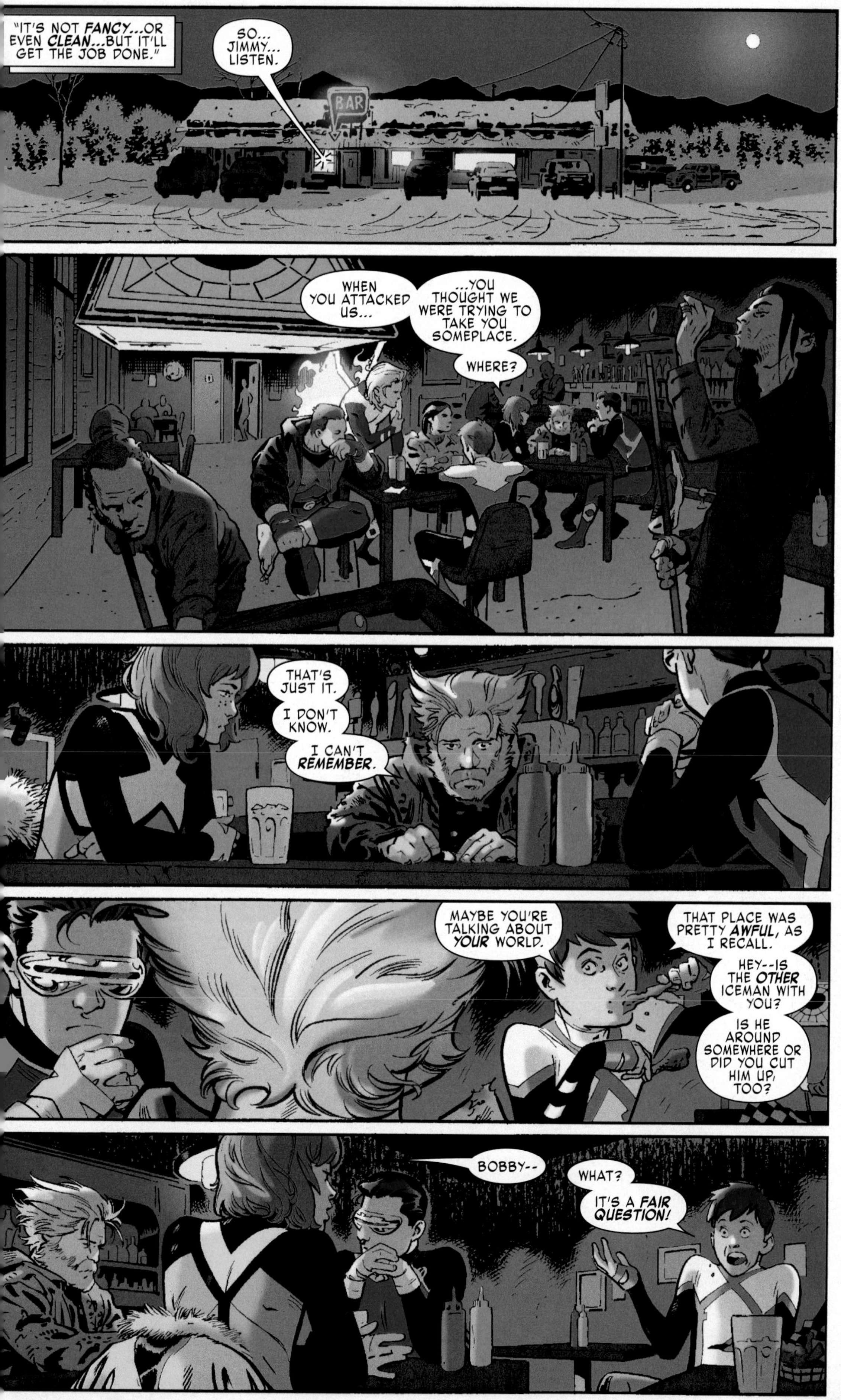
"IT'S NOT FANCY...OR EVEN CLEAN...BUT IT'LL GET THE JOB DONE."
SO... JIMMY... LISTEN.
BAR
WHEN YOU ATTACKED US...
...YOU THOUGHT WE WERE TRYING TO TAKE YOU SOMEPLACE.
WHERE?
THAT'S JUST IT.
I DON'T KNOW.
I CAN'T REMEMBER.
MAYBE YOU'RE TALKING ABOUT YOUR WORLD.
THAT PLACE WAS PRETTY AWFUL, AS I RECALL.
HEY--IS THE OTHER ICEMAN WITH YOU?
IS HE AROUND SOMEWHERE OR DID YOU CUT HIM UP, TOO?
BOBBY--
WHAT?
IT'S A FAIR QUESTION!

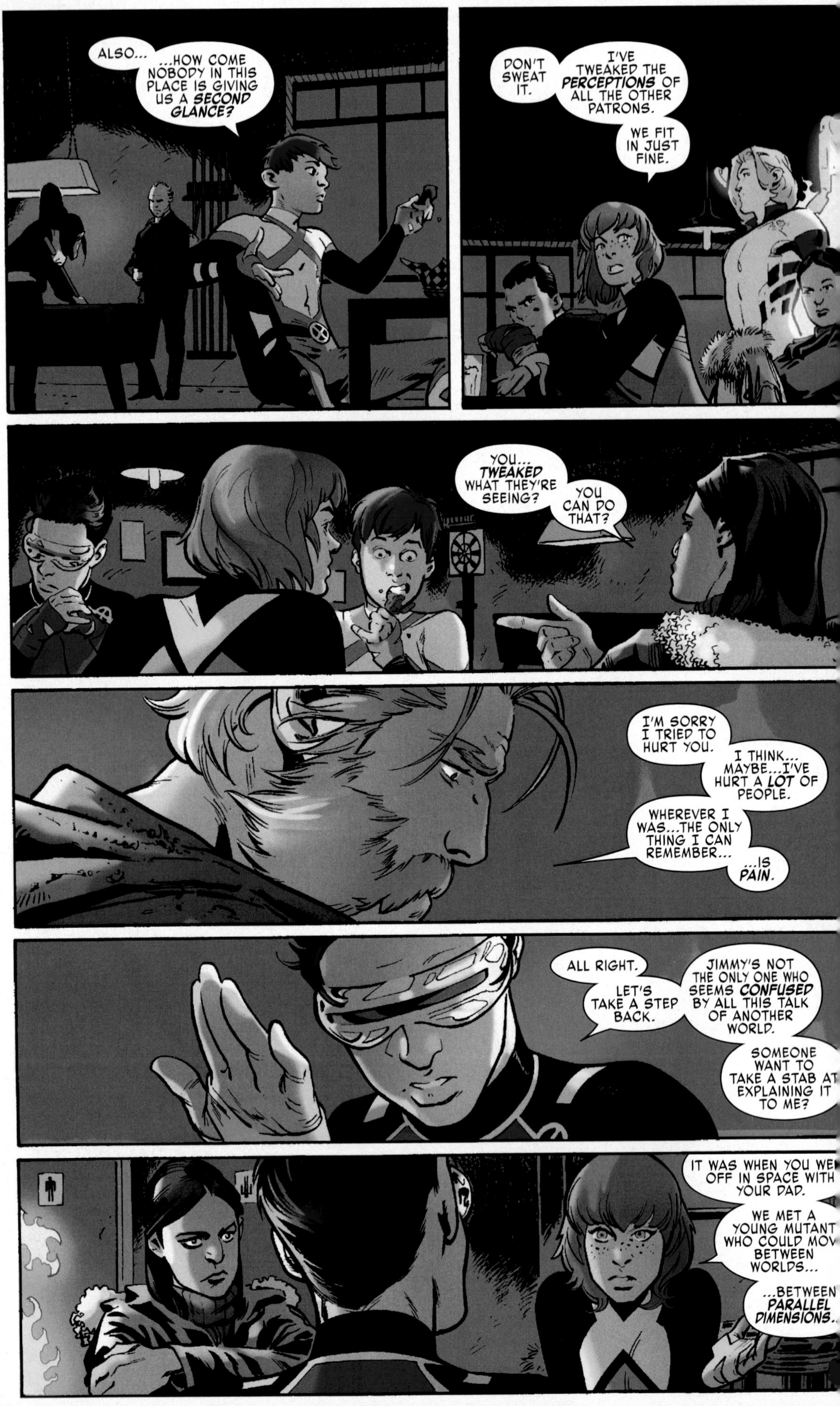

ALSO...
...HOW COME NOBODY IN THIS PLACE IS GIVING US A SECOND GLANCE?
DON'T SWEAT IT.
I'VE TWEAKED THE PERCEPTIONS OF ALL THE OTHER PATRONS.
WE FIT IN JUST FINE.
YOU... TWEAKED WHAT THEY'RE SEEING?
YOU CAN DO THAT?
I'M SORRY I TRIED TO HURT YOU.
I THINK... MAYBE...I'VE HURT A LOT OF PEOPLE.
WHEREVER I WAS...THE ONLY THING I CAN REMEMBER...
...IS PAIN.
ALL RIGHT.
LET'S TAKE A STEP BACK.
JIMMY'S NOT THE ONLY ONE WHO SEEMS CONFUSED BY ALL THIS TALK OF ANOTHER WORLD.
SOMEONE WANT TO TAKE A STAB AT EXPLAINING IT TO ME?
IT WAS WHEN YOU WE OFF IN SPACE WITH YOUR DAD.
WE MET A YOUNG MUTANT WHO COULD MOV BETWEEN WORLDS...
...BETWEEN PARALLEL DIMENSIONS.

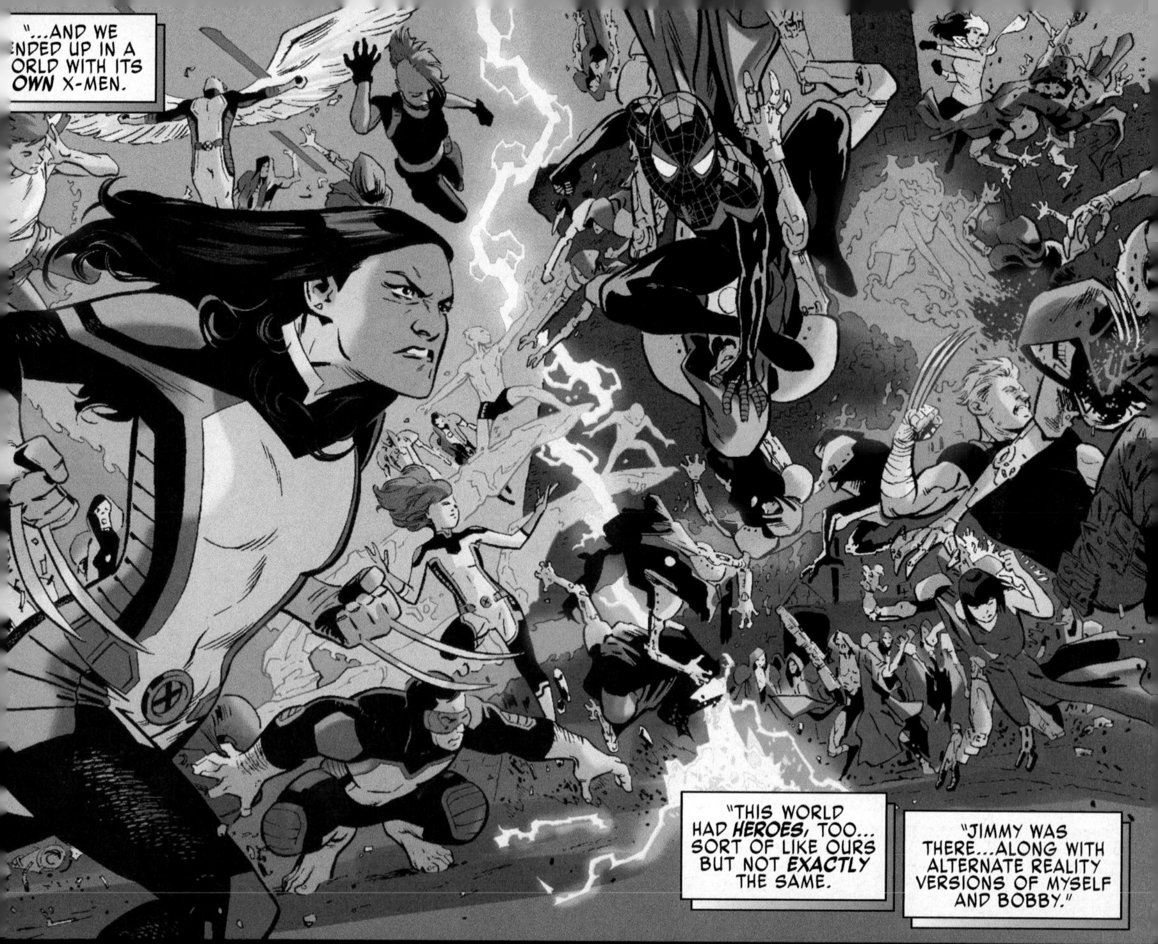
"...AND WE ENDED UP IN A WORLD WITH ITS OWN X-MEN.
"THIS WORLD HAD HEROES, TOO... SORT OF LIKE OURS BUT NOT EXACTLY THE SAME.
"JIMMY WAS THERE...ALONG WITH ALTERNATE REALITY VERSIONS OF MYSELF AND BOBBY."

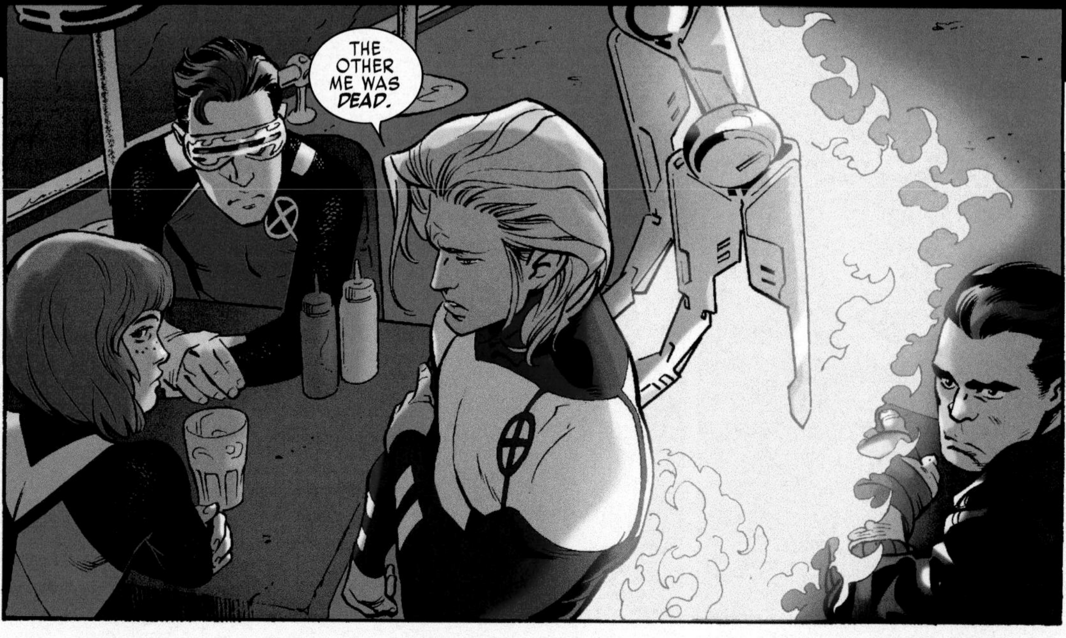
THE OTHER ME WAS DEAD.

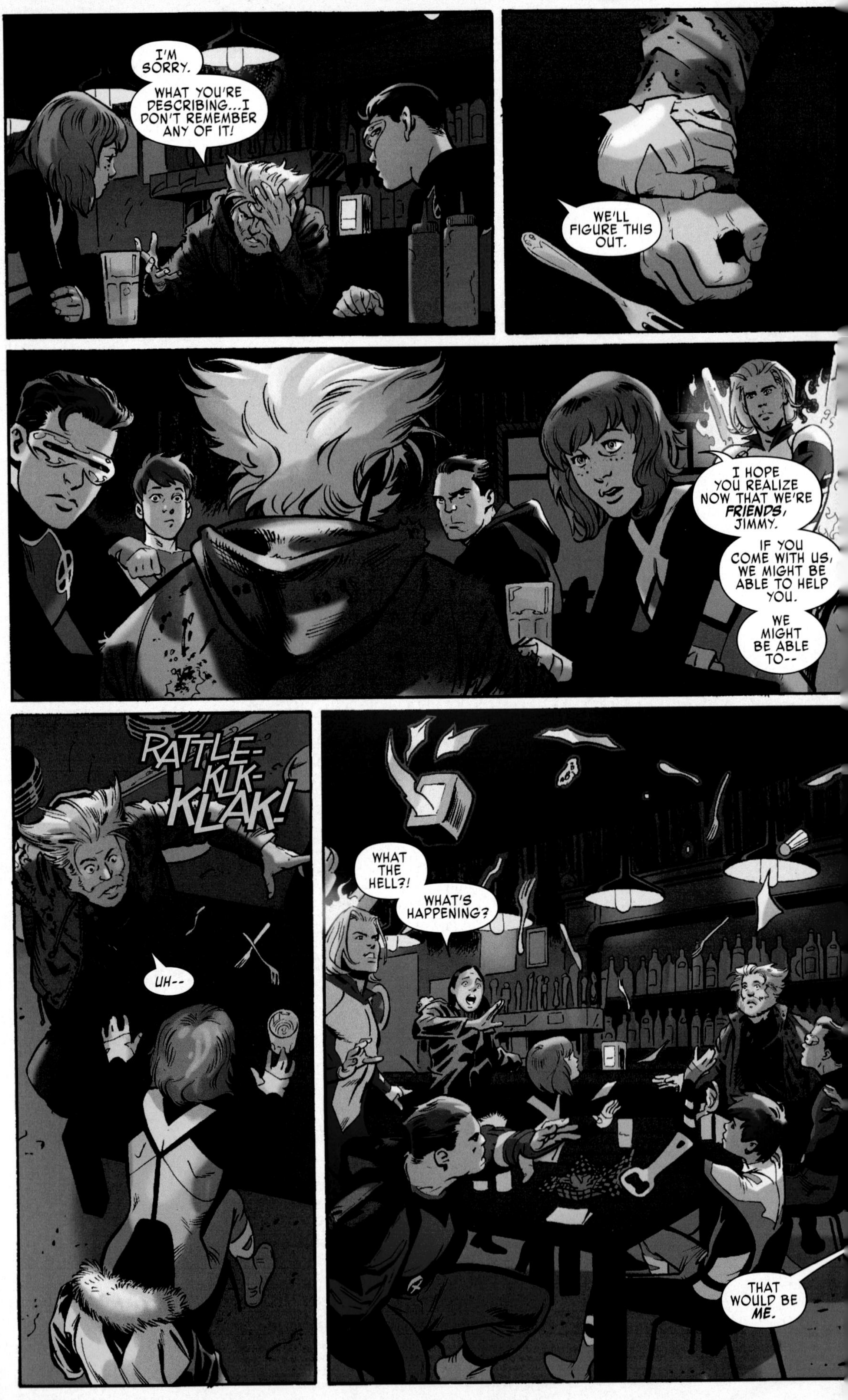
I'M SORRY.
WHAT YOU'RE DESCRIBING...I DON'T REMEMBER ANY OF IT!
WE'LL FIGURE THIS OUT.
I HOPE YOU REALIZE NOW THAT WE'RE FRIENDS, JIMMY.
IF YOU COME WITH US, WE MIGHT BE ABLE TO HELP YOU.
WE MIGHT BE ABLE TO--
RATTLE-KLIK-KLAK!
UH--
WHAT THE HELL?!
WHAT'S HAPPENING?
THAT WOULD BE ME.

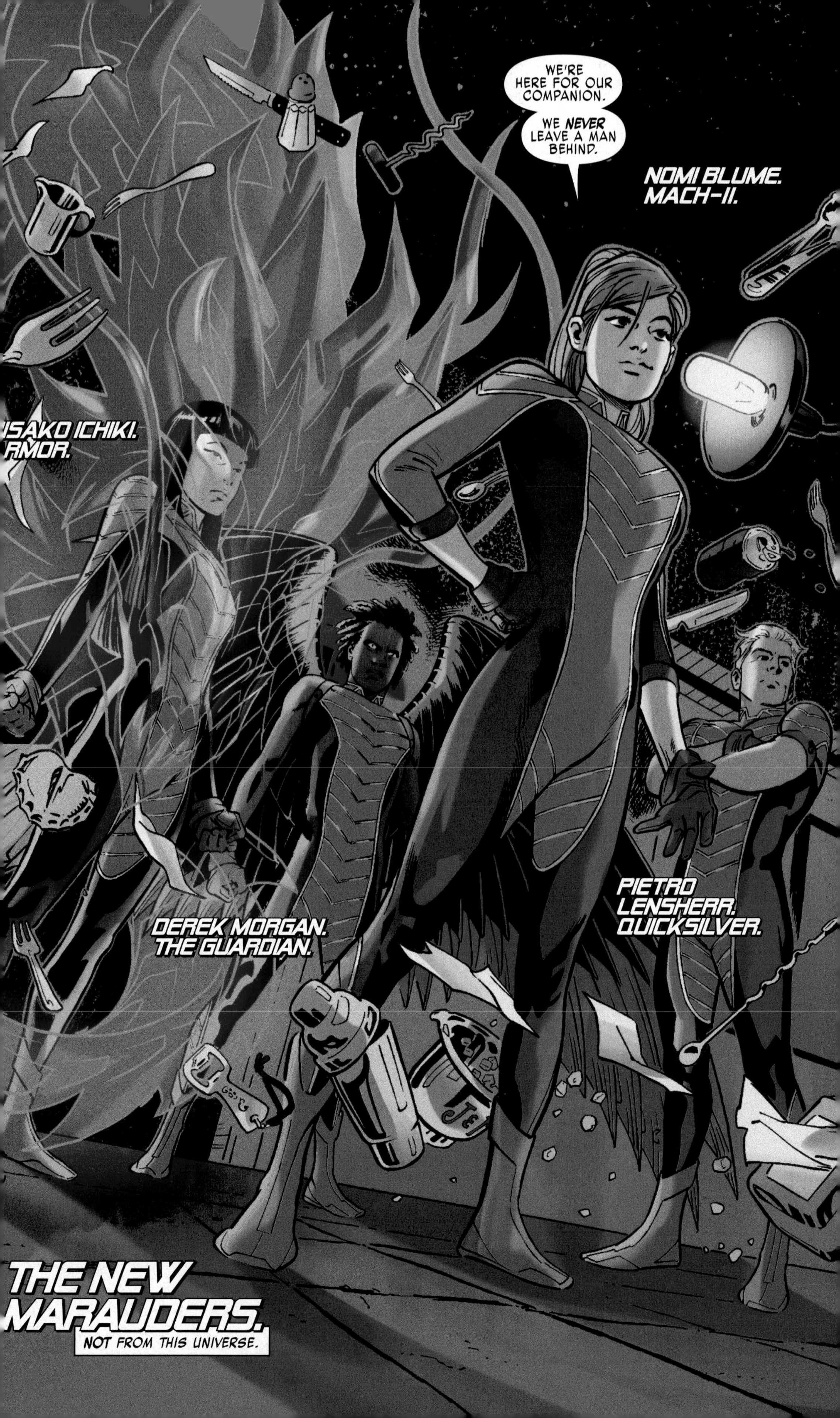

WE'RE HERE FOR OUR COMPANION.
WE NEVER LEAVE A MAN BEHIND.
NOMI BLUME. MACH-II.
ISAKO ICHIKI. RMOR.
DEREK MORGAN. THE GUARDIAN.
PIETRO LENSHERR. QUICKSILVER.
THE NEW MARAUDERS.
NOT FROM THIS UNIVERSE.

5

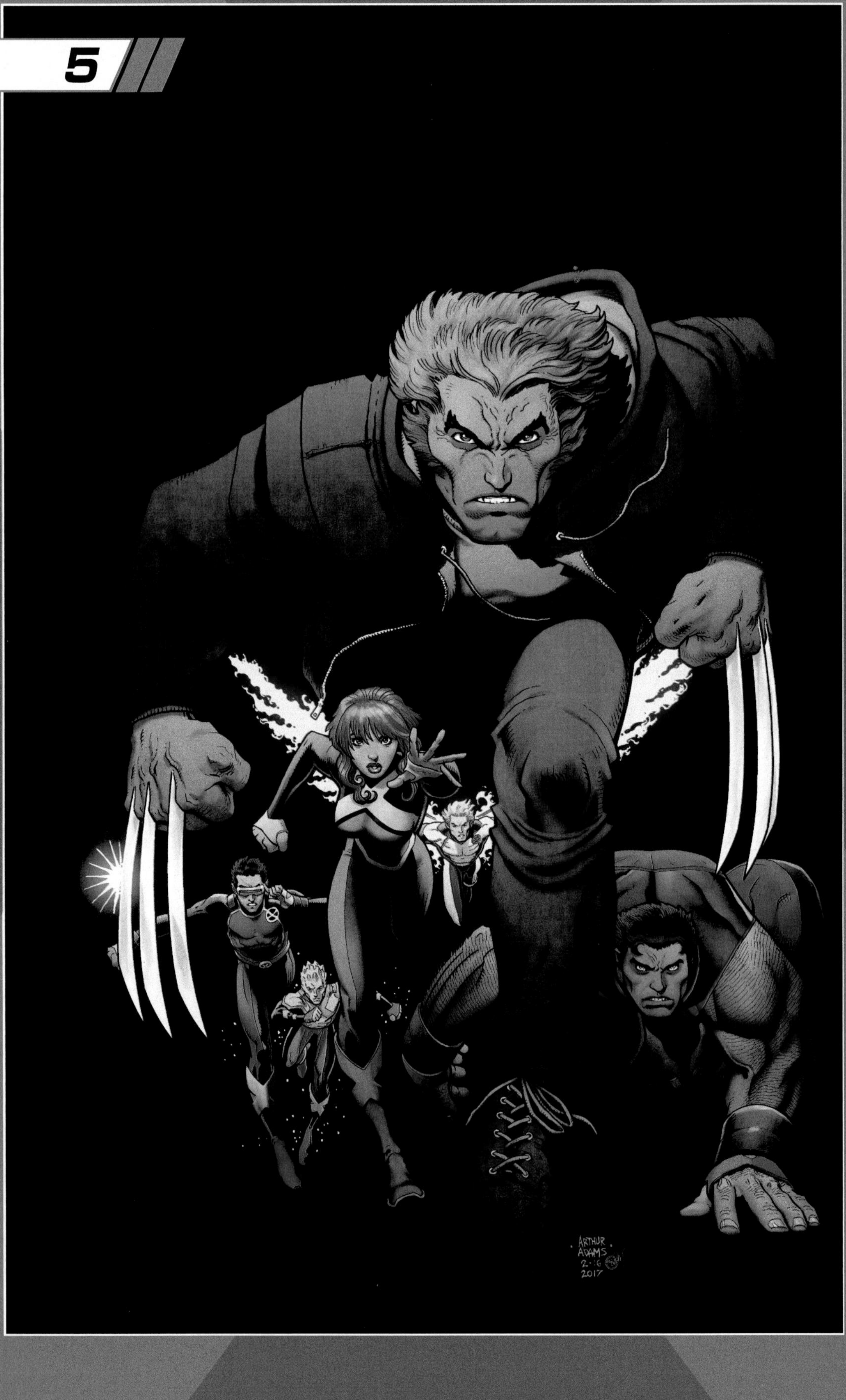
ARTHUR ADAMS
2-16
2017

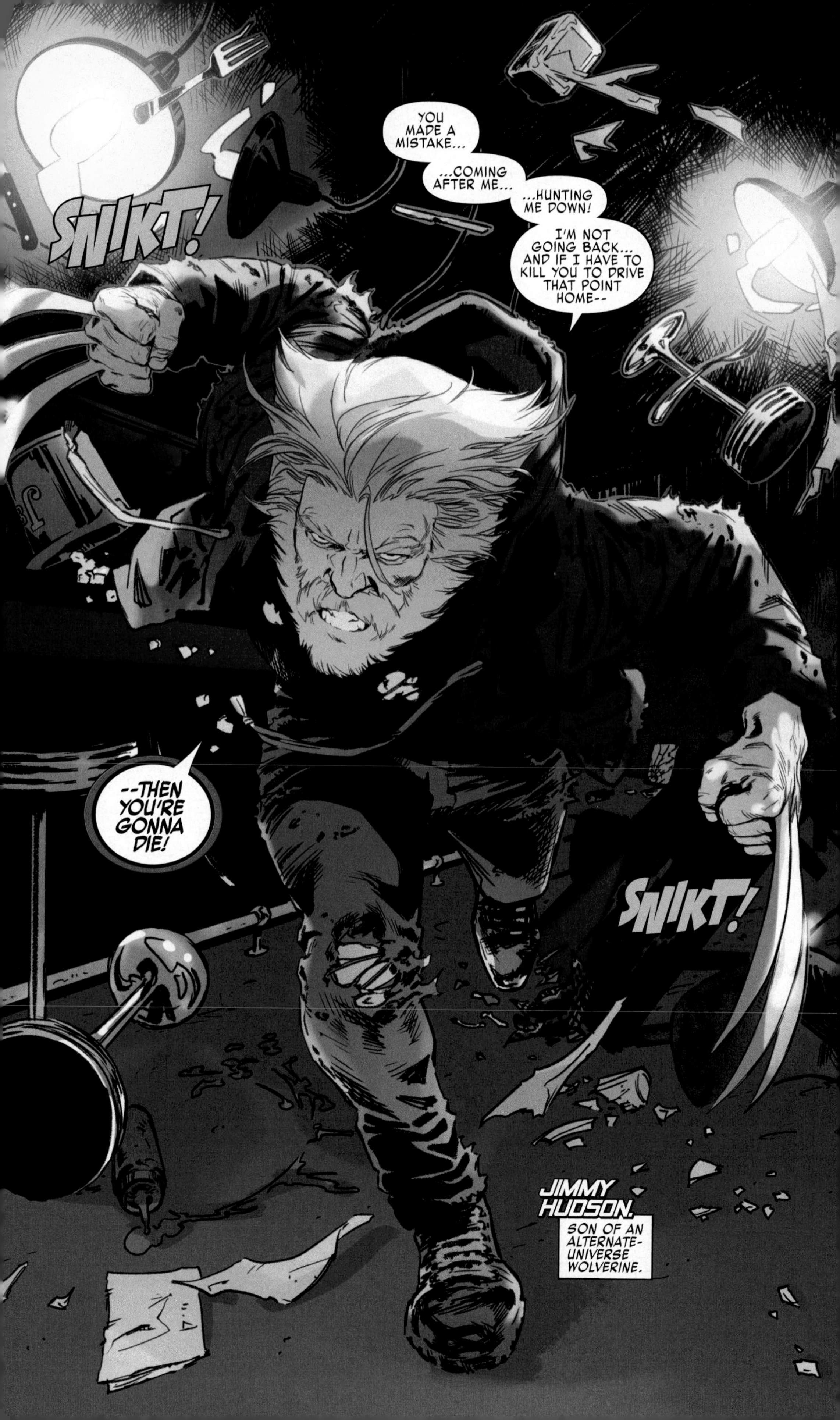
SNIKT!
YOU MADE A MISTAKE...
...COMING AFTER ME...
...HUNTING ME DOWN!
I'M NOT GOING BACK... AND IF I HAVE TO KILL YOU TO DRIVE THAT POINT HOME--
--THEN YOU'RE GONNA DIE!
SNIKT!
JIMMY HUDSON.
SON OF AN ALTERNATE-UNIVERSE WOLVERINE.

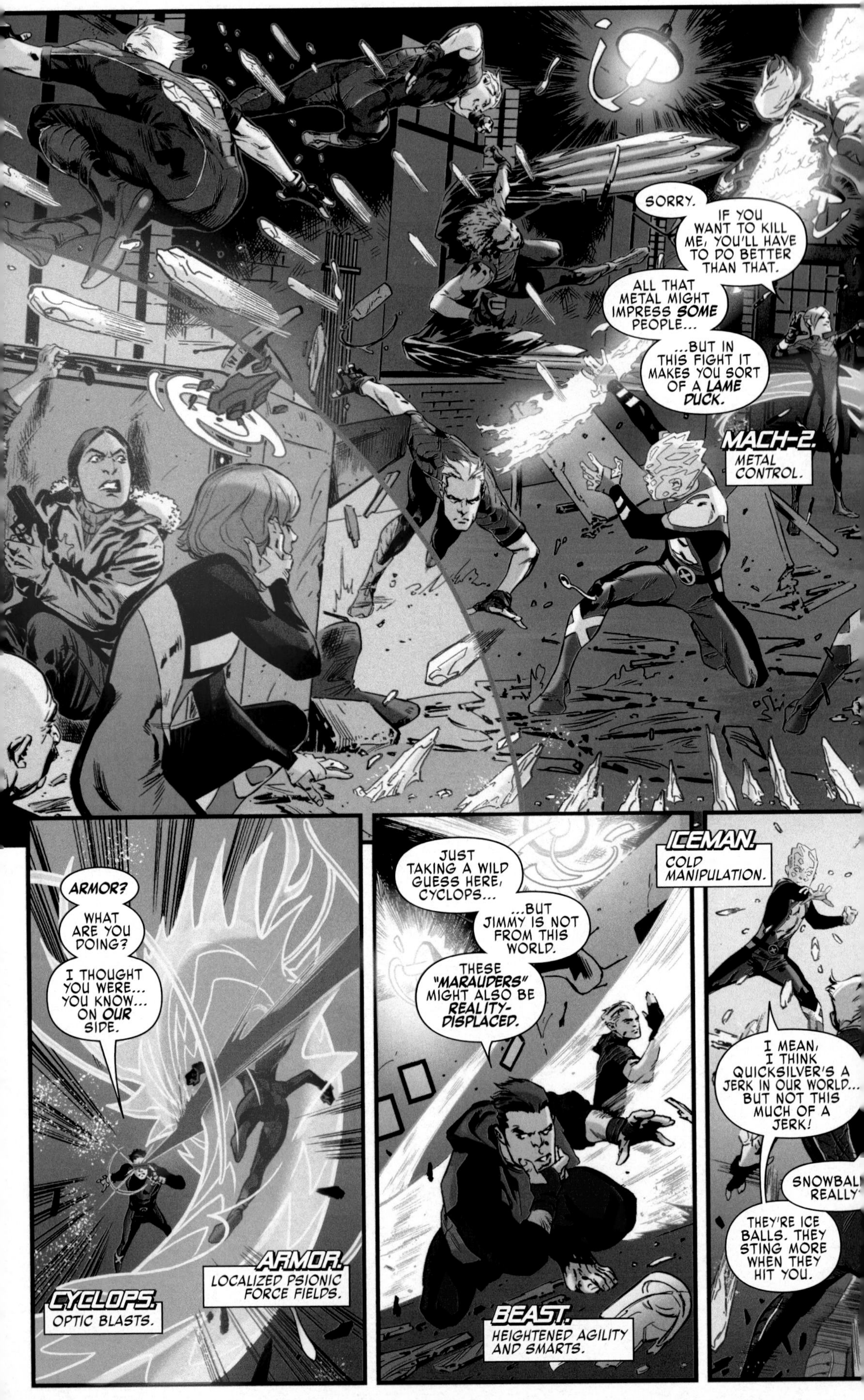

SORRY.
IF YOU WANT TO KILL ME, YOU'LL HAVE TO DO BETTER THAN THAT.
ALL THAT METAL MIGHT IMPRESS SOME PEOPLE...
...BUT IN THIS FIGHT IT MAKES YOU SORT OF A LAME DUCK.
MACH-2. METAL CONTROL.
ARMOR?
WHAT ARE YOU DOING?
I THOUGHT YOU WERE... YOU KNOW... ON OUR SIDE.
ARMOR. LOCALIZED PSIONIC FORCE FIELDS.
CYCLOPS. OPTIC BLASTS.
JUST TAKING A WILD GUESS HERE, CYCLOPS...
...BUT JIMMY IS NOT FROM THIS WORLD.
THESE "MARAUDERS" MIGHT ALSO BE REALITY-DISPLACED.
BEAST. HEIGHTENED AGILITY AND SMARTS.
ICEMAN. COLD MANIPULATION.
I MEAN, I THINK QUICKSILVER'S A JERK IN OUR WORLD... BUT NOT THIS MUCH OF A JERK!
SNOWBAL REALLY
THEY'RE ICE BALLS. THEY STING MORE WHEN THEY HIT YOU.

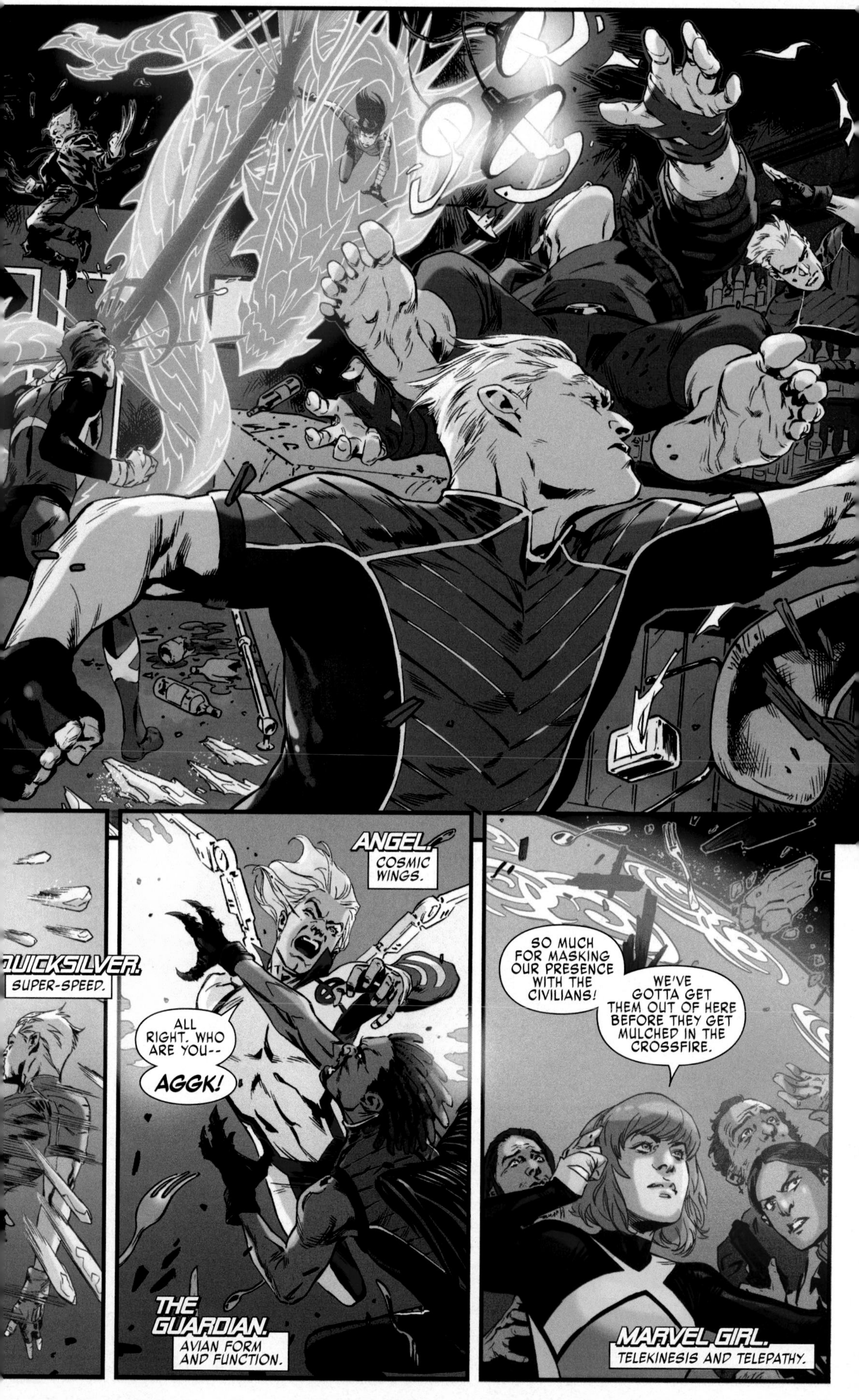
QUICKSILVER.
SUPER-SPEED.
ANGEL.
COSMIC WINGS.
ALL RIGHT. WHO ARE YOU--
AGGK!
THE GUARDIAN.
AVIAN FORM AND FUNCTION.
SO MUCH FOR MASKING OUR PRESENCE WITH THE CIVILIANS!
WE'VE GOTTA GET THEM OUT OF HERE BEFORE THEY GET MULCHED IN THE CROSSFIRE.
MARVEL GIRL.
TELEKINESIS AND TELEPATHY.

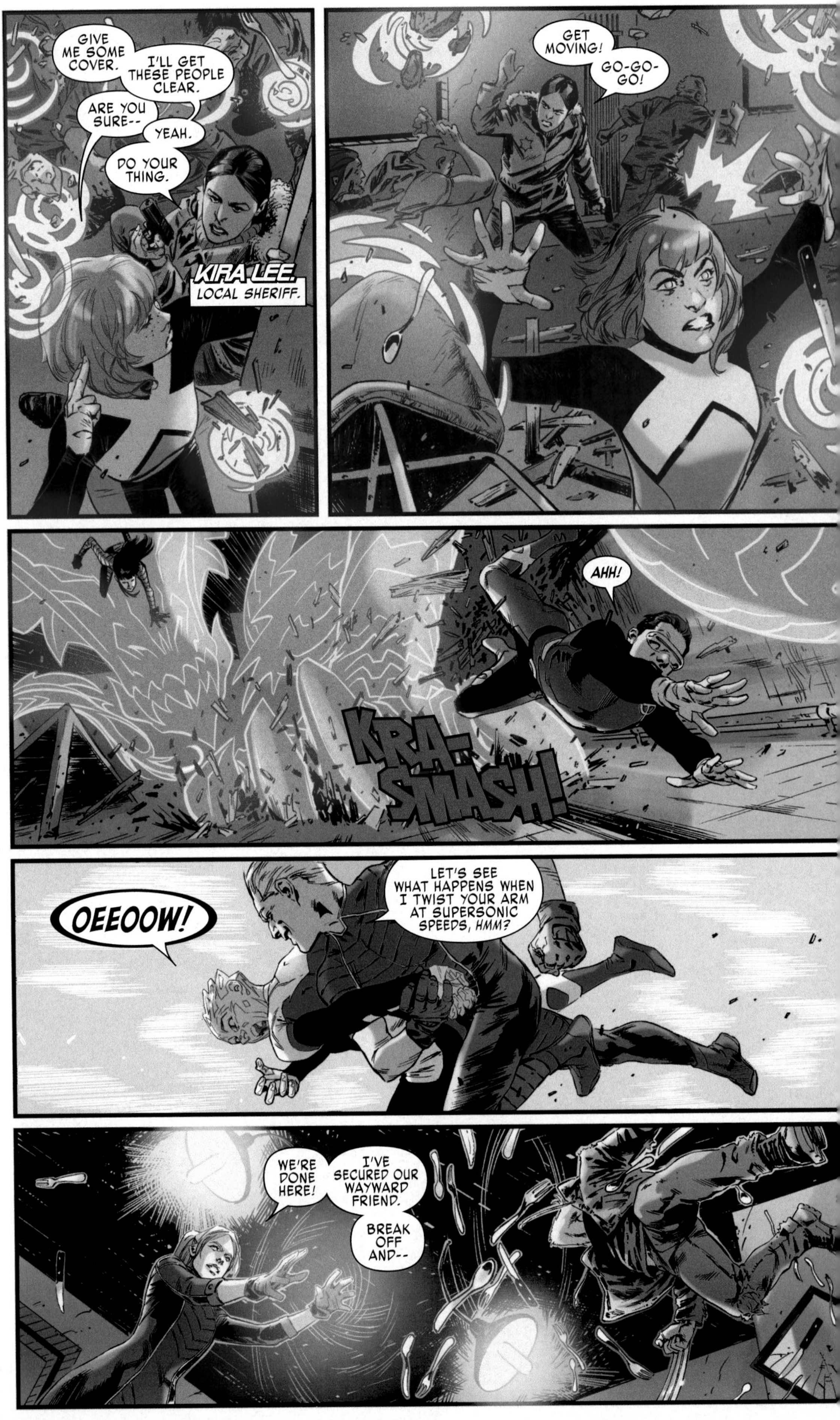
GIVE ME SOME COVER.
I'LL GET THESE PEOPLE CLEAR.
ARE YOU SURE--
YEAH.
DO YOUR THING.
KIRA LEE. LOCAL SHERIFF.
GET MOVING!
GO-GO-GO!
AHH!
KRA-SMASH!
OEEOOW!
LET'S SEE WHAT HAPPENS WHEN I TWIST YOUR ARM AT SUPERSONIC SPEEDS, HMM?
WE'RE DONE HERE!
I'VE SECURED OUR WAYWARD FRIEND.
BREAK OFF AND--

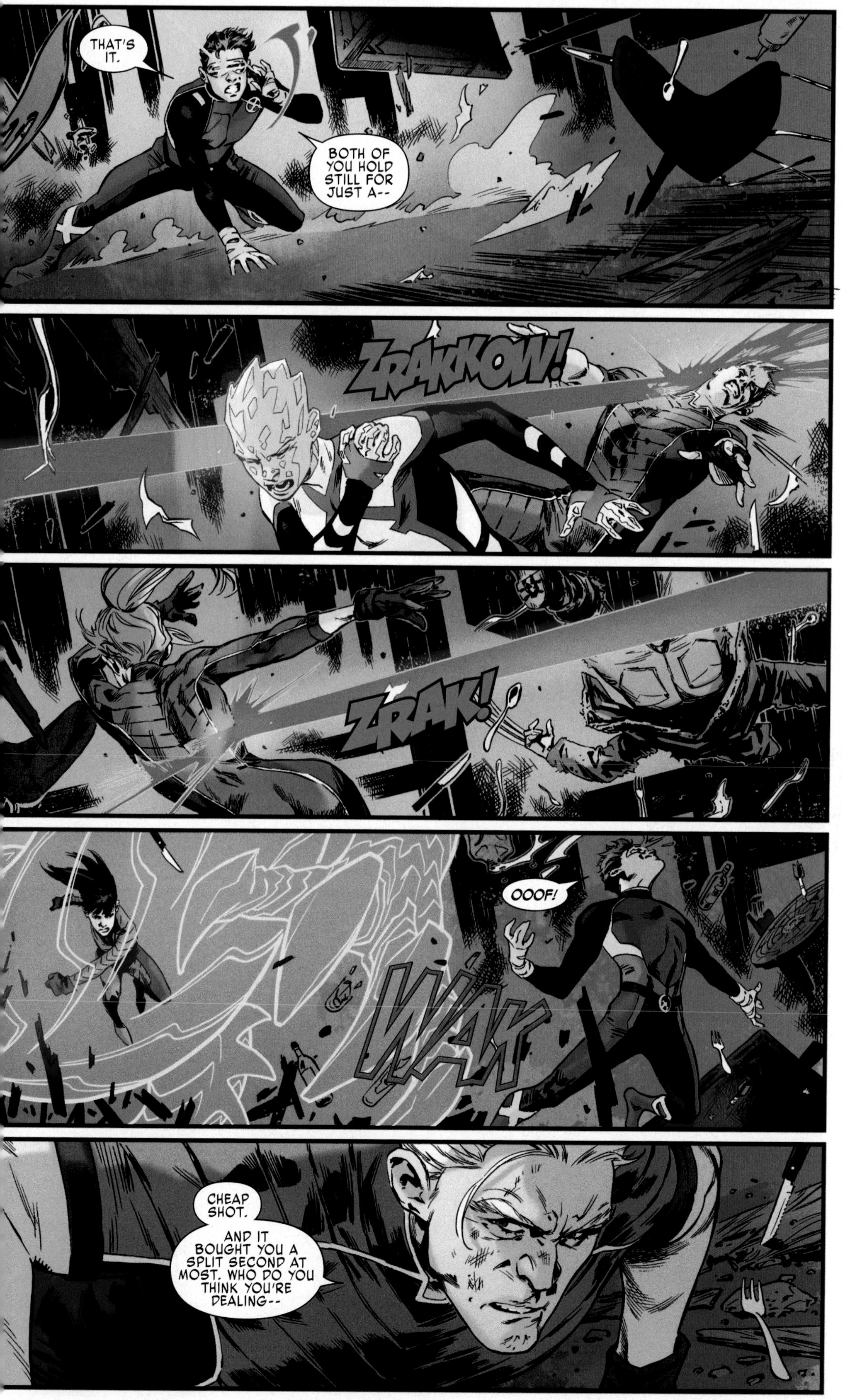
THAT'S IT.
BOTH OF YOU HOLD STILL FOR JUST A--
ZRAKKOW!
ZRAK!
OOOF!
WAK
CHEAP SHOT.
AND IT BOUGHT YOU A SPLIT SECOND AT MOST. WHO DO YOU THINK YOU'RE DEALING--

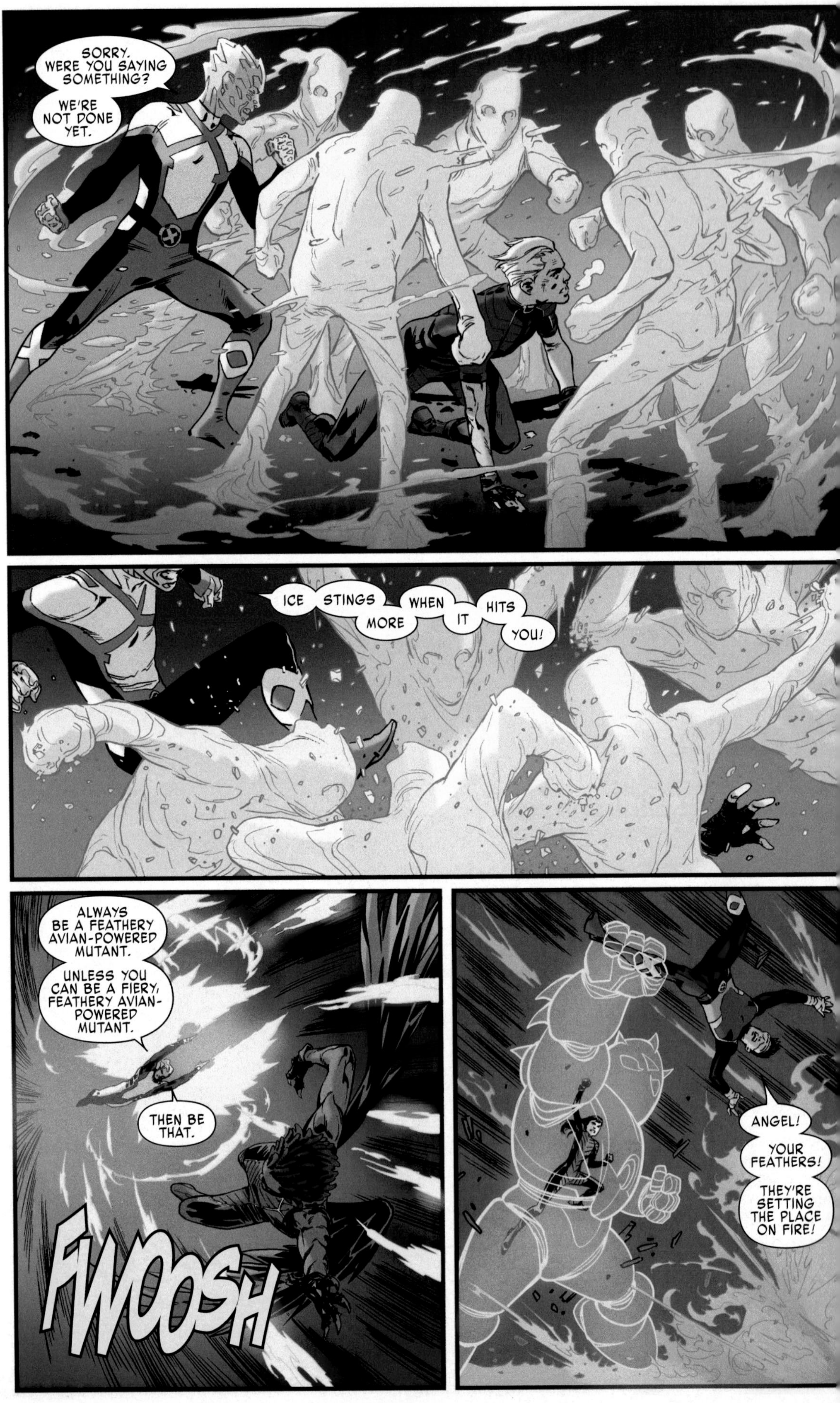
SORRY. WERE YOU SAYING SOMETHING?
WE'RE NOT DONE YET.
ICE STINGS MORE WHEN IT HITS YOU!
ALWAYS BE A FEATHERY AVIAN-POWERED MUTANT.
UNLESS YOU CAN BE A FIERY, FEATHERY AVIAN-POWERED MUTANT.
THEN BE THAT.
FWOOSH
ANGEL!
YOUR FEATHERS!
THEY'RE SETTING THE PLACE ON FIRE!

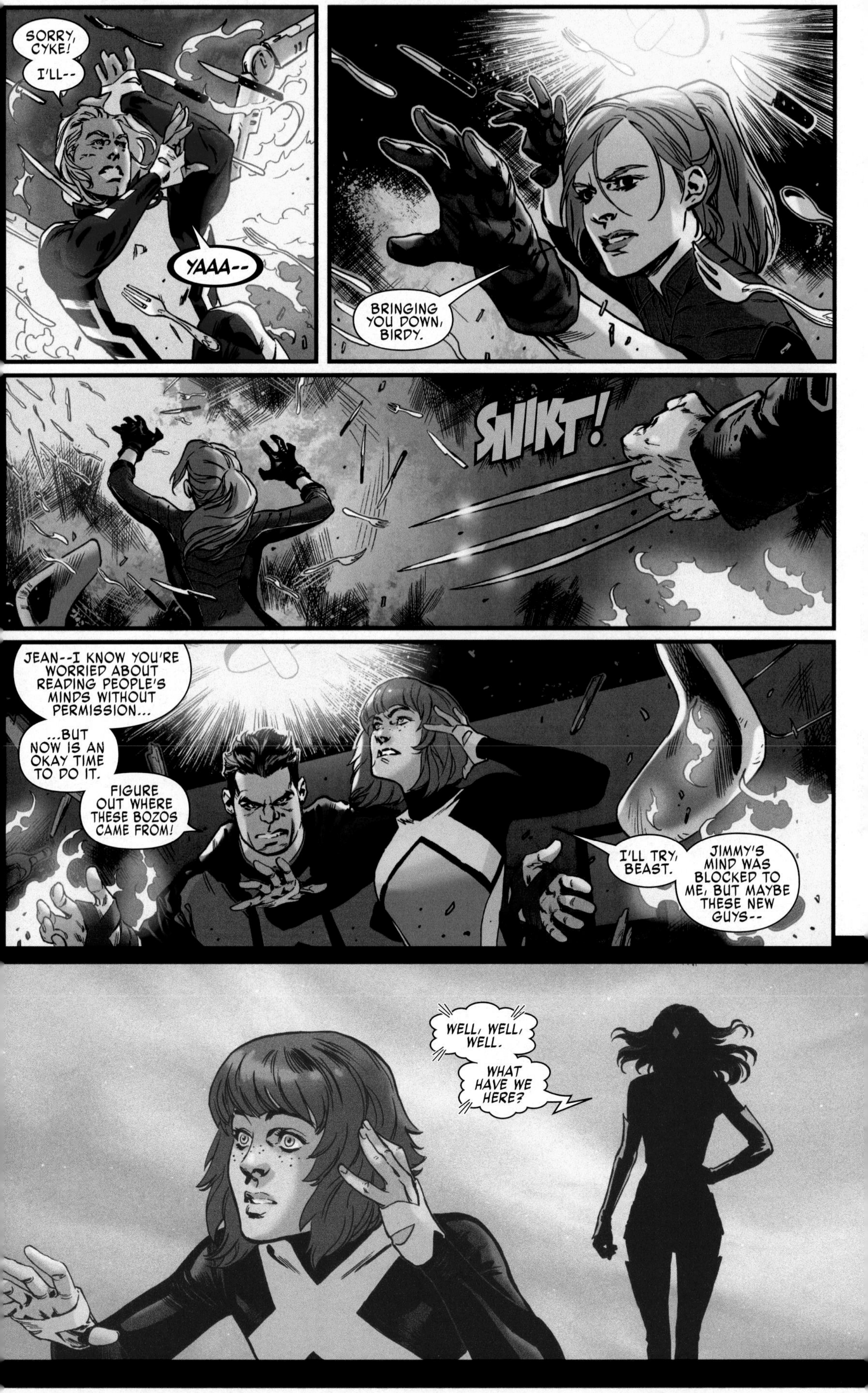
SORRY, CYKE!
I'LL--
YAAA--
BRINGING YOU DOWN, BIRDY.
SNIKT!
JEAN--I KNOW YOU'RE WORRIED ABOUT READING PEOPLE'S MINDS WITHOUT PERMISSION...
...BUT NOW IS AN OKAY TIME TO DO IT.
FIGURE OUT WHERE THESE BOZOS CAME FROM!
I'LL TRY, BEAST.
JIMMY'S MIND WAS BLOCKED TO ME, BUT MAYBE THESE NEW GUYS--
WELL, WELL, WELL.
WHAT HAVE WE HERE?

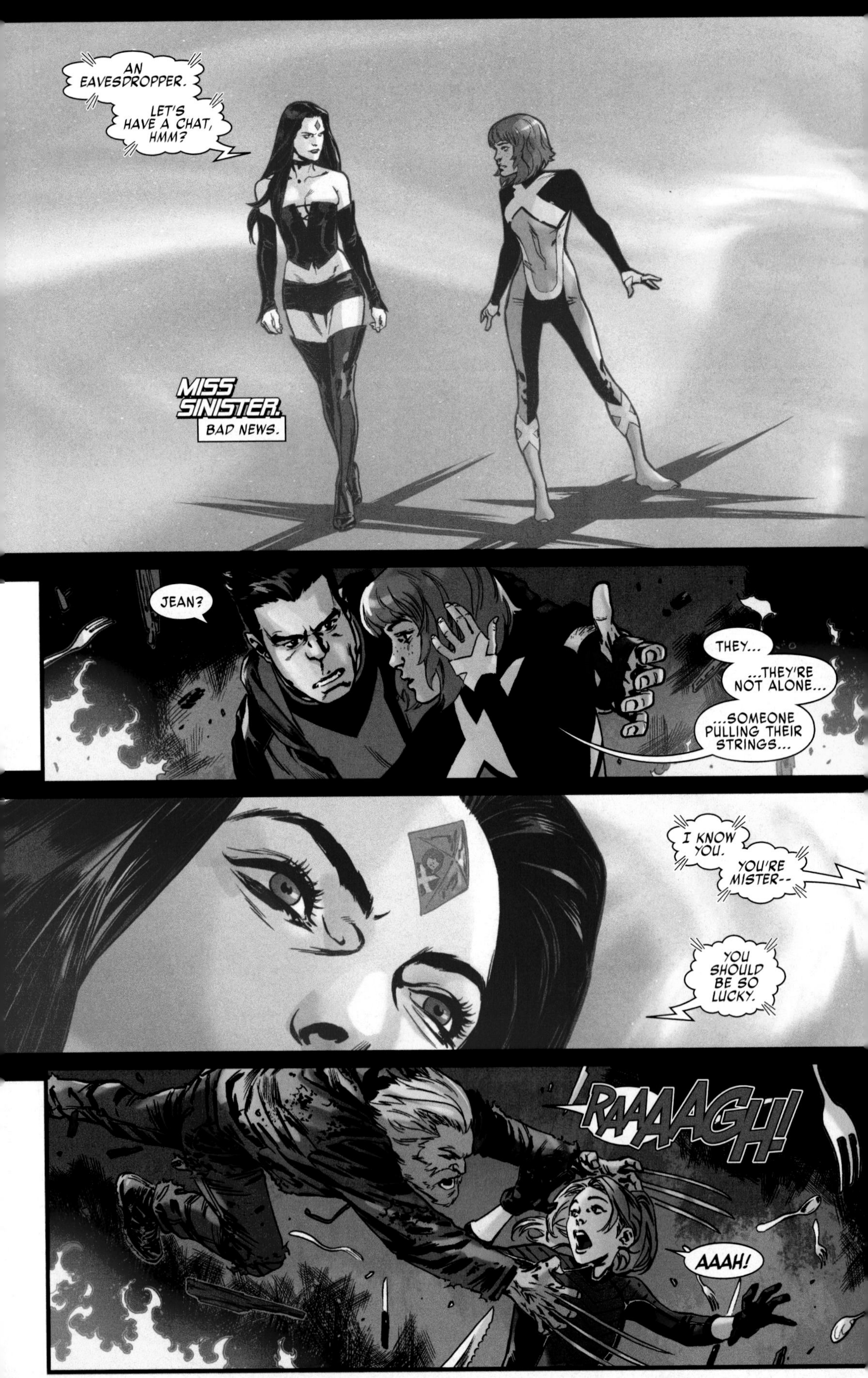
AN EAVESDROPPER.
LET'S HAVE A CHAT, HMM?
MISS SINISTER.
BAD NEWS.
JEAN?
THEY...
...THEY'RE NOT ALONE...
...SOMEONE PULLING THEIR STRINGS...
I KNOW YOU.
YOU'RE MISTER--
YOU SHOULD BE SO LUCKY.
RAAAAGH!
AAAH!

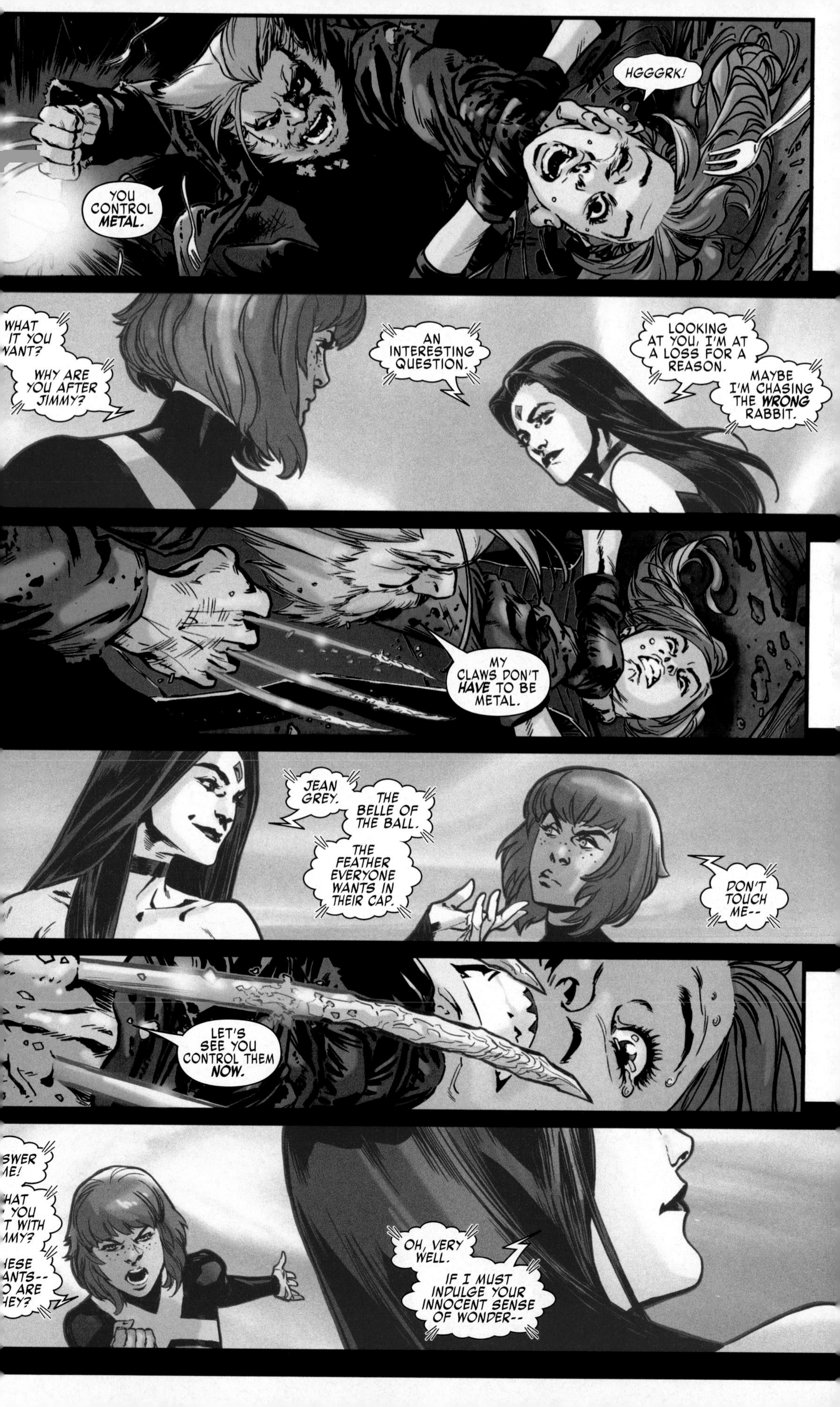

HGGGRK!
YOU CONTROL METAL.
WHAT IT YOU WANT?
WHY ARE YOU AFTER JIMMY?
AN INTERESTING QUESTION.
LOOKING AT YOU, I'M AT A LOSS FOR A REASON.
MAYBE I'M CHASING THE WRONG RABBIT.
MY CLAWS DON'T HAVE TO BE METAL.
JEAN GREY.
THE BELLE OF THE BALL.
THE FEATHER EVERYONE WANTS IN THEIR CAP.
DON'T TOUCH ME--
LET'S SEE YOU CONTROL THEM NOW.
SWER ME!
HAT YOU T WITH MMY?
HESE ANTS-- O ARE HEY?
OH, VERY WELL.
IF I MUST INDULGE YOUR INNOCENT SENSE OF WONDER--

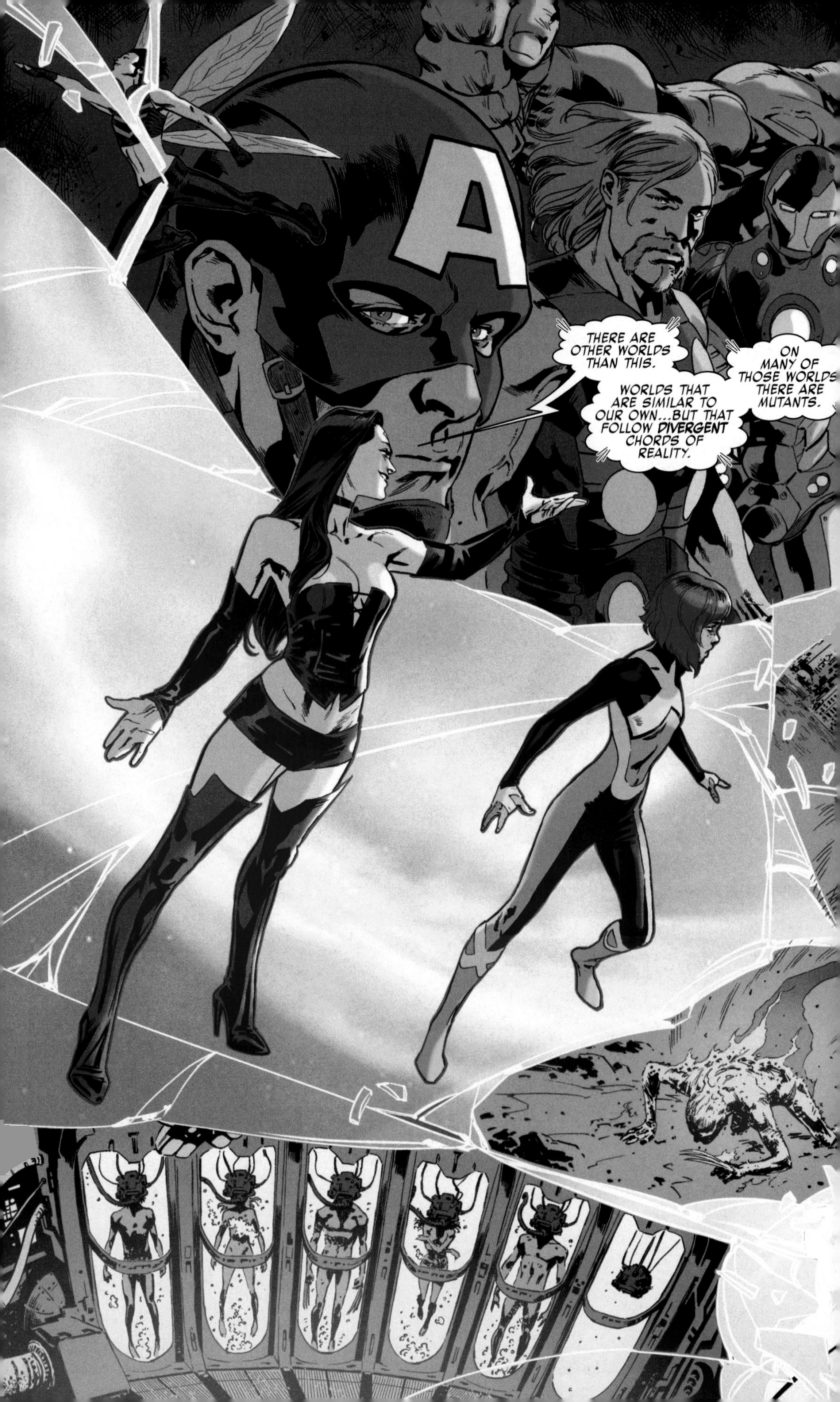
THERE ARE OTHER WORLDS THAN THIS.
WORLDS THAT ARE SIMILAR TO OUR OWN...BUT THAT FOLLOW DIVERGENT CHORDS OF REALITY.
ON MANY OF THOSE WORLDS THERE ARE MUTANTS.

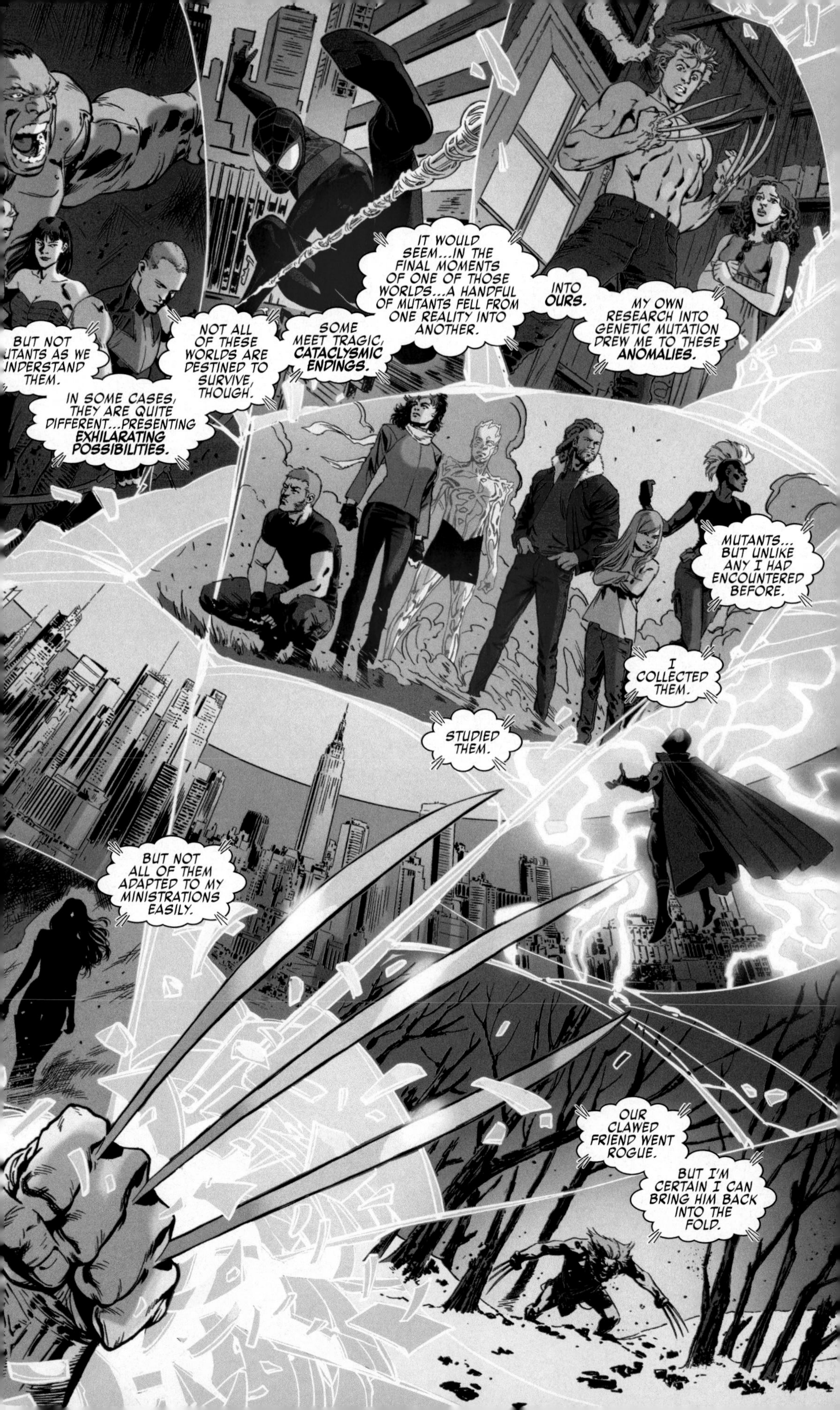
BUT NOT MUTANTS AS WE UNDERSTAND THEM.
IN SOME CASES, THEY ARE QUITE DIFFERENT...PRESENTING EXHILARATING POSSIBILITIES.
NOT ALL OF THESE WORLDS ARE DESTINED TO SURVIVE, THOUGH.
SOME MEET TRAGIC, CATACLYSMIC ENDINGS.
IT WOULD SEEM...IN THE FINAL MOMENTS OF ONE OF THOSE WORLDS...A HANDFUL OF MUTANTS FELL FROM ONE REALITY INTO ANOTHER.
INTO OURS.
MY OWN RESEARCH INTO GENETIC MUTATION DREW ME TO THESE ANOMALIES.
MUTANTS... BUT UNLIKE ANY I HAD ENCOUNTERED BEFORE.
I COLLECTED THEM.
STUDIED THEM.
BUT NOT ALL OF THEM ADAPTED TO MY MINISTRATIONS EASILY.
OUR CLAWED FRIEND WENT ROGUE.
BUT I'M CERTAIN I CAN BRING HIM BACK INTO THE FOLD.

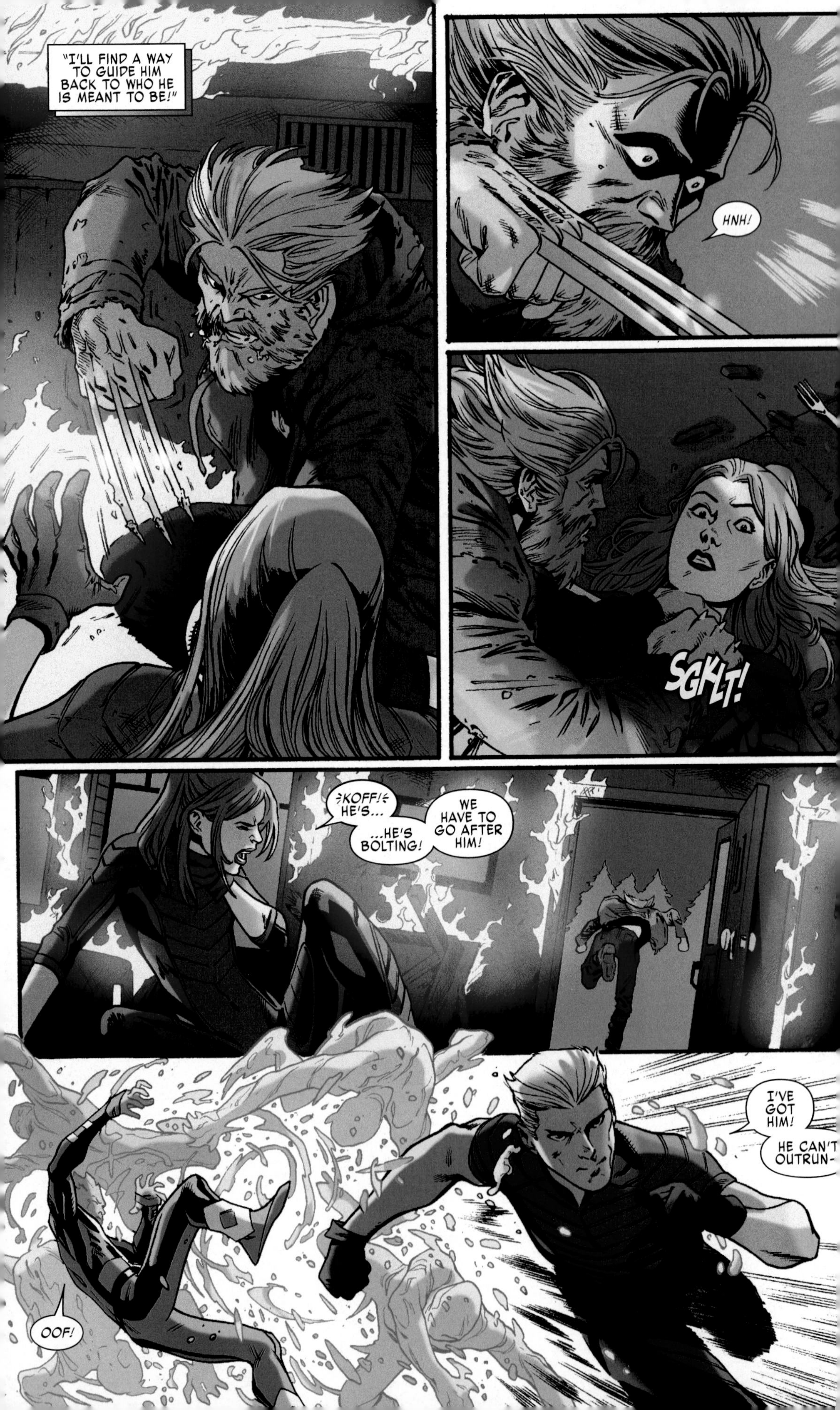
"I'LL FIND A WAY TO GUIDE HIM BACK TO WHO HE IS MEANT TO BE!"
HNH!
SGKLT!
KOFF! HE'S...
...HE'S BOLTING!
WE HAVE TO GO AFTER HIM!
I'VE GOT HIM!
HE CAN'T OUTRUN-
OOF!

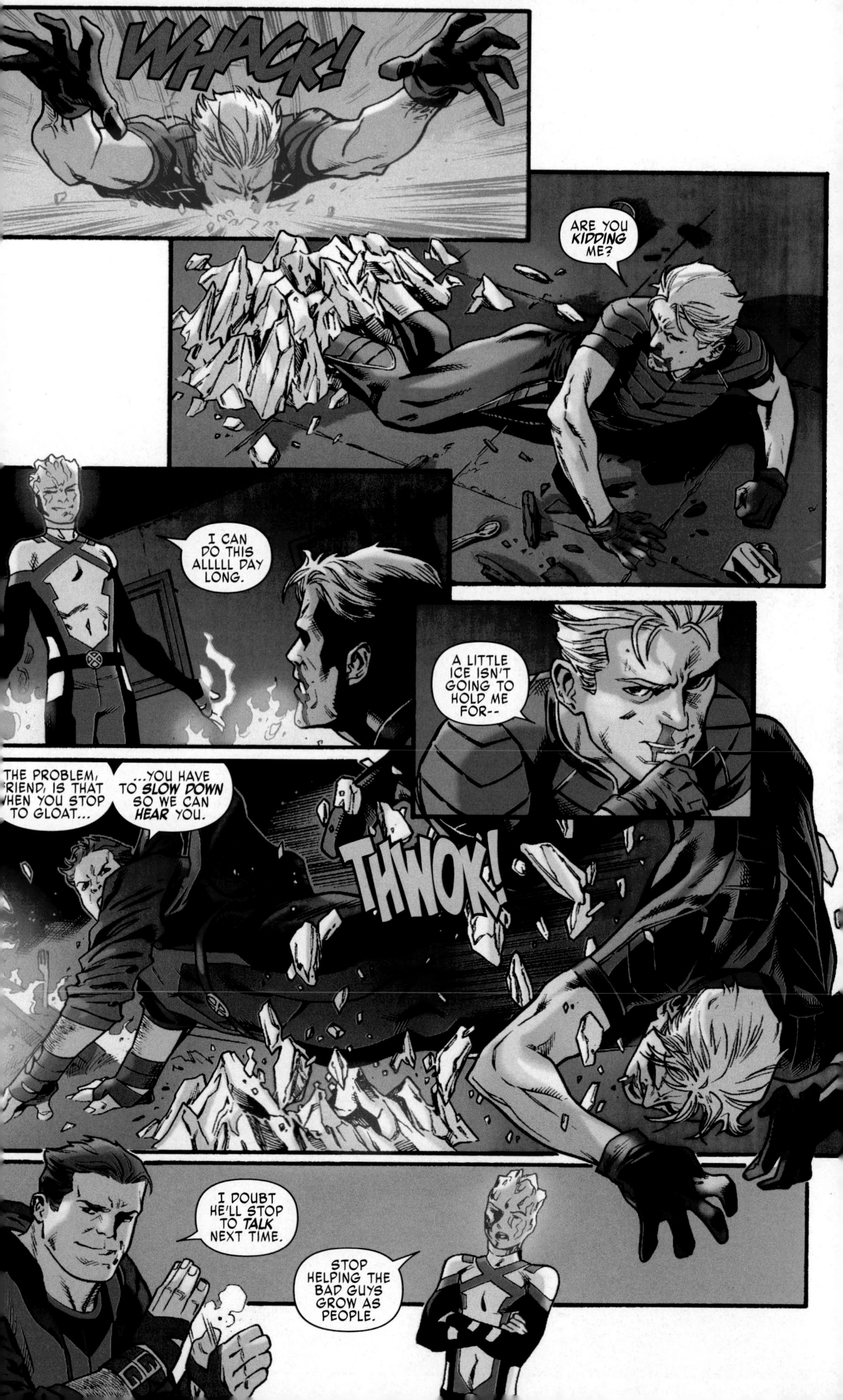
WHACK!
ARE YOU KIDDING ME?
I CAN DO THIS ALLLLL DAY LONG.
A LITTLE ICE ISN'T GOING TO HOLD ME FOR--
THE PROBLEM, FRIEND, IS THAT WHEN YOU STOP TO GLOAT...
...YOU HAVE TO SLOW DOWN SO WE CAN HEAR YOU.
THWOK!
I DOUBT HE'LL STOP TO TALK NEXT TIME.
STOP HELPING THE BAD GUYS GROW AS PEOPLE.

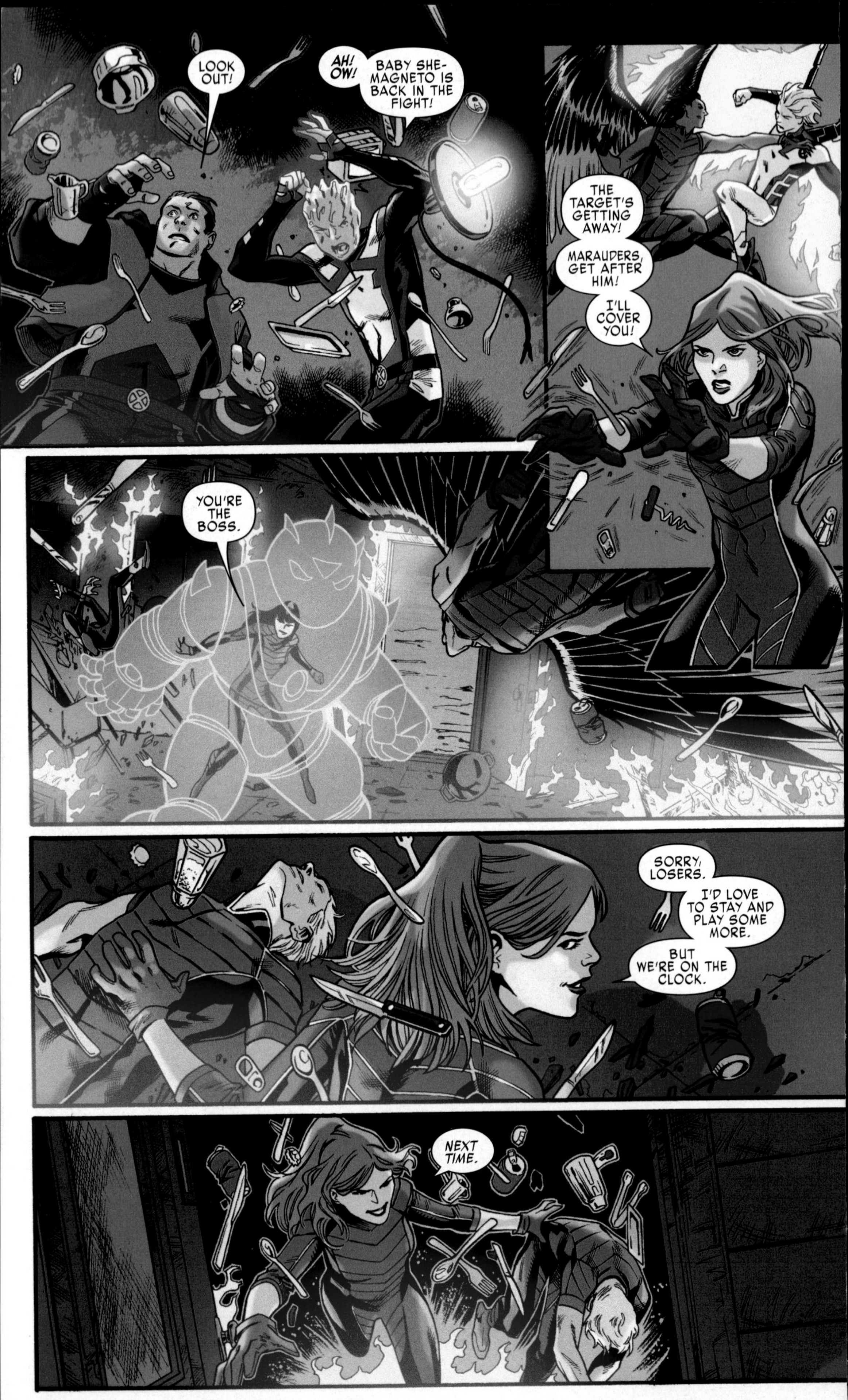

LOOK OUT!
AH! OW!
BABY SHE-MAGNETO IS BACK IN THE FIGHT!
THE TARGET'S GETTING AWAY!
MARAUDERS, GET AFTER HIM!
I'LL COVER YOU!
YOU'RE THE BOSS.
SORRY, LOSERS.
I'D LOVE TO STAY AND PLAY SOME MORE.
BUT WE'RE ON THE CLOCK.
NEXT TIME.

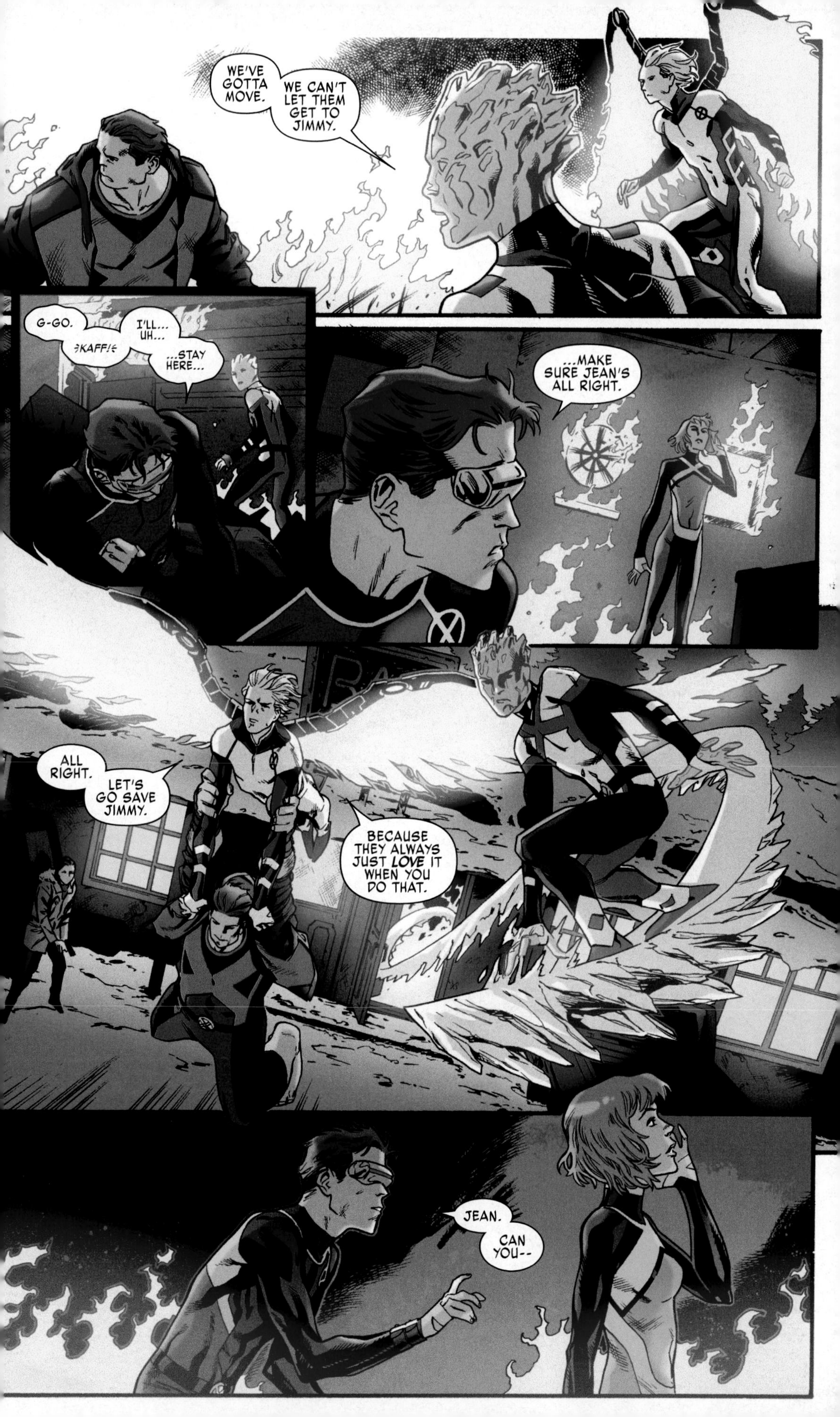
WE'VE GOTTA MOVE.
WE CAN'T LET THEM GET TO JIMMY.
G-GO.
⇒KAFF!⇐
I'LL... UH...
...STAY HERE...
...MAKE SURE JEAN'S ALL RIGHT.
ALL RIGHT.
LET'S GO SAVE JIMMY.
BECAUSE THEY ALWAYS JUST LOVE IT WHEN YOU DO THAT.
JEAN.
CAN YOU--

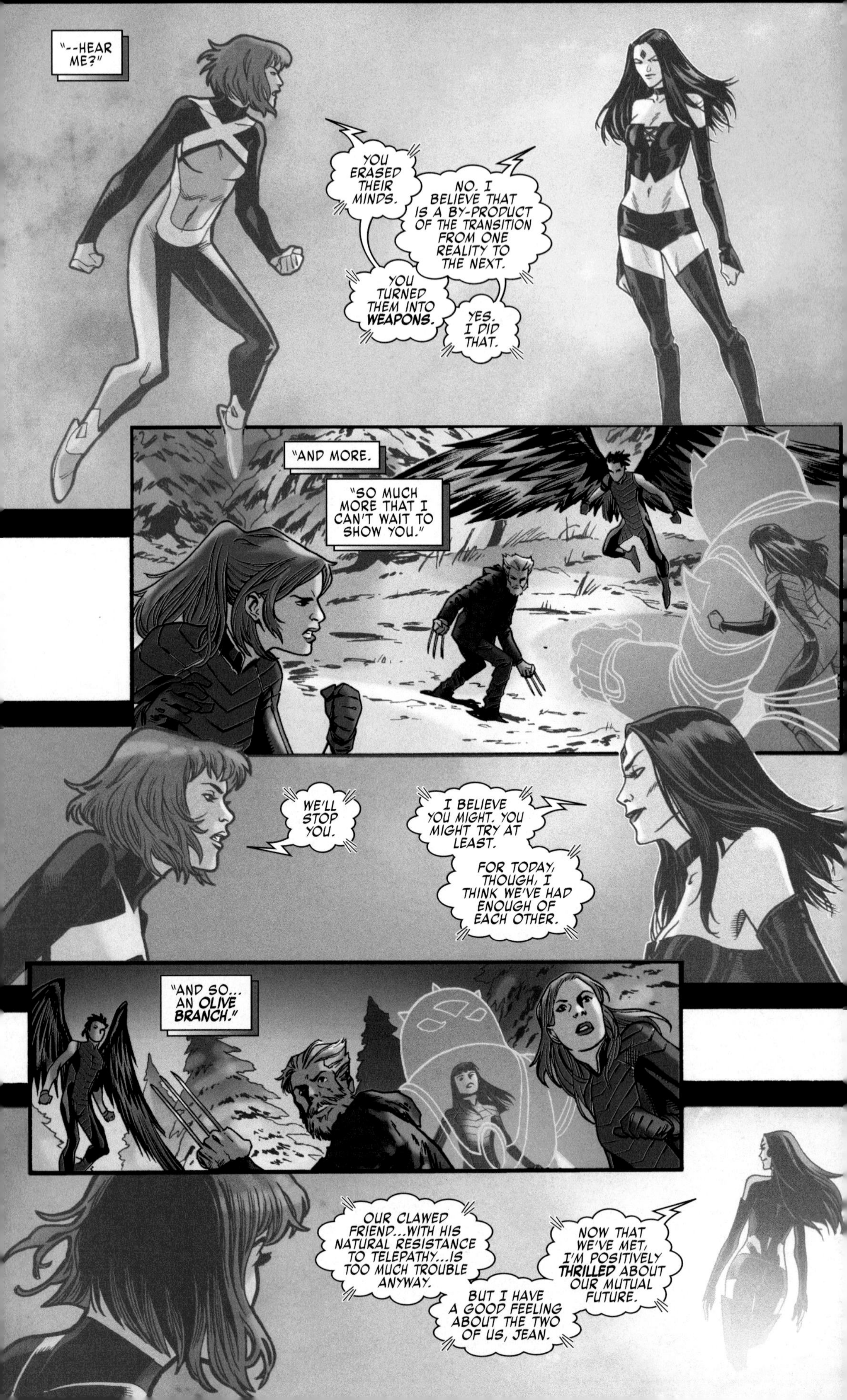
"--HEAR ME?"
YOU ERASED THEIR MINDS.
NO. I BELIEVE THAT IS A BY-PRODUCT OF THE TRANSITION FROM ONE REALITY TO THE NEXT.
YOU TURNED THEM INTO **WEAPONS.**
YES. I DID THAT.
"AND MORE.
"SO MUCH MORE THAT I CAN'T WAIT TO SHOW YOU."
WE'LL STOP YOU.
I BELIEVE YOU MIGHT. YOU MIGHT TRY AT LEAST.
FOR TODAY, THOUGH, I THINK WE'VE HAD ENOUGH OF EACH OTHER.
"AND SO... AN ***OLIVE BRANCH.***"
OUR CLAWED FRIEND...WITH HIS NATURAL RESISTANCE TO TELEPATHY...IS TOO MUCH TROUBLE ANYWAY.
BUT I HAVE A GOOD FEELING ABOUT THE TWO OF US, JEAN.
NOW THAT WE'VE MET, I'M POSITIVELY **THRILLED** ABOUT OUR MUTUAL FUTURE.

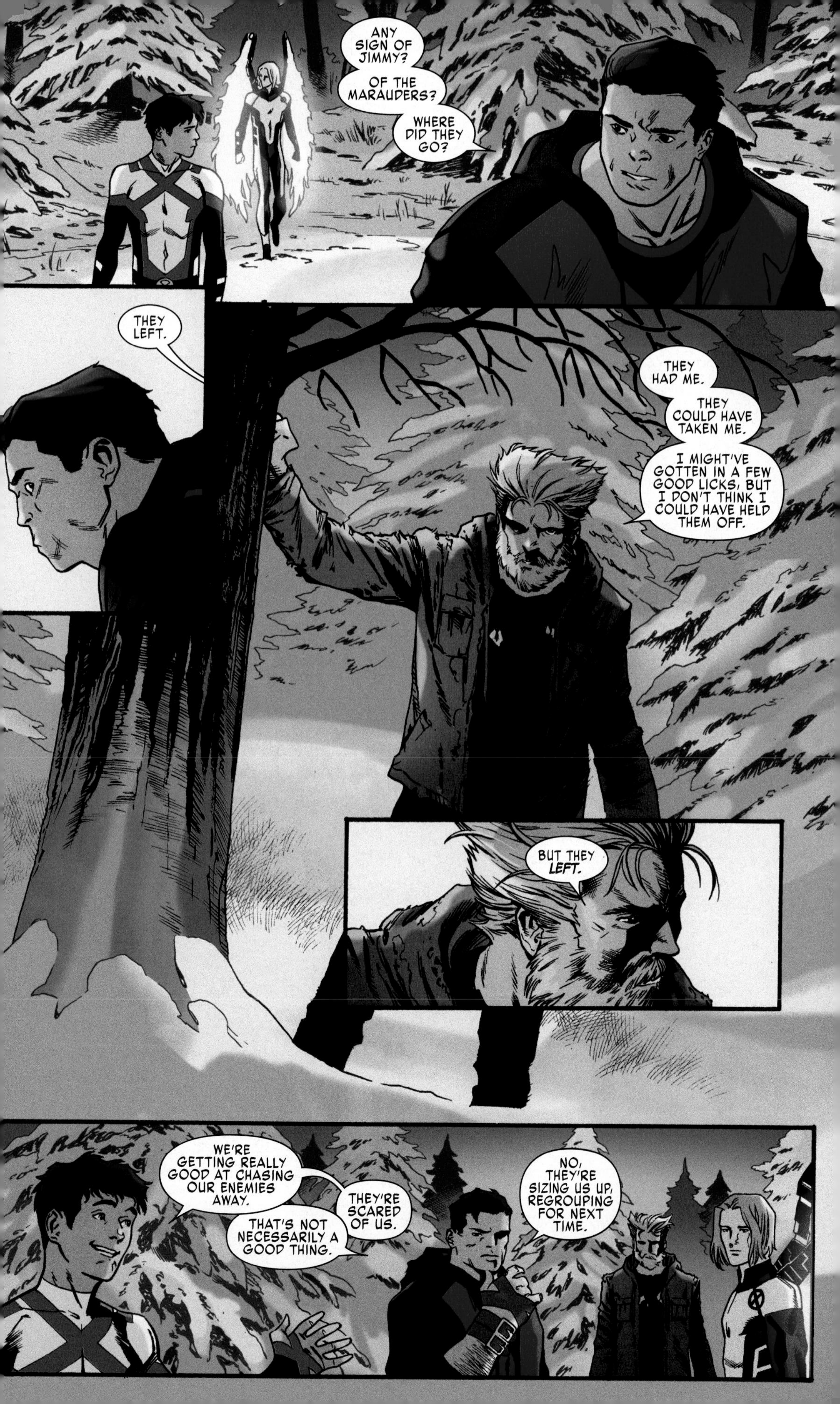
ANY SIGN OF JIMMY?
OF THE MARAUDERS?
WHERE DID THEY GO?
THEY LEFT.
THEY HAD ME.
THEY COULD HAVE TAKEN ME.
I MIGHT'VE GOTTEN IN A FEW GOOD LICKS, BUT I DON'T THINK I COULD HAVE HELD THEM OFF.
BUT THEY *LEFT.*
WE'RE GETTING REALLY GOOD AT CHASING OUR ENEMIES AWAY.
THEY'RE SCARED OF US.
THAT'S NOT NECESSARILY A GOOD THING.
NO, THEY'RE SIZING US UP, REGROUPING FOR NEXT TIME.

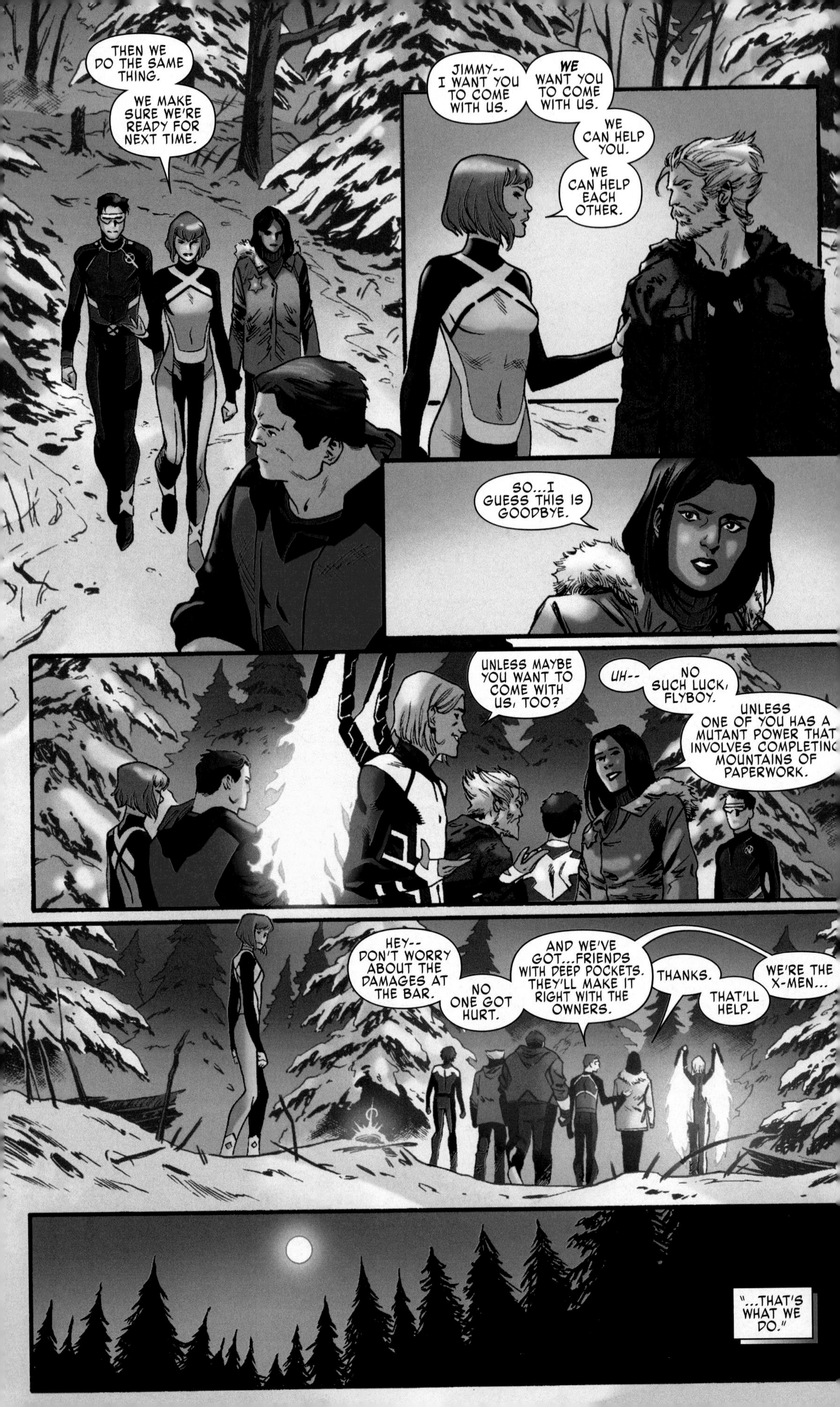

THEN WE DO THE SAME THING.
WE MAKE SURE WE'RE READY FOR NEXT TIME.
JIMMY-- I WANT YOU TO COME WITH US.
WE WANT YOU TO COME WITH US.
WE CAN HELP YOU.
WE CAN HELP EACH OTHER.
SO...I GUESS THIS IS GOODBYE.
UNLESS MAYBE YOU WANT TO COME WITH US, TOO?
UH--
NO SUCH LUCK, FLYBOY.
UNLESS ONE OF YOU HAS A MUTANT POWER THAT INVOLVES COMPLETING MOUNTAINS OF PAPERWORK.
HEY-- DON'T WORRY ABOUT THE DAMAGES AT THE BAR.
NO ONE GOT HURT.
AND WE'VE GOT...FRIENDS WITH DEEP POCKETS. THEY'LL MAKE IT RIGHT WITH THE OWNERS.
THANKS.
THAT'LL HELP.
WE'RE THE X-MEN...
"...THAT'S WHAT WE DO."

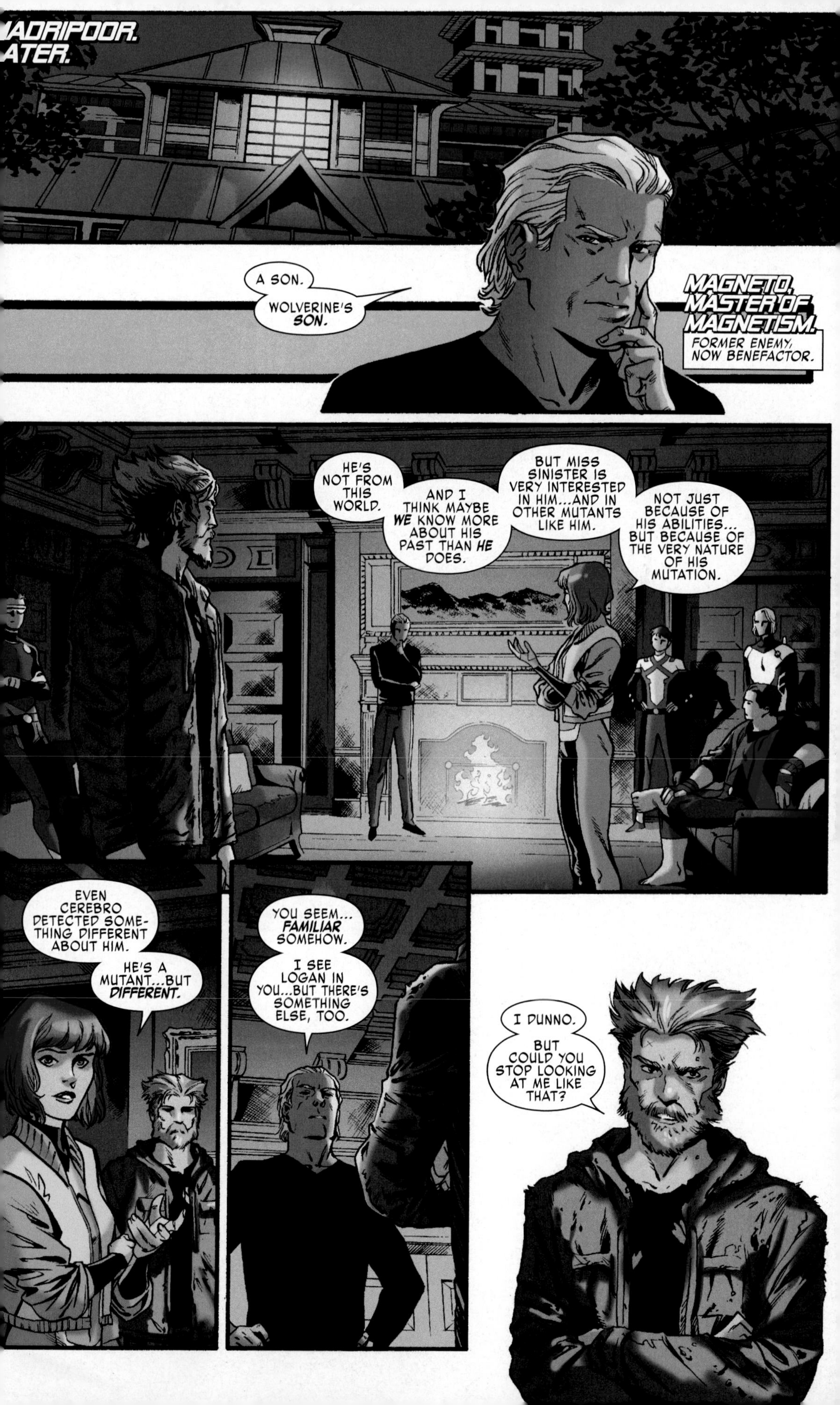
MADRIPOOR.
LATER.
A SON.
WOLVERINE'S SON.
MAGNETO, MASTER OF MAGNETISM.
FORMER ENEMY, NOW BENEFACTOR.
HE'S NOT FROM THIS WORLD.
AND I THINK MAYBE WE KNOW MORE ABOUT HIS PAST THAN HE DOES.
BUT MISS SINISTER IS VERY INTERESTED IN HIM...AND IN OTHER MUTANTS LIKE HIM.
NOT JUST BECAUSE OF HIS ABILITIES... BUT BECAUSE OF THE VERY NATURE OF HIS MUTATION.
EVEN CEREBRO DETECTED SOME-THING DIFFERENT ABOUT HIM.
HE'S A MUTANT...BUT DIFFERENT.
YOU SEEM... FAMILIAR SOMEHOW.
I SEE LOGAN IN YOU...BUT THERE'S SOMETHING ELSE, TOO.
I DUNNO.
BUT COULD YOU STOP LOOKING AT ME LIKE THAT?

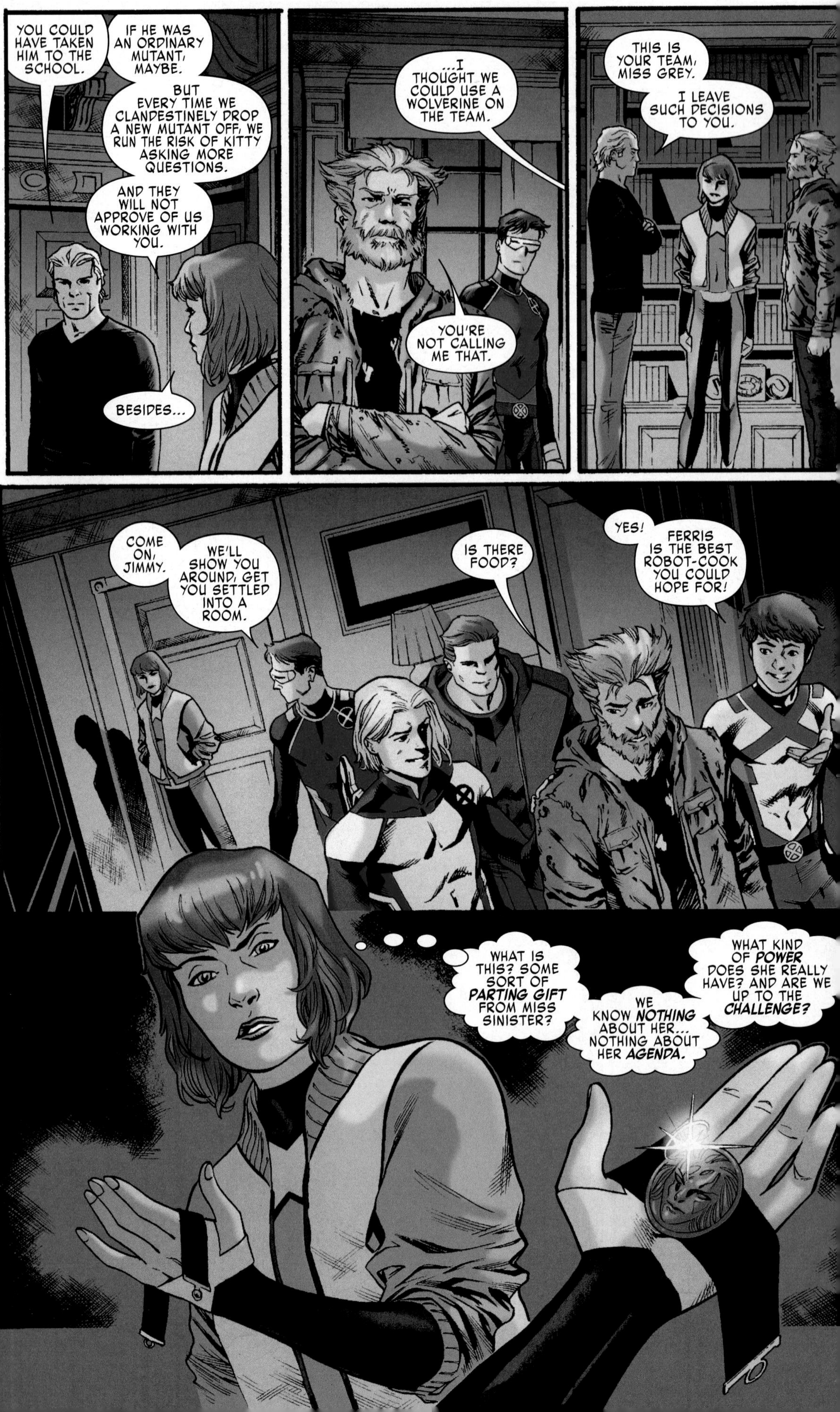

YOU COULD HAVE TAKEN HIM TO THE SCHOOL.
IF HE WAS AN ORDINARY MUTANT, MAYBE.
BUT EVERY TIME WE CLANDESTINELY DROP A NEW MUTANT OFF, WE RUN THE RISK OF KITTY ASKING MORE QUESTIONS.
AND THEY WILL NOT APPROVE OF US WORKING WITH YOU.
BESIDES...
...I THOUGHT WE COULD USE A WOLVERINE ON THE TEAM.
YOU'RE NOT CALLING ME THAT.
THIS IS YOUR TEAM, MISS GREY.
I LEAVE SUCH DECISIONS TO YOU.
COME ON, JIMMY.
WE'LL SHOW YOU AROUND, GET YOU SETTLED INTO A ROOM.
IS THERE FOOD?
YES!
FERRIS IS THE BEST ROBOT-COOK YOU COULD HOPE FOR!
WHAT IS THIS? SOME SORT OF PARTING GIFT FROM MISS SINISTER?
WE KNOW NOTHING ABOUT HER... NOTHING ABOUT HER AGENDA.
WHAT KIND OF POWER DOES SHE REALLY HAVE? AND ARE WE UP TO THE CHALLENGE?

#1 VARIANT BY **NEAL ADAMS** & **EDGAR DELGADO**

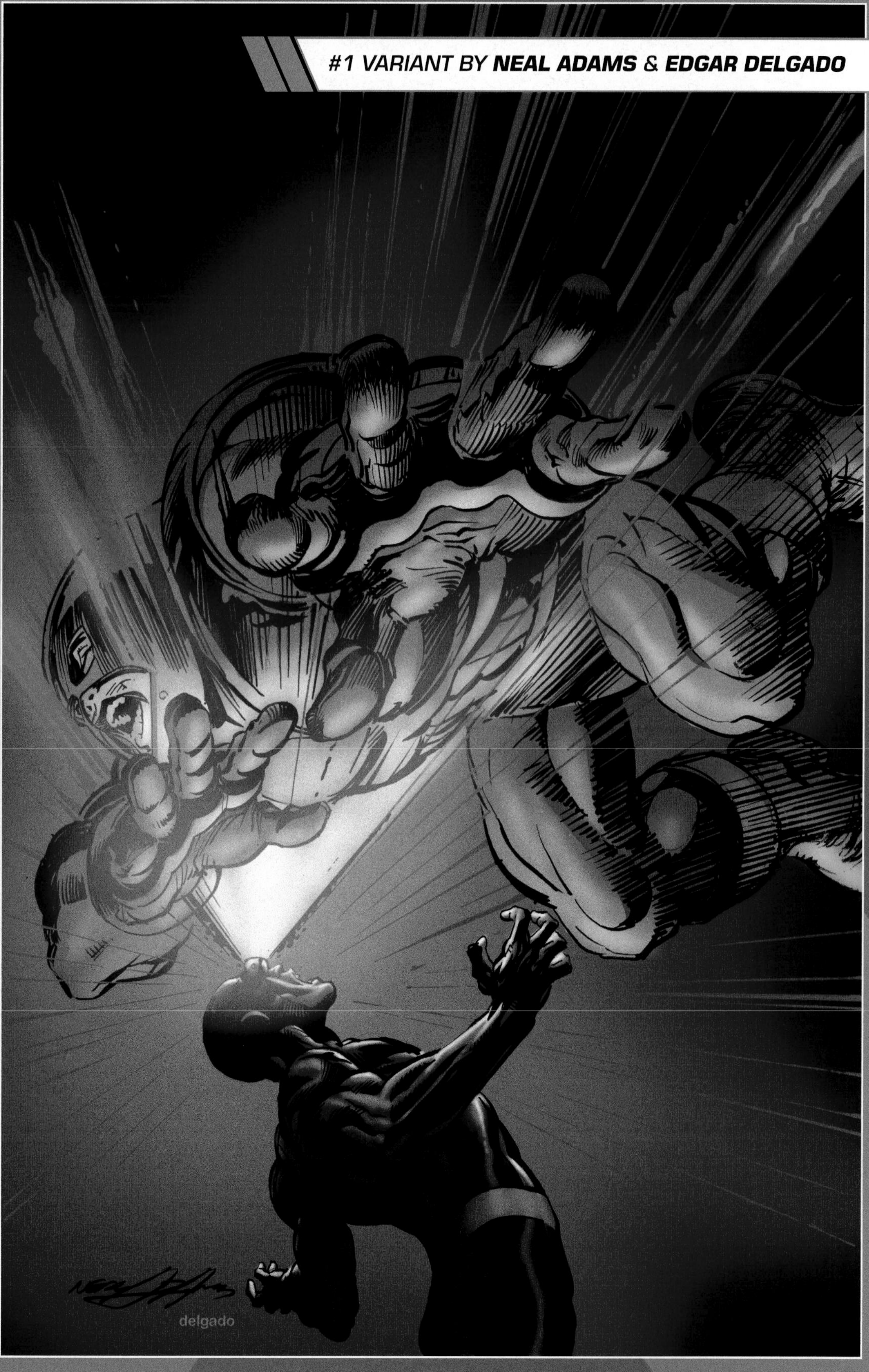

delgado

6

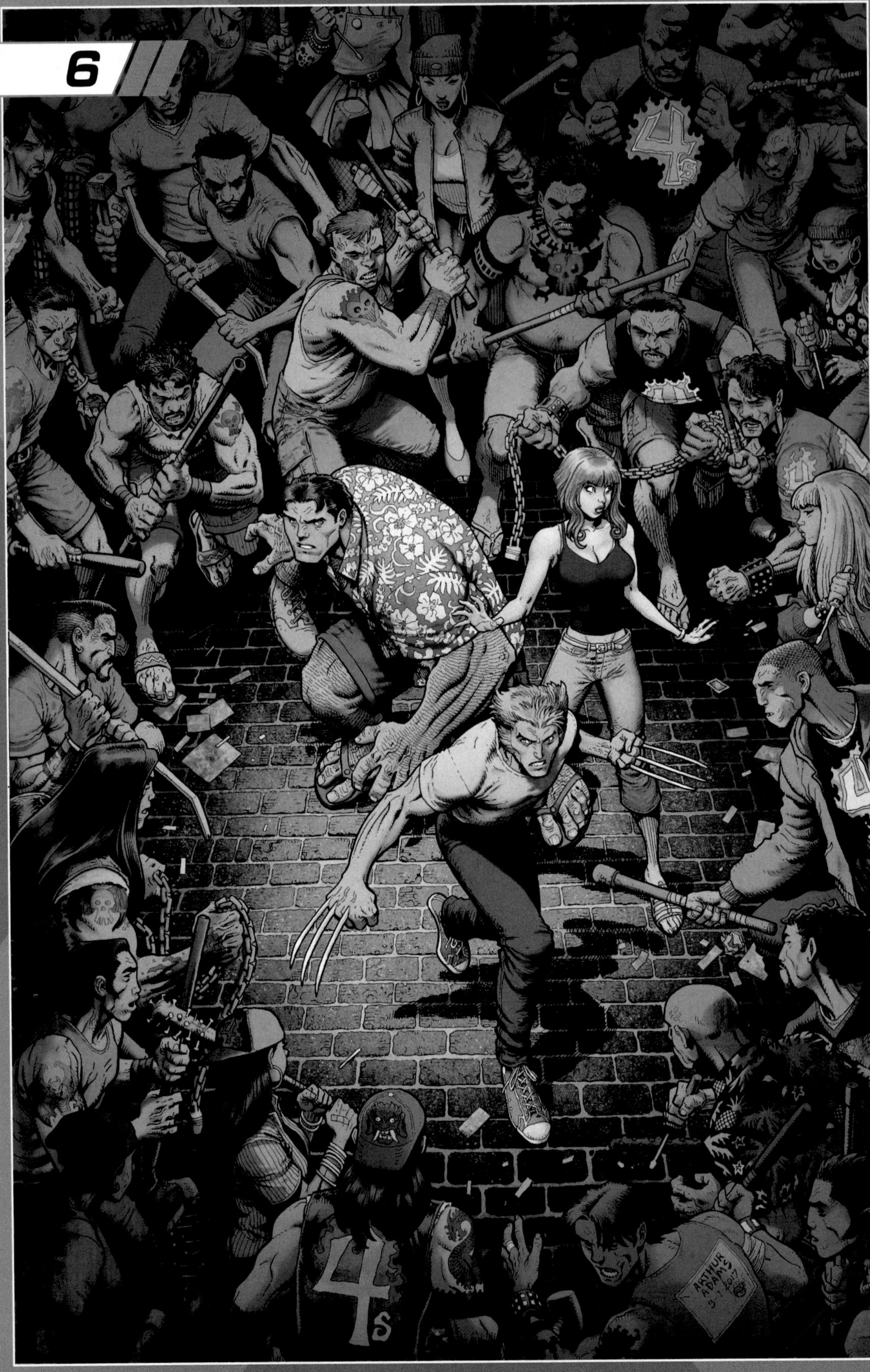
ARTHUR ADAMS

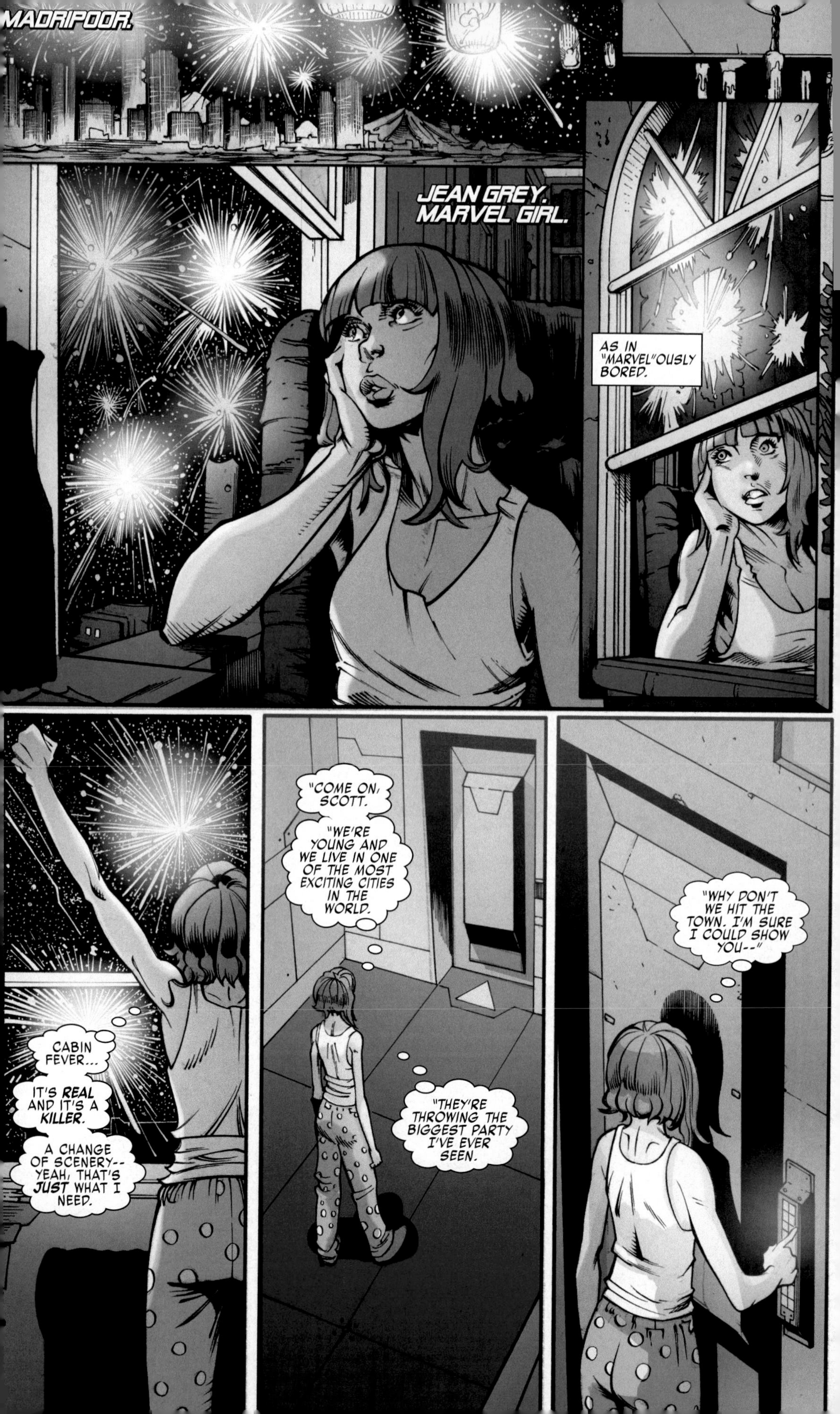
MADRIPOOR.
JEAN GREY. MARVEL GIRL.
AS IN "MARVEL"OUSLY BORED.
CABIN FEVER...
IT'S **REAL** AND IT'S A **KILLER**.
A CHANGE OF SCENERY-- YEAH, THAT'S **JUST** WHAT I NEED.
"COME ON, SCOTT.
"WE'RE YOUNG AND WE LIVE IN ONE OF THE MOST EXCITING CITIES IN THE WORLD.
"THEY'RE THROWING THE BIGGEST PARTY I'VE EVER SEEN.
"WHY DON'T WE HIT THE TOWN. I'M SURE I COULD SHOW YOU--"

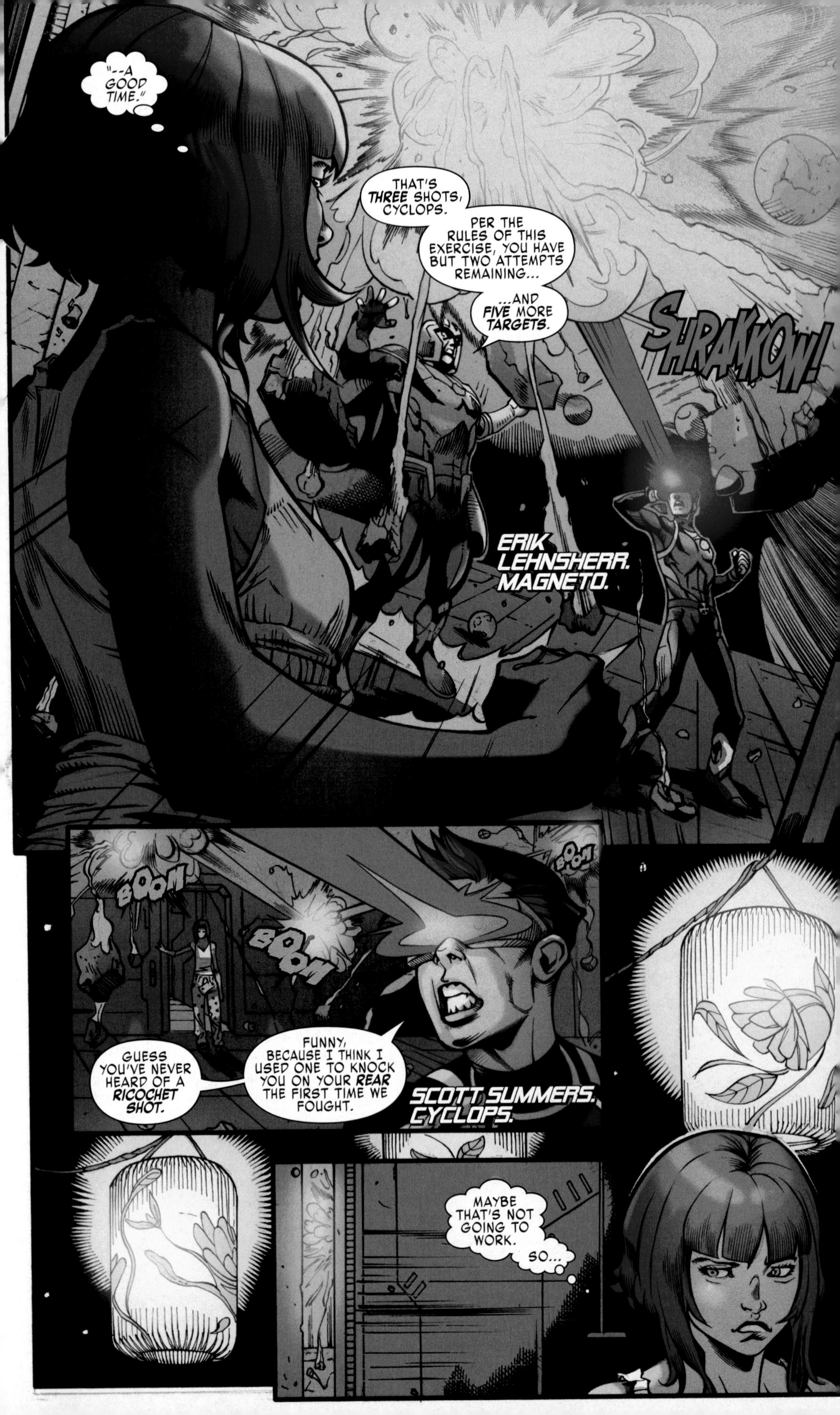
"--A GOOD TIME."
THAT'S THREE SHOTS, CYCLOPS.
PER THE RULES OF THIS EXERCISE, YOU HAVE BUT TWO ATTEMPTS REMAINING...
...AND FIVE MORE TARGETS.
SHRAKKOW!
ERIK LEHNSHERR. MAGNETO.
BOOM
BOOM
BOOM
GUESS YOU'VE NEVER HEARD OF A RICOCHET SHOT.
FUNNY, BECAUSE I THINK I USED ONE TO KNOCK YOU ON YOUR REAR THE FIRST TIME WE FOUGHT.
SCOTT SUMMERS. CYCLOPS.
MAYBE THAT'S NOT GOING TO WORK.
SO...

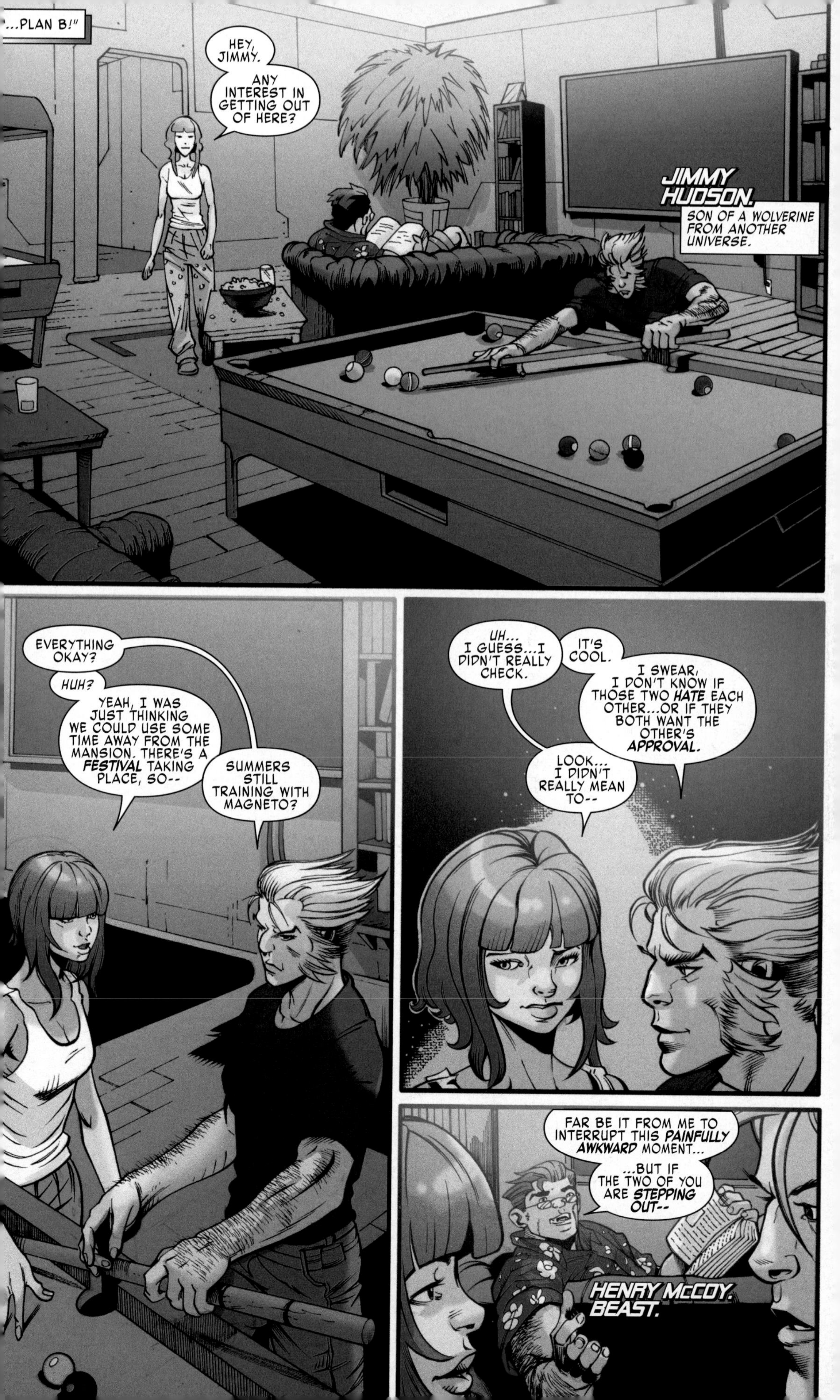
"...PLAN B!"
HEY, JIMMY.
ANY INTEREST IN GETTING OUT OF HERE?
JIMMY HUDSON.
SON OF A WOLVERINE FROM ANOTHER UNIVERSE.
EVERYTHING OKAY?
HUH?
YEAH, I WAS JUST THINKING WE COULD USE SOME TIME AWAY FROM THE MANSION. THERE'S A FESTIVAL TAKING PLACE, SO--
SUMMERS STILL TRAINING WITH MAGNETO?
UH... I GUESS...I DIDN'T REALLY CHECK.
IT'S COOL.
I SWEAR, I DON'T KNOW IF THOSE TWO HATE EACH OTHER...OR IF THEY BOTH WANT THE OTHER'S APPROVAL.
LOOK... I DIDN'T REALLY MEAN TO--
FAR BE IT FROM ME TO INTERRUPT THIS PAINFULLY AWKWARD MOMENT...
...BUT IF THE TWO OF YOU ARE STEPPING OUT--
HENRY McCOY. BEAST.

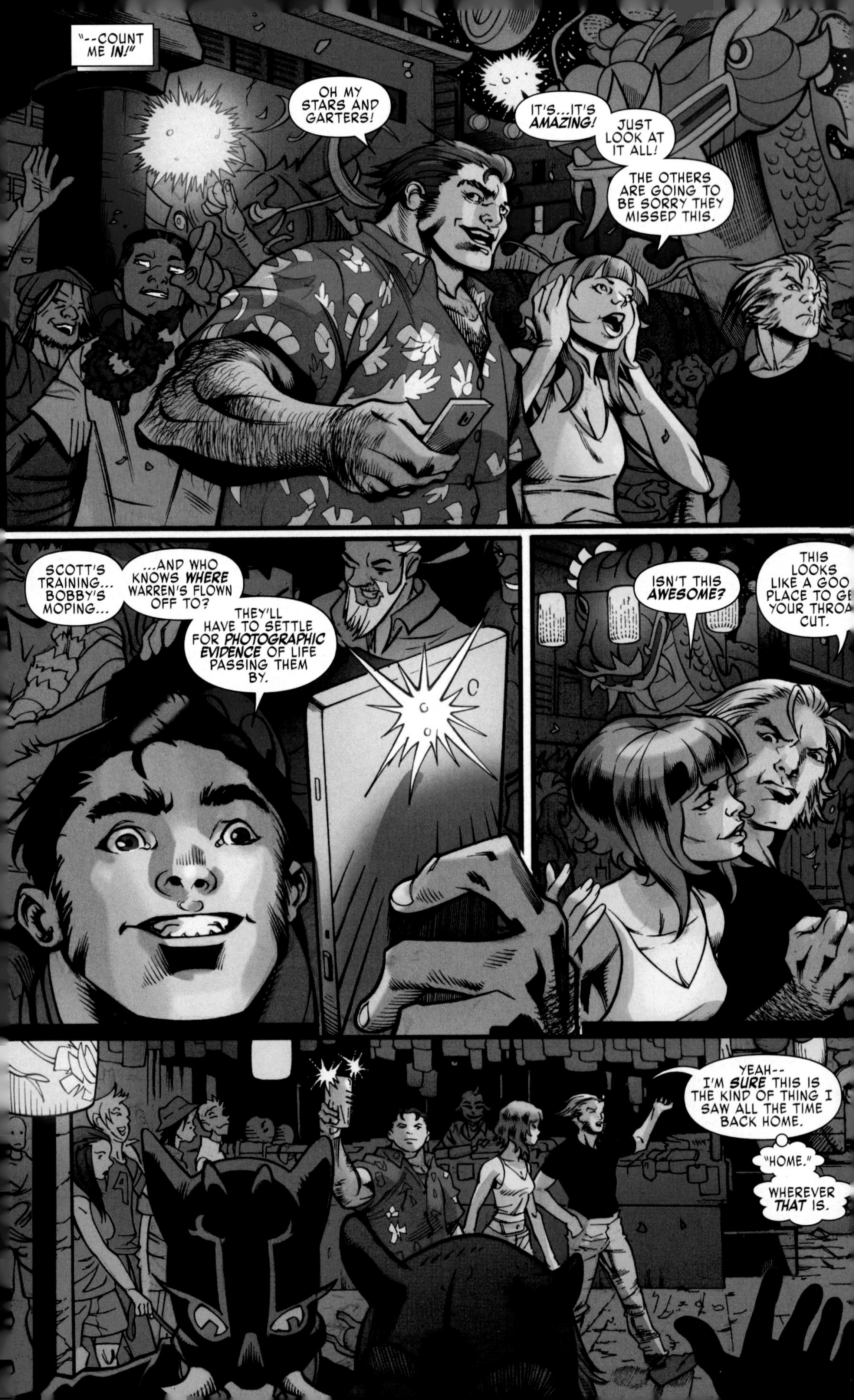
"--COUNT ME IN!"
OH MY STARS AND GARTERS!
IT'S...IT'S AMAZING!
JUST LOOK AT IT ALL!
THE OTHERS ARE GOING TO BE SORRY THEY MISSED THIS.
SCOTT'S TRAINING... BOBBY'S MOPING...
...AND WHO KNOWS WHERE WARREN'S FLOWN OFF TO?
THEY'LL HAVE TO SETTLE FOR PHOTOGRAPHIC EVIDENCE OF LIFE PASSING THEM BY.
ISN'T THIS AWESOME?
THIS LOOKS LIKE A GOO PLACE TO GE YOUR THROA CUT.
YEAH-- I'M SURE THIS IS THE KIND OF THING I SAW ALL THE TIME BACK HOME.
"HOME."
WHEREVER THAT IS.

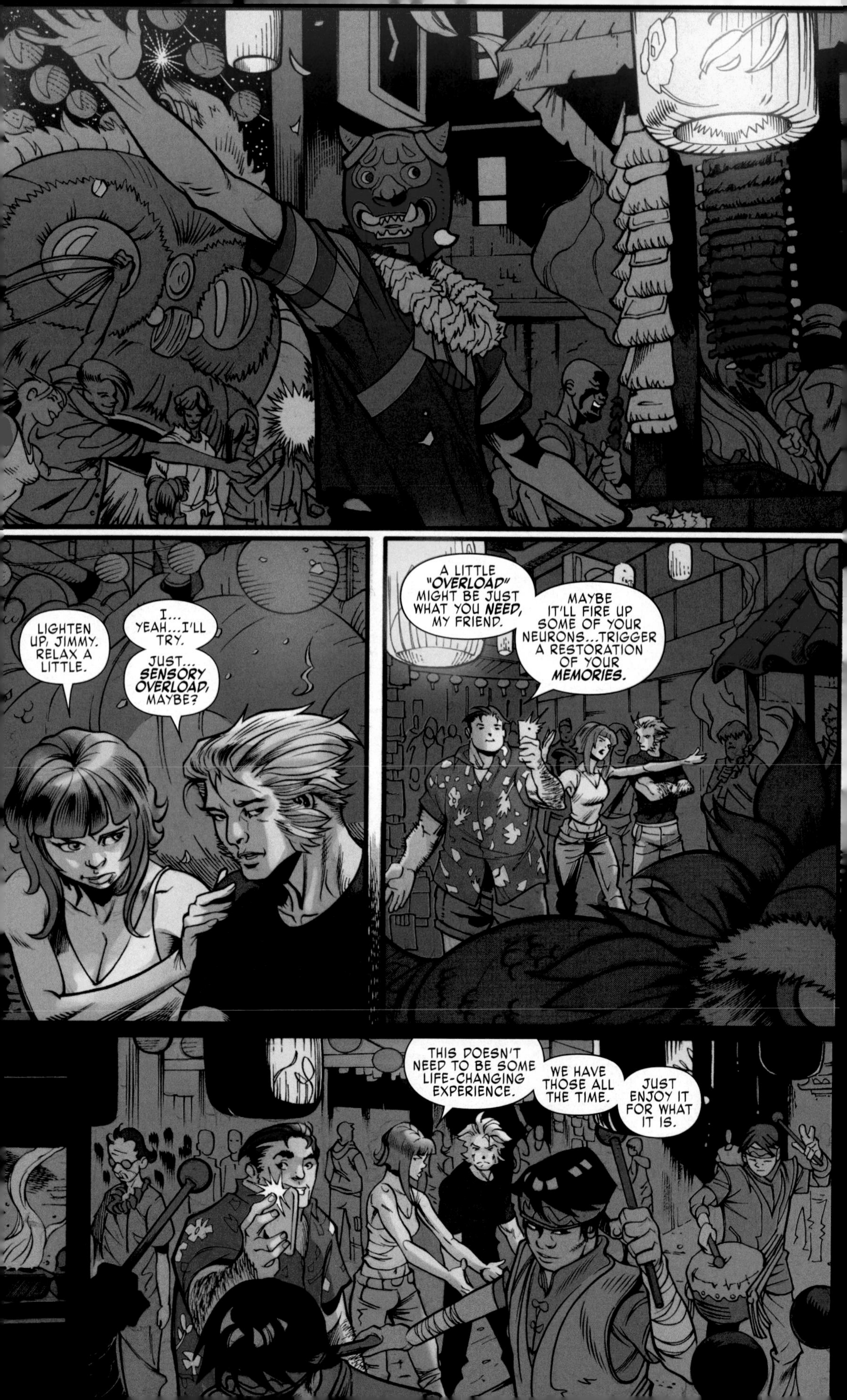
LIGHTEN UP, JIMMY. RELAX A LITTLE.
I... YEAH...I'LL TRY.
JUST... SENSORY OVERLOAD, MAYBE?
A LITTLE "OVERLOAD" MIGHT BE JUST WHAT YOU NEED, MY FRIEND.
MAYBE IT'LL FIRE UP SOME OF YOUR NEURONS...TRIGGER A RESTORATION OF YOUR MEMORIES.
THIS DOESN'T NEED TO BE SOME LIFE-CHANGING EXPERIENCE.
WE HAVE THOSE ALL THE TIME.
JUST ENJOY IT FOR WHAT IT IS.

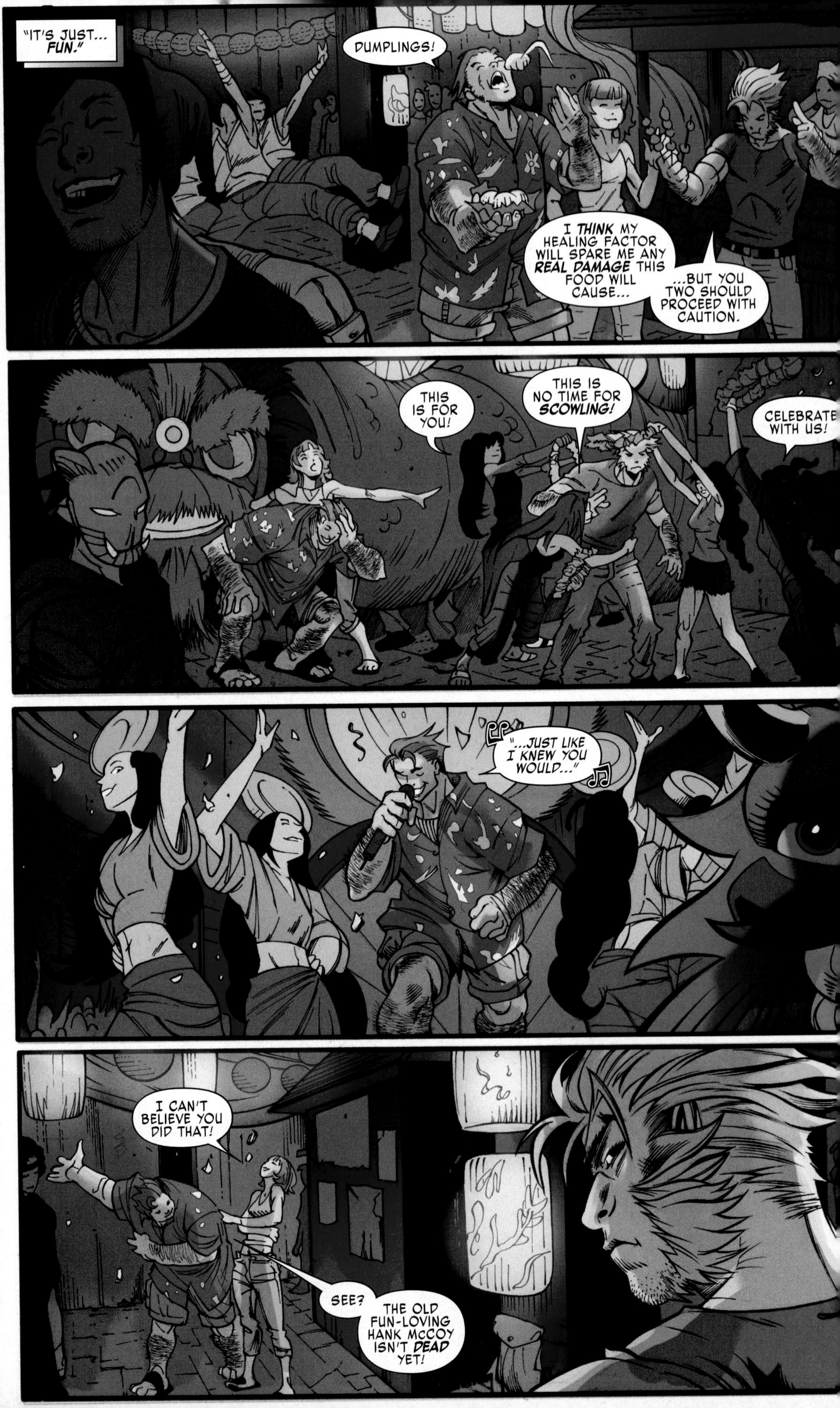
"IT'S JUST... FUN."
DUMPLINGS!
I THINK MY HEALING FACTOR WILL SPARE ME ANY REAL DAMAGE THIS FOOD WILL CAUSE...
...BUT YOU TWO SHOULD PROCEED WITH CAUTION.
THIS IS FOR YOU!
THIS IS NO TIME FOR SCOWLING!
CELEBRATE WITH US!
"...JUST LIKE I KNEW YOU WOULD..."
I CAN'T BELIEVE YOU DID THAT!
SEE?
THE OLD FUN-LOVING HANK McCOY ISN'T DEAD YET!

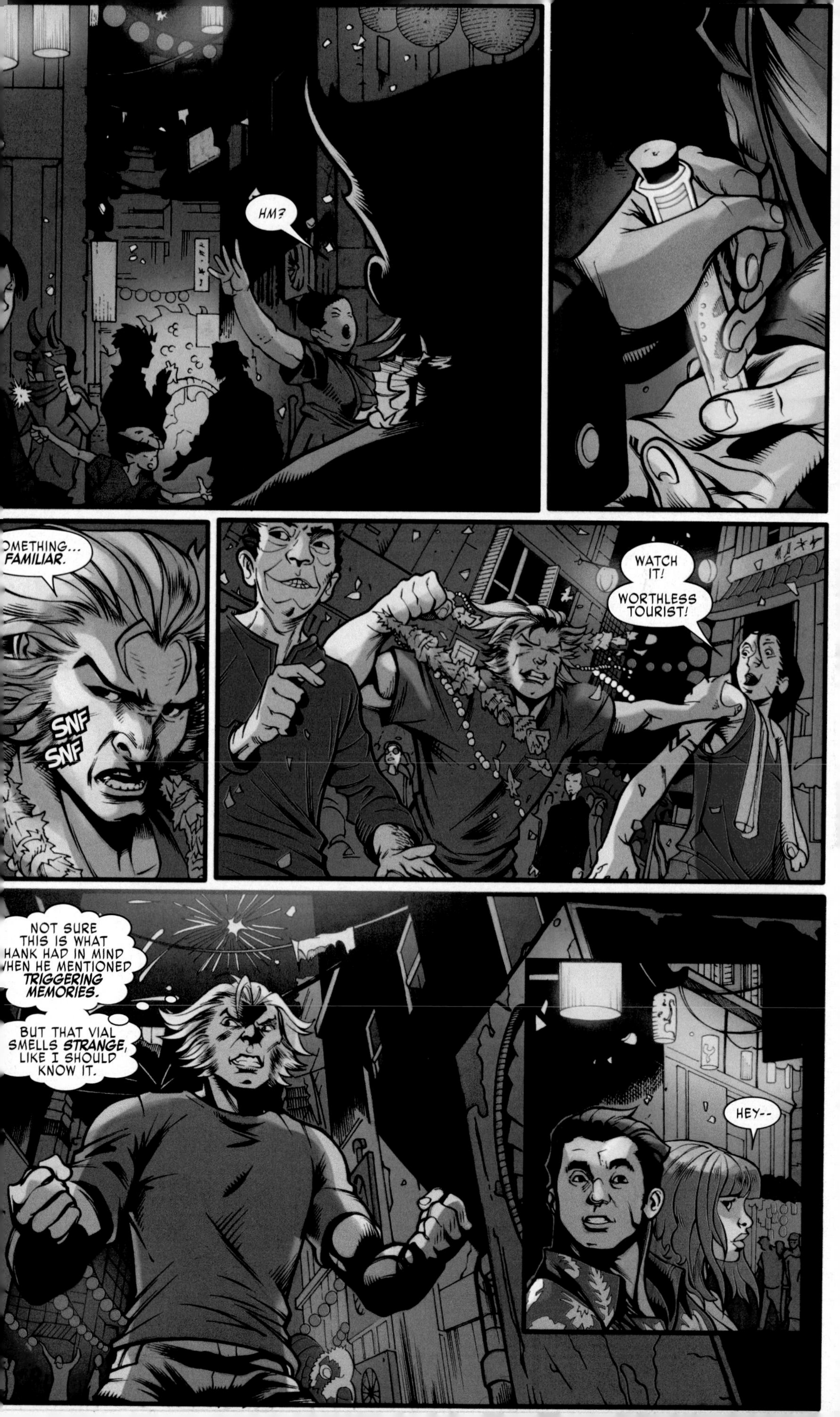
HM?
OMETHING... FAMILIAR.
SNF SNF
WATCH IT!
WORTHLESS TOURIST!
NOT SURE THIS IS WHAT HANK HAD IN MIND WHEN HE MENTIONED TRIGGERING MEMORIES.
BUT THAT VIAL SMELLS STRANGE, LIKE I SHOULD KNOW IT.
HEY--

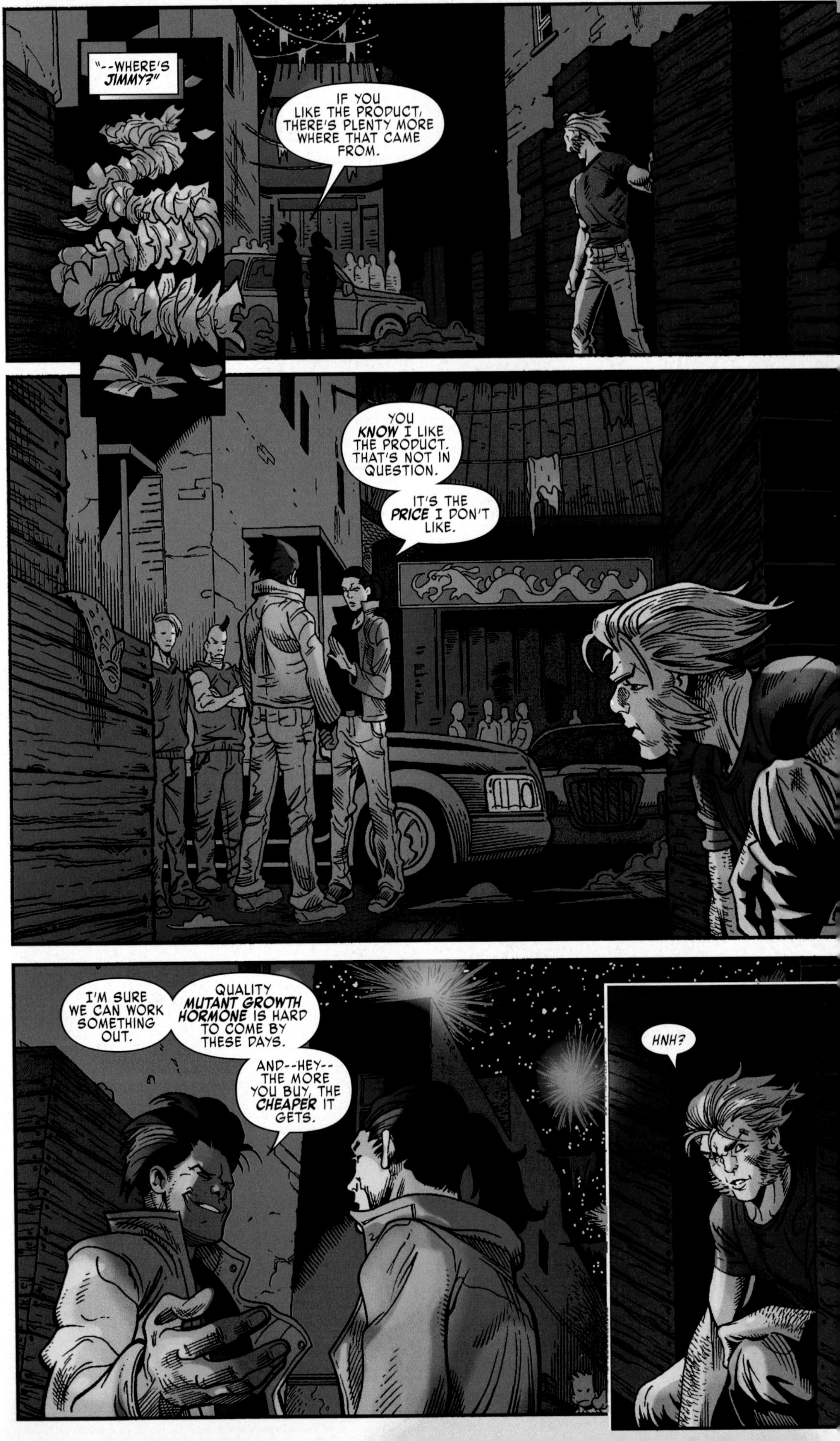
"--WHERE'S JIMMY?"
IF YOU LIKE THE PRODUCT, THERE'S PLENTY MORE WHERE THAT CAME FROM.
YOU KNOW I LIKE THE PRODUCT. THAT'S NOT IN QUESTION.
IT'S THE PRICE I DON'T LIKE.
I'M SURE WE CAN WORK SOMETHING OUT.
QUALITY MUTANT GROWTH HORMONE IS HARD TO COME BY THESE DAYS.
AND--HEY--THE MORE YOU BUY, THE CHEAPER IT GETS.
HNH?

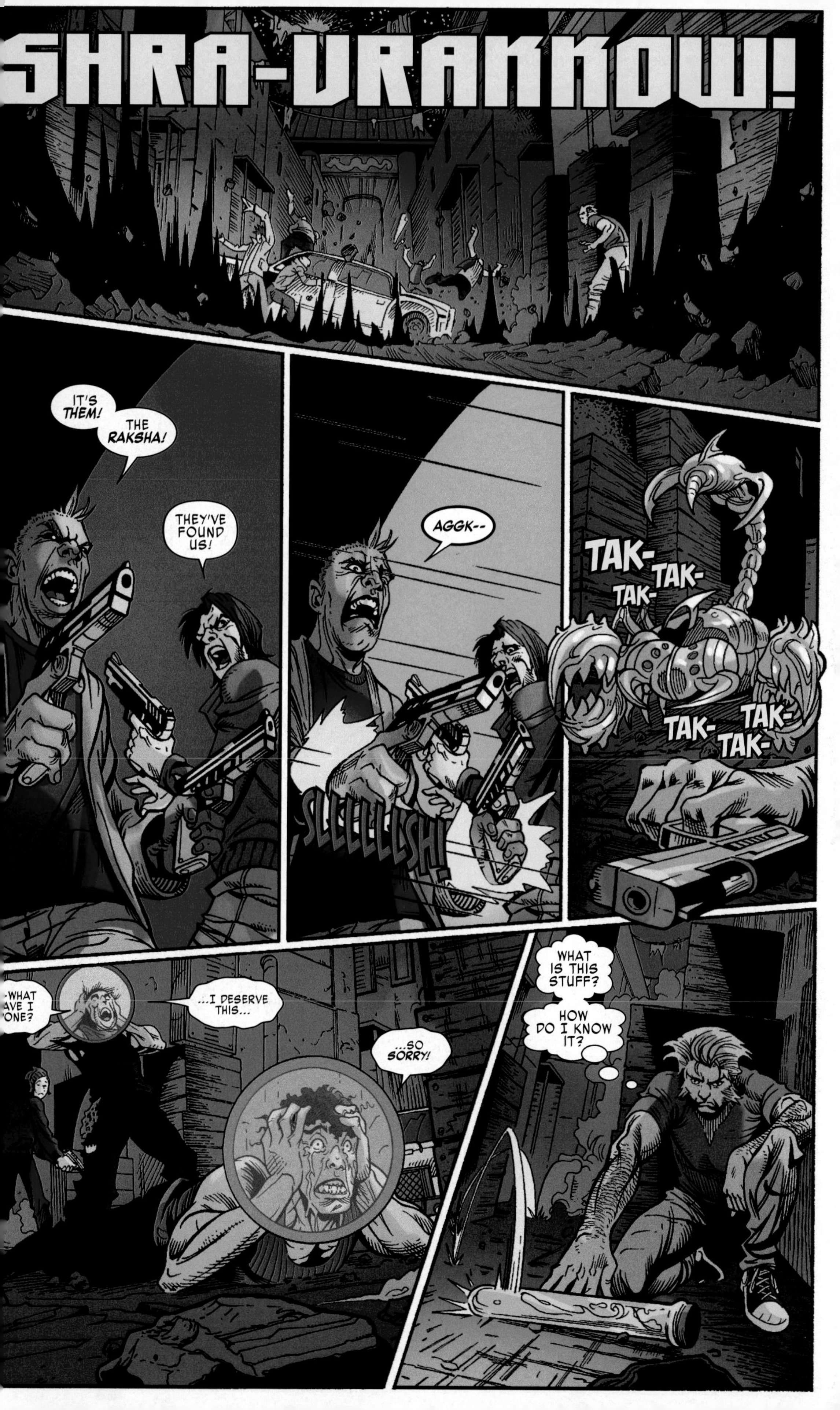
SHRA-VRAKKOW!
IT'S THEM!
THE RAKSHA!
THEY'VE FOUND US!
AGGK--
SLEEEEESH!
TAK-TAK-TAK-
TAK-TAK-TAK-
-WHAT AVE I ONE?
...I DESERVE THIS...
...SO SORRY!
WHAT IS THIS STUFF?
HOW DO I KNOW IT?

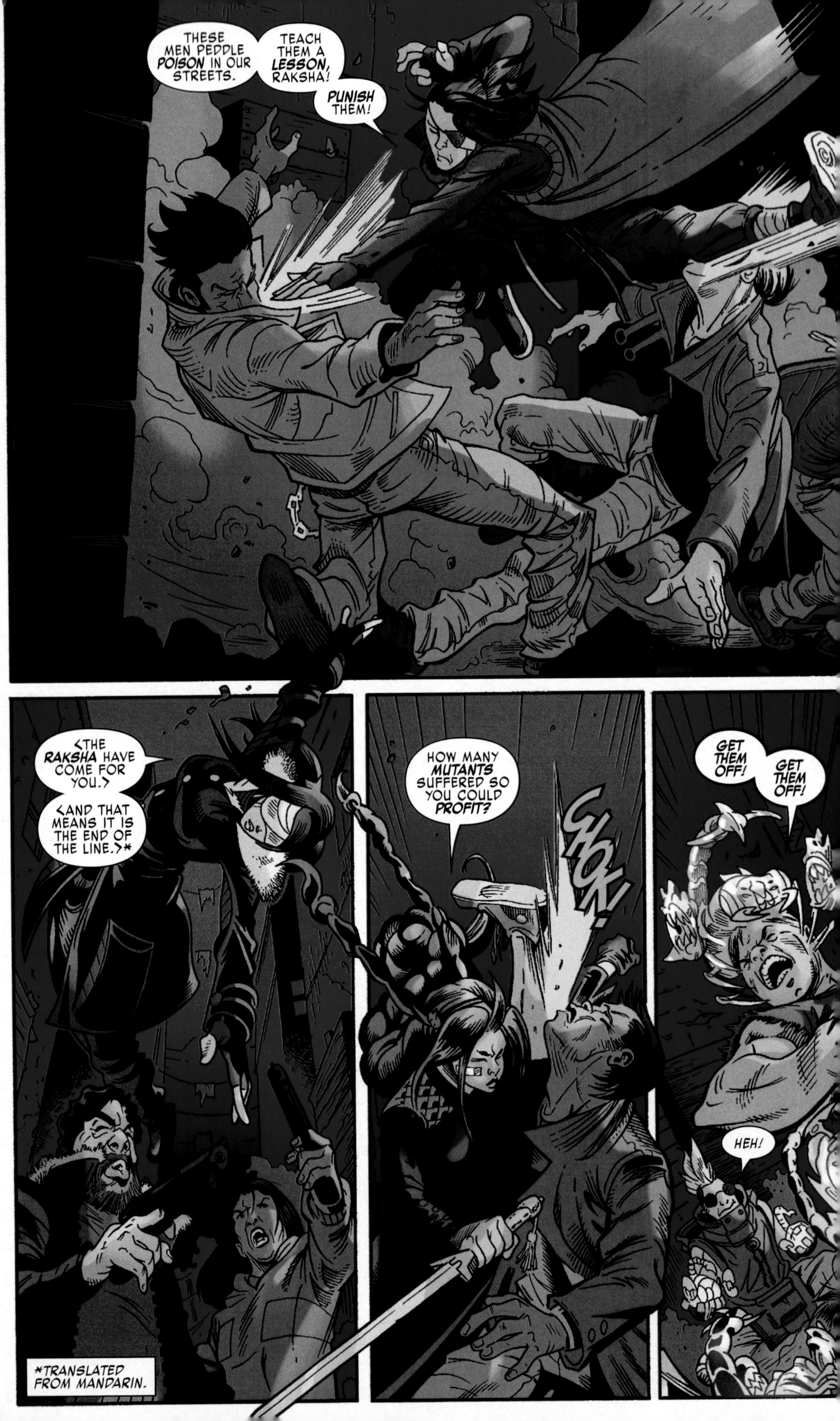
THESE MEN PEDDLE POISON IN OUR STREETS.
TEACH THEM A LESSON, RAKSHA!
PUNISH THEM!
<THE RAKSHA HAVE COME FOR YOU.>
<AND THAT MEANS IT IS THE END OF THE LINE.>*
*TRANSLATED FROM MANDARIN.
HOW MANY MUTANTS SUFFERED SO YOU COULD PROFIT?
CHOK!
GET THEM OFF!
GET THEM OFF!
HEH!

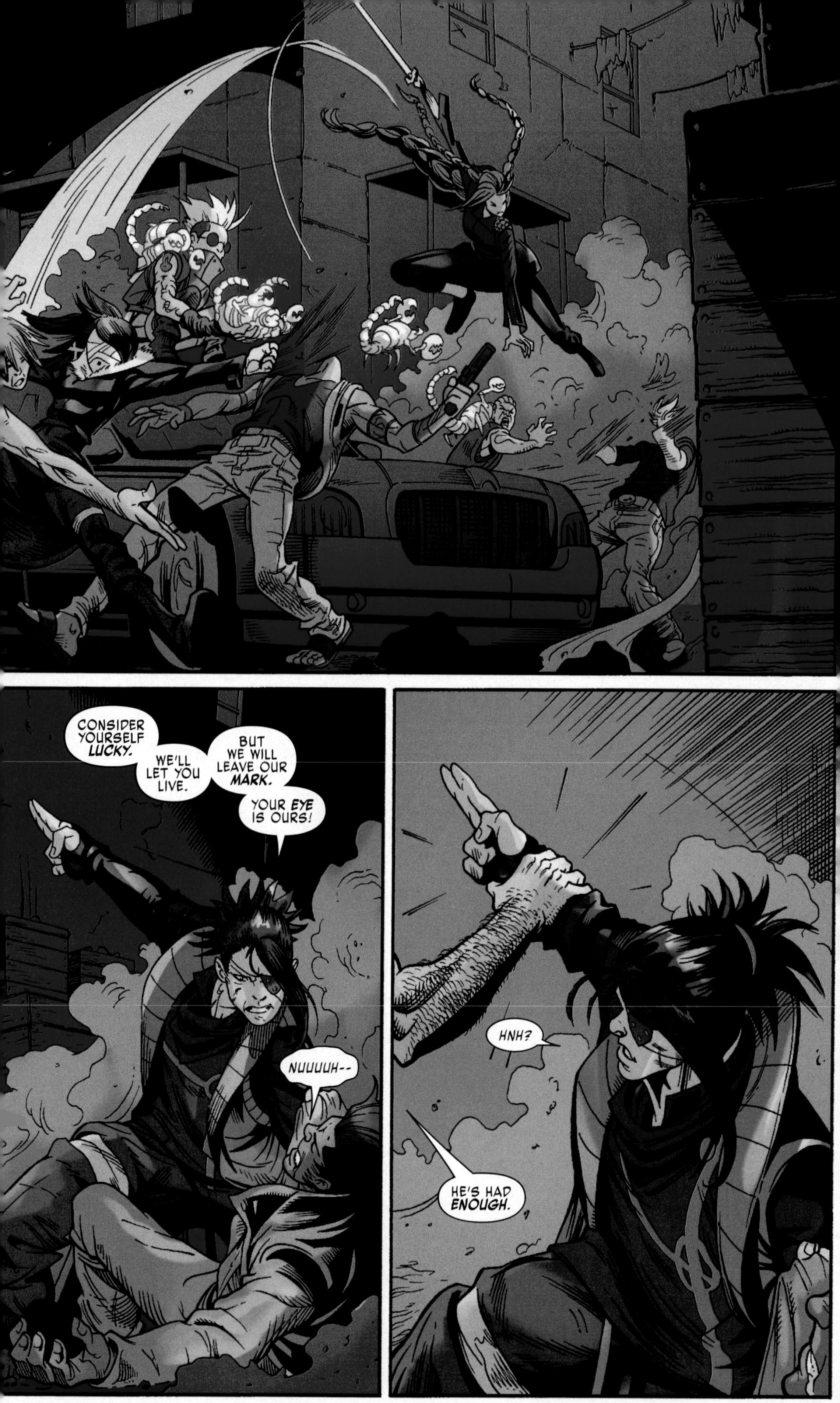
CONSIDER YOURSELF LUCKY.
WE'LL LET YOU LIVE.
BUT WE WILL LEAVE OUR MARK.
YOUR EYE IS OURS!
NUUUUH--
HNH?
HE'S HAD ENOUGH.

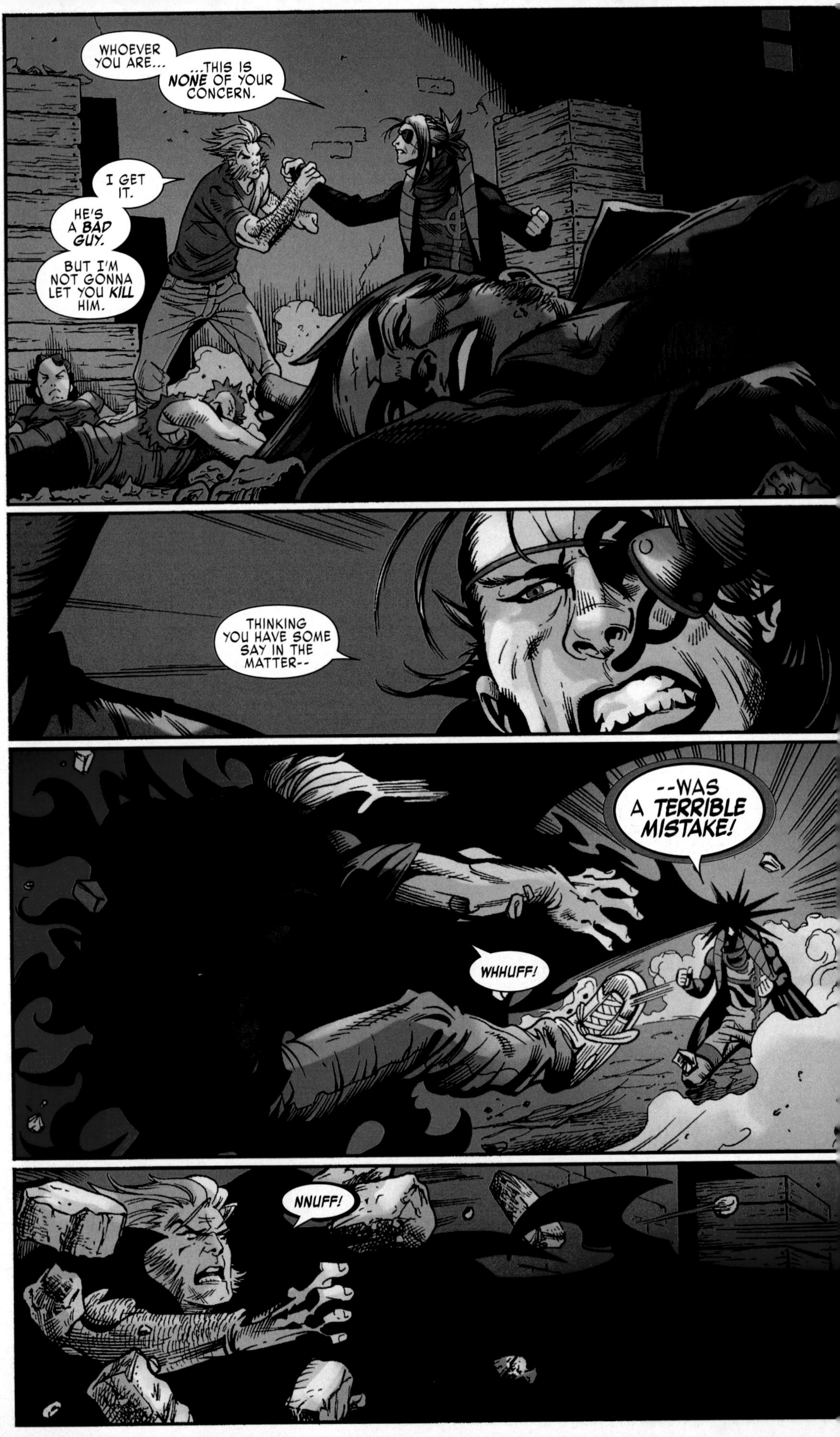
WHOEVER YOU ARE...
...THIS IS NONE OF YOUR CONCERN.
I GET IT.
HE'S A BAD GUY.
BUT I'M NOT GONNA LET YOU KILL HIM.
THINKING YOU HAVE SOME SAY IN THE MATTER--
--WAS A TERRIBLE MISTAKE!
WHHUFF!
NNUFF!

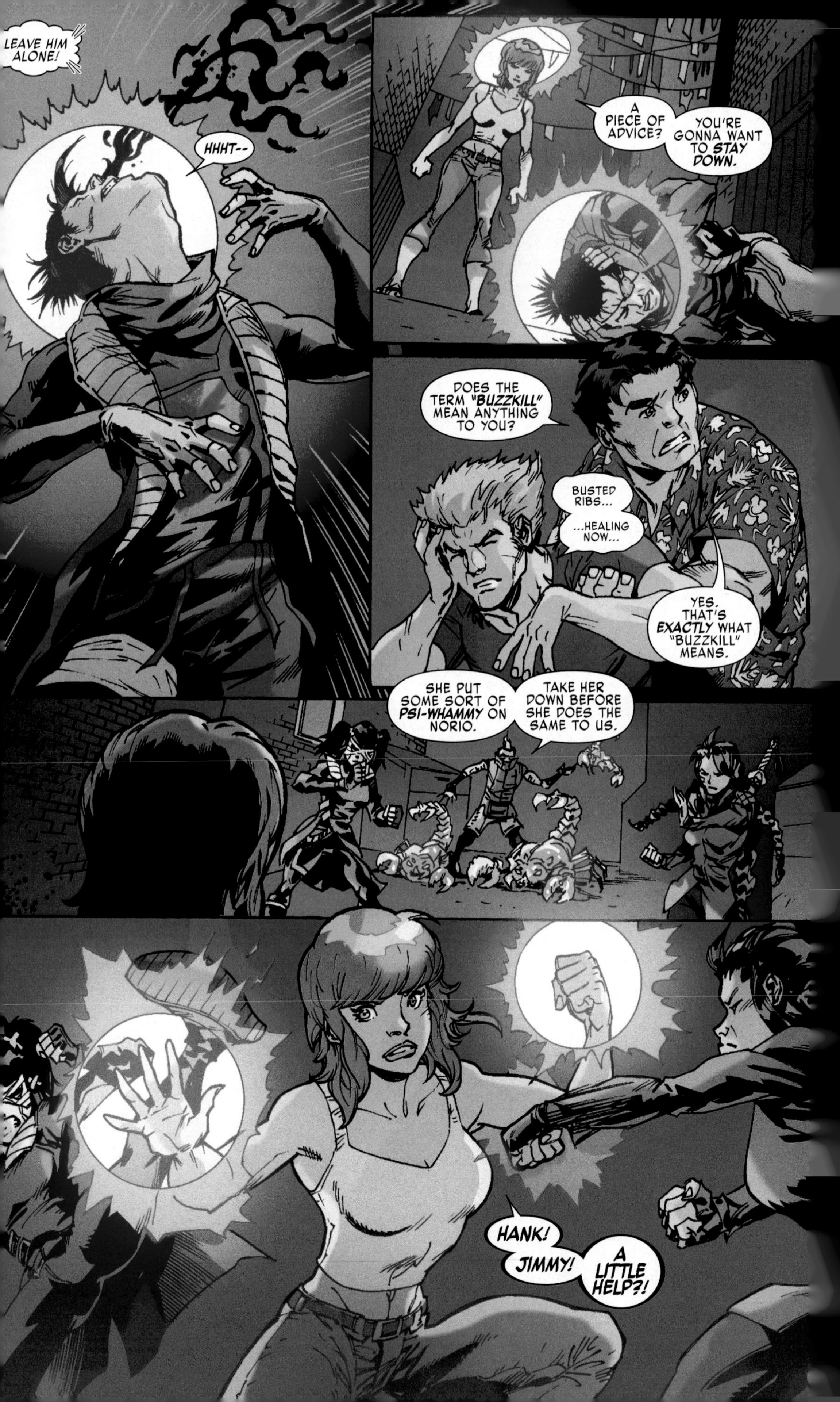
LEAVE HIM ALONE!
HHHT--
A PIECE OF ADVICE?
YOU'RE GONNA WANT TO STAY DOWN.
DOES THE TERM "BUZZKILL" MEAN ANYTHING TO YOU?
BUSTED RIBS...
...HEALING NOW...
YES. THAT'S EXACTLY WHAT "BUZZKILL" MEANS.
SHE PUT SOME SORT OF PSI-WHAMMY ON NORIO.
TAKE HER DOWN BEFORE SHE DOES THE SAME TO US.
HANK!
JIMMY!
A LITTLE HELP?!

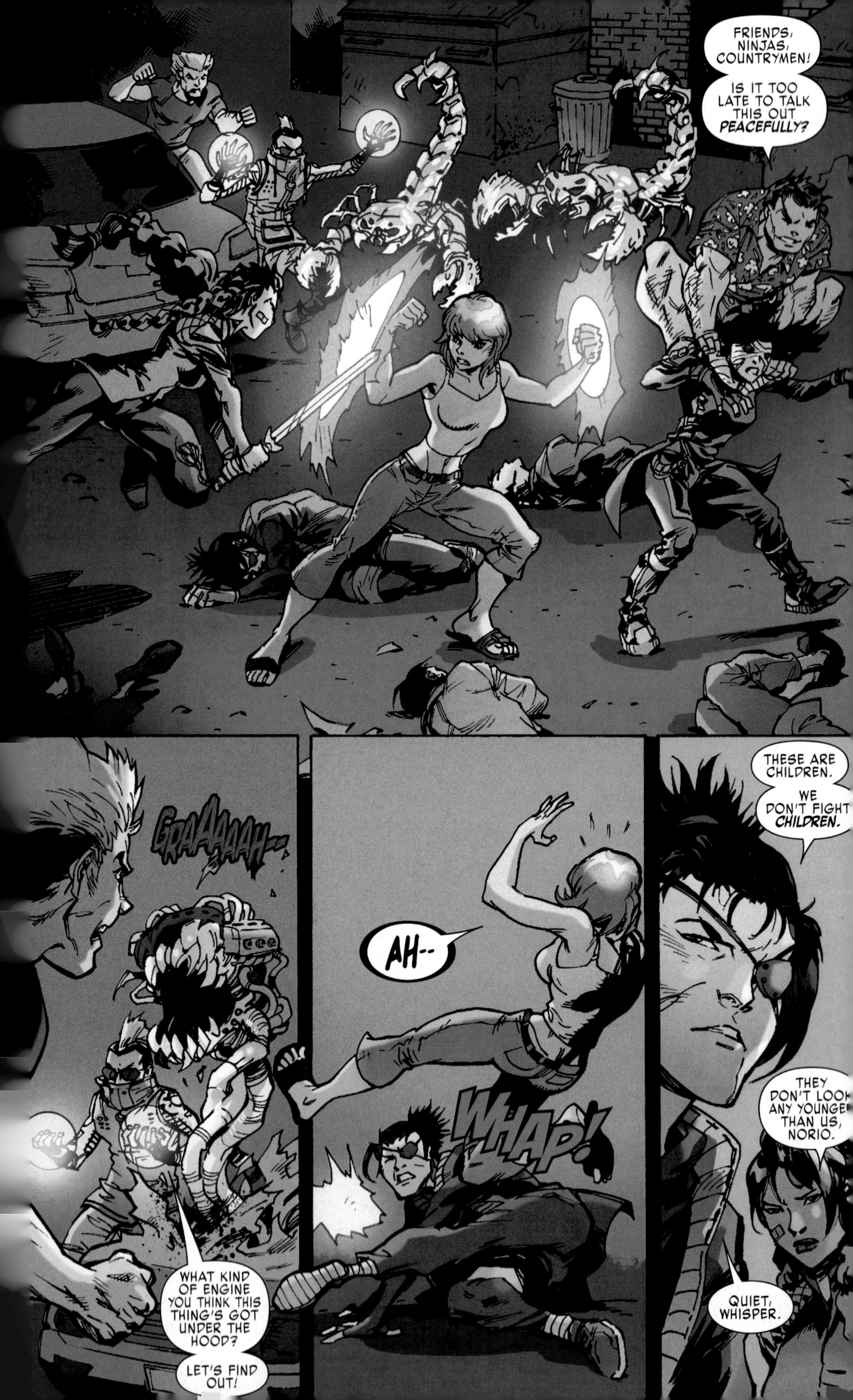

FRIENDS, NINJAS, COUNTRYMEN!
IS IT TOO LATE TO TALK THIS OUT PEACEFULLY?
GRAAAAAH--
WHAT KIND OF ENGINE YOU THINK THIS THING'S GOT UNDER THE HOOD?
LET'S FIND OUT!
AH--
WHAP!
THESE ARE CHILDREN.
WE DON'T FIGHT CHILDREN.
THEY DON'T LOOK ANY YOUNGE THAN US, NORIO.
QUIET, WHISPER.

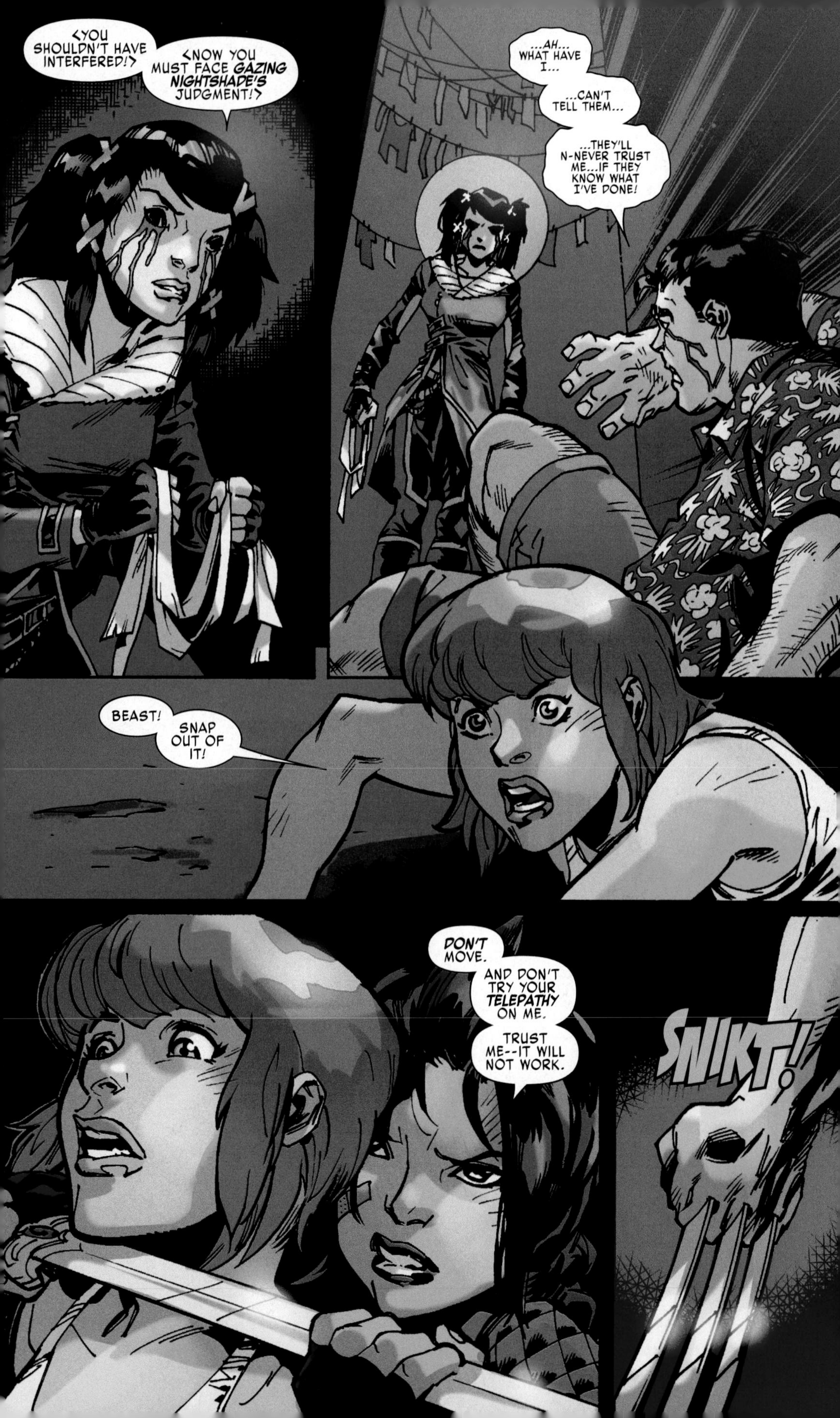

<YOU SHOULDN'T HAVE INTERFERED!>
<NOW YOU MUST FACE GAZING NIGHTSHADE'S JUDGMENT!>
...AH... WHAT HAVE I...
...CAN'T TELL THEM...
...THEY'LL N-NEVER TRUST ME...IF THEY KNOW WHAT I'VE DONE!
BEAST!
SNAP OUT OF IT!
DON'T MOVE.
AND DON'T TRY YOUR TELEPATHY ON ME.
TRUST ME--IT WILL NOT WORK.
SNIKT!!

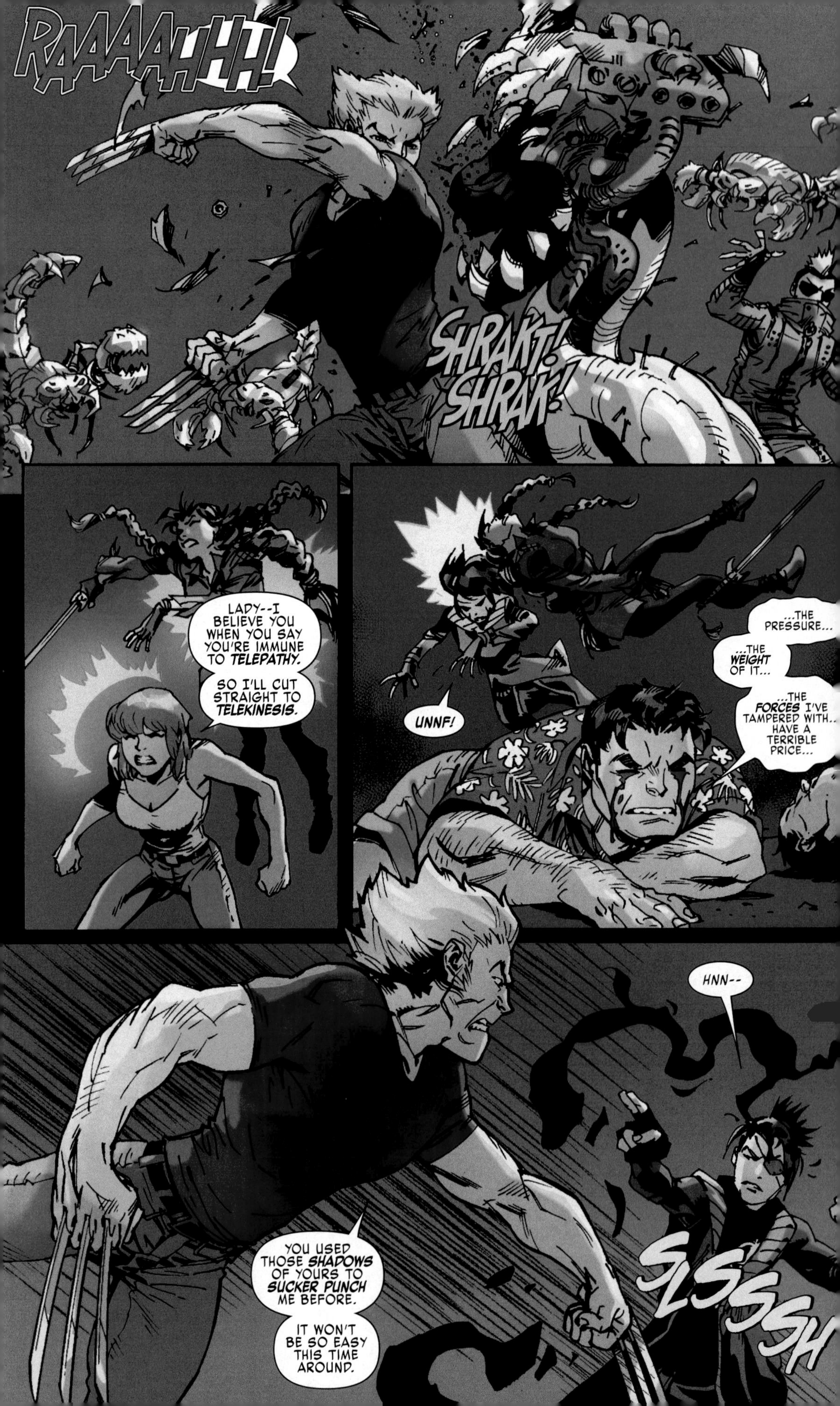
RAAAAHHH!
SHRAKT! SHRAK!
LADY--I BELIEVE YOU WHEN YOU SAY YOU'RE IMMUNE TO TELEPATHY.
SO I'LL CUT STRAIGHT TO TELEKINESIS.
UNNF!
...THE PRESSURE...
...THE WEIGHT OF IT...
...THE FORCES I'VE TAMPERED WITH... HAVE A TERRIBLE PRICE...
HNN--
YOU USED THOSE SHADOWS OF YOURS TO SUCKER PUNCH ME BEFORE.
IT WON'T BE SO EASY THIS TIME AROUND.
SLSSSH

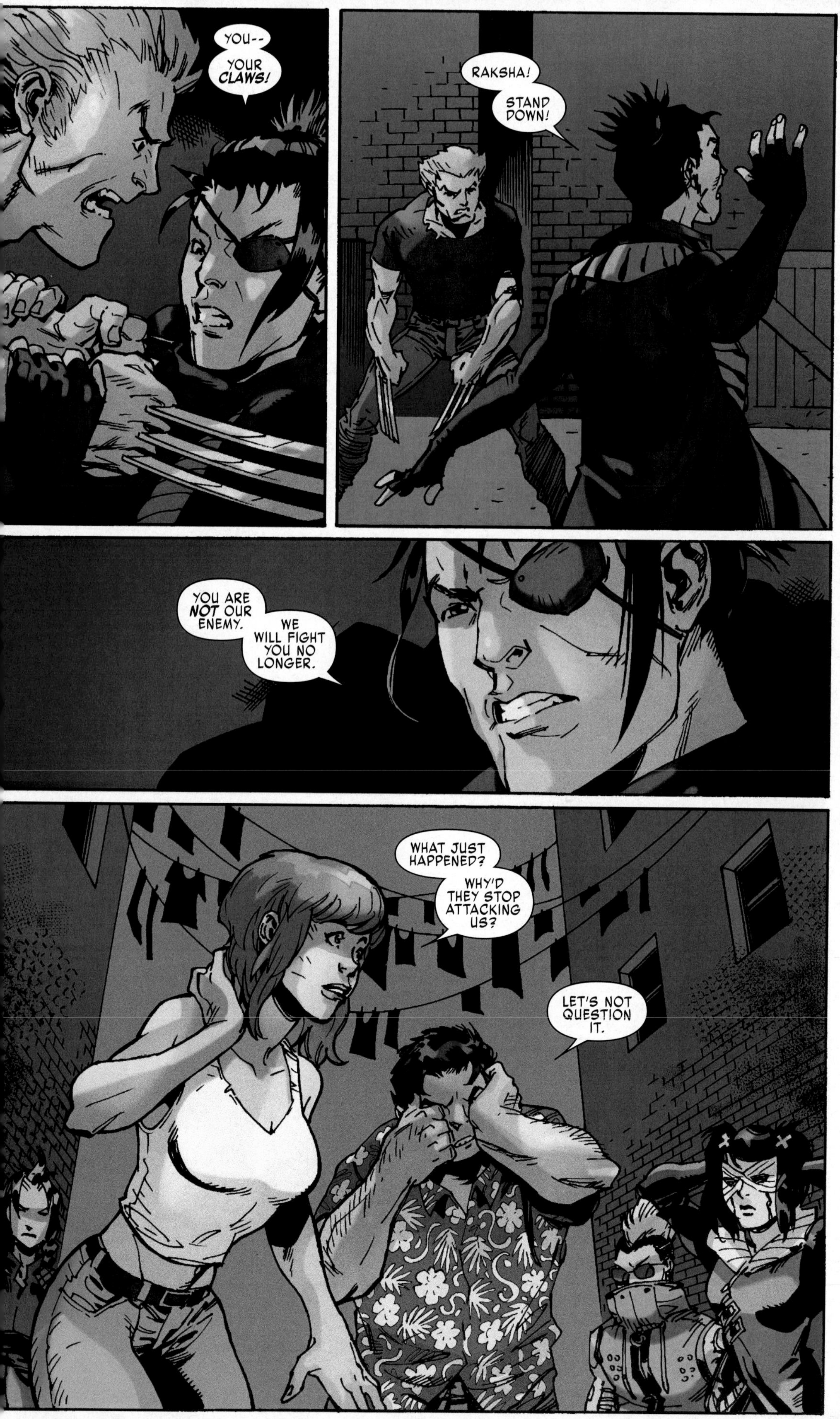
YOU--
YOUR CLAWS!
RAKSHA!
STAND DOWN!
YOU ARE NOT OUR ENEMY.
WE WILL FIGHT YOU NO LONGER.
WHAT JUST HAPPENED?
WHY'D THEY STOP ATTACKING US?
LET'S NOT QUESTION IT.

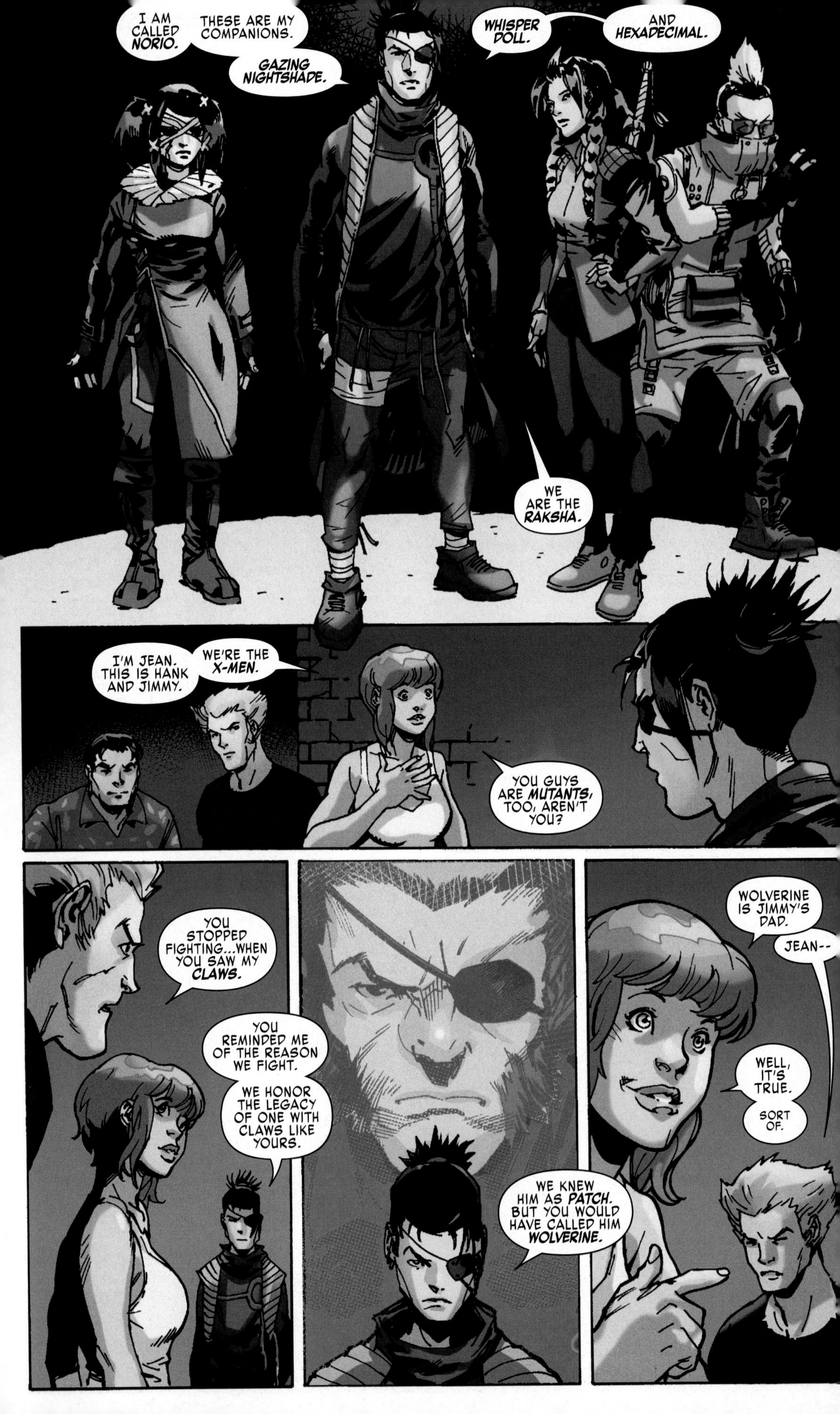
I AM CALLED NORIO.
THESE ARE MY COMPANIONS.
GAZING NIGHTSHADE.
WHISPER DOLL.
AND HEXADECIMAL.
WE ARE THE RAKSHA.
I'M JEAN. THIS IS HANK AND JIMMY.
WE'RE THE X-MEN.
YOU GUYS ARE MUTANTS, TOO, AREN'T YOU?
YOU STOPPED FIGHTING...WHEN YOU SAW MY CLAWS.
YOU REMINDED ME OF THE REASON WE FIGHT.
WE HONOR THE LEGACY OF ONE WITH CLAWS LIKE YOURS.
WE KNEW HIM AS PATCH. BUT YOU WOULD HAVE CALLED HIM WOLVERINE.
WOLVERINE IS JIMMY'S DAD.
JEAN--
WELL, IT'S TRUE.
SORT OF.

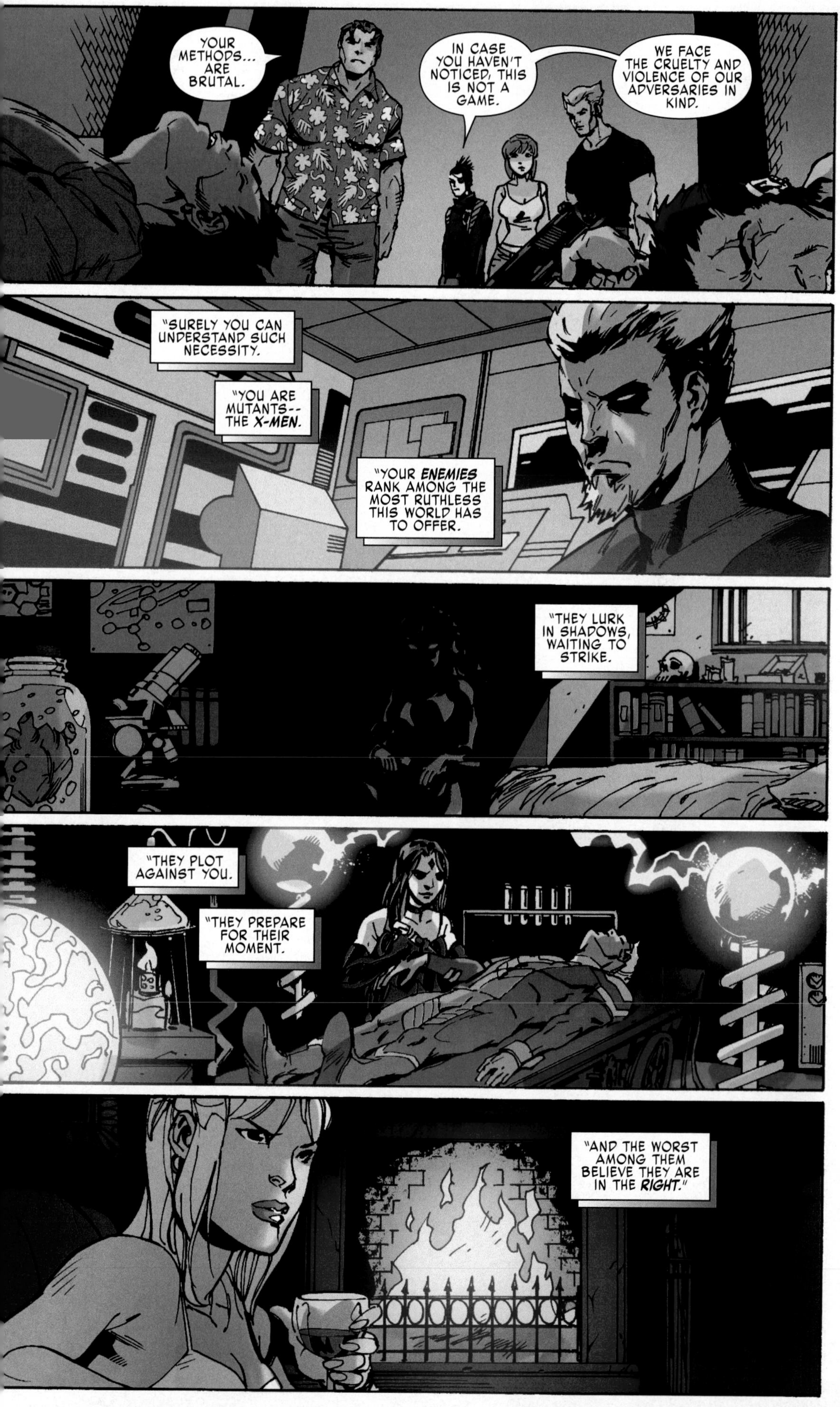
YOUR METHODS... ARE BRUTAL.
IN CASE YOU HAVEN'T NOTICED, THIS IS NOT A GAME.
WE FACE THE CRUELTY AND VIOLENCE OF OUR ADVERSARIES IN KIND.
"SURELY YOU CAN UNDERSTAND SUCH NECESSITY.
"YOU ARE MUTANTS--THE X-MEN.
"YOUR ENEMIES RANK AMONG THE MOST RUTHLESS THIS WORLD HAS TO OFFER.
"THEY LURK IN SHADOWS, WAITING TO STRIKE.
"THEY PLOT AGAINST YOU.
"THEY PREPARE FOR THEIR MOMENT.
"AND THE WORST AMONG THEM BELIEVE THEY ARE IN THE RIGHT."

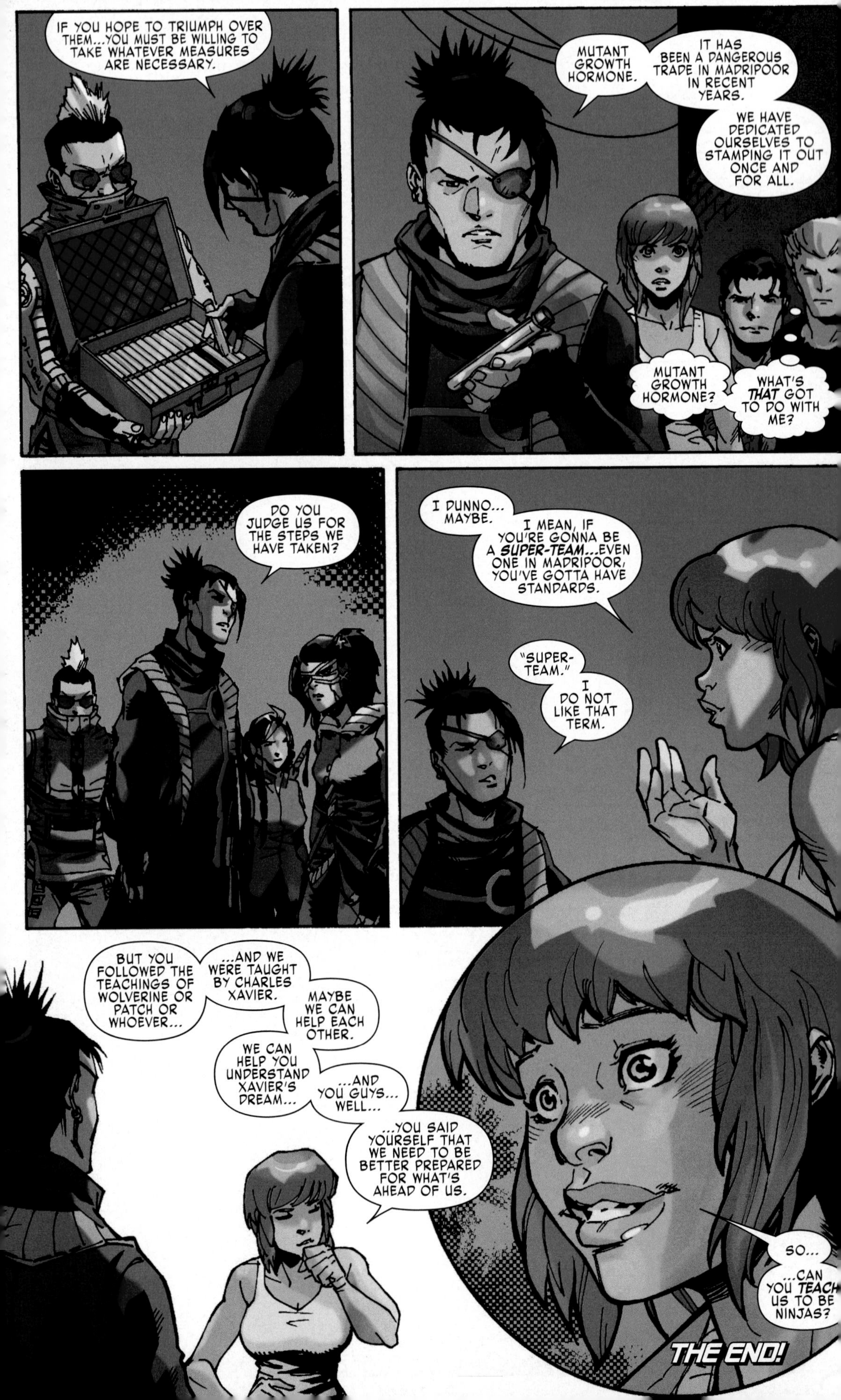
IF YOU HOPE TO TRIUMPH OVER THEM...YOU MUST BE WILLING TO TAKE WHATEVER MEASURES ARE NECESSARY.
MUTANT GROWTH HORMONE.
IT HAS BEEN A DANGEROUS TRADE IN MADRIPOOR IN RECENT YEARS.
WE HAVE DEDICATED OURSELVES TO STAMPING IT OUT ONCE AND FOR ALL.
MUTANT GROWTH HORMONE?
WHAT'S *THAT* GOT TO DO WITH ME?
DO YOU JUDGE US FOR THE STEPS WE HAVE TAKEN?
I DUNNO... MAYBE.
I MEAN, IF YOU'RE GONNA BE A *SUPER-TEAM...*EVEN ONE IN MADRIPOOR, YOU'VE GOTTA HAVE STANDARDS.
"SUPER-TEAM."
I DO NOT LIKE THAT TERM.
BUT YOU FOLLOWED THE TEACHINGS OF WOLVERINE OR PATCH OR WHOEVER...
...AND WE WERE TAUGHT BY CHARLES XAVIER.
MAYBE WE CAN HELP EACH OTHER.
WE CAN HELP YOU UNDERSTAND XAVIER'S DREAM...
...AND YOU GUYS... WELL...
...YOU SAID YOURSELF THAT WE NEED TO BE BETTER PREPARED FOR WHAT'S AHEAD OF US.
SO...
...CAN YOU *TEACH* US TO BE NINJAS?
THE END!

MORE THINGS TO COME IN X-MEN BLUE

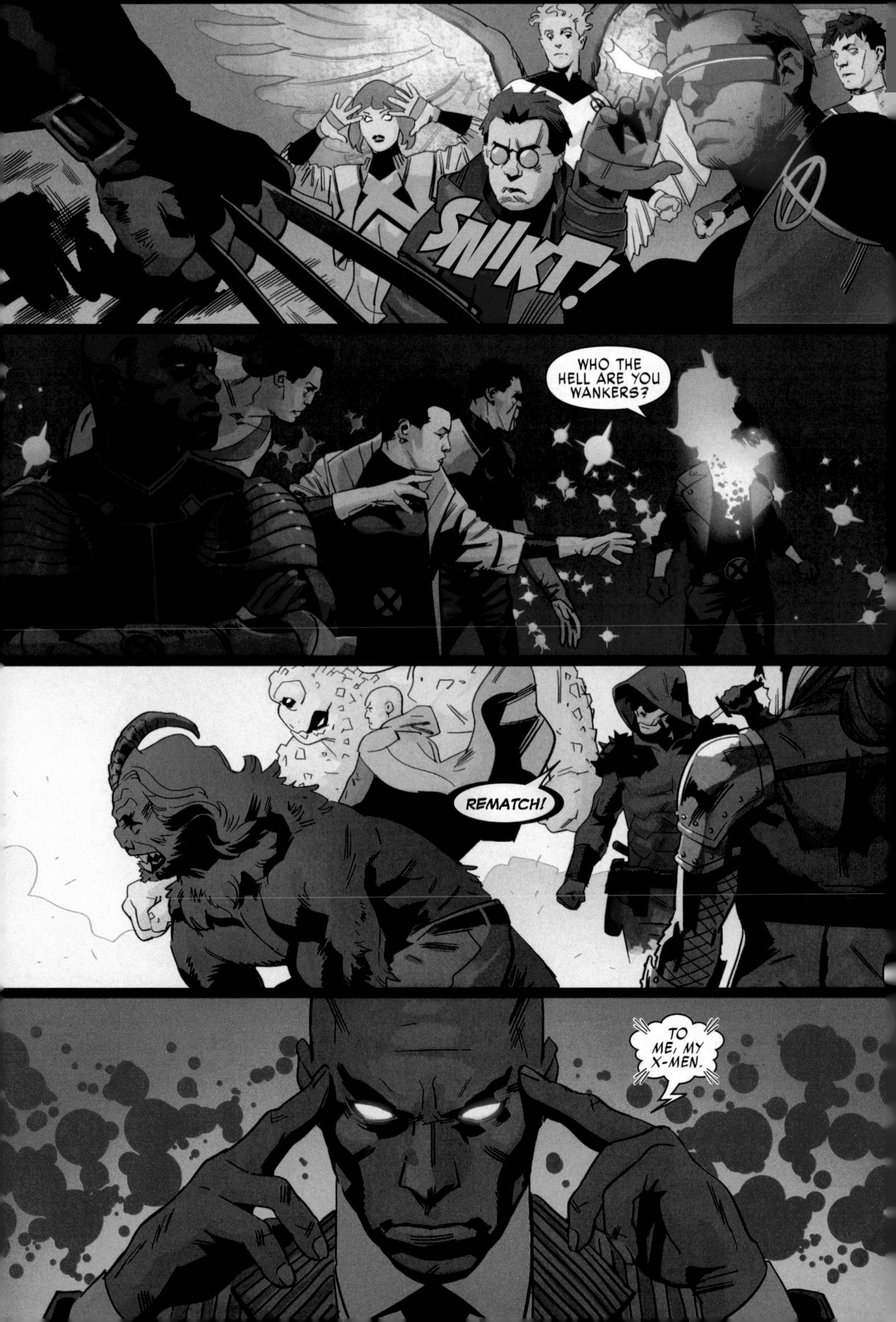
SNIKT!
WHO THE HELL ARE YOU WANKERS?
REMATCH!
TO ME, MY X-MEN.

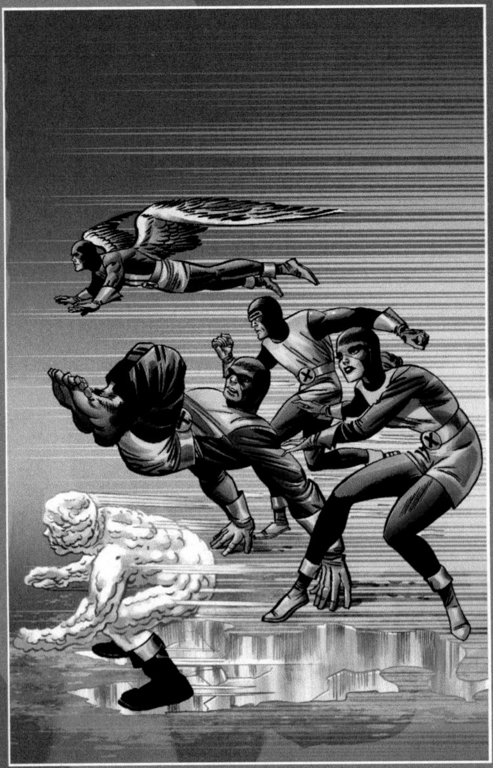

#1 JACK KIRBY 100TH ANNIVERSARY VARIANT BY **JACK KIRBY, PAUL REINMAN** & **PAUL MOUNTS** WITH **JOE FRONTIRRE**

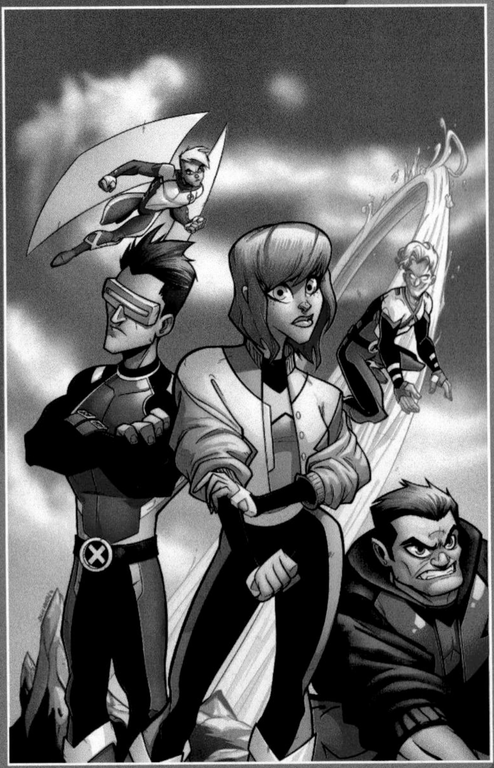

#1 VARIANT BY **BILLY MARTIN** & **EDGAR DELGADO**

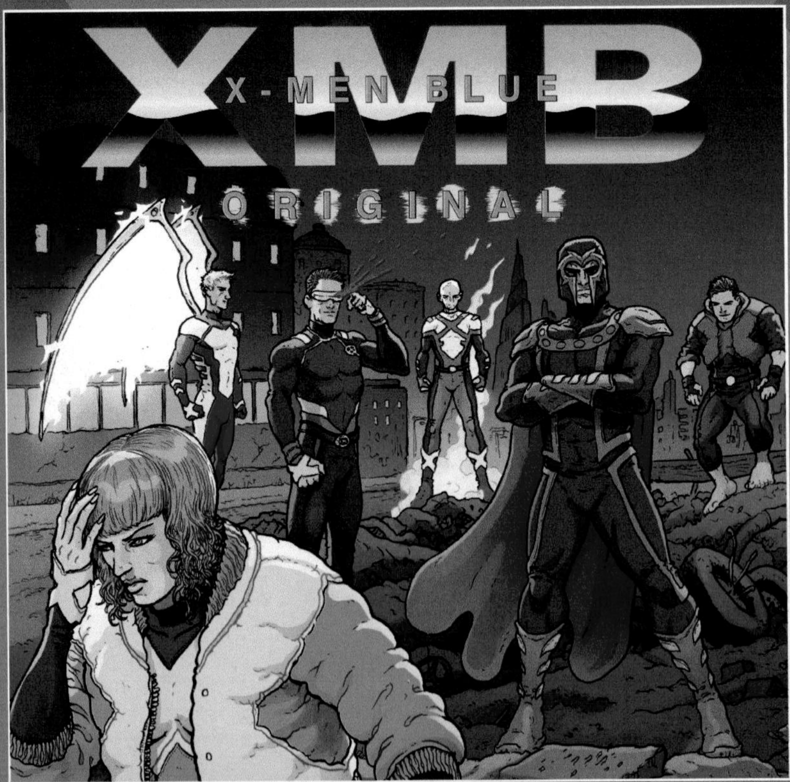
XMB
X-MEN BLUE
ORIGINAL

#1 HIP-HOP VARIANT BY **RAMON VILLALOBOS** & **TAMRA BONVILLAIN**

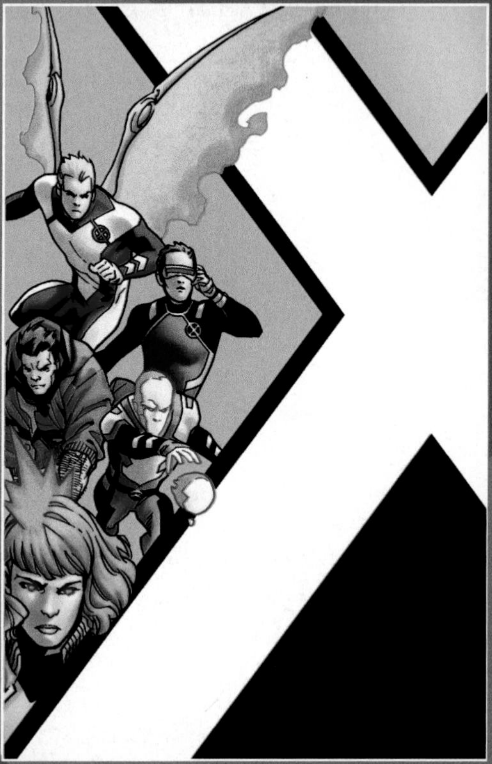

#1 CORNER BOX VARIANT
BY **LEONARD KIRK**
& **MICHAEL GARLAND**

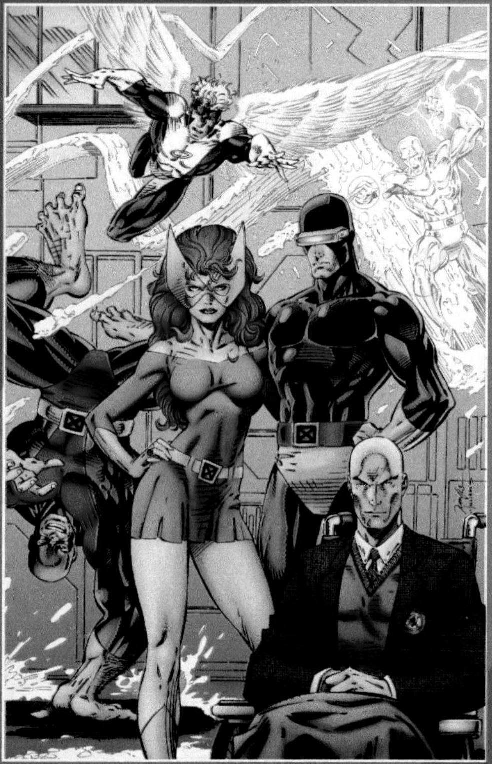

#1 REMASTERED VARIANT
BY **JIM LEE, SCOTT WILLIAMS**
& MORRY HOLLOWELL

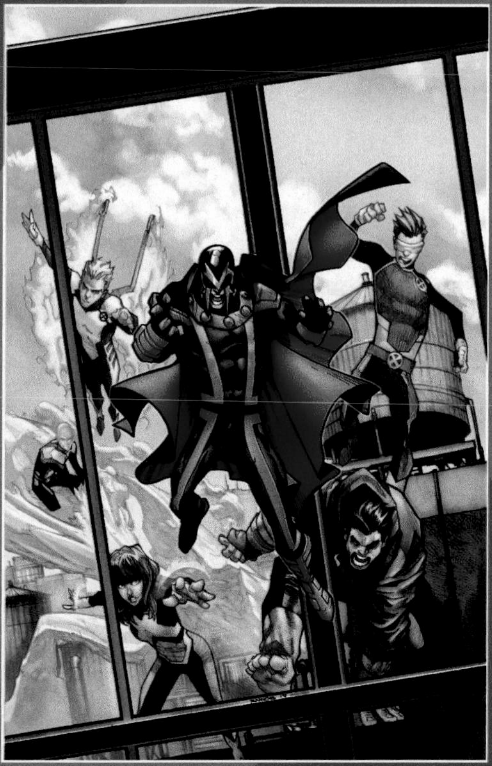

#2 VARIANT
BY **HUMBERTO RAMOS**
& **EDGAR DELGADO**

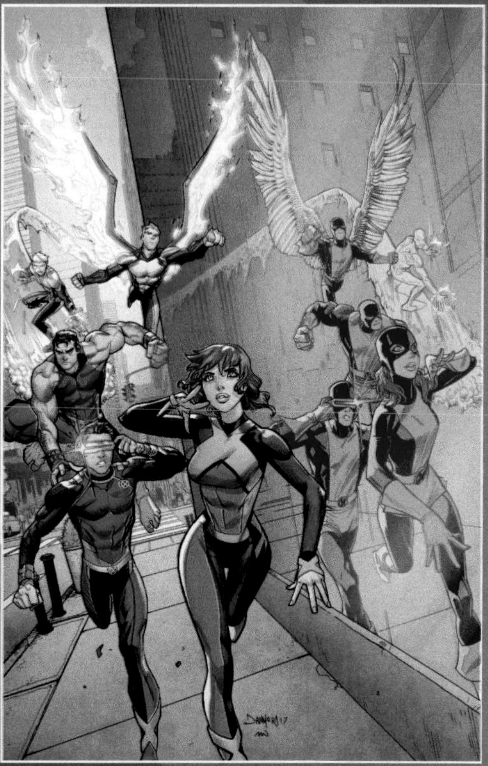

#3 VARIANT
BY **DAN MORA**
& **NOLAN WOODARD**

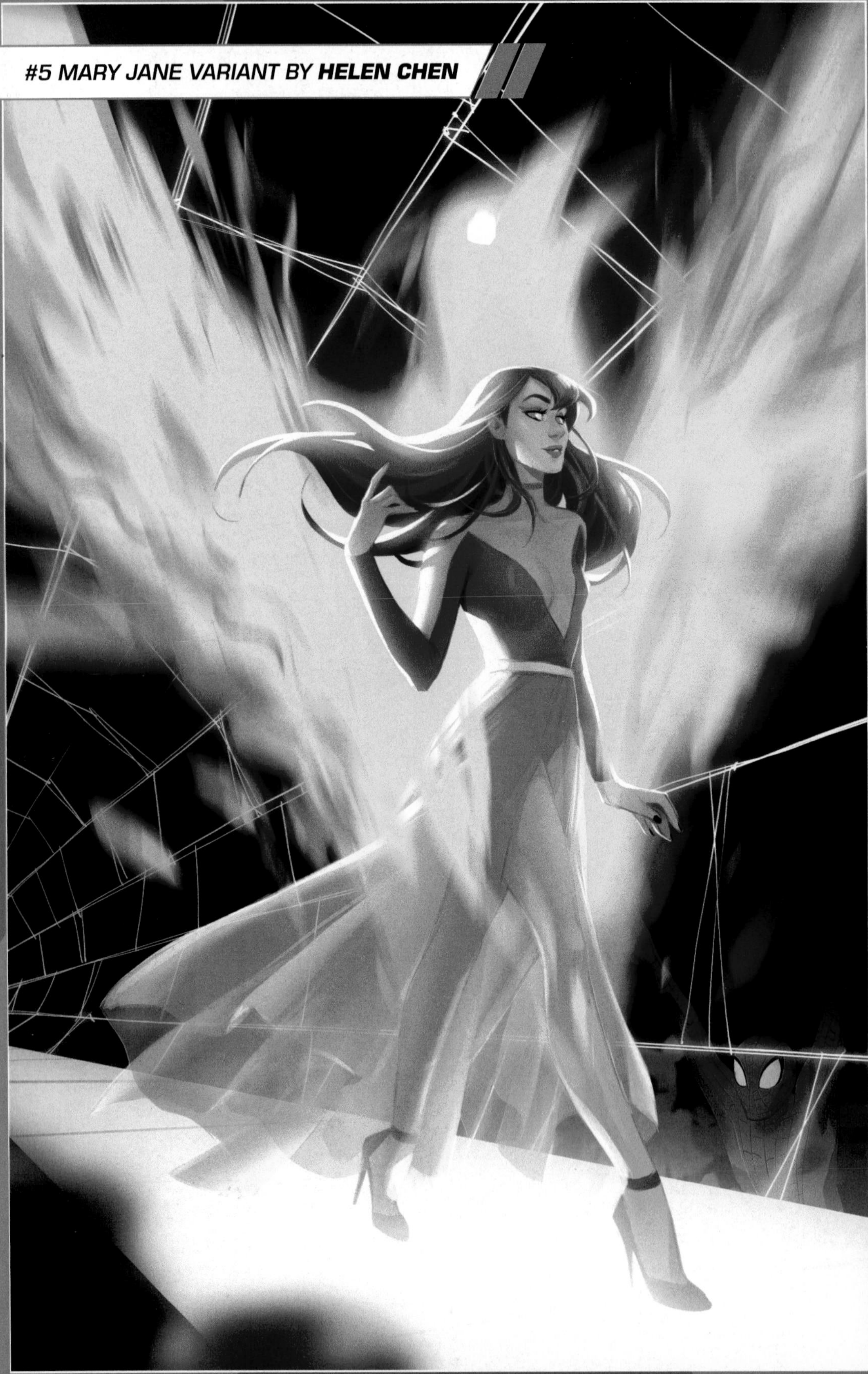

#5 MARY JANE VARIANT BY **HELEN CHEN**